Nietzsche's Jewish Problem

Nietzsche's Jewish Problem

Between Anti-Semitism and Anti-Judaism

Robert C. Holub

Princeton University Press

Princeton and Oxford

Copyright © 2016 by Princeton University Press
Published by Princeton University Press, 41 William Street, Princeton, New Jersey 08540
In the United Kingdom: Princeton University Press, 6 Oxford Street, Woodstock, Oxfordshire
OX20 1TW

press.princeton.edu

ISBN 978-0-691-16755-8
Library of Congress Control Number 2015943620

British Library Cataloging-in-Publication Data is available

This book has been composed in Sabon Next LT Pro and Helvetica Neue LT Std

Printed on acid-free paper. ∞

Printed in the United States of America

10 9 8 7 6 5 4 3 2 1

For Bini
SP

Contents

All citations from Nietzsche's writings and correspondence are noted parenthetically in the text according to the standards established in current Nietzsche scholarship. Abbreviations used in this study are given below.

When there is no indication in the text, parenthetical citations for published and unpublished writings will include the abbreviation for the work, an indication of where in the work the citation occurs, and the volume and page number in the critical edition. Letters will include the addressee or sender, the date of the letter, the number of the letter, and the volume and page number in the critical edition.

I have consulted various sources for translations, modifying for the sake of accuracy and consistency. In cases where no translation exists, I translated myself.

KGW = Kritische Gesamtausgabe der Werke = Friedrich Nietzsche, *Werke: Kritische Gesamtausgabe*, planned ca. 50 vols., ed. Giorgio Colli, Mazzino Montinari, et al. (Berlin: de Gruyter, 1967–).

KGB = Kritische Gesamtausgabe Briefwechsel = Friedrich Nietzsche, *Briefwechsel: Kritische Gesamtausgabe*, 24 vols., ed. Giorgio Colli, Mazzino Montinari, et al. (Berlin: de Gruyter, 1975–2004).

KSA = Kritische Studienausgabe = Friedrich Nietzsche, *Sämtliche Werke: Kritische Studienausgabe*, 15 vols., ed. Giorgio Colli and Mazzino Montinari (Berlin: de Gruyter, 1980).

KSB = Kritische Studienausgabe Briefe = Friedrich Nietzsche, *Sämtliche Briefe: Kritische Studienausgabe*, 8 vols., ed. Giorgio Colli and Mazzino Montinari (Berlin: de Gruyter, 1986).

Published Works

SGT = Sokrates und die griechische Tragoedie (Socrates and Greek Tragedy)

GT = Die Geburt der Tragödie (The Birth of Tragedy)

NJ = Ein Neujahrswort (A Message for the New Year)

MD = Mahnruf an die Deutschen (Admonition to the Germans)

UB = Unzeitgemässe Betrachtungen (Untimely Meditations)

DS = David Strauss, der Bekenner und der Schriftsteller (David Strauss, the Confessor and the Writer)

HL = Vom Nutzen und Nachtheil der Historie für das Leben (On the Advantage and Disadvantage of History for Life)

SE = Schopenhauer als Erzieher (Schopenhauer as Educator)

WB = Richard Wagner in Bayreuth (Richard Wagner in Bayreuth)

MA = Menschliches, Allzumenschliches (I und II) (Human, All Too Human)

    VM = Vermischte Meinungen und Sprüche (Mixed Opinions and Sayings)

    WS = Der Wanderer und sein Schatten (The Wanderer and His Shadow)

M = Morgenröthe (Dawn)

IM = Idyllen aus Messina (Idylls from Messina)

FW = Die fröhliche Wissenschaft (The Gay Science)

Z = Also sprach Zarathustra (Thus Spoke Zarathustra)

JGB = Jenseits von Gut und Böse (Beyond Good and Evil)

GM = Zur Genealogie der Moral (On the Genealogy of Morals)

WA = Der Fall Wagner (The Case of Wagner)

GD = Götzen-Dämmerung (Twilight of the Idols)

AC = Der Antichrist (The Antichrist)

EH = Ecce homo

NW = Nietzsche contra Wagner

DD = Dionysos-Dithyramben (Dionysian Dithyrambs)

Unpublished Writings and Fragments

Nachlass = Nachlass (Literary Remains)

WM = Die Nachlass-Kompilation "Der Wille zur Macht" (The Compilation from the Literary Remains "The Will to Power")

GMD = Das griechische Musikdrama (The Greek Music Drama)

ST = Socrates und die Tragödie (Socrates and Tragedy)

DW = Die dionysische Weltanschauung (The Dionysian Worldview)

GG = Die Geburt des tragischen Gedankens (The Birth of Tragic Thought)

BA = Ueber die Zukunft unserer Bildungsanstalten (On the Future of Our Educational Institutions)

CV = Fünf Vorreden zu fünf ungeschriebenen Büchern (Five Prefaces to Five Unwritten Books)

PHG = Die Philosophie im tragischen Zeitalter der Griechen (Philosophy in the Tragic Age of the Greeks)

WL = Ueber Wahrheit und Lüge im aussermoralischen Sinne (On Truth and Lies in an Extramoral Sense)

Many books and essays have been written on Friedrich Nietzsche's relationship with Jews and Judaism. In 1995 I made a contribution to this topic with an article titled "Nietzsche and the Jewish Question."[1] At that point I recognized that much previous scholarship had misconstrued Nietzsche's views because it tended to evaluate his statements through the distorting lens of the Holocaust and therefore failed to situate them in the context of the nineteenth century. There was often something at stake in these examinations of Nietzsche's attitudes toward the Jewish Question, something that went well beyond his actual statements about Jews and his personal relationships with persons of Jewish heritage. Some scholars appeared intent on condemning Nietzsche as a racist or, if the commentators were Germans writing during the Third Reich, recruiting him for their cause—although we should remember that there was a healthy contingent of Nazi ideologues who disputed Nietzsche's foundational place in the National Socialist philosophical canon. Especially in the postwar period the majority of scholars believed that he should be relieved of any association with Judeophobic sentiments and Nazi affiliation, and therefore composed one-sided apologies for him, emphasizing factors such as his opposition to the anti-Semitism of Wilhelmine Germany and the unhealthy influence of Wagnerian anti-Jewish thought, which he "overcame" after his break with the Meister. But in dealing with these issues, scholars were frequently inclined to ignore the context for Nietzsche's statements and actions. In their portrayals they failed to present an accurate picture of Nietzsche's views on Jews and Judaism, more often offering arguments that accused or excused for reasons extraneous to Nietzsche's intentions and motivations.[2]

My article tried to remedy this situation by looking more closely at biographical, intellectual, and historical context. I pointed out, for example, that Nietzsche's attitude toward anti-Semitism could not be understood without considering his conflicted relationship with his sister, his brother-in-law, and his publisher, Ernst Schmeitzner, and that his notion of anti-Semitism was quite different from ours. Indeed, for Nietzsche anti-Semitism had a specific referent in political agitation during the early 1880s and thus encompassed both more and less than hatred of Jews. I tried to make sense out of the various contradictions in Nietzsche's statements and actions, but concluded, somewhat indecisively, that on the basis of the evidence we have, his views on Jews and Judaism resist any sort of simple conclusion:

> Because he was involved in several different discourses about the Jews—at the very least a general cultural discourse, a religious historical discourse, and a political discourse—and because his evaluation of the Jews inside of these discourses was hardly monolithic, we have encountered a wide range of statements and apparently contradictory opinions. Nietzsche held different, and sometimes inconsistent, views about Jews he met socially or casually, about antisemitism as a political movement, about Jews as a cultural and religious group in nineteenth-century German and European society, and about the ancient Jews as the founders of a religious tradition. There is no single image of the Jews in his writings, and if we try to harmonize his remarks on the Jewish Question without considering textual and historical context, then we will perforce draw even more confusing conclusions.[3]

With this statement the matter for me was settled: there is no definitive resolution to the Jewish Question in Nietzsche's writings because there are too many contradictions, too many contextual factors, and too many discourses to which he was responding in various ways at various moments in his life.

This essay on "Nietzsche and the Jewish Question" was part of a larger project I had undertaken in the early 1990s involving Nietzsche's response to social and scientific issues central to the life of an intellectual in the late nineteenth century. In the social sphere I planned to examine Nietzsche's response to education, the German Question, the "social question," women's emancipation, and colonialization; in the realm of the natural sciences I wanted to look at his dialogue with such phenomena as thermodynamics, Darwinism and evolution, and eugenics.[4] I produced a small volume for the Twayne series, also published in 1995, which amounted to a preliminary study,[5] and I planned to devote myself to this project over the next few years. But after completing a good deal of research and some writing on this project, I was enticed into academic administration, assuming first the position of dean of the Undergraduate Division at Berkeley, then provost at Tennessee, and finally chancellor at UMass Amherst. For about a decade, I achieved very little progress on my research and writing. But in 2012, when I returned to the faculty and took up a professorial position at Ohio State University, I renewed my interest in Nietzsche's participation in discourses of the nineteenth century. I found that there had been a great many studies published in the interim that furthered the notion of Nietzsche as a "timely meditator" and contributor to discourses of his own era, and I was gratified that so much work had been accomplished on what I considered an essential deficiency in our understanding of Nietzsche, especially in the Anglophone world.[6] I began researching and writing again, but when I reached the point where I was going to revise and expand on my original thoughts on "Nietzsche and the Jewish Question," I was forced to pause and reconsider.

I recognized that my previous views on Nietzsche were too derivative of earlier scholarship that was faulty or incomplete, and not nuanced enough in grasping the significance of the texts I was analyzing. I do not believe that I was fundamentally inaccurate in my general contentions, but I saw that I had been woefully inadequate in my contextualizing of Nietzsche's views on Jews and Judaism. Many of the points I had argued could have been made with greater precision; many of the confusions I harbored about Nietzsche and the Jewish Question could have been disentangled by a more careful consideration of the sources and a better knowledge of the biographical and historical context. From previous accounts I had taken over, for example, the notion that Nietzsche must have been exposed to, and influenced by, anti-Jewish thought in his youth without sufficient attention to Nietzsche's juvenilia, letters, and surroundings. I had believed without question that Nietzsche was just a callow youth who had fallen under the spell of Richard Wagner, and that the composer's pronounced Judeophobia infected the young man like a virus. And I had echoed the repeated accusations in the research that Nietzsche's sister Elisabeth was primarily responsible for Nietzsche's reputation as an anti-Semite, that she had falsified his writings and correspondence to make him into an anti-Jewish racist in the spirit of her husband, Bernhard Förster, the propagator of the infamous Anti-Semites' Petition in the early 1880s. Reading more carefully and more widely, checking sources and new scholarship, I found that several aspects of Nietzsche's views on Jews and Judaism had been too hastily formulated in the 1995 essay, and that I could resolve at least some contradictions in the earlier piece that I considered simply the manifestation of conflicted sentiments in Nietzsche himself. Above all, I soon recognized that the chapter I sought to revise for my study would be inadequate to deal with everything I had learned in the interim about this topic. At that point I decided to compose this monograph and present to the many readers interested in Nietzsche a more complete, more scholarly, more differentiated, and more accurate account of his dealings with Jewry.

The "problem" to which the title of this book refers revolves largely around the phenomenon of "anti-Semitism." Normally if we speak of "Nietzsche's anti-Semitism," we simply mean the sentiments in his writings that express hatred of, or bias against, Jewry. But I shall argue in the chapters that follow that there is a particular sense attached to anti-Semitism for Nietzsche, as well as for many of his contemporaries, that does not exactly match our current understanding of the term. When we consider what Nietzsche understood by anti-Semitism, we form a somewhat different and more differentiated view of his relationship with Jews and Judaism. There is little question that Nietzsche considered himself an adversary of the political anti-Semitism that arose in Germany in the 1880s. If we consider only his antagonism to this crude racist movement, he surely qualifies as an anti-anti-Semite. But prior to his opposition to political anti-Semitism, he was himself involved with anti-Jewish thought, in particular when he was a Wagnerian disciple from approximately 1868 until 1876. His involvement with anti-Jewish prejudice, however, predates his acquaintance with Wagner and continues well past his break with him. Nietzsche thus partakes of "anti-Semitism" in the sense of the word today: he exhibits definite prejudices about Jewry throughout his mature years, although his evaluation of features he associates with Jewry changes over time and sometimes goes against the grain of nineteenth-century opinion. In this study I therefore find it necessary to distinguish two somewhat contradictory attitudes by using "anti-Jewish" or "Judeophobic" to describe Nietzsche's negative bias toward Jews and Judaism, and to apply "anti-Semitic" to him and to others only when it relates clearly to the political anti-Semitism of the late nineteenth century. This distinction is heuristic since anti-Semitism of the 1880s is not a completely new phenomenon; it inherits and intensifies many of the anti-Jewish attitudes of the eighteenth and early nineteenth century. But it does help to clarify the two most outstanding features of Nietzsche's sentiments toward Jews and Judaism: a rejection of anti-Semitism in the narrower sense of the political racist movement that arose in Germany around 1880 and the simultaneous embrace of many anti-Jewish motifs, some of which were employed by the very anti-Semites he detested. On some occasions, publicly and privately, Nietzsche also expressed an admiration for ancient and modern Jewry, and one of my central tasks is also to elucidate what these positive expressions signify in their historical context. In general I understand my study as one that clarifies for the reader Nietzsche's views on this important topic. The issues are complex, and Nietzsche is not always free from contradiction. But if his utterances are properly contextualized, then he is more consistent than he otherwise appears to be. In sum, I hope to shed new light on a controversial subject that has been misunderstood, oversimplified, and sometimes manipulated by previous scholarship.

The first chapter serves as an introduction to Nietzsche's "anti-Semitism." It traces his fate as an "anti-Semite" from the first appearance of political anti-Semitism in the 1880s through the postwar era, when Nietzsche was exonerated from connections with anti-Jewish thought. As we might suspect, the trajectory is anything but straightforward. In his own time he was initially suspected of anti-Semitic leanings because of various personal associations, most notably his brother-in-law and his publisher, both of whom were leaders of the fledgling anti-Semitic movement in Germany. Moreover, although Nietzsche broke with Wagner in his own mind in the years 1876–78, the German reading public still considered him an acolyte of the Wagnerian cultural mission, and he thus continued to be identified with the racist proclivities of the Meister. During the second half of the 1880s, because of his pronouncements against political anti-Semitism, the anti-Semites of his own time rejected him, often considering him a supporter of the Jews. None of the major anti-Semites in the nineteenth century regarded Nietzsche as an ally or confederate. Conservative racists began to interest themselves again in Nietzsche around the turn of the century, but his reputation as a philosopher harboring anti-Jewish sentiments was bolstered considerably only during the First World War, when his writings were recruited in support of the war effort. During the Weimar Republic (1919–33) he was claimed by many political persuasions as a precursor—from socialists to fascists—but his reputation as a right-wing advocate of racism was solidified only after Hitler came to power, and he was eventually, albeit at times uneasily, integrated into the Nazi pantheon as a forerunner. After the war scholars made a concerted effort to cleanse his reputation and to blame his sister Elisabeth for his renown during the Third Reich. The evidence shows, however, that Elisabeth did not try to fashion her brother into an anti-Semite, although many critics today continue to regard her as the main reason Nietzsche was integrated so readily into the National Socialist camp. Today his reputation, especially in the Anglophone world, is largely one of an anti-anti-Semite who was misunderstood as "anti-Semitic" because of distortions, manipulations, and insufficient attention to what he wrote.

The second chapter examines Nietzsche's early life and dispels the notion that he was raised and educated in an environment that foisted anti-Jewish sentiments onto him. If we examine the documents at hand, we find very little evidence of early exposure to anti-Jewish ideas, either at home or in the schools he attended. There are remarkably few mentions of Jews or Judaism in the five volumes of juvenilia that comprise almost everything he wrote in his childhood and youth. It is unlikely that he had any personal acquaintance, or even casual contact, with Jews or Judaism in the places he lived for the first two decades of his life, although we must assume that he gained exposure to some knowledge about the Jewish religion and the Old Testament from the schools he attended and the churches in which he worshiped. He probably encountered some anti-Jewish thought in fairy tales, lore, and church doctrine, but it evidently made little or no impression on him. Even at the university in Bonn, where he matriculated for two semesters beginning in 1864, we find no evidence of any contact with Jews or reflections on Jewry. Only when Nietzsche transferred to the University of Leipzig the following year do we encounter the initial indications that he had adopted anti-Jewish attitudes. There appear to have been two sources of his newly found "cultural" anti-Jewish orientation. He was exposed to Jewish merchants at the Leipzig fair, responding with racial slurs and snide racist asides to what some fellow students considered a Jewish "invasion" of the city, and the students with whom he began to associate in his philological studies uttered anti-Jewish remarks, which he then emulated. We find that in the second half of the 1860s Nietzsche's letters to his mother and sister contain several anti-Jewish comments, although their letters to him throughout his years of university study were devoid of any racist sentiments. This chapter thus establishes that prior to his integration into the circle of Wagnerians, Nietzsche had begun to develop the type of anti-Jewish biases that we then encounter with some consistency throughout his sane life.

In the third chapter I examine anti-Jewish sentiments in Nietzsche's relationship with Richard Wagner and in his early nonphilological writings. Wagner was an unabashed Judeophobe and a major inspiration for the anti-Semitic movement of the 1880s. Nietzsche made his acquaintance in 1868 and quickly became an inner member of the Wagnerian circle, frequently visiting the Meister in Tribschen, where he lived with his paramour and later spouse Cosima, who was also fiercely anti-Jewish. In 1869 Wagner had republished one of the central tracts of anti-Jewish thought in the German world, *Judaism in Music*, and Nietzsche was able to witness firsthand the public reaction, much of which was adverse and hurt the Wagnerian cause. Nietzsche dedicated himself nonetheless to supporting Wagner's cultural mission and adopted an openly negative attitude toward contemporary Jewry. In an early preparatory lecture for *The Birth of Tragedy* (1872) Nietzsche included a direct attack on the Jewish press, but when Wagner and Cosima read it, they were perturbed and admonished him not to be so open in his anti-Judaism. Nietzsche accepted Wagner's conviction that the Jews are a united and vindictive people, that they possess significant power in Germany and throughout Europe, and that they should therefore be treated with extreme caution. In his published writings from 1872 to 1876 Nietzsche, following the dictates of the Wagners, eliminated all direct reference to Jews and Judaism, adopting instead a "cultural code" to make his anti-Jewish views obvious to contemporaries. *The Birth of Tragedy* and its reception indicate clearly the extent of the anti-Jewish discourse in Nietzsche's circles, and in the *Untimely Meditations* (1873–76) it is possible to discern a continuation of anti-Jewish motifs and references, albeit without any direct mention of Jews. Nietzsche's Wagnerian outlook on Jewry persists through the last *Untimely Meditation*, *Richard Wagner in Bayreuth* (1876), in which his growing ambivalence toward his mentor does not prevent him from including obvious Judeophobic stereotypes.

Chapter four deals with Nietzsche's so-called aphoristic middle period, when he moved away from Wagnerian ideology and began to express a more differentiated view of Jews and Judaism. After his break with Wagner in the middle of the decade, we can discern a noticeable attempt on Nietzsche's part to include more favorable remarks about Jews, especially in his published writings. He may have done so out of conviction, but it is also possible that he was attempting to distinguish himself publicly from his former mentor, who was renowned for this anti-Jewish convictions. Nietzsche appears to have retained the clichéd opinions he had harbored since the 1860s, but he now reevaluates formerly negative characteristics as positive features. In his notebooks and letters, however, we continue to find racist slurs or questionable statements about contemporary Jewry. We thus detect a continuity with Nietzsche's earlier sentiments, which he either retains in a revised assessment of "Jewish features" or espouses in nonpublic documents. In this chapter I also consider Nietzsche's relationship with a trio of acquaintances and admirers of Jewish heritage: Paul Rée, an author who, like Nietzsche, dealt with psychological and moral reflections; Siegfried Lipiner, who was a great admirer of Nietzsche's works, and for whom Nietzsche for a time also had considerable regard; and Josef Paneth, a Viennese scientist who reported on his conversations with the philosopher in letters to his bride in early 1884. In each case the affiliation with Judaism was precarious: Rée was Jewish only by virtue of ancestry; he was born a Protestant and made no public or private statements about his parents' former religion. Lipiner and Paneth both came from the extended Pernerstorfer Circle, a group consisting mostly of assimilated Jews studying at the University of Vienna. Lipiner converted in 1881, apparently out of conviction; Paneth was more sensitive to his religious heritage but considered himself a scientist first and foremost. In all three cases previous observers have misunderstood the import of the Jewish dimension of these relationships. At one point or another Nietzsche evidences anti-Jewish prejudices in dealing with each of these individuals.

Chapter five clarifies the historical context of anti-Semitism in Germany in the 1880s and what this movement meant for Nietzsche both personally and ideologically. The anti-Semitism with which Nietzsche was confronted has to be understood in large part as a movement opposing the citizenship rights Jews had recently gained in the Second Empire and as a reaction against the National Liberal Party, with which Bismarck had ruled Germany from 1871 to 1879, and the financial dealings of wealthy German Jews in the period immediately following the Franco-Prussian War. It continued a tradition of anti-Jewish sentiment that dates back many centuries and borrows ideologemes from eighteenth-century notions of race and narrow romantic nationalism. But it was also a crude and virulently racist political movement that had significant negative implications for Nietzsche personally. It estranged him from his sister because of her fiancé and later husband, Bernhard Förster, who was a leading voice of German anti-Semitism; it alienated him from his publisher, Ernst Schmeitzner, who printed anti-Semitic materials and became active politically in anti-Semitic parties in Saxony; and he suspected that his association with anti-Semitism was in part responsible for the miserable sale of his writings and hence his financial difficulties and failure to achieve any discipleship among Germans. I discuss in some detail three moments of anti-Semitic involvement that are centrally important for understanding Nietzsche's relationship to Jewry: his relationship with his publisher, and in particular Nietzsche's contribution of poems to the anti-Semitic journal Schmeitzner published; the anti-Semitism of the Försters (sister and brother-in-law), who eventually left Germany to found a racially pure colony, Nueva Germania, in Paraguay; and his brief confrontation in early 1887 with the *Anti-Semitic Correspondence* and its editor Theodor Fritsch, a notorious anti-Semite, whose notoriety in racist circles extended from the 1880s into the Weimar Republic. I demonstrate that Nietzsche's virulent reaction against political anti-Semitism had personal as well as philosophical roots and did not mean that he abandoned anti-Jewish sentiments. Indeed, Nietzsche, along with his contemporaries, drew an important distinction between the vulgar and counterproductive activities of the anti-Semitic political movement, which they opposed, and the need to find a suitable resolution to the Jewish Question in Germany, which often involved anti-Jewish prejudices and perspectives.

In my final chapter I focus on the Jewish dimension of Nietzsche's writings in the last two years of his sane life. The central issues for Nietzsche's consideration of Judaism in 1887 and 1888 involve the origins of morals and the history of religion, in particular the role historical Judaism plays in early Christianity. Nietzsche's introduction of Judaism as a priestly religion in the first essay in the *Genealogy of Morals* (1887) brings him into close association with anti-Semitic thought despite his own rejection of the anti-Semitic movement of his times. Especially noteworthy is his juxtaposition of a Jewish, slave morality and the values of a noble stratum associated with Aryans and fair-haired peoples. The struggle between these value systems and the victory of Jews in this lengthy historic confrontation parallels a popular anti-Semitic narrative on a grander scale. In connection with Judeo-Christian history, I analyze central sources Nietzsche consulted for his views on Judaism and early Christianity—Paul de Lagarde, Ernest Renan, and Julius Wellhausen are the three most important influences—and show then how he adapted these sources to his own purposes in discussions in *Twilight of the Idols* (1889) and especially in *The Antichrist* (1895). Although Nietzsche does acquire a more differentiated view of Jewish history, his general evaluation of Judaism's role in the degeneration of the Roman world and the decadence of contemporary Europe remains unaltered. Consistently Jewish values are considered to be the single most important factor in the degeneration of the species and the dismal plight of contemporary society. I then look at Nietzsche's uncritical reception of Louis Jacolliot's translation and commentary on "The Traditions of Manu," which occupied an important place in his thoughts on comparative religion in 1888 in published works and in his notebooks. Nietzsche affirms in his positive reception of Jacolliot's fabrications a linguistic and ethnographic narrative about the origins of Judaism that was otherwise associated with the very nineteenth-century anti-Semitism he detested.

My brief conclusion summarizes the most important findings in this study and then takes up the issue of Nietzsche's connection with National Socialism and its anti-Jewish ideology. Previous speculation on this issue is largely nugatory; it is impossible to predict exactly how Nietzsche would have reacted to the rise of an ultranationalist and overtly anti-Semitic political movement. We can find parallels in his ideas and those of fascist Germany; we can also easily discern aspects of National Socialism that stand in stark contrast to Nietzsche's stated beliefs. But we cannot—and should not—view his remarks on historical and contemporary Jewry through the lens of later events, ideas, and ideologies. Indeed, the point of this book is that we must situate Nietzsche in his own era, as someone reacting to events and ideas of the late nineteenth century, if we are going to come to a real understanding of his complex views on Jews and Judaism.

I am indebted to many individuals and institutions for this study. I began reflecting on Nietzsche as a graduate student at the University of Wisconsin–Madison in the 1970s, and I recall specifically the seminar on Nietzsche I took with Reinhold Grimm. Perhaps the most seminal proposition for the course of my intellectual activity—and also for this study—was a statement made by my *Doktorvater*, Jost Hermand, who on more than one occasion emphasized that no individuals are "ahead of their times," although, as he hastened to add, they may appear to be so, since so many are often "behind their times." At Berkeley I was blessed for over a quarter of a century with numerous colleagues who exerted a tremendous influence on my thought and assisted me greatly in my development. I am especially grateful to Ohio State University and to the current faculty members in Germanic Languages and Literatures for welcoming me so graciously into their midst, and to the institution for providing me with the funding and leisure to pursue my research. Paul Reitter, who was my student at Berkeley and now is my colleague at Ohio State, was a careful and attentive reader of the manuscript and provided encouragement for me to write the study in the first place. The library staff at Ohio State has been extremely helpful and patient with someone who had engaged only sporadically in scholarly pursuits for the past decade. I would also like to thank my editor at Princeton University Press, Fred Appel, for his encouragement and professionalism, and the anonymous readers of the manuscript, whose suggestions I have endeavored to incorporate in the final product. Dawn Hall's expert copyediting made the manuscript a better book. On a personal level my three beautiful daughters—Madelaine, Shoshanah, and Natalie—probably interrupted my work as much as they assisted it, but somehow without them I doubt I could have persevered so well. Finally, I owe more than I can say—and in more ways than I can say—to my wife Sabine, to whom I dedicate this book.

Columbus, September 2014

Nietzsche's Jewish Problem

CHAPTER ONE

The Rise and Fall of Nietzschean Anti-Semitism

REACTIONS OF ANTI-SEMITES PRIOR TO 1900

Discussions and remarks about Jews and Judaism can be found throughout Nietzsche's writings, from the juvenilia and early letters until the very end of his sane existence. But his association with anti-Semitism during his lifetime culminates in the latter part of the 1880s, when Theodor Fritsch, the editor of the *Anti-Semitic Correspondence*, contacted him. Known widely in the twentieth century for his *Anti-Semites' Catechism* (1887), which appeared in forty-nine editions by the end of the Second World War, Fritsch wrote to Nietzsche in March 1887, assuming that he harbored similar views toward the Jews, or at least that he was open to recruitment for his cause.[1] We will have an opportunity to return to this episode in chapter five, but we should observe that although Fritsch erred in his assumption, from the evidence he and the German public possessed at the time, he had more than sufficient reason to consider Nietzsche a like-minded thinker. First, in 1887 Nietzsche was still associated with Richard Wagner and the large circle of Wagnerians, whose ideology contained obvious anti-Semitic tendencies. Nietzsche's last published work on Wagner, the deceptive encomium *Richard Wagner in Bayreuth* (1876), may contain the seeds of Nietzsche's later criticism of the composer, but when it was published, it was regarded as celebratory and a sign of Nietzsche's continued allegiance to the Wagnerian cultural movement. Nietzsche's break with Wagner occurred gradually during the 1870s, although it may have been punctuated by particular affronts, but from Nietzsche's published writings we can detect an aggressive adversarial position only with the treatises composed in 1888, *The Case of Wagner*, which appeared in that year, and *Nietzsche contra Wagner*, which was published in 1895 after his lapse into insanity. Nietzsche's closest friends retained their connection to Wagner; Franz Overbeck, for example, the Basler professor of New Testament Exegesis and Old Church History who had been close to Nietzsche since their time together on the faculty of the Swiss institution,[2] was the head of the local Wagner society, and Malwida von Meysenbug,[3] with whom Nietzsche was on good terms for almost two decades, was a fervent adherent of Wagner. The break with Wagner that Nietzsche felt so strongly was almost impossible to perceive from the outside. Second, Nietzsche appeared to be closely associated with anti-Semitism through his brother-in-law, Bernhard Förster, who was a member of the extended Wagner circle. Förster, a Gymnasium teacher in Berlin, was well known for his anti-Semitic convictions and one of the initiators of the notorious Anti-Semites' Petition in 1880, which demanded severe restrictions on rights for Jews and Jewish immigration. He married Nietzsche's sister Elisabeth in 1885 and left with her the following year to found a pure German colony in Paraguay. Third, Nietzsche's publishers were known for their anti-Semitic proclivities; both Wilhelm Fritzsch, who was originally Wagner's publisher, and Ernst Schmeitzner, with whom Nietzsche worked from the third *Untimely Meditation* until the third part of *Thus Spoke Zarathustra* (1883–85), were involved with anti-Semitic agitation. In *Schmeitzner's International Monthly*, whose subtitle after 1882 was *Journal for the General Association Combating Judaism*, we find frequent advertisements for Nietzsche's writings;[4] any reader of this journal might well assume that Nietzsche harbored the same racist sentiments as his publisher. Finally, we should not discount that Nietzsche's early writings, which adopted many of the Judeophobic motifs found in Wagner's critique of modernity, and his later works, which implicated the Jews in slave morality and decadence, could easily have convinced Fritsch—as well as others—that Nietzsche's interest in anti-Semitic politics was greater than it actually was. An outsider unacquainted with Nietzsche's journals and private remarks in correspondence would have been completely justified in concluding that Nietzsche was a potential participant in the widespread and disparate movement that encompassed not only professors like Heinrich von Treitschke or court officials like Adolf Stöcker but also the well known philosopher and socialist Eugen Dühring and the celebrated cultural figure Richard Wagner.

In general, however, Nietzsche's relationship to Jews and Judaism was infrequently thematized in commentary written during his lifetime and into the first decade of the twentieth century. Although it is likely that some individuals, like Fritsch, simply assumed Nietzsche harbored anti-Semitic convictions, Nietzsche's remarks on Jews were infrequent and ambiguous enough that they did not constitute an emphasis in these initial discussions of his thought. In the early years of his reception Nietzsche was much more appealing for his general oppositional attitude, and accordingly he was read and admired by many writers and critics who identified with his polemics against the status quo and his vaguely defined vision of the future. In some instances he received praise from aesthetically inclined writers, and often they highlighted his early work on Greek tragedy, his emphasis on the irrational creativity of the Dionysian, and his criticism of philistinism in German culture. For many of these Nietzsche enthusiasts, *Thus Spoke Zarathustra* (1883–85), Nietzsche's most literary work, provided both inspiration and the possibility to flaunt one's exegetical skills. Others placed his observations on morality in the center of their reception. Nietzsche was often considered a keen observer of the foibles in Wilhelmine society and someone who did not hesitate to expose the hypocrisy of middle-class norms while envisioning a new, emancipatory, and more natural moral code. Those who opposed Christianity, or who believed that Christianity had betrayed its original teachings and mission, could admire Nietzsche for his ruthless criticism of the Church and its oppressive restriction on human development. Nietzsche especially intrigued members of politically oppositional groups, even if Nietzsche excoriated the groups' doctrines in his writings. We find an eager reception among anarchists and non-Marxist socialists, despite Nietzsche's overt and repeated rejection of their doctrines. In a little-known play from 1902 titled *Children: A High School Comedy*, the son of a staid member of the middle class reports to a classmate: "Nietzsche is nonsense, father says, a hack and a social democrat."[5] Because of the conservative nature of German society, Nietzsche's adversarial profile made him initially more attractive to the left. This attraction extended well beyond German borders; in the initial commentary in the United States, for example, Nietzsche is appreciated as a man sympathetic to the working-class struggle and a champion of individual liberties. Indeed, translations of Nietzsche's writings in the United States very likely appeared first in *Liberty*, the anarchist journal Benjamin Tucker edited.[6] What fascinated leftist and left-leaning intellectuals about Nietzsche was not his views on socialism, anarchism, or feminism, but rather his vivid expressions of contempt toward the institutions of middle-class society, which they also rejected. Nietzsche could be an uncomfortable confederate, and even admirers admitted that his philosophy had glaring shortcomings, but long before he became identified with the anti-Semitic racism of the political right, we find him serving as an inspiration for intellectuals of the left, for aesthetically minded individuals outside of mainstream culture, and for outsiders to Wilhelmine society.[7]

Among those early commentators were writers and thinkers who were Jewish or from Jewish backgrounds. But for the most part they too studiously avoided discussions of anti-Semitism in Nietzsche's thought. Even Max

Nordau, cofounder with Theodor Herzl of the World Zionist Organization and a searing critic of Nietzsche's philosophy, skirts any possible relationship to Judeophobic sentiments in Nietzsche's writings. In *Degeneration* (1892), Nordau does emphasize the role Jews play in the origins of slave morality and cites relevant passages from the *Genealogy of Morals* (1887), in which Jews and "Israel" are blamed for overthrowing a previous moral system of values, obviously preferable to Nietzsche and identified with aristocratic norms as well as superior physical strength and will. He recognizes as well that Nietzsche's influence has extended to individuals we today associate with anti-Semitism, noting that Julius Langbehn's *Rembrandt as Educator* (1890) is modeled on Nietzsche's early *Untimely Meditation, Schopenhauer as Educator* (1874). But among the many intellectual sins Nietzsche commits, according to Nordau, anti-Semitism is not included. He accuses Nietzsche of "insane gibberish," of "wild assertions," of "delirious sallies," and of "fabulous stupidity and abecedarian ignorance"; his system is characterized as "a collection of crazy and inflated phrases"; Nordau describes him as an egomaniac and a sadist, who was "obviously insane from birth, and his books bear on every page the imprint of insanity"; and he is associated with megalomania, mysticism, false individualism, and aristocratism. But Nordau never comments on Nietzsche's relationship to the Judeophobic tendencies of the era.[8] Nordau, of course, may have considered it obvious that Nietzsche was anti-Semitic. In the works of other Jewish writers of the era we find this association asserted with the same sort of evidence Nordau produces. In Bernard Lazare's study *L'Antisémitisme: Son histoire et ses causes* from 1894, for example, Nietzsche is grouped together with Eugen Dühring as part of "Christian anti-Semitism":

> After Dühring, Nietzsche, in his turn combated Jewish and Christian ethics, which according to him are the *ethics of slaves* as contrasted with *the ethics of masters*. Through the prophets and Jesus, the Jews and the Christians have set up low and noxious conceptions which consist in the deification of the weak, the humble, the wretched, and sacrificing to it the strong, the proud, the mighty.[9]

Lazare's reference to Nietzsche is fleeting, however; although he is included in this survey of anti-Semitic tendencies of the times, his work does not warrant more than this brief mention. We might justifiably conclude that for most early commentators, both Jewish and non-Jewish, Nietzsche's attitude toward the Jews was of little interest.[10] There may have been general and tacit agreement that he had much in common with more noted anti-Semites of the Wilhelmine period, but other items in his writings attracted more attention, and for those concerned with prominent anti-Semites, there existed a sufficiently large selection and variety of anti-Jewish writing from which to choose without needing to have recourse to Nietzsche.

The only critics of Nietzsche who seemed overly concerned about his attitude toward the Jews before the turn of the century were the anti-Semites themselves. As we will see later, after receiving an unequivocal rebuke from Nietzsche in two letters, Fritsch not only ceased courting him for the anti-Semitic cause but also published an extremely harsh criticism of his thought, especially regarding the Jewish Question. Once Nietzsche's assault on the anti-Semitic movement in his late works became better known, other anti-Semitic commentators followed suit. One of the most vituperative accounts of Nietzsche's philosophy occurred in 1896 in five consecutive issues of the *Modern Spirit of the People*, a journal that was published for only six years, from 1894 to 1899, and was subsequently relaunched as *Personalist and Emancipator* by its guiding spirit, Eugen Dühring, continuing publication until 1922, a year after Dühring's death. The article, "Friedrich Nietzsche, Part of the Jewish and Lunatic Question," was authored by "–t –n," but the anonymity was lifted in 1931 when the author, Dühring's disciple Ernst Jünemann, republished the essay in a short book format.[11] By the time Jünemann's original essay appeared Nietzsche had started to attract considerable attention among his compatriots after nearly two decades of neglect during the 1870s and 1880s. In the same year that the serialized critique of Nietzsche was published, Heinrich Mann wrote that Nietzsche was such "a modish philosopher" (*Modephilosoph*) that it was difficult to assess his true importance.[12] Three years prior to Mann's utterance, the sociologist Ferdinand Tönnies composed a pamphlet titled "Nietzsche Nitwits" in which he criticized Nietzsche's views on morality and all those who mindlessly borrowed them. And in 1897 Tönnies would write a text rebuking *The Nietzsche Cult*, which had appropriated Nietzsche in the false hopes of liberation.[13] Jünemann is therefore writing in the initial phases of Nietzsche's burgeoning popular reception in Germany, and he feels justified in dealing at the outset with the reasons that Nietzsche was suddenly being accorded such widespread attention. In keeping with the anti-Semitic tenor of the journal, he attributes Nietzsche's fame to Jewish advocates:

> The writings of Friedrich Nietzsche, who several years ago fell into a state of deep derangement, are currently being purchased and read with great enthusiasm by the public since Hebrew advertisements in particular have propped him up, and Jewish opinion, as is well known, is unfortunately fashionable, which is evidence of how low the intellectual and moral level of today's dominating social powers has sunken.[14]

The author, who is transparently acting as the mouthpiece for his mentor, feigns regret at having to take up this topic at all, but rationalizes that since Nietzsche is currently influencing so many people and therefore exercising an unhealthy effect on German society, he must deal with subjects that in themselves have no "internal value." Much of the article is spent on an account of Nietzsche's illogical conclusions and apodictic claims, and because Dühring and his thought are the foundation for the periodical, throughout Jünemann portrays Nietzsche as the lesser intellect who envies the superior philosophical insights of Dühring, trying unsuccessfully to present arguments and hypotheses that challenge his more renowned Berlin rival.

Jünemann describes Nietzsche's philosophical trajectory as a steady decline into insanity and Judeophilia. After a promising beginning when he was engaged productively with Richard Wagner and Arthur Schopenhauer, he strayed from the nationalist and anti-Semitic path in his aphoristic period and descended into irrational argumentation and pandering to Jewish interests in his last writings. In the fourth part of his article Jünemann argues at length that Nietzsche stole his most important insights in his later works from Dühring, but modified them in such a way to make them a virtual parody of the original; ultimately, they amount to little more than an "unsuccessful attempt at plagiarism."[15] But Jünemann reserves his most venomous attacks for Nietzsche's perverse, because supportive, relationship to Jews and Judaism. He claims that despite some apparently critical remarks about Jews, they remain for Nietzsche "a non plus ultra of intellectual abilities and powerful will"; they are the true bearers of culture and the creator of values. In reality, of course, Jünemann maintains that Jews are "the opposite of what Nietzsche believes them to be, namely parasites destructive of peoples, culture, and morals." Fortunately, continues Jünemann, anti-Semitic doctrine has penetrated far enough into contemporary German thought that its assertions and teachings have become common knowledge, and "every normally thinking and perceiving individual can confirm the correctness of these claims on every Hebrew specimen that crosses his path." Ultimately we are left with the choice of believing that Nietzsche is "the greatest psychologist" and nature is a "comedian," or considering nature to be true and honest and Nietzsche to be "spiritually and morally defective."[16] To a large extent Nietzsche's philosophy is reduced to either illogical nonsense or regarded as propaganda for Jewish interests. At one point his writings are compared to a "Jewish junk shop."[17] Jünemann suggests what amounts to almost a conspiracy between Nietzsche and the Jews. Nietzsche achieves fame and popularity only when he repudiates Wagner and jumps on the Jewish bandwagon; he then receives favorable coverage in the press and even monetary sponsorship of his collected works: "the publication of the many volumes appears to have been made possible only through Jewish money." Since Nietzsche could no longer profit from these alleged subsidies, Jünemann draws Elisabeth into his account, claiming that Jewish interests similarly funded her Nietzsche biography. Indeed, so complete is Jünemann's rejection of Nietzsche that he censures even Elisabeth's husband, Bernhard Förster, the darling of other anti-Semitic periodicals such as Fritsch's *Anti-Semitic Correspondence*. Förster, Jünemann contends, is a "reactionary anti-Semitic agitator," the proponent of an "anti-Semitic Jewishness and Judaism" that harmonizes well with Jewish blood and has the effect of "watering down genuine anti-Hebraism and weakening it to the point of inefficacy."[18] Jünemann's attacks culminate in the speculation that Nietzsche himself is Jewish, or at least that he has "Jewish blood" in his ancestry. In this manner Jünemann can more easily account for the numerous Jewish traits he detects in Nietzsche's writings: "impudent self-indulgence that knows no bounds; cruelty; crude powers of discernment; abject worship of power and authority; a low, servile morality and mentality." Jünemann concedes that he does not know Nietzsche's family tree, but he concludes nonetheless from his intellectual proclivities that he must have had Jewish ancestors: "His forefathers were pastors, which does not mitigate against this assumption, since baptized Hebrews used to prefer turning to the theological trade. The family is also supposed to have emigrated from Poland, and it is well known that one finds many Hebrews there."[19] In contrast, therefore, to many casual observers who assumed a loose affiliation between Nietzsche and anti-Semitism, the anti-Semitic press not only rejects any connection with Nietzsche but also even considers his works, his reputation, and his family to be infected with the worst aspects of Jewishness.[20]

INITIAL ATTEMPTS TO INTEGRATE NIETZSCHE BY THE RIGHT

Still some right-wing and *völkisch* nationalists, racists and anti-Semites, and proto–National Socialists found Nietzsche appealing, even prior to World War I, despite the difficulties they encountered reconciling his statements about Jews and race with the convictions they would have preferred him to hold. His attractiveness to the radical right can be explained as part of the oppositional animus almost everyone detected in his work. We should recall that until the advent of the Third Reich, radical nationalists and racists, like socialists, communists, and anarchists, considered themselves part of an adversarial movement aimed at overthrowing the status quo, whether it was

Wilhelmine Germany or, later, the Weimar Republic. Nietzsche's rhetorical assaults on the smug social order of his era had the potential to be just as provocative for the right as for the left. The difficulties right-wing intellectuals had in integrating Nietzsche into their worldview are evident in one of the earliest, more sympathetic discussions of his thought by a right-wing ideologue, Adolf Bartels's essay from 1902, "Friedrich Nietzsche and Germanness." Bartels, who composed the most influential *völkisch* history of German literature in 1901–2 and was extolled throughout the Third Reich for his exemplary accomplishments, recognizes that the radical right must struggle fiercely to retain Nietzsche—"we will not let Friedrich Nietzsche be robbed from us"—but that his many deprecatory statements about Germans and Germany make it a problematic appropriation. Bartels assures his readers, however, that Nietzsche's negative remarks about Germany have nothing in common with similar pejorative statements by Jewish writers, such as Heinrich Heine or Ludwig Börne, since these latter utterances are the consequence of racial hatred. Nietzsche's comments, although misguided, superannuated, and sometimes simply erroneous, are the result of a highly spiritual and ideal temperament. Bartels even concedes that his criticisms of the Second Empire in his early writings may have some justification, but as time went on he committed injustices toward his own people, "while simultaneously he did not tire of singing the praises of Israel, although he very well knew its true nature." Nietzsche, according to Bartels, after an initially sound period of national awareness, was gradually caught in the snares of the Enlightenment, and his turn toward Europeanism and away from German patriotism was the result of a mode of thought inimical to nationalism. With respect to the Jews Nietzsche recognized the purity, vitality, and strength of their race, as well as their potential to acquire a dominant position in European affairs. Despite this recognition, he did not advocate, as the anti-Semitic movement had from its very inception, resistance to Jewish hegemony. Bartels thus denounces Nietzsche's passivity in the face of the Jewish threat to German sovereignty, and in closing he cites a longer passage from *The Birth of Tragedy* (1872), composed at a time when Nietzsche had not yet succumbed to his unfortunate turn against his own people. Bartels acknowledges in this essay that Nietzsche is no anti-Semite, although he does account for his rejection of anti-Semitism in part as a reaction against his brother-in-law, and credits him with recognizing the Jews as a race that can easily obtain power over Europe and its nations.[21]

Subsequent *völkisch* commentators invented various strategies to overcome the obvious failings Bartels detected in Nietzsche's writings. Particularly in the Weimar period Nietzsche increasingly provided a fascination for the racist right wing as he became associated with thematic complexes recognizable in retrospect as protofascist. Nietzsche's style made him more easily adaptable for the political purposes for which he was harnessed. Apart from his essayistic writings of the early 1870s, which were more obviously infused with German nationalism and anti-Jewish motifs and therefore presented fewer difficulties for the radical right, his subsequent works were composed in such a fashion that they were susceptible to many interpretations. The aphoristic writings of the late 1870s and early 1880s seem to invite the reader to pick and choose aphorisms or short sections most suitable to a given perspective or ideological direction. Similarly, *Zarathustra* with its highly symbolic passages and its biblical style suggests the need for exegesis, and over the course of the decades has been perhaps the most malleable of Nietzsche's texts. The later writings, although more essayistic in character, still lack the cohesion of more traditional linear argumentation, while the notebooks, filled with aphorisms, sketches, excerpts from other writers, and thoughts in various stages of completion, are open to many different appropriations. Moreover, Nietzsche ranges widely in the topics he included in his published and unpublished writings, from philosophical reflections on truth and epistemology to arguments on morality and religion, to observations on women and politics. The stylistic ambiguity in Nietzsche and the diverse substantive issues he broached contributed to his favorable reception from a wide spectrum of philosophical, aesthetic, and political directions over the past century and a quarter. In the realm of culture he has been viewed as an inspiration for aestheticism, futurism, impressionism, expressionism, modernism, Dadaism, and surrealism. In philosophical circles he has allegedly influenced phenomenology, hermeneutics, existentialism, poststructuralism, and deconstruction. On the political front he has been considered a promoter of anarchism, fascism, libertarianism, liberal democracy, and—despite his pointed polemics against the most modern manifestation of slave morality—socialism. Observers have often noted that Nietzsche's texts are much like the Bible in that they can serve as evidence for diverse and even antagonistic positions. As Kurt Tucholsky, the most renowned satirist from the Weimar Republic, commented: "Who cannot claim [Nietzsche] for their own? Tell me what you need and I will supply you with a Nietzsche citation: ... for Germany and against Germany; for peace and against peace; for literature and against literature—whatever you want."[22] When opponents of *völkisch* interpretations of Nietzsche accuse the radical right of citing him out of context, they miss the point. Nietzsche himself, through stylistic and substantive strategies, decontextualized his own ideas, aiding their adoption from eager acolytes of various stripes, adhering to disparate perspectives.

Bartels emphasized that Nietzsche was a writer whose reception was disputed, and that the right should not allow him to be robbed from them. Like many others, he assumed that Nietzsche's natural home was the Germanophilic tradition that, in Bartels's view, he had regrettably abandoned in the 1870s. There are probably several reasons that the right did not want to relinquish Nietzsche to the leftist and aesthetic opposition, where he had also found allies, and certainly the enormous popularity he acquired during the first three decades of the twentieth century was a motivation for wanting to claim him for one's own cause. But there were several more specific developments that brought Nietzsche closer to *völkisch* values and made his allegedly anti-Jewish views a popular topic. Perhaps most important was the advent of the First World War. It was evident to all commentators that Nietzsche had championed war, battle, *agon*, struggle, and related notions repeatedly in his writings. While many interpreters simply considered statements concerning these terms part of a metaphorical register unrelated to actual military conflict, World War I began a longer association of Nietzsche and the goals of German militaristic and right-wing segments of society who were ultrapatriotic and at the same time xenophobic. Often the irrational hatred of foreigners extended to elements in German society considered nonnative, in particular the Jewish population. As a result his works, or portions of his works, could be read in a new chauvinistic light. His *Zarathustra*, which had sold so poorly in its first editions,[23] became requisite reading for German soldiers. It has been reported that 150,000 copies of a durable wartime edition were distributed to the troops, and 40,000 volumes were sold in 1917 alone.[24] Nietzsche had finally been accepted by the Germans, but ironically as the visionary proponent of a narrow-minded German patriotism. Nietzsche also became known increasingly as an inspiration for celebrated fascist or right-wing personalities. The Italian dictator Benito Mussolini had long been an enthusiastic reader of Nietzsche, and he regarded his fascist movement as the concretization of a national "will to power." Oswald Spengler, one of the most influential nationalist philosophers in the Weimar Republic and author of the two-volume *Decline of the West* (1918, 1923), proclaimed that along with Goethe, Nietzsche was his greatest inspiration: "Goethe gave me method, Nietzsche the questioning faculty—and if I were asked to find a formula for my relation to the latter I should say that I made of his 'outlook' (*Ausblick*) an 'overlook' (*Überblick*)."[25] And although we have no evidence that Adolf Hitler ever read a line of Nietzsche's philosophy, he certainly did not mind being associated with Nietzsche's sister and with the Nietzsche Archives in Weimar. Finally, right-wing Nietzscheans could take comfort in their ready inclusion in the activities of the Nietzsche

Archives. It would be a vast exaggeration to claim that right-wing elements controlled the Archives' program during the Weimar Republic. But certainly Nietzsche's sister Elisabeth, although she was no longer an anti-Semite and never became a National Socialist, welcomed contributions, monetary and otherwise, from diverse ideological perspectives, including a generous gift from Mussolini;[26] and her mother's family, the Oehlers, who were integrated into management positions, leaned further to the right and eventually became active party members. In addition, the board of directors for the Archives, while pluralist, especially in the early years of the Weimar Republic, contained several right-wing appointees, including Spengler, who joined the board in 1923. From 1914 until the end of the Weimar Republic, radical nationalist and *völkisch* observers could easily discern an appreciable expansion in Nietzsche's right-wing profile.

NIETZSCHE AND THE RIGHT IN THE WEIMAR REPUBLIC

The demise of the Second Empire and the Hohenzollern dynasty, the outbreak of World War I, and the imposition of a democratic republic on Germany by the victorious nations opened up new interpretive possibilities for right-wing Nietzsche enthusiasts and different strategies for connecting him with anti-Semitism. While the anti-Semitic movement of his own time had viewed him as an unsympathetic rival for attention, decrying him as a philo-Semite who betrayed the nationalist cause, in the Weimar Republic Nietzsche became a prescient thinker who justifiably expressed dissatisfaction with the half-hearted measures of the Wilhelmine era. Nietzsche's acceptance by the right wing is evidenced in many ways. Arno Schickedanz, for example, who later served in the "Rosenberg Office,"[27] in a book whose title betrays its *völkisch* and anti-Semitic content, *Social Parasitism in the Life of the People* (1927), simply includes a citation from Nietzsche (incorrectly quoted) to bolster his case for the ineluctability of the racist cause.[28] In Franz Haiser's *The Jewish Question from the Standpoint of Master Morality* (1926), a citation from *Zarathustra* supplies the motto for the entire book, and Haiser devotes a short chapter to Nietzsche, excusing his failings as a product of his era: "Nietzsche died much too early; for the chaos that he created was even more confused than the ruins of the heathen world out of which Christ established his empire." He admits that Nietzsche is frequently "culturally leftist and contradictory," but in an attempt to bind him to his compatriots he asserts, "only the German is able to comprehend completely Nietzsche's greatness." Although opponents of the Jews on the right may often harbor convictions that differ from his, Haiser concludes nonetheless that Nietzsche provides the appropriate direction for his movement and "is irreplaceable for us."[29] Finally, we could instance a collection like *Clarification: 12 Authors and Politicians on the Jewish Question*, published shortly before the demise of the Weimar Republic in 1932. Unusual about this volume is that it contains a variety of different vantage points; not all of the contributors are pro-Nazi or even right wing; three are Jewish. Of the contributors only Nietzsche, however, was no longer alive at the time of its publication, and the section devoted to his views consists of excerpts drawn from *On the Genealogy of Morals* (1887) and *The Antichrist* (1895).[30] The intent of the volume is obviously to recruit Nietzsche for anti-Semitism. In the first essay, which serves to an extent as an introduction, Ernst Johannsen, who edited the Nietzsche selections, admits that Nietzsche's writings are "rich enough" to support many different arguments, but in *The Antichrist* Nietzsche is incontrovertibly anti-Semitic: he is "the most profound adversary of the Jews that one can imagine!" Citing further from *Beyond Good and Evil* (1886), Johannsen concludes again that his remarks should be considered Judeophobic. He exhibits a "love-hate" relationship with his fellow Germans, but "in the course of his observations he provides a serious assessment of anti-Semitism, in which his un-Christian, highly political position becomes unambiguously clear." Johannsen asserts that Nietzsche supported enmity against the Jews as understandable and even necessary, and he concludes that those who find Nietzsche in opposition to anti-Semitism simply quote him out of context.[31] In *Clarification*, as in other texts from the Weimar period, we encounter a confirmation of Nietzsche's adherence to anti-Semitism. In contrast to the anti-Semites of his own era, most right-wing Weimar critics went out of their way to select Nietzsche's most provocative anti-Jewish statements or to interpret more equivocal utterances in a manner favorable to their cause, integrating them into a coherent, Judeophobic worldview.

By the end of the Weimar Republic the right wing had succeeded in constructing a Nietzsche interpretation that rivaled leftist, moderate, and aesthetic views. We should recall, of course, that Nietzsche's *völkisch* credentials were never unchallenged by some elements of the radical right. Jünemann's book appeared in 1931, and Nietzsche continued to be unacceptable and unaccepted by many anti-Semites and National Socialists even during the Third Reich. But by the end of the 1920s his right-wing credentials had achieved widespread acceptance. Crucial as a culmination for the rehabilitation of Nietzsche on the right and for the transition of Nietzsche studies into the National Socialist era was Alfred Baeumler's *Nietzsche the Philosopher and Politician* from 1931. Unlike many of the official philosophers in the Third Reich, Baeumler had acquired a reputation and a position during the Weimar Republic. He had written on Kant, Hegel, Kierkegaard, and Bachofen before he turned to Nietzsche in the early 1930s. Closely associated with Alfred Rosenberg, one of the chief racist ideologues of the Third Reich, Baeumler joined the anti-Semitic Fighting League for German Culture in 1930, declared his allegiance to National Socialism before the elections in 1932, and entered the party after Hitler assumed power in January 1933. From the so-called Rosenberg Office, responsible for the education of party members, he served as principal liaison with German universities.[32] His Nietzsche monograph was the most important National Socialist work on the philosopher and was reprinted several times before the end of the Second World War. In addition, Baeumler was the editor of several popular editions of Nietzsche's writing, composing afterwords and commentaries from his *völkisch* perspective.[33] Nietzsche was also the subject of many occasional remarks in Baeumler's talks.[34] While Nietzsche served to legitimize Baeumler in philosophical circles of the radical right, he, in turn, with his Nietzsche interpretation helped to secure the philosopher's legitimacy among radical nationalists and racists. He argued that Nietzsche's anti-German remarks must be understood in the context of Bismarck's rule and the Second Empire; his views could then be more easily harmonized with the ideology of the Third Reich, which was similarly critical of Wilhelmine political practices. "The German state of the future will not be the continuation of Bismarck's creation," Baeumler announces, "but it will be shaped in the spirit of Nietzsche and the Great War." Reconciling Nietzsche's assaults against anti-Semitism with the policies and practices of National Socialism was a more difficult task, and Baeumler, like many Nazi commentators, is compelled to employ strained arguments that are never entirely convincing. It is noticeable that the Jewish Question is seldom broached in his book, and when it is, it is mentioned only in passing and absent any insistence on Nietzsche's anti-Semitism. Baeumler is convinced, however, that Nietzsche did not have a high regard for Jews. After citing Nietzsche's contention that he has known Jews with tact and *délicatesse*, but no Germans (EH, Warum ich so gute Bücher schreibe, Der Fall Wagner 3, KSA 6.363), and after recalling his laudatory comments about Georg Brandes, a Jewish scholar in Denmark who delivered the first lectures on his thought, Baeumler contends: "In his innermost being he was disinclined toward the Jews, in whom he saw the real priestly constitution, and even the flattery that he experienced from them could not alter his opinion." Nietzsche uses the Jews rhetorically, Baeumler claims, as he had used the French: as a foil to the Germans in order to goad them to greatness. Despite his highly deprecatory utterances about Germans, Baeumler explains that "all of that is not Nietzsche's real thoughts about the Germans; they are only exaggerations in the heat of battle. Everything is said with calculation."[35] From Baeumler's presentation we are thus left with the bald avowal of Nietzsche's furtive patriotism and his dislike of the Jews, as well as a few flimsy explanations of why he often writes favorably about the Jewish people. But on the whole Baeumler leaves little doubt that for him Nietzsche is an important anticipator of the National Socialist state, and that his views on Jews and Judaism are, despite appearances, really in accord with prevailing anti-Semitic positions.

NIETZSCHE IN THE THIRD REICH

By the end of the Weimar Republic the basic strategies for bringing Nietzsche into the anti-Semitic fold were thus well established. Although a few philosophers under National Socialism continued to argue against Nietzsche's appropriation for the anti-Jewish cause,[36] most integrated him as a precursor of the Third Reich by pointing to his early works when he was still associated with Wagner, or by citing from his late writings, where Jews are identified with slave morality and the decline of the heroic—and hence Germanic—worldview. His remarks about the anti-Semitic movement itself or his favorable comments on Jews were attributed to personal circumstances or his strained relationship to the zeitgeist. In the initial year of National Socialist rule, Gottlieb Scheffler categorizes Nietzsche accordingly as a "theoretical anti-Semite," who grounded his anti-Christianity on anti-Semitism. In spite of his numerous Jewish friendships, Nietzsche regarded the Jewish people as the "party of all decadence instincts," and the "history of Israel" as the "typical history of the denaturalization of natural values."[37] Heinrich Härtle, Baeumler's successor in the Rosenberg Office, was both more differentiated and more crucial for Nietzsche's Nazi appropriation. In contrast to Baeumler, Härtle includes a section on "the Jews" in his book on Nietzsche, *Nietzsche and National Socialism*, which appeared in 1937. He recognizes first that many of Nietzsche's views result from chance occurrences in his private life: "his attacks on anti-Semitism are conditioned by personal influences, anti-Semitic enemies, and Jewish 'friends.'" Furthermore, Nietzsche's putatively Lamarckian assumptions led him to believe that Jews could be assimilated into German culture, a position that Härtle claims has now been superseded by modern biological race theory. With regard to the essence of Judaism, however, Nietzsche made, in Härtle's view, important contributions to our understanding. He anticipated racist theorists like

Schickedanz in considering the Jews as parasites on the human species. In connection with Nietzsche's discussion of Jewish values, Härtle finds that "Jewishness was never assaulted more sharply." Although Nietzsche does not do justice to the anti-Semitic movement of his own time and proposed solutions to the Jewish Question that differ from those of National Socialism, in his philosophy of values he is the "primeval enemy of everything Jewish."[38] Other National Socialist ideologues, such as Heinrich Römer, reached identical conclusions without any of Härtle's caveats. In "Nietzsche and the Problem of Race" Römer brings Nietzsche into close association with the theories of Arthur de Gobineau, whose *Essay on the Inequality of the Human Races* (1853–55) was the most important early work to hypothesize the superiority of the Aryan race. Römer points out that Nietzsche and Gobineau were contemporaries, which is not entirely accurate; Gobineau, born in 1816, belonged to a previous generation and is contemporary with Richard Wagner, who was a genuine admirer of his writings. Nietzsche did read Gobineau, but it was Wagner's *Bayreuther Blätter* that lionized his theories, and there is little evidence that Nietzsche showed a similar enthusiasm for this type of racism. Römer, however, while admitting that Nietzsche rejected the racist thought of his own times, represented by the anti-Semitic movement—he did so "out of personal and other reasons"—nonetheless claims that Nietzsche was "in his own manner the most ardent anti-Semite that ever lived: he is the most ruthless revealer of the pernicious role that Judaism played in the intellectual development of Europe, which it played above all as Christianity." Indeed, in reviewing Nietzsche's "grandiose struggle against a millennium of decline and degeneration," Römer finds that Nietzsche was an advocate of "racial hygiene" avant la lettre: "To be sure Nietzsche did not yet have the word, but he had the substance no matter what he named it: struggle against decadence, or revaluation of values, or cultivation and breeding, or overman, or 'purification of the race.'"[39] Like Scheuffler, Härtle, Baeumler, and a host of other Nazi Nietzsche enthusiasts, Römer assesses Nietzsche as an essentially anti-Semitic philosopher whose demands accord well, mutatis mutandis, with those of National Socialism.[40]

The philosophers in the Third Reich were not the only observers who believed that Nietzsche was well suited to the anti-Semitic cause. In the United States Crane Brinton, a Harvard historian who served for a time during World War II as chief of research and analysis in the Office of Strategic Services in London, composed in 1941 an introduction to Nietzsche's life and works that agreed wholeheartedly with contemporary German sentiments.[41] Brinton does recognize that National Socialist exegetes do not always quote accurately when they seek to enlist Nietzsche as an ally. He notes, for example, that Härtle, in citing a passage from the *Genealogy* in which Nietzsche mentions the "blond Teuton beast," omits Nietzsche's parenthetical qualification: "although between the old Germans and ourselves there exists scarce a psychological, let alone a physical, relationship."[42] Although he concedes that on occasion Nazi interpretations have to bend Nietzsche's words to their own purposes, he finds, nonetheless, ample evidence in his own readings that substantiates the connection between the philosopher and his fascist admirers. Like Römer, Brinton believes that Nietzsche "dabbled in notions of *Rassenhygiene*" (race hygiene) and that "occasionally he comes very close indeed to the Nazi program." Likewise his works are a veritable treasure trove for National Socialist Judeophobia:

> Scattered through Nietzsche's work is a good deal of material suitable for anti-semitic use. Nietzsche himself had Jewish friends—if one may use the word friendship of any relation between Nietzsche and another human being—and some Jewish writers have for years been among the most ardent and uncritical of Nietzscheans. Yet most of the stock of professional anti-semitism is represented in Nietzsche: the Jews are intellectuals with a grievance, hence destroyers of what makes for stability in society; they run the press and the stock-exchange, to the disadvantage of the slower-witted but more honest and healthy Gentiles; they are parasites, decadents; they are responsible for the three great evils of modern civilization—Christianity, Democracy, Marxism.

Even when Nietzsche endeavors to compliment the Jews or to be fair to them, he winds up, according to Brinton, providing "good ammunition for Nazi leaders, who have only to excise a few of his qualifying phrases."[43] Brinton devotes less space and energy to exploring Nietzsche's putative anti-Semitism and his relationship to the Jewish Question than he does to other topics that connect Nietzsche with National Socialism. But it is fair to conclude that in this important and influential monograph Brinton, like his Nazi counterparts, establishes firmly Nietzsche's anti-Semitic credentials.

FALSE ACCUSATIONS AGAINST ELISABETH FÖRSTER-NIETZSCHE

We have seen thus far how Nietzsche, originally spurned by anti-Semites as a friend of the Jews, an opponent of their movement, and a renegade from German nationalism, was eventually transformed after the First World War into a staunch proponent of anti-Semitism. In several post–World War II versions of this transformation critics assign Nietzsche's sister Elisabeth a seminal role. Henning Ottmann, author of an important study of philosophy and politics in Nietzsche's writings, claims that Nietzsche's appearance in the "ancestral chain of the fathers of anti-Semitism" is a *chronique scandaleuse* in its own right." At the source of this "scandal" are Elisabeth and her falsifications, which included not only inaccurate presentations of his works, but also literal falsifications of texts—although Ottmann adds parenthetically that they occur mostly in the form of "fabrications and manipulation" in the correspondence. Relying on the research of Karl Schlechta, who had worked in the Nietzsche Archives during the Third Reich and edited a popular postwar edition of Nietzsche's works, Ottmann asserts that among the falsified letters were some that appeared to make concessions to anti-Semitism and that even praised Elisabeth's husband, Bernhard Förster, as an "honorable personality."[44] Ottmann's endeavor to make Elisabeth the primary cause for Nietzsche's inclusion among the forerunners of fascism is one of many such attempts in the postwar years. In the *Cambridge Companion to Nietzsche*, for example, the volume's editors refer to "Elisabeth Förster-Nietzsche, and her fascistic and racist compatriots," claiming Elisabeth's edition of *The Will to Power* (1901, 1906) was arranged in a fashion emphasizing themes that appeared "friendly to the ideals of National Socialism."[45] Later in the same volume R. J. Hollingdale, repeating the canards of earlier scholarship, abuses Elisabeth for her commercialism (although he himself enjoyed obvious commercial success with his various Nietzsche translations), and contends that "as far as she could she imposed Förster's values," that is, anti-Semitism and proto-Nazism, on the Nietzsche Archives "and adapted Nietzsche in accordance with them."[46] Perhaps the most virulent assault on Elisabeth, however, occurs in an essay by Weaver Santaniello, who labels Elisabeth a "proto-fascist," "a virulent Christian anti-Semite," and "a staunch supporter of Hitler and the Nazis."[47] According to Santaniello there is a direct line from Wagner and Elisabeth to the Third Reich; the "process of manipulating Nietzsche ... began with Elisabeth and culminated with Hitler."[48] The extent to which Elisabeth's Nietzsche is equated with the most pernicious parts of Nazism in the mind of the wider reading public, especially in the Anglophone world, is perhaps shown best in Paul Strathern's *Nietzsche in 90 Minutes*, when he asserts that after Nietzsche's mental collapse Förster-Nietzsche began "doctoring her brother's unpublished notebooks, inserting anti-Semitic ideas and flattering remarks about herself."[49] Even writers for the *New York Times* uncritically parrot these views: Simon Romero, reporting on Nueva Germania today, describes Elisabeth's post–South American activities: "While Nietzsche derided anti-Semitism and expressed disdain in correspondence with his sister for the anti-Semitic character of Nueva Germania, she went on to reinvent his legacy after his death in 1900, transforming the philosopher into a kind of prophet for the Nazi propaganda machine."[50] From scholarly treatises to newspaper accounts, Elisabeth has been censured not only for falsifying her brother's writings but also for making him more palatable to the worst parts of National Socialist ideology, in particular anti-Semitism.

There are ample reasons to associate Elisabeth with anti-Semitism, and there is even some circumstantial evidence to support the claim that she welcomed her brother's inclusion as a precursor of the Third Reich. Elisabeth grew up in the same environment as her brother, one in which there was an absence of Jews, but in the larger German society there was a good deal of unreflected anti-Jewish sentiment. In the 1870s she attached herself to the Wagnerians, and even after her brother distanced himself from the celebrated composer, her social life and connections revolved around Bayreuth and its extended circles. Once Nietzsche retired from university life, and she was no longer called upon to assist with his household, she became attracted to an ambitious and industrious anti-Semitic Wagnerian, Bernard Förster, eventually marrying him on Wagner's birthday in 1885 and settling with him in the *völkisch*, utopian colony, Nueva Germania, in Paraguay. During her involvement with Förster, she almost assuredly absorbed and echoed his racist views, especially since one of the aims of the colonial enterprise was to escape a "Jewified" Germany. After the collapse of the colony and her husband's suicide, she returned to Germany, where she took charge of her insane brother, his published writings, and his literary remains, and through cunning, deceit, and perseverance helped to promote Nietzsche into a cult figure of the early twentieth century, and the archives that housed Nietzsche himself until his death in 1900, and Nietzsche's manuscripts thereafter, into a cultural center of German life. She took charge of publishing his complete works, dismissing one editor after another when they disagreed with her or countered her wishes, and allowed portions of her brother's writings to remain unpublished for many years, while publishing other parts under titles or arranged in collections that were neither authorized by Nietzsche nor philologically sound. From early on persons working with her in the Nietzsche Archives discovered that she was suppressing certain letters penned by her beloved "Fritz" that portrayed her in an unfavorable light, and even before her death in 1935 there was either suspicion of, or evidence for, numerous forgeries, distortions, or deceptions. Politically Elisabeth, like her brother, was hostile to democracy: before 1918 she leaned toward monarchism; during the Weimar Republic she made no secret of her conservative proclivities and of her animosity toward the parliamentary order. She admired Mussolini and spoke favorably of his fascist regime when it came to power in Italy.[51] And she was flattered by the attention Hitler showered on her and the Archives in the early 1930s, speaking admiringly of him when he was appointed chancellor in January 1933. When she died on November 9, 1935, the official organs of National Socialism sang her praises, and Hitler himself attended her funeral.[52]

Still, the notion that Elisabeth is chiefly responsible for her brother's integration into the pantheon of National Socialist philosophers and for his inclusion as a seminal anti-Semitic thinker has scant merit.[53] One indication of how inconsequential Elisabeth was for Nietzsche's reputation during the Third Reich is that she is rarely mentioned by the chief ideologues dealing with her brother's thought. None of the studies we have briefly reviewed above include her as a source or inspiration. The letters she doctored or forged play no role in the arguments of National Socialist interpretations, which depend entirely on either published and authorized writings or texts that Elisabeth did not manipulate. Ottmann's accusation of invented positive statements about Förster is odd, since we find Nietzsche favorably inclined toward his brother-in-law in letters that are certainly genuine. In October 1885, for example, Nietzsche writes to Overbeck that Förster "was not unsympathetic," and that he has "something sincere and noble in his being." He goes on to compliment him on his practical abilities: "it surprises me how he continuously accomplishes many things and how easily he does it" (Nr. 636, KSB 7.101–2). Like most commentators who blame Elisabeth for Nietzsche's fascist celebrity, Ottmann misunderstands the nature of Elisabeth's falsifications of the correspondence. As assistants in the Nietzsche Archives in 1937, Schlechta and Wilhelm Hoppe discovered that there existed no original manuscripts for thirty-two letters that Elisabeth had included in the fifth volume of Nietzsche's collected letters, which appeared in 1909. All but two of these letters were addressed to his sister; two were supposedly written to his mother. The letters are falsifications, but they are not entirely fiction. It seems that Elisabeth took letters or drafts of letters and doctored them to make them appear that Nietzsche had sent them to her. In addition, Elisabeth also added and subtracted phrases or entire paragraphs from these letters. As it turns out, several letters that Schlechta at first considered forgeries are real and were taken verbatim into the standard critical edition of Nietzsche's correspondence edited by Giorgio Colli and Mazzino Montinari. Several other letters are based on existing drafts and are credible at least as actual correspondence from Nietzsche's pen. Others have such mundane and innocuous content that it is difficult to understand why Elisabeth would have included them in her edition if they were not authentic; they certainly add nothing of any significance to the ideological record, and anti-Semitism plays no part in them whatsoever.

A careful examination of Elisabeth's actions indicates that her motivation in doctoring the correspondence was primarily personal, not ideological; quite simply stated, she falsified letters to make it appear that she was as close to her brother in the 1880s as she was during the previous decade, when she actually did participate intimately in his intellectual and private life. There is only one obvious example of her manipulating a document with anti-Semitic references. It is a letter Nietzsche purportedly wrote to his mother on December 29, 1887. The authoritative Colli/Montinari edition includes this entry as a draft consisting of four paragraphs, the first of which is fragmentary; no actual letter was discovered. The earlier edition from 1909, which Elisabeth edited, includes the three nonfragmentary paragraphs, which may raise the suspicion that Elisabeth suppressed the initial paragraph.[54] Our suspicion may be heightened by the fact that in this first paragraph Nietzsche writes of anti-Semitism ruining his reputation, his sister, and his friends; he continues by maintaining that the unwanted association with the anti-Semitic party—he is likely referring to the mention of his name and Zarathustra in the *Anti-Semitic Correspondence*—is the only thing standing in the way of his fame, and that it is most fortunate that this party has now begun to attack him: "only it occurs ten years too late" (Nr. 967, KSB 8.216–17). Although it is impossible to tell whether Nietzsche deleted his angry remarks on anti-Semitism before sending the letter, his mother's answer to him makes no reference to these matters (January 17, 1888, Nr. 514, KGB 3/6.147–48). In addition, we know from other examples in his correspondence that often Nietzsche's drafts differed quite a bit from the actual letters, especially with respect to matters that were apt to be controversial. Nietzsche frequently deleted items that might upset his correspondent, or that might cause strains in their relationship. In particular Nietzsche often spared his mother from receiving angry or disturbing sentiments. We therefore have no reason to suspect that Elisabeth did not alter this particular piece of correspondence by excluding the fragmentary initial paragraph, but from the evidence we possess we can also imagine very well that the copy she published in her edition was taken from a genuine letter.[55] We should note, however, that with regard to anti-Semitism Elisabeth's edition of the correspondence contains several letters in which Nietzsche expresses his antipathy to that movement, and he accuses her of "committing a great stupidity" by marrying Förster and involving herself—and him—with someone who will always be known for his anti-Semitism.[56] In the last letter Schlechta suspects is doctored, Nietzsche even writes of his sudden admiration for the young Kaiser (Nietzsche is referring to Wilhelm II) for opposing anti-Semitism and the conservative *Kreuzzeitung*, remarking that his sister should emulate him, and that the Kaiser would certainly understand the principle of the will to power.[57] There is no instance in his correspondence or in his writings and notebooks in which Elisabeth made Nietzsche appear favorably inclined toward anti-Semitism or adversely disposed toward Jews and Judaism. At times she appears to be solely concerned with her own image as it was reflected in her brother's comments, but anyone who has examined the actual manipulations could not possibly conclude that she was promoting a view of her brother as anti-Jewish or as someone who had sympathy with the burgeoning anti-Semitic movement of the early 1880s.

It is difficult to sustain the claim that Elisabeth made her brother appear anti-Semitic in other areas as well. In her numerous writings on Nietzsche she avoids bringing him into association with the anti-Semitic movement because she knew that he was virulently opposed to it. On numerous occasions in her biography and in other essays she informs her reader of Nietzsche's antipathy to any form of anti-Jewish sentiment. In contrast to Wagner, Elisabeth writes, "my brother was never an anti-Semite; in addition, he was never completely convinced that 'Germany, Germany' should be placed above everything;[58] he always recognized that the Jews had done a great service for the intellectual movement in Germany, especially at the beginning of the century."[59] Similar sentiments can be found in other books and articles. Indeed, Elisabeth may be more justifiably accused of excusing or concealing her brother's anti-Jewish proclivities. As someone acquainted with Wagner and the Wagnerians, she knew very well that Nietzsche had adopted much of the racist attitude of the Meister, and that many of Nietzsche's student friends also harbored Judeophobic views. Citing anti-Jewish remarks in Nietzsche's letters from the early 1870s, however, Elisabeth claims that they reflect "Wagner's views, and not his own."[60] And although she developed an animosity toward Paul Rée, she, unlike the Wagnerians, never mentions Rée's Jewish heritage. Before 1933 the Nietzsche Archives that she founded was also not a primary source of Nietzschean anti-Semitism. Prior to the Third Reich, the Archives leaned to the right, sometimes far to the right, but it maintained active relations with Nietzsche scholars and enthusiasts from all political perspectives. In 1925, for example, the one and only issue of *Ariadne*, the yearbook of the Nietzsche Society, contained contributions from Ernst Bertram, André Gide, and Thomas Mann. The following year the expanded board of directors included such prominent persons as the

French author and Nobel laureate Romain Rolland and the German publisher Anton Kippenberg, founder of the celebrated Insel Publishing House.
The chairman was Arnold Paulssen, a high official from Thüringen in the
left liberal German Democratic Party.[61] Indeed, in 1923 Oswald Spengler
was appointed to the board of directors for the Archives to offset politically
a perception of left liberal domination, represented by the presence of both
Harry Graf Kessler and Paulssen.[62] Above all, Elisabeth at this point in her
life was not an anti-Semite herself, despite her marriage to Förster, and despite her later adulation of Mussolini and Hitler. Throughout the Weimar
years she maintained a friendship with Ernest Thiel, a Swedish banker and
industrialist brought up as an Orthodox Jew.[63] She supported Jewish scholarship on Nietzsche, especially when it concurred with her views. A case in
point is Paul Cohn's book *Concerning Nietzsche's Demise*, which appeared in
1931 and to which Elisabeth contributed an appendix with letters she wrote
to Cohn.[64] Finally, there is considerable evidence that Elisabeth had disavowed her former convictions long before she began dealing seriously with
her brother's writings and the Archives. In her Nietzsche biography she
claims that she temporarily adopted anti-Semitic positions out of respect
for her husband, while he was away in South America and needed someone
to defend him in Germany. But she adds that anti-Semitism "was always
unpleasant for me" and that she "did not have the slightest reason" to be an
anti-Semite.[65] Hitler's rise to power evidently did not alter this conviction.
In April 1933 she wrote to Andreas Heusler: "Only the persecution of the
Jews that Minister Goebbels wrenched from our excellent Chancellor seems
to me a bad blunder and is very unpleasant for me. I am certain that it has
not been pleasant for our splendid Chancellor Adolf Hitler and that he will
do everything to ameliorate this mistake of his fellow party members." And
a few days later she reiterates these feelings: "I am not entirely in agreement
with the anti-Jewish movement, even though I would have reason to approve of it, since as widow of the first leader of the anti-Semites I have been
treated very badly by the Jewish press."[66] Indeed, Erich Podach, who was
anything but an apologist for Elisabeth, notes that she was critical of Max
Oehler for suppressing the name of a Jewish author, Albert Levy, who wrote
on Nietzsche and Stirner; she had no patience with such opportunism: "To
be sure at no time did she ignore the political tendencies that might be favorable for her, but when push came to shove, she not only demonstrated a
civil courage that was seldom seen in those times and supported her friends,
but also she, the widow of Bernhard Förster, wrote anti-anti-Semitic peti-
tions."[67] It is difficult to admire Elisabeth Förster-Nietzsche's political opinions; she obviously embraced views that are loathsome to postwar supporters

of democracy, equality, and cosmopolitanism, and some of her positions were proximate to those of avowed National Socialists. But with regard to anti-Semitism she not only did not try to fashion her brother as a Judeo-phobe; in public and private statements she herself was free from overt, biologically based notions of racism.[68]

NIETZSCHE'S POSTWAR REHABILITATION

Although Elisabeth was not responsible for her brother's association with the anti-Semitism of the National Socialist regime, she played a pivotal role in the postwar era when Nietzsche scholars and enthusiasts endeavored to extricate him from his racist reputation. As we have seen, Nietzsche had undergone a transformation from anti-anti-Semite to anti-Semite during the first four and a half decades of the twentieth century, but we should recognize that not everyone considered him a racist at the close of the Second World War. Many enthusiastic readers regarded his views on Jews and Judaism to be of relatively little importance for an understanding of his work and were unconcerned with Elisabeth and her alleged manipulations. The members of the Frankfurt School, for example, continued to admire Nietzsche while in exile in the United States, and although the scholars most closely associated with the Institute of Social Research were themselves Jewish, and although several prominent members wrote or conducted research on topics related to racism, anti-Semitism, or authoritarian views, they continued to hold Nietzsche in high regard, ignoring entirely the racially informed reception history sketched above. Similarly, authors like Thomas Mann or philosophers like Karl Löwith esteemed Nietzsche, and we have to assume that many intellectuals in the Third Reich who are associated with "inner emigration" valued Nietzsche for qualities other than his views for or against the Jewish people. After the war, as the European intellectual world split into opposing Cold War camps, the Communists in the East disparaged Nietzsche. While many unorthodox socialists had acclaimed Nietzsche during the first half of the twentieth century, the communist left had little use for him or his philosophy,[69] and they contributed to his image as a fascist during World War II.[70] Their rejection of Nietzsche became even more obdurate after 1945 as part of the Cold War. The communists, however, avoided or downplayed the topic of racism, and anti-Semitism was an especially sensitive subject because of Stalin's anti-Semitic campaign in the early 1950s.[71] Thus the foremost authority on German culture during the immediate postwar years, Georg Lukács, never mentions Jews, Judaism, or anti-

Semitism in his influential chapter "Nietzsche as the Founder of Irrational-
ism of the Imperialist Period" in *The Destruction of Reason* (1954).[72] Although
Lukács himself was of Jewish heritage, his analysis focuses on class, since
racism was for him and for orthodox practitioners of Marxism only epiphe-
nomenal and a diversion from the real, materialist conflicts in society.
Lukács cites Nietzsche's biologism and his proximity to Gobineau, but contends that he did not place any emphasis on Aryan supremacy, and that he
is really more of a precursor to Spengler than to Rosenberg. He continues
by expressing regrets that this lineage is now being used by postwar apolo-
gists as a means of denazifying Nietzsche, since the exact nature of his racism places Nietzsche in the same company as other irrational racist theorists of the imperialist period, from Gobineau and Chamberlain to Spengler
and Rosenberg.[73] Lukács obviously knows very well about the nuances of
Nietzsche's position vis-à-vis the Jews and anti-Semitism, but ideological
constraints, both external and internal, prevent him from exploring the
issue in any detail.

The agenda regarding Nietzsche in the non-Communist West was much
different, and it involved perforce the reputation he had gained—deservedly
or not—as an anti-Jewish thinker. Class-based issues were of no consequence,
but racism was, especially as the enormity of National Socialist crimes
against the Jews of Europe became public. To extricate Nietzsche from his
fascistoid image, Nietzsche enthusiasts had to provide an explanation for
how he had been recruited so readily for the nefarious purposes of the Third
Reich. In their efforts Elisabeth became indispensible. She was a person
closely connected with Nietzsche and his writings, who came to exercise a
domineering influence over his works and reception, and who had also tam-
pered with manuscripts, fabricated evidence about Nietzsche and his life,
and defied the accepted traditions and persons of the scholarly community.
Karl Schlechta, perhaps the scholar chiefly responsible for rehabilitating
Nietzsche's damaged reputation in German-speaking countries, had known
Förster-Nietzsche personally, discovering quite early on, as we have seen,
that she was responsible for falsifications in her brother's correspondence.
In the "Philological Afterword" to his important 1956 edition, Schlechta
produces the usual litany of complaints about Nietzsche's sister: she had no
understanding for her brother's philosophy; she was interested only in producing volumes quickly and in spreading Nietzsche's fame; she illicitly
published *The Will to Power* from notes in Nietzsche's literary remains that
were not meant for publication, or at least not in that form or under that
title. As we have seen, he established that Elisabeth falsified a significant number of letters, making it appear that correspondence destined for others was

actually written to her, although he left many issues regarding these falsifications unclarified. In the afterword Schlechta only hints at the ideological ramifications of Förster-Nietzsche's actions: the falsifications "built the foundation upon which his sister based her certainly fateful Nietzsche legend," he writes ominously, and the reader is left to imagine what that legend could entail.[74] In talks and essays written shortly after the publication of his edition, Schlechta is more suggestive about the consequences of Elisabeth's malicious deeds. Speaking of "the catastrophe that lies behind us," he argues that the reason Nietzsche was made coresponsible for it was primarily owing to his obsessively ambitious sister, who hitched her wagon to the fate of the Third Reich, producing simplistic editions and portrayals of her brother. Here the connection between philological shenanigans and political responsibility is more or less explicit. As an extra bonus, in the process of repudiating Elisabeth, Schlechta's own archival discoveries become tantamount to antifascist resistance. Reporting about his exposé in 1937 to the committee charged with oversight of the scholarly work of the Archives, Schlechta writes: "Here Frau Förster-Nietzsche, who had been honored only two-and-a-half years before with a state funeral, which the Führer himself attended, was exposed as a swindler."[75] The reader of Schlechta's explanations should have no trouble drawing the appropriate conclusion: by concocting her own Nietzsche legend, Elisabeth perpetrated a political act that besmirched her brother's reputation by entwining his fate with National Socialism.

Schlechta never directly accuses Elisabeth of promoting a connection between her brother and anti-Semitism. His aims, however, are obvious: (1) to accuse Elisabeth of falsifications that led to her brother's Nazification, (2) to present himself as the resistance fighter, heroically opposing a venerated figure in the Third Reich, and (3) to justify the need for his newly published edition of Nietzsche's writings. On a much smaller scale and without the need for self-promotion, Richard Roos performed an analogous function for Nietzsche in France. Like Schlechta, Roos is centrally concerned with Elisabeth's editorial practices, and his particular focus is the last works, which are particularly difficult to disentangle because of Nietzsche's somewhat less than stable mental condition, and the plethora of plans and projects he sketched in his notebooks during the last two years of his sane life. Criticizing Elisabeth for originally publishing *The Antichrist* as part of *The Will to Power*, which is entirely justified based on several statements Nietzsche actually made, Roos goes on to cite other falsifications in that work and other late texts. Almost all relate to the exclusion of specific derogatory comments about Christianity.[76] A few exclusions might also have caused political difficulties since they were criticisms directed at Wilhelm II. In general, Roos, like many scholars in the postwar discussions, aims to discredit Elisabeth's oversight of her brother's writings, but when discussing her philological peccadillos, he makes only minor claims for ideological bias among the various exclusions and falsifications, and certainly none that would connect Nietzsche with Nazism.[77] Indeed, almost all of the passages that Elisabeth excluded from publication could plausibly have served, in her mind at least, to damage Nietzsche's reputation because they contain direct assaults on Jesus and the Christian religion, or on the Prussian monarchy. In an essay dealing with Elisabeth as "the abusive sister," however, he is more explicit about her purportedly fascist proclivities. Her influence, we are told, has been "sometimes baneful, often embarrassing, and almost always contrary to the ideas and interests of her brother."[78] Roos leaves no doubt that Elisabeth's influence is primarily responsible for bringing Nietzsche into the proximity of the Nazis, whose assumption of power was "opportune" for her: "In effect, the Nietzsche that Bäumler and Rosenberg made the prophet of the party coincides perfectly with her portrayal of him. Henceforth [after Hitler's assumption of power] any attack on the tradition of the Nietzsche Archives was able to be considered a manifestation hostile to Nazi doctrine."[79] By specifically mentioning Rosenberg, who was responsible for much of Nazi race theory, Roos makes it appear that Elisabeth's image of her brother partook of the Aryan supremacy and anti-Semitism promoted during the Third Reich. At the close of his essay Roos reproduces damaging documents that demonstrate Elisabeth's enthusiasm for Hitler and the National Socialist regime, thereby advancing the notion by innuendo that Elisabeth's own political activities brought Nietzschean philosophy into association with a political regime he would have detested.

The individual who did the most to connect Elisabeth with Nietzsche's Nazi affiliation, including anti-Semitism, and who contributed most to the decontamination of Nietzsche during the postwar period was Walter Kaufmann. His impact on Nietzsche's reception in the United States cannot be overestimated, not only because his monograph *Nietzsche: Philosopher, Psychologist, Antichrist* went through four editions since it first appeared in 1950, but also because his many translations and editions of Nietzsche's writings made the philosopher accessible to a wide Anglophone audience.[80] Kaufmann is the most explicit of the postwar rehabilitators in denying any connection between Nietzsche and anti-Jewish sentiments and in accusing Elisabeth of promoting a National Socialist affiliation with his philosophy. Nietzsche was not a protofascist, argued Kaufmann; he was an existentialist concerned with the creativity of the human spirit and with a strengthening of individualism. That others have not recognized Nietzsche's intentions has to do with the "Nietzsche legend," whose main proponent was his sister Elisabeth, a woman unsuited to be her brother's interpreter and apostle.[81] The "two most common forms" of this legend can be traced back to Elisabeth and consist of the notion that "Nietzsche's thought is hopelessly incoherent, ambiguous, and self-contradictory" and that "Nietzsche was a proto-Nazi." In Kaufmann's account, after her unsuccessful venture in South America with her anti-Semitic husband, Elisabeth returned to Germany and "realized that her brother's star had meanwhile begun its steep ascent." It was at this point that Elisabeth Förster became Elisabeth Förster-Nietzsche. She acquired the rights to her brother's works, sometimes through unscrupulous means; carefully controlled the publication of his literary remains, thereby withholding texts from the public; and issued interpretations of his works using Nietzsche's writings not yet in the public domain and therefore possessing an authority that could not be easily challenged. Kaufmann, like Schlechta and Roos, more often cites faulty philology than pernicious ideology in his discussions of Elisabeth's misdeeds, and although he does not focus on her falsifications, he makes it clear to the reader that she is generally not trustworthy. He complains at length about her editorial practices, in particular her withholding of *Ecce Homo* (1908) from publication. This misdeed had "fateful" implications, Kaufmann claims, since "the book contains explicit repudiations of many ideas that were meanwhile attributed to Nietzsche and have been associated with him to this day."[82] And he is especially outraged at the publication of *The Will to Power* as Nietzsche's magnum opus, although in a strange turnabout he himself edited and translated an English edition of the same work in 1967 and even followed in his arrangement of the English text the previously published German editions. In the editor's introduction to the translation he endeavors to explain why he would render into English a text whose very existence contributed so extensively to the Nietzsche legend he despises. But his explanation is simply that now that all of Nietzsche's later writings have been published—and Kaufmann had a hand in all of these publications—"*The Will to Power* should be made accessible, too, for those who cannot read these notes in the original German."[83] It is difficult to make sense of this explanation; if Elisabeth falsified her brother's thought by selecting aphorisms from different years and different contexts, and then placing them under rubrics that are unauthorized and contrary to Nietzsche's subsequent plans for the book, why would Kaufmann validate Elisabeth's work and thereby contribute to the legend he is at such pains to debunk?[84]

Kaufmann's discussion of the ideological dimension of Elisabeth's activity is similar to Schlechta's and Roos's in that accusations are made more by suggestion and innuendo than by philological proof and logical argumentation. Elisabeth, as we have seen, is held responsible for propagating a "Nietzsche legend" that harmonized well with tenets of National Socialism, and Kaufmann leaves no doubt that part of this legend entails a connection with anti-Semitism. He accuses Elisabeth of "bringing the heritage of her late husband to her interpretation of her brother's works," although he never cites from "her interpretation" to provide evidence for this claim.[85] If this "heritage" is not delineated clearly enough in the monograph, Kaufmann clarifies when, quoting himself in the introduction to *The Will to Power*, he inserts in brackets after the word "husband": "a prominent anti-Semite whose ideology Nietzsche had excoriated on many occasions."[86] Kaufmann insists that Nietzsche abhorred anti-Semitism. He admits that "anti-Semitic Teutonism," which he equates with "proto-Nazism," was "one of the major issues in Nietzsche's life, if only because his sister and Wagner, the two most important figures in his development, confronted him with this ideology."[87] But he cites extensively passages from letters and published writings that demonstrate Nietzsche's unequivocal rejection of anti-Semitism. He also dismisses the suggestion that Nietzsche's statements may have had a personal dimension, a common contention we have observed in Nazi interpretations: "His contempt for anti-Semitism was not prompted by the man who took his sister away from him: Nietzsche's position had been established unmistakably about the time of his breach with Wagner, and *Human, All-Too-Human* (1878) leaves no doubt about it."[88] For Kaufmann, Elisabeth's manipulation of her brother's thought, which then became associated with the anti-Semitism of the Nazis, is summed up symbolically in the hyphenated last name she assumed: "Förster-Nietzsche. The irony of this name suggests almost everything that could be said against her: the gospel she spread was indeed Förster first and Nietzsche second." He further maintains that she never accepted her brother's break with Wagner, and that she "doggedly persuaded the Nazis to accept her brother as their philosopher, and that it was in response to her insistent invitations that Hitler eventually visited the *Nietzsche-Archiv*—on a trip to Bayreuth."[89] These claims are offered without evidence. They are odd, especially since we have already seen that in her books and essays Elisabeth distinguishes very sharply between her brother's views on anti-Semitism and Wagner's. From the record we possess it is also evident that although Elisabeth did not object to Nietzsche's appropriation by the Nazis, she generally supported anyone who praised her brother provided they did not oppose her views. Finally, in Kaufmann's discussion of *The Will to Power* he asserts that Elisabeth and Heinrich Köselitz (Peter Gast), the editors of the work, eliminated "unkind comments" on anti-Semitism and the German Reich, but he adds that "there is no reason whatever for believing that the hitherto withheld material includes anything of significance that would have corroborated Frau Förster-Nietzsche's version of her brother's thought."[90] The inference is obvious: Elisabeth's "version" of Nietzsche is implicitly branded as anti-Semitic and supportive of the Third Reich, but there is nothing in his writings, or in the notebooks that would support the "Nietzsche legend" she purportedly advanced. Despite his philological differences with Schlechta, Kaufmann joins his German colleague and the French scholar Roos in placing the blame for Nietzsche's Nazi appropriation squarely at the feet of his sister. In the process all three intimate that Elisabeth promoted an image of Nietzsche that connects him with anti-Semitism and racism.

Although Elisabeth played no role in making her brother a racist and anti-Semite, she was nonetheless extremely important in removing any stigma of anti-Jewishness from him after the Second World War. It is worth noting that Schlechta, Roos, and Kaufmann had great familiarity with the textual situation surrounding Nietzsche's works and literary remains, as well as his correspondence, and that they never produce a shred of evidence in their works that Elisabeth had doctored anything Nietzsche wrote, or invented anything and attributed it to her brother, that would make him appealing to the anti-Semitic fanatics in the Third Reich. Their accusations are subtle and associative, entailing mostly her marriage to Förster and her later activities in the Nietzsche Archives. By emphasizing these personal involvements, leaving vague the notion of what sort of textual manipulation she perpetrated, and confirming that Nietzsche became a precursor of Nazi ideology, they create the impression that Elisabeth bears responsibility for illicitly moving her brother into the anti-Semitic camp. Later postwar commentators, as we have seen, who have no direct acquaintance with, or interest in, philological details, have been less circumspect in their accusations, maintaining against the textual record that Elisabeth's manipulations led to Nietzsche's inclusion as an anti-Semite, and against the historical record that she encouraged anti-Semitic interpretations of his work. Today there are few scholars who do not indict Elisabeth for Nietzsche's Nazi affiliation and anti-Semitism and believe that Nietzsche himself was largely free from nationalist and racist inclinations. If we are going to achieve a comprehensive view regarding Nietzsche's relationship to Jews, Judaism, and anti-Semitism, however, we will have to pay closer attention to both textual and contextual factors than scholars have in the past. We will have to understand, first of all, what sort of features and statements in his writings led many readers, both anti-Semites and their adversaries, to include him among anti-

Jewish thinkers. In some instances historical and personal circumstances may be decisive for our assessment. It will be important to account for both the atmosphere in Germany during his lifetime and the persons with whom Nietzsche most closely associated, as well as the individuals he read who were most influential in his intellectual development. Second, we must gain a better understanding of the value and import of various positions regarding racial and religious bias in Nietzsche's era. It is essential, for example, that we come to understand "anti-Semitism," both the expression itself and the political movement of the 1880s, as a historical phenomenon, and see how it related to Nietzsche in his professional and personal life. In the post–World War II era, the situation seemed clear: anti-Semitism signified simply a hostility or hatred of the Jews, and the rejection of anti-Semitism is associated with a liberal tolerance for religious and/or racial difference. In the following chapters, however, we have to exercise caution not to project backward our own meanings and associations onto Nietzsche's time, treating his statements and views ahistorically. It is crucial that we cease observing him through the distorting lens of National Socialism and its eliminationist policies toward the Jewish population of Europe. In short, if we want to reach an understanding of where Nietzsche stood on these critical issues, we must endeavor to avoid the very errors we have seen committed in this overview of the rise and fall of the image of Nietzsche as an anti-Semite.

CHAPTER TWO

Youthful Remarks and Encounters

RÖCKEN AND NAUMBURG

There was nothing remarkable in Nietzsche's ancestry or in his place of birth with respect to Jews and Judaism. Nietzsche was born into a family known for its Protestant pastors: his father, his father's father, and his mother's father all had ministries in one or another location in Saxony, and his other male ancestors had held mostly middle-class occupations. At various points in his life Nietzsche insisted that he was descended from Polish nobility, especially during the last years of his sane existence, but a thorough investigation of Nietzsche's family tree has found Germans extending back into the seventeenth century.[1] The claims we have seen advanced by first-generation anti-Semites that Nietzsche has Polish-Jewish blood are therefore just as fictional as Nietzsche's insistence that he was the descendant of Polish aristocrats. Nothing in his forefathers' past indicates an extensive preoccupation with Jews or the Jewish tradition. In his book on *Nietzsche and the Jews* (1998), Siegfried Mandel has pointed out that Nietzsche's paternal grandfather, Friedrich August Ludwig Nietzsche (1756–1826), who eventually assumed the position of superintendent in Eilenburg, had written a book titled *Gamaliel, or the Everlasting Endurance of Christianity* in 1796.[2] The book partakes of the Enlightenment tradition in Protestant theology, and since the title figure occupies a place in both the Jewish and Christian tradition—he was the grandson of Hillel the Elder, one of the most renowned rabbis in the Jewish heritage—we might suspect that Nietzsche, once he was old enough to study the history of early Christianity and its transition from Jewish doctrines and practices, had been acquainted with it. Gamaliel might also have appealed to Nietzsche since he was reputed to be the teacher of Paul the Apostle. Both the transition from Judaism to Christianity and the role of Paul in institutionalizing Christianity were central concerns for Nietzsche in the late 1880s. But the name Gamaliel occurs nowhere in Nietzsche's writings, neither in works nor notes nor correspondence, so we must conclude that there is no Jewish connection through his grandfather's theology. The town where Nietzsche was born, Röcken in Saxony-Anhalt, also gives us no clues about Nietzsche's relationship to Jews and Judaism. At the time of Nietzsche's birth in 1844 Röcken was a tiny village; Karl Ludwig Nietzsche, Friedrich's father, had received the parsonage there through the influence of the Prussian king, Friedrich Wilhelm IV, whom he had met while he was a tutor for the three daughters of the Duke of Saxe-Altenburg. Neither Röcken nor the town of Pobles, where Nietzsche's mother had lived in the pastor's house, were likely to have had any Jewish inhabitants, and it is probably fair to say that most of the villagers had no firsthand experience of Jews or Jewish life. The only knowledge they had would have come from the Bible, its interpretations by their pastors, or folk legends and lore. We know from the history of Jewish persecution that the absence of personal contact with Jews often goes hand in hand with irrational fears and prejudice. It is unlikely that the views of progressive Protestants during the Enlightenment, including perhaps Nietzsche's own grandfather, penetrated into the Saxon villages where Nietzsche lived during his initial years on earth.

Outside the provincial atmosphere in which Nietzsche was born and spent his early childhood, the Jewish Question was very much alive. In 1842 Bruno Bauer had published an essay, "On the Jewish Question," that appeared in book form the following year and occasioned a response from Karl Marx in the year of Nietzsche's birth. These texts by Bauer and Marx should be understood in the context of the ongoing discussion of Germany as a "Christian State," a notion that had apparently become popular in titles and chapter headings in the early 1840s.[3] But the controversies among radical leftists during the "pre-March" period were only a fraction of the contributions to a vast literature on the question of Jewish emancipation and related issues, numbering some 2,500 works published in the timespan from 1815 to 1850.[4] The push for Jewish emancipation in Germany, whose spearhead was the Hamburg lawyer Gabriel Riesser, reached a climax in the revolutionary years 1848 and 1849, assisted by the liberal spirit in parliaments in separate German states, as well as the democratic aspirations of the German federal representatives in St. Paul's Church in Frankfurt. Indeed, during the tumultuous years of the 1848 Revolution, for the first time in German history we find Jewish politicians elected and deliberating on the fate of their co-religionists. By 1849 a significant number of German Jews were officially "emancipated," meaning that they were granted full citizenship status and no longer subject to the great variety of restrictive laws under which most Jews had lived in different German territories. The Jews of Prussia and other German states, of course, had already experienced emancipation earlier in the century. In the wake of Napoleonic conquests, many Jews in Germany became subject to the more liberal French *code civil*, which in effect liberated them from the prohibitions German laws enforced, and an official edict on March 11, 1812, granted Jews in Prussia extensive new rights, although they were still excluded from the civil service and the military. The Wars of Liberation, however, fought by coalition armies against the French occupiers, meant precisely the opposite of liberation for most of the Jewish residents of the affected regions. At the Congress of Vienna and in the ensuing years of the Metternich Restoration Period, the emancipation of the Jews was systematically canceled, and most German states reverted to older statutes regarding their Jewish inhabitants. The emancipation of 1848–49 suffered a similar fate. It was enacted in only a small number of territories and impacted a tiny fraction of the German Jewish population at the time. As a consequence of the defeat of the revolution and the reinstitution of traditional leadership, emancipation was weakened or eliminated. In Prussia, for example, the revised constitution of 1850 reestablished the Christian religion as a prerequisite for most positions in culture or education.[5] During the 1860s, when Nietzsche was first a pupil at the Gymnasium and then studying at Bonn and Leipzig, various German states granted Jews the full rights of citizenship. A law of full equality, passed by the North German Confederation in July 1869, was then extended to the entirety of the Second Reich in 1871, and German Jews would remain emancipated until new restrictions ensued in the Third Reich.

It is unlikely that discussions and activity surrounding Jewish emancipation penetrated very far into the consciousness of the inhabitants of Saxon villages in the 1840s and 1850s. In Prussian Saxony, where Nietzsche was born and lived until he moved to Bonn to attend the Prussian Rhineland university, Jewish inhabitants constituted a mere 0.3 percent of the population in 1848, and this proportion had not increased since the end of the Napoleonic Wars. There were severe restrictions on Jewish residency in many parts of Saxony, and as a result Jewish communities were either small or nonexistent, and there was little chance for Gentiles to have contact with Jews and almost no public discourse concerning Jewish emancipation. Naumburg, where the Nietzsche family took up residence in 1850 following the untimely death of Nietzsche's father Karl Ludwig the previous year, is a case in point. In comparison to Röcken, Naumburg was a metropolis, comprising around 14,000 inhabitants with a large middle class and on a newly built railway line that ran from Halle to Erfurt. The military and the Superior

Provincial Court were the most important institutions for the city. During most of Nietzsche's childhood, however, there were no Jewish residents. It is possible that Nietzsche was acquainted with the history of the Jewish population in Naumburg, which was typical of many cities of moderate size in central Germany. There was a flourishing Jewish presence in the fourteenth century and perhaps a Jewish population as early as the eleventh century, as evidenced by the existence of a "Jewish Alley" (*Judengasse*), dedicated houses for Jews, a synagogue, and a Jewish bath. Jews were accused of plotting to set fire to the town during the Black Death, but they survived this persecution and persisted as a community into the fifteenth century. Officially, twenty-two Jewish families, which meant approximately 110 Jewish individuals, were permitted in the city in 1410, but in 1454 Jews were forced to wear a special hat, and their numbers were reduced. Although the community was well connected with the ecclesiastical authorities, in 1494 the city council on the advice of the imperial elector Friedrich the Wise expelled all Jews from Naumburg "for all eternity," the local bishop receiving compensation of sixty gulden for his incurred losses until 1803. The Peter-Paul's Fair quite likely brought Jewish merchants back to the city starting in the sixteenth or seventeenth century, and we have records of a great increase in taxes on Jewish traders during the first quarter of the eighteenth century. By 1804 there were evidently over six hundred Jews participating in the fair, and a reestablishment of the Naumburg Jewish community appeared to be in the offing. Naumburg's incorporation into Prussia as the result of the compromises at the Congress of Vienna, however, and the resulting customs laws, put an end to the fair, and the municipal council, harkening back to the restrictive measures of 1494, forbade any Jewish settlement until 1859. The census in 1861 lists nine Jewish residents out of a population of 13,917.[6] Nietzsche may not have been familiar with all details of Naumburg's history regarding the Jews, but he almost certainly was acquainted with the Jewish figures on the hood screen or jube in the Naumburg Cathedral. Although other churches depicted Jews more grotesquely or cruelly battering Jesus, Naumburg's Jewish figures are nonetheless distinctly Jewish and designated as different by dint of their Jewish hats.[7] We have no record of Nietzsche's reactions to these figures or to any of the historical occurrences regarding Jews in the city in which he lived for most of his childhood, but it would be unlikely that he remained completely ignorant of the history of the Jewish presence in Naumburg.

From the evidence that we have, Nietzsche therefore had very limited exposure to actual Jews, and his knowledge of Judaism and the history of Jews in Germany or in general is apt to have been restricted to very conventional sources. We encounter no reference to Jews or Judaism in any correspondence prior to his enrollment at the university; Jews are not mentioned in preuniversity years in his juvenilia; there are no remarks about Jews in any memoirs of individuals acquainted with him during the first two decades of his life. In her biography of Nietzsche, his sister Elisabeth confirms this general impression: "We ourselves, that is, my brother and I, did not meet a single Jew in our entire childhood or early youth." She does mention that their Aunt Rosalie, who was a member of the Nietzsche household until her death in 1867, was an enthusiastic supporter of Julius Stahl, a "Jewish" representative to the Prussian General Assembly,[8] but Stahl, a conservative professor of law at Würzburg and Berlin, had converted to Protestantism in 1819 and became a radical opponent of Jewish emancipation. The general absence of references to Jews makes the inclusion of an anti-Jewish refrain in Nietzsche's notebooks from 1861–62 all the more remarkable. In a poem or song whose first two lines are the refrain "O Engelmann, o Engelmann / Just look at this rascal" ("*O Engelmann, o Engelmann / So seht doch mal den Bengel an*"), the following lines complete one of the stanzas:

Schmeißt doch den Juden Itzig raus
Zum Tempel 'naus
Das rabenschwarze Kantorhaus! (Nachlass 1861–62, 11[36], KGW I 2.312–13)

(Throw the Jew Itzig out, out of the temple, the raven-black cantor house)

None of the other stanzas contains an obvious reference to Jews. The first line after the refrain in this particular stanza alludes to a common anti-Jewish song popular in the second half of the nineteenth century. In the Neustettin Pogrom in 1881, for example, the mayor, in an endeavor to calm the masses bent on attacking the Jewish population, asked the city band to play patriotic songs, but after an agitator finished riling up the crowd, "the band intoned the song popular at that time: 'Throw him out, the Jew Itzig.'"[9] It is reported in 1880 that the noted anti-Semitic politician Ernst Henrici employed the song after a speech.[10] And we even find it mentioned as part of a puppet show, in which a Jew named Abraham, who is trying to collect money owed to him, is beaten to death by Kasperl, who then drags him away singing the Judeophobic ditty.[11] We can make sense of the song as part of common folk traditions in the latter half of the nineteenth century by understanding it as a response to Jews gaining economic power in post-1848 Germany, which in turn became an overworked theme in the political anti-Semitic propaganda of the 1880s. The Jew has to be thrown out because he threatens German propriety; the Kasperl play makes it explicit that

Jewish usury must be punished with death. How Nietzsche came into possession of this song, why he copied it in his notebook in the early 1860s, and what he thought about the anti-Jewish content—if he gave it a second thought—is open to speculation. But the inclusion of this stanza, as innocuous as it may appear, gives an indication of the type of anti-Jewish sentiments that circulated in the public sphere Nietzsche inhabited, even in the absence of a Jewish presence.

BONN

When Nietzsche began his theological studies at the University of Bonn, he resided for the first time outside of Prussian Saxony. Although the part of the Rhineland to which Bonn belonged had been awarded to Prussia as a result of compromises at the Congress of Vienna, so that Nietzsche technically remained under Prussian authority, he encountered a somewhat different and more liberal tradition in the western part of Germany. The likelihood of an encounter with Jews in Bonn was appreciably higher than in Naumburg or at Schulpforta, the nearby preparatory school Nietzsche attended. The Jewish student Harry Heine, who later became the celebrated author Heinrich Heine, was enrolled at the University of Bonn for a year in 1819, and in 1835 a young Karl Marx, likewise of Jewish heritage, matriculated as a law student; so it is very likely that a handful of Jewish students were in attendance in 1864, when Nietzsche arrived in the city.[12] Among the faculty the Jewish mathematician Rudolf Lipschitz was appointed the same year Nietzsche matriculated, and in 1866 a Jewish classical scholar, Jacob Bernays, was named the successor to Friedrich Ritschl, who was both Bernays's former professor and the classicist under whom Nietzsche studied at Bonn and then Leipzig. Bernays is said to have been Ritschl's favorite student at Bonn, and Nietzsche, twenty years Bernays's junior, assumed that place of honor for a later generation of budding classical philologists. Prior to his appointment in Bonn, Bernays had held a position at the Jewish Theological Seminary in Breslau, and Nietzsche mentions in a letter to his family that he had intended to go to Breslau, but now that "one of the professors on whose account I wanted to go to Breslau has left Breslau" (KSB 2.105), he had canceled those plans. We have to assume that Nietzsche is referring to Bernays, whom Ritschl had likely recommended, and who worked on topics that were directly in Nietzsche's field of interest. At Bonn, however, we have no indication that Nietzsche met any Jewish students or professors; he makes no reference to Jews whatsoever. The city of Bonn, like most German urban centers, had a checkered history of Jewish relations. After Jews were martyred in the wake of the First Crusade, we have reason to believe that a Jewish quarter was established in the twelfth century, but during the Black Death the community was again violently dissolved. In the ensuing centuries the Jews experienced similar changes in fortune, at times establishing themselves and gathering wealth through cattle dealing and usury, at other times being persecuted and expelled. There was a Jewish ghetto established in the eighteenth century; the grandfather of the noted nineteenth-century writer and political activist Ludwig Börne resided in these quarters. Not until Napoleon's time were the Jews emancipated, and the community had several hundred members by the time Nietzsche arrived on the scene.[13] But there is no indication that Nietzsche took any particular notice of Jewish life in Bonn during the single year that he attended the university.

The university in Bonn had been established in 1818 in the spirit of Prussian educational reform, but soon thereafter it was subject to the repressive measures of the Metternich Restoration. Ernst Moritz Arndt, a famous patriotic poet from the first two decades of the nineteenth century, had received an appointment to the history faculty in 1818, but he was shortly thereafter relieved of his official duties because of his political views, which continued to support a unified Germany and opposed the separate rulers of the German principalities and states. He was rehabilitated only after the death of the Prussian king, Friedrich Wilhelm III, in 1840, after which he served as rector of the university in 1841, and as a professor until his retirement in 1854. Even after he retired from the university, he remained active in the civic life of Bonn until his death in 1860, just four years before Nietzsche began his studies at the Rhineland university. Arndt's legendary advocacy for Germany was combined with a virulent anti-French attitude and a healthy dose of Judeophobia. Indeed, Jews were identified at various points with the French, with cosmopolitans, and with the left. Violating the racial purity of the nation, Jews are for Arndt a bastardized people and compared in different passages with flies, gnats, and vermin. As a delegate to the National Assembly in 1848, Arndt did not publicly advocate for the persecution of the Jews, but he was openly opposed to a policy of unrestricted emancipation.[14] Nietzsche was certainly conscious of Arndt's reputation as a proponent of German unity. Indeed, shortly after his arrival in Bonn he made a visit to the recently deceased poet's gravesite, and in the following year he mentions in several letters his attendance at the 1865 "national Arndt festival," where a memorial monument depicting the celebrated German patriot was dedicated (to Franziska and Elisabeth Nietzsche, to Oskar Wunderlich, to Carl von Gersdorff, May 29, 1865, June 1865, August 4, 1865, Nr. 468, 471, 476, KSB 2.59, 69, 76).[15] For most of the student body and the general population, many of whom, like Arndt, enthusiastically embraced the concept of a unified Germany, expressions of anti-Jewish sentiments would assuredly not have detracted from a celebrated individual's renown or importance. Whether Nietzsche knew firsthand about Arndt's remarks regarding Jews is impossible to determine. But it is safe to say that if he did, it would not have diminished his enthusiasm for this former professor and for his accomplishments as a writer and citizen in Bonn.

We can therefore detect no significant modification in Nietzsche's attitude toward Jews and Judaism during his year in Bonn; his exposure to actual Jews was minimal, and we find no evidence of a preoccupation with Jews or Jewish issues in his notebooks or correspondence. It is quite possible, however, that Nietzsche took some interest in the topic of tolerance and religious prejudice during his initial year as a university student. We have indirect evidence that he involved himself with Gotthold Ephraim Lessing's drama *Nathan the Wise* (1779) during this period. In a letter Carl von Gersdorff wrote to Nietzsche in December 1864, his friend mentions "works about *Nathan the Wise*" that Nietzsche had obviously cited in a previous letter that we no longer possess (Nr. 91, KGB I 3.23). Lessing was a quite controversial figure for anti-Jewish thinkers, especially for the wave of anti-Semitic agitators that flourished around 1880. It is not hard to understand why. He was renowned for his close friendship with Moses Mendelssohn, the most prominent member of the Jewish community in Germany during the late eighteenth century and the model for the title figure of his last play. In one of his earliest dramas, titled simply *The Jews* (1749) and written prior to his acquaintance with Mendelssohn, Lessing had already advocated for tolerance and humane treatment toward members of the Jewish faith. His later theological writings continued in this vein of enlightened liberality. His final dramatic work, *Nathan the Wise*, would become the most celebrated German theatrical production to portray Jews and Judaism in a positive light; consequently, after the Second World War it frequently opened theaters throughout Germany. Because of his enlightened views on Jews and religion, ultranationalists and Judeophobes of the late nineteenth century decried Lessing, and he himself was frequently considered Jewish, or at least partially Jewish. In Nietzsche's published works, notebooks, and correspondence Lessing plays no substantive role, and he is never mentioned in connection with his views on Jews or religious tolerance. That the twenty-year-old showed an interest in this celebrated play is thus remarkable. Noteworthy also is that the two commentaries on the drama he mentioned to Gersdorff were both highly supportive of Lessing's liberal proclivities. In the short monograph by Kuno Fischer, whose history of modern philosophy Nietzsche would appreciate and cull frequently in the 1870s and 1880s, the author identifies "self-denial" as the most genuine characteristic of religion according to Lessing, and, defending the playwright against detractors who claimed he deprecated Christianity while lauding Judaism, he offers trenchant reasons that the lead character had to be Jewish.[16] The essay by David Friedrich Strauß, whom Nietzsche would attack a few years later in his first *Untimely Meditation, David Strauß, the Confessor and Writer* (1873), similarly claims that Lessing's theme will be generally relevant as long as there are arguments concerning "fanaticism and tolerance" or "bigotry and enlightenment."[17] Nietzsche's interest in Lessing's play about religious tolerance and two liberal commentaries suggests that he was fairly open-minded toward the Jewish Question as he began the third decade of his life.

LEIPZIG

Nietzsche's exposure to Jews and to anti-Jewish sentiments would increase dramatically over the next few years, however, establishing a structure of perception and attendant clichés that he would never entirely abandon. After leaving Bonn, Nietzsche traveled back to Naumburg to recuperate from an illness, but before his initial semester at the University of Leipzig, he accompanied his friend and fellow student, Hermann Mushacke, to his home in Berlin. It was Nietzsche's first visit to the city that would soon become the capital of the Second Empire, and he would return to Berlin only occasionally and for brief periods during the rest of his life. In a retrospective of his first two years in Leipzig written in August 1867, Nietzsche recalls the time he spent with Mushacke's family as very pleasant. He seems to have become instant friends with Mushacke's father, the Gymnasium teacher Eduard Mushacke, who has usually been connected to Nietzsche studies only insofar as he was a friend of Max Stirner, the pseudonym taken by the philosopher and anarchist Johann Kaspar Schmidt. For over a century there has been speculation about whether Nietzsche was acquainted with or influenced by the anarchist tradition, since there is some resemblance in their ideas about individualism and the state. Nietzsche's sister Elisabeth, who had a proprietary interest in maintaining her brother's originality, and who certainly did not desire his works associated with the circle of left-Hegelian individualism, maintained that he had never read Stirner.[18] Franz Overbeck, however, who was Nietzsche's closest associate during his Basel years, and who was actively engaged in a dispute with Elisabeth over her brother's legacy, asserts the contrary and estimates that the influence was considerable.[19] Curiously we find no reference to Stirner in any of Nietzsche's writings or notebooks, nor does his name appear in his correspondence, and several of his closest acquaintances, when queried by Elisabeth, stated that Nietzsche had never mentioned Stirner. The search for a tangible connection has led some investigators to Mushacke, who was probably a member of the Berlin Young Hegelians, a group to which the young Friedrich Engels belonged for a time, and who therefore knew Stirner and possibly mediated something of Stirner's thought or even lent one of Stirner's books to the young student visiting his son. We know that the elder Mushacke and Nietzsche became rather close during this short stay, since Nietzsche informs his mother that Mushacke extended the permission of familiar address to him (October 22, 1866, Nr. 483, KSB 2.90). In his retrospective account he also gives some information regarding the themes that this "amiable man" had broached: "his insights into the higher administration of schools, his anger about Jewish Berlin, his memories from the times of the Young Hegelians: in short, the entire pessimistic atmosphere of a man who has glimpsed a great deal behind the scenes" (Nachlass 1867–68, 60[1], KGW I 4.509). Significant here is again the climate that surrounded Nietzsche, rather than any particular views on Jews or Judaism. On his first trip to the Prussian capital he is already exposed to an individual, otherwise pleasant, respectable, and knowledgeable, who exhibits an open antipathy toward the Jews and associates them with adverse aspects of urban existence.[20] Nietzsche is uncritical of this anti-Jewish remark, as he would be toward most Judeophobic utterances he encountered throughout his life.

With his matriculation at the University of Leipzig, his residence in a city famous for its trade fairs, and his acquisition of a circle of friends among the students, Nietzsche begins to develop more pronounced opinions regarding Jews in contemporary German life. In some aspects the city of Leipzig did not distinguish itself very much from Nietzsche's earlier domiciles. It was the first place Nietzsche had lived that was not under Prussian rule—Leipzig remained part of the Kingdom of Saxony after the Congress of Vienna—and it was a somewhat larger city than Nietzsche had previously experienced—it numbered approximately 100,000 inhabitants at the beginning of the Second Reich in 1871. But its history of Jewish relations, like those of most German municipalities, was decidedly mixed, with alternating periods of acceptance and banishment. An organized Jewish community dated back to the thirteenth century, but it appears it was disbanded during the Black Death when Jews were accused of poisoning wells. They returned at some point but were banished again under instigation from Martin Luther by the Elector of Saxony, Johann Friedrich I, in 1536. Jews participated continuously in the Leipzig fairs, however, which were held three times annually. By the end of the seventeenth century, Jews were given permission to hold services during fairs, and a few years later they were again granted permanent residence. By the time Nietzsche arrived in 1865, there was a significant Jewish presence in Leipzig; the first Jew was granted citizenship in 1839, a synagogue was built in 1855, and a cemetery was established in 1864.[21] More significant for Nietzsche and his fellow students at the university was the large influx of Jewish traders and merchants during the fairs. These Jews brought economic prosperity to Leipzig, not least through the taxes they paid to conduct business in the city, but they also disrupted the normal life of some residents, especially students, some of whom were forced to relinquish their domiciles temporarily to house the itinerant traders. Nietzsche was likely exposed for the first time not only to a significant number of Jews in one place but also to anti-Jewish slurs and comments from his university colleagues. These anti-Jewish sentiments certainly did not emanate from Nietzsche's dissertation adviser, Friedrich Ritschl, who had married a Jewish woman, Sophie Guttentag, daughter of the chief physician at Breslau's Jewish Hospital.[22] Indeed, Nietzsche felt great respect and admiration for Frau Ritschl and exchanged letters with her, as well as with her husband. But some of his fellow students slipped easily into anti-Jewish clichés. We have already seen that the Mushacke household harbored denigratory views about Jewish Berlin, but we find evidence of several other students, among them Nietzsche's childhood friend from Naumburg, Wilhelm Pinder,[23] and his closest friends from Leipzig, Carl von Gersdorff and Erwin Rohde, who freely produce anti-Jewish utterances.

None of Nietzsche's friends was engaged in Judeophobic activities; their racist comments are made in passing and are part of a general cultural climate in which it was accepted that Jews are to be regarded as inferior and undesirable human beings. Pinder, for example, writing from Berlin during the Austro-Prussian War, reports how the common people in the city crowded around the pillars on which news is publicly posted to read the latest official reports from the battlefield. Pinder places himself in the position of an observer of this activity: "Then one furtively observes the impression that the news makes on the gathered masses, rejoices when a Jew, who dares to cry out: 'but all that is not true' is properly treated with a beating" (July 9, 1866, Nr. 127, KGB I 3.114). The casual nature of these remarks—Pinder further relates how he strolls down the main street, visits a café, and buries himself behind a wall of newspapers—indicates that neither he nor his reader should give a second thought to a Jew being roughed up for questioning the official news on the war. Indeed, Pinder rejoices (*freut sich*) at the thought of the thrashing and exhibits no compassion or concern for the mistreated human being. Paul Deussen, a fellow student of Nietzsche at both Schulpforta and Bonn who would later become an eminent Sanskrit scholar and the founder of the Schopenhauer society, is much more academic in his remarks.[24] As a philologist he appreciates the Hebrew language, and although the Jewish people exhibit "oriental barbarism," he at least appreciates their unique place in history, the venerable quality of their holy texts, and their deeply ethical substance (August 1866, Nr. 129, KGB I 3.125). Gersdorff, whom Nietzsche had met in Pforta and whose intention to study in Leipzig was probably the main impetus for Nietzsche's transfer from Bonn, is much less kind in his considerations of Jews. Adopting a perspective that would become common in anti-Semitic writings of the early 1880s, he accuses Jews of promoting and then profiting from military hostilities with fraudulent financial maneuvers. Writing to Nietzsche from Görlitz at the end of March in 1866, just two and a half months before the outbreak of the Austro-Prussian War, he fulminates against dishonest Jewish dealings: "Stockmarket Jews mobilize army corps, although they know very well that we are still truly enjoying the deepest peace, and use contemptible deception to sell off low-priced securities: in short, it is a time of swindle in every sense of the word" (Nr. 115, KGB I 3.82–83). When Gersdorff travels to the Bavarian city Fürth, he invariably describes it with the epithet "Jew-city" (August 17, 1866, Nr. 132, KGB I 3.136), referring no doubt to the long tradition of tolerance for Jews among the Christian population of the Bavarian municipality.[25] And when Gersdorff writes to Nietzsche in 1868 regarding Julius Frauenstädt, the Jewish editor of the works of Arthur Schopenhauer, he includes his uncle's comments, which claim Frauenstädt to be "a superficial, vain Jewish rascal whose chief concern is to obtain profit from the literary remains of the master" (August 12, 1868, Nr. 283, KGB I 3.286). As far as we can tell, Nietzsche had never been exposed to such a variety of deprecatory remarks about Jews during the first two decades of his life, in particular from his closest friends and associates.

Nietzsche's response was hardly a repudiation of these casual anti-Jewish statements; in his correspondence he showed himself more than willing to participate in this sort of commonplace racist banter. We should recall that he was hardly a child or an impressionable teenager when he was studying at Leipzig; he matriculated at the Saxon university when he was twenty-two years old and left Leipzig only when he received a position at Basel in his twenty-fifth year. From his reading he knew about religious tolerance, as his preoccupation with *Nathan* evidences, and we have no reason to suspect that he had prior negative experience with Jews. Quite the contrary: the one Jewish individual we are certain he knew, Sophie Ritschl, was a woman he sincerely admired. And from his notebooks we can determine that he definitely recognized her Jewish ancestry (Nachlass 1867–68, 60[1], KGW I 4.519). Nonetheless, when writing to his mother and sister about his experiences during the Leipzig fair, he emphasizes the unsavory impact of the Jewish tradespeople who descend on the city. He complains that he is unable to make progress on his book because of the disruption, and tries to relax by walking through the streets: "The food that you get in restaurants is hardly appetizing at present. Moreover, everywhere it is teeming with revolting, insipid apes and other merchants. So that I really long for the termination of this intermezzo. Finally Gersdorff and I found a tavern where we didn't have to countenance oily butter and Jewish mugs [*Judenfratzen*], but where we are regularly the only customers" (April 22, 1866, Nr. 502, KSB 2.125). Five days later he grouses in a similar vein to Mushacke in Berlin: "Everywhere the food is very bad and just as expensive; in the theater *The African Woman*[26] is still playing; and everywhere you look there are Jews and associates of Jews [*Juden und Judengenossen*]" (Nr. 504, KSB 2.127–28). And writing again to his mother and sister on the final day of the fair in October 1868, Nietzsche expresses relief that the turmoil is coming to an end and that he will soon be relieved of "the smell of fat and the numerous Jews" (Nr. 593, KSB 2.326). In these early letters we may have the impression that Nietzsche's disparaging remarks about Jews are more thoughtless decoration than the expression of a deep-seated conviction. In his early years Jews have a traditional field of association in Nietzsche's mind; they are identified with merchants and money, with unsavory food, ugliness, and occasionally cleverness. The remarks and associations in Nietzsche's letters—and very likely in his casual conversations—are significant for at least two reasons. They do not show that Nietzsche was on the road to becoming a rabid anti-Jewish polemicist—which was the fate of several of his contemporaries—but they do indicate that in his early years he blended in rather inconspicuously with a climate of anti-Jewish biases that flourished almost everywhere around him. Nietzsche never opposed anti-Jewish statements or sentiments coming from his friends, and he did not hesitate to employ them to spice up his own accounts of his travails in Leipzig during the fair season. He could have known better—and perhaps did know better—with regard to Jews and Judaism from his readings and from his personal acquaintances. But his comments demonstrate that he succumbed to the easy path of parroting the prejudices of a noxious German Judeophobia. Second, these remarks are noteworthy because they occur prior to Nietzsche's acquaintance with Richard Wagner. The notion that Wagner, who had harbored strong anti-Jewish convictions since the 1840s, was principally responsible for infecting Nietzsche with a disdain for Jews and Judaism is simply false. The seeds of anti-Jewish bias were already very deeply implanted in the young Leipzig philologist by the time he met Wagner in November 1868. With regard to Jews and Judaism, Wagner's influence, as we shall see, represents much more of continuity in ideology than a fundamental shift in beliefs.

The foundation for Nietzsche's anti-Jewish outlook in his Leipzig years must have emanated from personal contact with friends and acquaintances. During his student years there is no evidence that Nietzsche read or pursued authors who exhibited Judeophobia or texts that contained Judeophobic themes, or that he was exposed to any anti-Jewish sentiments in his readings. As a young adult he was an enthusiastic reader of Emerson's essays, and he was impressed early by Friedrich Albert Lange's *History of Materialism* (1866), but neither Emerson nor Lange deal with Jewish topics or themes, and neither is known for racist utterances. In the 1860s Nietzsche appears to have read and appreciated Eugen Dühring's *The Value of Life* (1865),[27] and, as we have seen, Dühring was one of the most vocal anti-Semites during the 1880s. But in his early writings Dühring had not yet developed, or at least expressed, his hatred of Jews and their religion. Similarly, Nietzsche was impressed with Heinrich von Treitschke and mentions his political pamphlet on the "Future of the Middle States," which appeared shortly after the conclusion to the Austro-Prussian War (to Carl von Gersdorff, August 1866, Nr. 517, KSB 2.159), but again Treitschke's anti-Semitism and the "Berlin Anti-Semitism Controversy" he unleashed in the 1880s[28] was a future development; his pamphlet, written in the spirit of the National Liberal Party, contains no mention of Jews or Jewish emancipation. Nietzsche's notebooks from his time at the university, especially in his last two years in Leipzig, contain predominantly reflections and exercises relating to topics from classical philology, indicating that he was devoting most of his time to his academic studies and specialization. There are many topics in the ancient world, of course, that relate to Jews and Judaism, but Nietzsche does not appear to have taken an interest in them. His published philological writings, almost all of which were researched during his years at Leipzig under Ritschl's tutelage, include longer treatises on the poet Theognis of Megara, who wrote during the sixth century BC, and the sources of Diogenes Laërtius, as well as shorter essays on Greek lyric poetry and the Contest of Homer and Hesiod,[29] but none of these topics has an obvious relationship to Jews in the ancient Mediterranean region. Only after Nietzsche received his appointment at Basel and began lecturing and writing on tragedy did he insert in his writings remarks on how modern Judaism represents a continuation of tendencies in Attic society or invidious comparisons of Semitic values with those found in Roman or Greek culture.

One possible exception in Nietzsche's general reading from the 1860s was the philosopher Arthur Schopenhauer. Nietzsche's interest in Schopenhauer would flourish during his years as a Wagnerian disciple and would wane considerably after he broke off his relationship with the composer, but Nietzsche discovered Schopenhauer well before he became a member of Wagner's entourage. If we believe Nietzsche's account, he happened upon Schopenhauer's chief philosophical work, *The World as Will and Representation* (1818/19, 1844), by chance browsing in a local antiquarian shop in Bonn: "I don't know what demon whispered to me: 'Take this book home with you.' In any case it occurred despite my usual habit of not rushing into the purchase of books" (Nachlass 1867–68, 60[1], KGW I 4.513). Although there is some reason to believe that this account is apocryphal,[30] there is no doubt that Nietzsche, like many young intellectuals of his generation, became an avid reader and admirer of the philosopher of pessimism. Schopenhauer's relationship to Jews and Judaism followed a pattern frequently encountered in the nineteenth and twentieth centuries among German Gentiles. Jews were among his closest friends and supporters; from the impoverished student Josef Gans, whom Schopenhauer had met and befriended in Berlin, to the lawyer Martin Emden and the linguist and writer David Ascher, two men from the initial wave of Schopenhauer enthusiasts in the 1850s, the philosopher did not appear to have any personal animus against Jews. Indeed, although the relationship was at times strained, he even entrusted his literary remains and legacy to a Jew, Julius Frauenstädt, to whom, as we have seen, some Germans attributed dubious motives. We should recall, however, that Richard Wagner, whose contributions to anti-Semitic thought are indubitable, relied heavily on several Jewish musicians and attracted considerable Jewish support for his operas, and that even Wilhelm Marr, the probable inventor of the term "anti-Semitism," married women of Jewish origins on three separate occasions.[31] In Schopenhauer's most rigorous philosophical texts Jews and Judaism are not commonly topics,[32] but they do play a slightly greater role in various places in his essays collected under the title *Parerga and Paralipomena* (1851). Taken as a whole Schopenhauer wrote relatively sparsely on the Jewish Question and Jewish history. In his latest biography the subject does not even appear until the final pages of a five-hundred-page tome, and then it is handled quickly on a page and a half of text and in a long footnote.[33] A writer could make more of the topic if inclined toward anti-Semitism, as was Maria Groener in her 1920 monograph *Schopenhauer and the Jews*, published in a series on Germany's Leading Men and Judaism,[34] and there is enough material for a small book if one considers all the evidence exhaustively.[35] But generally Schopenhauer had little to say about the Jews of his own era and their religious heritage.

What he did say, however, could easily have served to expand and reinforce the anti-Jewish worldview Nietzsche was beginning to develop as a student. Most of Schopenhauer's remarks on Judaism criticize the very essence of that religion. It is characterized by "realism and optimism," which he views as features closely related to theism in general. Since Schopenhauer's philosophical views, like Brahmanism and Buddhism, which he extolls in comparison to the Jewish faith, "have as their fundamental characteristics idealism and pessimism," he is invariably ill disposed toward Judaism. Schopenhauer comments favorably only on the single most important correction to Jewish optimism, the fall from grace in the Garden of Eden, calling it a "pessimistic element that is required in the interests of the most obvious and palpable truth."[36] We will see that Nietzsche, in a different context, regards the fall as the essential Semitic myth in contrast to the Aryan myth of Prometheus's defiance of the gods. In other passages Schopenhauer expounds on the deficiencies of Judaism as a religious doctrine: it is "the crudest of all religions because it is the only one that has absolutely no doctrine of immortality." He is fond of emphasizing that the wretched nature of the Jewish religion is part of its very foundation, claiming that the absence of an afterlife and the alleged immanence of Judaism account for the contempt experienced by the Jews on the part of adherents to all other religions in the ancient world.[37] Schopenhauer also supplies an alternative and unflattering commentary on Exodus based on his reading of Tacitus: Pharaoh expelled the Jewish people, "a sneaking dirty race afflicted with filthy diseases (scabies) that threatened to prove infectious," and sent soldiers to pursue them only because they had stolen golden vessels from the temples. With "the murderer Moses at their head" the Jews acquired their "promised land" by "ruthlessly murdering and exterminating all the inhabitants, even the women and children" solely because they were an uncircumcised people and did not believe in Jehovah. This account again demonstrates how disdained Jews were in the ancient world—once more Schopenhauer attributes it to the absence of any existence beyond this life—and why they were regarded "as cattle, as the dregs of humanity, but as great masters in lying."[38] Schopenhauer's most disparaging remarks about Jews occur in his discussion of Judaism's putative disregard for the humane treatment of animals.

Citing the hegemony over the animal kingdom granted to human beings in the opening passages of Genesis, Schopenhauer exclaims: "Holy Ganga! Mother of our race! Such stories have on me the same effect as do Jew's pitch and *foetor Judaicus*! The fault lies with the Jewish view that regards the animal as something manufactured for man's use."[39] The Latin phrase "foetor Judaicus" (Jewish stench) recurs throughout Schopenhauer's discussion, and the association of Jews with unpleasant odors was certainly not foreign to Nietzsche, as we have already witnessed from his Leipzig correspondence. Schopenhauer's point, of course, is that animals are more similar to human beings than they are different because they have a will and cerebral intelligence. Contemporaries, he maintains, are too "befuddled through *foetor Judaicus*" to recognize the inherent equality among the species, and in Schopenhauer's view it is high time that in Europe "Jewish views on nature were brought to an end." Schopenhauer thus posits, as Nietzsche would in the late 1880s, a fundamental continuation of Jewish values in the Christian world, which the philosopher of pessimism dubs at one point "Jewish-Christianity" (*Juden-Christenthum*).[40] Nietzsche's continuity, found in his writings from 1887 and 1888, would involve a radically different moral attitude, but he certainly follows Schopenhauer in assigning blame to Judaism for current ills in Christian Europe. We have no direct evidence that Nietzsche read the passages in Schopenhauer's writings relating to Jews and Judaism. But as an avid and enthusiastic student of Schopenhauer, it is more than likely that he absorbed these anti-Jewish thoughts along with others he encountered during his years in Leipzig.

Schopenhauer's evaluation of the situation of Jews in contemporary society is colored by his views of the essential qualities of the Jewish religion, but it also represents a response to demands for emancipation, which were sounded in various European nations during the nineteenth century. The Jews are personified in Schopenhauer's view by the wandering Jew Ahasuerus; they have no homeland and are condemned by their crime against the Savior to wander the earth. The Jews live "parasitically" from the peoples whose nations they inhabit, and at the same time they are inspired by the liveliest patriotism for their own nation. "The Fatherland of the Jews," Schopenhauer informs his reader, "is the rest of the Jews," and for this reason "it would be absurd to want to concede to them a share in the government or administration of any country." On the other hand, Schopenhauer also believes that they should enjoy the same civil rights as other citizens in a given society. He thus proposes a compromise position with regard to emancipation, advocating for equality in civil rights (*bürgerliche Rechte*), while at the same time denying them "any share in the running of the State." Likewise,

Schopenhauer assumes an intermediate position with regard to the status of Judaism. He does not believe that Jews are defined solely by religion: "it is an extremely superficial and false view to regard the Jews merely as a religious sect." But he also does not regard them as a biologically defined race, which would have been an unusual view considering when Schopenhauer was writing. Instead, he uses the somewhat superannuated concept of a "Jewish nation" as the "correct expression" for defining contemporary Jews. With regard to their religious beliefs, Schopenhauer contends that "monotheism is part of their nationality and political constitution and is with them a matter of course"; indeed, "monotheism and Judaism are interchangeable terms." Accordingly the resolution to the "Jewish Question" for Schopenhauer is conversion, which is the same solution proposed by many of the pro- and anti-Jewish writers of the eighteenth and early nineteenth centuries. "Reasonable Jews" will readily relinquish a faith that brings them neither advantage nor honor, even if they do not take Christianity very seriously. To accelerate this process one should encourage unions of Gentiles and Jews, and in the space of a century few Jews will remain and the curse of Ahasuerus will be lifted. If Jews were fully emancipated now, however, they would shun conversion and remain Jews: thus a further argument against Jewish emancipation is that it would interfere with the easiest solution to the larger Jewish Question. Until they are fully assimilated by conversion to Christianity, they "are and remain a foreign, oriental race, and so must always be regarded merely as domiciled foreigners."[41] Schopenhauer's views on Jewish emancipation thus harken back to a time that predates Nietzsche's exposure to Jews and anti-Jewish sentiments. Nonetheless, their status as parasites and as a foreign element in Germany resonated well with racist notions developed in the second half of the nineteenth century and propagated by individuals close to Nietzsche. His suggestion that Jewish-Gentile marriages were a remedy for the contemporary Jewish Question could very well have had an impact on Nietzsche, as we will see in chapter four. Important for our present concerns, however, is that here, too, Nietzsche's exposure to anti-Jewish thought did not begin with his association with Wagner, but rather prepared him for that association.

CHAPTER THREE

The Wagnerian Vanguard

NIETZSCHE PRO-WAGNER

We saw in chapter one that Nietzsche's sister has often been considered responsible for the anti-Semitic reputation her brother acquired during the first half of the twentieth century. Similarly, scholars and critics have often blamed Richard Wagner for inculcating the young, impressionable Nietzsche with anti-Jewish thought. There is some circumstantial evidence for this claim. By the time Nietzsche was introduced to Wagner, the composer was already firmly ensconced in Judeophobic themes and rhetoric, and with the advent of the Second Reich his animus against the Jews only increased. His consort and then wife Cosima[1] was perhaps even more strident in her anti-Jewish convictions than Wagner, and Nietzsche became particularly close to her; indeed, the exchange of letters between Nietzsche and Cosima is much more extensive and personal than the correspondence between Wagner and his young acolyte. Furthermore, the close personal bond between Wagner and Nietzsche was anything but a relationship of peers. Wagner was born in the same year as Nietzsche's father; by the time he knew Nietzsche, he had composed a half dozen operas, published several longer theoretical texts, participated in a revolution, resided in various countries in exile, married, had several affairs, and was living "in sin" with the wife of another man who had conducted the premieres of two of his operas in the 1860s. Nietzsche, by contrast, had tried his hand at musical composition and written a few amateurish poems; he had hardly spent any time outside of Saxony; his life experience consisted mostly of readings in classical philology and a few academic essays. Moreover, Wagner was notoriously charismatic, attracting devotees wherever he went. Although Nietzsche would later endeavor to portray them as equals engaged in struggle with each other—the very title *Nietzsche contra Wagner* (1895) places the two on the same level—it was in reality a relationship where Nietzsche played a very subservient role.[2] This inequality, however, does not mean that Nietzsche was somehow deprived of his powers of discernment and compelled to obey the Meister without question, adopting his every opinion and bias. Scholars who hold Wagner accountable for Nietzsche's anti-Jewish sentiments are fond of portraying Nietzsche as coming "under the maestro's spell" or of "being bowled over by the 'fabulously lively and fiery' Wagner," and consider his Judeophobic remarks as concessions meant to impress Richard and Cosima, or to signal his alliance with the Wagnerian cause.[3] Accordingly, Nietzsche is regarded as finding "his own identity" only after his break with Wagner, which was a painful process, "so deep had Wagner penetrated his own self, albeit as an alien and self-alienating force." In this psychological account Wagner becomes the foreign invader infiltrating an internal core of being that ultimately rejects him in a heroic struggle for authenticity.[4] We should recall that Nietzsche was hardly an impressionable and callow youth when he associated with Wagner; he was twenty-four years old when they met and just months away from becoming one of the youngest men to receive a professorship at a German-speaking university. As we have seen, although he personally had minimal contact with Jews or with the Jewish tradition, he had been subjected to—and employed— derogatory clichés for several years prior to making Wagner's acquaintance. Judeophobia was not well developed in his writing or thought, but it formed an unstated background for his intellectual endeavors, ready to be activated by the right person. Wagner was that person, and we should conceive of his influence over Nietzsche as one of directing an already latent anti-Jewish attitude into an active prejudice. No doubt Wagner had a tremendous and decisive impact on Nietzsche in the third decade of his life and continued to exercise, frequently *ex negativo*, an influence until the outbreak of insanity. But the anti-Jewish sentiments in Nietzsche's early works of the 1870s, while not sui generis, were part of his own maturation process and should be considered as his conscious and deliberate endeavor to parallel and thereby contribute to the goals his friend and mentor articulated.

At first it was all about the music. Nietzsche was introduced to Wagner's music by his friend Gustav Krug, the most musically perceptive member of the three-person club "Germania" that Nietzsche formed with two other local teenagers in Naumburg in the early 1860s. He showed little enthusiasm for Wagner at this point, and even in his first Leipzig years he expressed doubts about the composer. In 1866 he reports to Carl von Gersdorff, probably his closest friend during this period, that he has "mixed feelings" about the piano score of Wagner's *Walküre* (1870):[5] "The great beauties and virtues are balanced out by ugliness and deficiencies that are just as great" (October 11, 1866, Nr. 523, KSB 2.174). Two years later he seems to have gained an appreciation for Wagner, possibly influenced by his reading of Schopen-hauer and the more general acceptance of Wagner's music in Schopenhauer-ian circles. Writing to fellow philology student Erwin Rohde, he alludes to Otto Jahn's critical appraisal of Wagner as a modern dilettante, but disagrees with his former professor in Bonn: "one cannot be astounded enough how significant every single artistic ability of this man is, how much inexhaust-ible energy is paired with multi-faceted artistic talents" (October 8, 1868, Nr. 591, KSB 2.322). By October 1868 he expresses unqualified admiration for both *Tristan und Isolde* (1865) and the overture to the *Meistersinger* (1868): "I cannot bring myself to take a coolly critical view of this music; every fiber, every nerve quivers inside me, and for a long time I have not had such a sustained feeling of rapture as I had from that overture" (to Rohde, Nr. 596, KSB 2.332). The final stage in his conversion to Wagnerian discipleship occurred shortly thereafter. Wagner had heard of Nietzsche's enthusiasm for him through Sophie Ritschl, who was friends with Wagner's sister, Ot-tilie Brockhaus, the wife of the Leipzig orientalist Hermann Brockhaus. One of Brockhaus's students, Ernst Windisch, was given the task of inviting Nietzsche to meet Wagner. Although the originally scheduled meeting did not take place as planned—Wagner was in Switzerland—Nietzsche, along with Windisch, was subsequently invited to the Brockhaus residence for a Sunday gathering. He wrote to Rohde that he had assumed he was being included in a larger reception and, in a rather amusing passage, describes the elaborate preparations he took for this momentous occasion. Much to Nietzsche's surprise, however, the gathering at the Brockhaus's consisted of "no one except the immediate family, Richard Wagner and us." Wagner played for them from the *Meistersinger*, and they discussed their mutual ad-miration for Schopenhauer. Nietzsche describes Wagner to Rohde as "a fab-ulously vivacious and fiery man who speaks very rapidly, is very witty, and livens up this sort of very private gathering." Friendly relations must have been established almost immediately since Nietzsche refers to him in his letter as "Richard."[6] A further indication of their intimacy is that Wagner read to Nietzsche from his autobiography, and when his young visitor was leaving, he shook his hand warmly and invited him back for further discus-sions of music and philosophy (November 9, 1868, Nr. 599, KSB 2.335–42).

JUDAISM IN MUSIC

From this point until sometime in the mid-1870s, Nietzsche was a Wagne-rian. He was involved with more than an admiration of the musical prowess of the Meister and his operatic masterpieces; he also partook in the ideological dimensions surrounding Wagner's cultural ambitions and his vision for a renaissance in German art. When Nietzsche received his professorship at Basel in 1869, he became a frequent visitor at Tribschen,[7] where Wagner, Cosima, her children, and their children lived until 1872, and from Basel he carried on a lively correspondence with both Richard and Cosima. It was a decisive moment in Wagner's anti-Jewish crusade. In 1850 he had published in the *New Journal for Music* an anonymous diatribe against Jews titled "Judaism in Music" under the name "K. Freigedank" (K. Freethought). Despite prudent advice from friends and even from Cosima not to republish this essay, Wagner decided in 1869 to reissue the original text as a pamphlet, divulging his authorship and adding a brief prefatory statement, as well as a commentary on his fate and further thoughts as a lengthy addendum. Wagner must have conceived the idea in 1868, since Cosima mentions in her first diary entries in January 1869 that her paramour is "completing his essay on the Jews";[8] the first copies arrived at the Wagner residence in March, and for well over a year Cosima notes reactions of various sorts, from outraged newspaper articles to disruptions of performances at Wagner's operas. Nietzsche arrived in Basel to take up his professorial post in April of 1869, and soon thereafter he began his frequent visits to Tribschen. He thus had firsthand knowledge of both the essay and the widespread reaction it occasioned. Nietzsche himself never commented on "Judaism in Music," but from his correspondence with Gersdorff we can ascertain that he approved of the racist message. In March 1870 Gersdorff wrote to him and mentioned Nietzsche's "insistent advice" to read the pamphlet. Gersdorff reported that he is now astounded and ashamed that he could have believed the accounts of Wagner in the "Jewified" press for such a long time; after reading Wagner's invective against the Jews, he now harbors "the firm conviction" that he is "a genius in the truest sense of the word: 'Judaism in Music' has opened my eyes completely" (Nr. 82, KGB II 2.164). The essay must have made quite an impression on Gersdorff since he wrote to Nietzsche in November 1872 that in order to practice his Italian, he is translating it for his Italian teacher, who has now also acquired a high opinion of Wagner (Nr. 381, KGB II 4.131). Nietzsche's response to Gersdorff in 1870 indicates how firmly allied he is with Wagner's sentiments regarding the Jews. "That we are now also in agreement with regard to Richard Wagner is for me completely reliable evidence of how we belong together. Because it isn't easy and demands a vigorous, manly courage not to be led astray by the alarming racket." Nietzsche goes on to admit that there are "decent and intelligent" people in the opposing party, by which he likely means those people who do not share these views on the Jews. He then adds that "Schopenhauer must raise us up above this conflict theoretically, just as Wagner does it practically, as an artist." Many people of "modern times" (*Jetztzeit*), Nietzsche comments, find every note in Wagner an abomination, just as they do Schopenhauer's asceticism and denial of the will; and he continues: "Our 'Jews'—and you know how widely this concept extends—in particular despise Wagner's idealistic manner" (March 11, 1870, Nr. 65, KSB 3.104–5). From this exchange with Gersdorff we can see that not only did Nietzsche himself subscribe to the Meister's anti-Jewish ideology, he also encouraged others to engage with it and expressed obvious approval when they too shared his (and Wagner's) views.

"Judaism in Music" is one of the pivotal documents in the history of German anti-Semitism. Its racist themes form a bridge between the Judeophobic discussions in the period prior to the 1848 revolution and the rise of anti-Semitism as a political movement with definite racist dimensions in the 1880s. At issue in the original core text from 1850 is the extent to which Jews can be considered Germans; its personal background, however, concerns slights perceived by Wagner on the part of what he regarded as the Jewish music establishment in the 1840s. It is not coincidental that it is published directly after the revolutionary period, since, as we have seen, the issue of Jewish emancipation was hotly debated in those very years. But the essay also includes, especially in its later rendition, several elements that were frequently repeated by anti-Semitic agitators of the Second Empire: the alleged Jewish control over finance and press; Jewish vindictiveness; and the dire necessity to eliminate Jewish influence one way or another for the salvation of the German people. As in the prerevolutionary years, in the 1860s Jewish emancipation was a crucial topic, and Cosima's diary entry on January 20, 1869—"he [Richard Wagner] continues to insist that the emancipation of the Jews has stifled all German impulses"[9]—gives an indication of Wagner's views at the time of German unification. Indeed, it appears that Wagner felt compelled to reissue this essay not only to clarify his evolving views on Jews, revolution, and nationalism but also because of the similarity in the political constellation in 1850 and 1869. In both periods the liberal majority had succeeded in securing Jewish emancipation, although quite a few of the patriotic supporters of the revolution in 1848 and of the drive toward unification in 1870–71 were uncomfortable with this outcome of their political activity. Some observers even suspected that Jews had used the liberal political movement in an illicit fashion to secure their own emancipation and subsequently abandoned or undermined the nationalist cause. Wagner certainly alludes to the ambivalence in his own views on this matter when he writes that only as a theoretical political tenet was there general support for Jewish emancipation. "When we strove for emancipation of the

Jews, however, we were really more the champions of an abstract principle than of a concrete case: ... our zeal for equal civil rights for Jews was much more the consequence of a general idea than of any real sympathy; for, with all our speaking and writing for Jewish emancipation, we always felt instinctively repelled by any actual, operative contact with them." Significant here is that Wagner, by using the first person plural, includes himself among those who abstractly favored emancipation, but that he simultaneously lays the foundation for opposing emancipation when he descends from the heights of theoretical reflection into the reality of Germans and Jews in the nineteenth century.[10]

Championing Jewish emancipation and refraining from expressing openly "our natural repugnance against the Jewish nature" are acts of nineteenth-century political correctness, and Wagner's essay initially seeks to smash this taboo and explore why this antipathy obtains. First, however, he inverts the discourse on emancipation. Like so many of his fellow Judeophobes, Wagner asserts that it is the Germans who require emancipation from the Jews, not the Jews in Germany. "The Jew," he asserts, "is already more than emancipated: he rules, and will rule as long as money remains the power before which all our doings and our dealings lose their force." The natural disdain for the Jews does not relate to their financial prowess, but to inborn qualities of Jewishness. In the first instance Wagner disparages the outward appearance of Jews, "which, no matter to what European nationality we belong, has something disagreeably foreign to that nationality: instinctively we wish to have nothing in common with a man who looks like that." The second aspect of the Jewish constitution that arouses contempt is his speech. While the discussion of outward appearance appears gratuitously included to debase Jewry, speech relates more directly to Wagner's main concern, since it is later associated with song, and hence innate ability in music. Wagner's point is initially that Jews, because they enter into an organic community of native speakers, never completely master a foreign tongue. Semitic speech is always foreign to the German ear, since it retains a "hissing, grating, buzzing, bungling aural impression" and exhibits the character of "an insufferable bewildering blabbering." Wagner proceeds logically: if Jews cannot even talk properly, how can they be suitable for song? "Very naturally, in song—the most vivid and indisputable expression of an individual's personal sentience—the repulsive composure of the Jewish nature reaches for us its climax." The Jews, Wagner recognizes, possess their own musical tradition, which is associated with the ceremonial music sung and chanted in religious services in the synagogue. But this tradition is ill suited for higher cultural achievement. "Who has not been seized with a feeling of the greatest revulsion," Wagner asks rhetorically, "of horror mingled with absurdity, at hearing that gurgle, yodel, and cackle, which defies sense and sound, and which no intentional caricature can distort more repugnantly than it presents itself here in complete, naïve seriousness?" Despite the complete unsuitability of Jews for music, they have nevertheless been able to assert themselves in musical life and now determine public taste in this most widely appreciated of modern art forms. Jewish domination over something foreign to the essence of the Jew has been made possible because of money. Not all Jews are alike, Wagner concedes. Assimilated and cultured Jews have endeavored to rid themselves of the traits of their more vulgar co-religionists. But this endeavor has been futile: "Alien and apathetic stands the educated Jew in the midst of a society he does not understand, with whose inclinations and aspirations he does not sympathize, whose history and evolution have always been indifferent to him." Even Felix Mendelssohn-Bartholdy, a talented composer who has valiantly tried to overcome his inherent limitations, is for Wagner only a tragic figure, powerless to achieve real virtuosity and eminence. More offensive is Giacomo Meyerbeer, whom Wagner never mentions by name in the pamphlet, but whom he considers typical for the Jewish "tone-setter" who translates Jewish jargon into popular operas, and who amounts to little more than a pathetic musical entrepreneur, bereft of talent, yet setting the trend for the modern musical epoch.[11]

Quite obviously Wagner drifts into personal vendetta in his discussion of Mendelssohn and especially in his attack on Meyerbeer. Nietzsche therefore may not have been able to identify with all elements of "Judaism in Music," and certainly he lacked Wagner's personal experience in the world of nineteenth-century music. But he nonetheless found much in the essay that validated his own observations, confirming the platitudes he exchanged with his friends, or that could be easily adopted as part of his patriotic worldview from the early 1870s. The remarks about Jewish physical appearance accorded very well with his own pronouncements concerning Jewish merchants at the Leipzig fair, or at least with the stereotypes he employed when discussing them with his family and friends. With regard to Jewish speech patterns Nietzsche would develop along the lines of Wagner's discussion a parallel concern for the German language and its debasement in the mouths of "foreign" elements. One easy target was Berthold Auerbach, a noted German Jewish author, whose "Village Stories" were popular fare in the mid-nineteenth century. Nietzsche was not apt to have heard favorable comments about Auerbach from Wagner or Cosima. Although Auerbach was a fervent patriot and longtime advocate of German unity, Cosima writes dismissively concerning a poem he composed regarding the Siege of Strasbourg during the Franco-Prussian War; her commentary excludes Auerbach from the genuine German community: "only a German being demonstrates his steadfastness in death and conquest, and that is great" (September 2, 1870, Nr. 121, KGB 2.2.240).[12] And a diary entry from Cosima in May 1870 denigrates an article by Auerbach on nature: "An article by Berthold Auerbach (no genius he!) about woods is printed in the newspaper; R. [Richard Wagner] says he found it unreadable on account of its affected closeness to Nature: 'These fellows are a real nuisance' (the Jews)."[13] As a young man Nietzsche had written sympathetically about Auerbach's "Village Story" *Barfüßele* (Little Bare-Footed One) (1856), recommending it in February 1862 to his mother and stating that he was charmed by it (Nr. 296, KSB 1.199). But once he had learned to be more circumspect about complimenting Jewish writers, he comments quite differently on Auerbach. In his lectures on education in 1872 he recommends the study of "our great poets" so that pupils will acquire the appropriate "physical loathing for the beloved and much-admired 'elegance' of style of our newspaper manufacturers and novels." The "young man" will no longer need to ask "whether Auerbach and Gutzkow are really poets, for their disgust at both will be so great that he will be unable to read them any longer, and thus the problem will be solved for him" (BA II, KSA 1.684).[14] In his first *Untimely Meditation* (1873) he recalls reading a pamphlet by Auerbach titled "On the German People," "in which every expression was un-German, wrongheaded, and false, and which in general was comparable to a soulless word mosaic held together with international syntax" (DS 11, KSA 1.222).[15] The putative influence of Hegel and Heine in Auerbach leads to "a natural foreignness in the German language on national grounds," and the result is "a jargon that is reprehensible in every word and phrase" (Nachlass 1873, 27[38], KSA 7.598). Auerbach is exemplary for the "impoverishment and enervation" of the German language, which are in turn symptoms of a "general atrophy of the spirit in Germany" (Nachlass 1874, 37[7], KSA 7.834). Finally, Nietzsche concludes: "Auerbach can neither tell tales nor think; he just pretends to do so. He is in his element, when he can swim in an insipid, garrulous mawkishness; but we dislike being in his element" (Nachlass 1874, 37[4], KSA 7.830). The animus Nietzsche displays toward Auerbach, as well as his associations with "jargon," foreignness, and internationalism, surely reflects a modification in Nietzsche's worldview toward Jews in German society.

"Judaism in Music" also provided Nietzsche with a ready model for dealing with the musical world of Jewish composers, influencing both Nietzsche's written comments and behavior. Meyerbeer's compositions, as we might expect, are treated as the antithesis of genuine German music. In his lectures on education Nietzsche remarks on the perversion of the German spirit by a culture focused on the momentary and the superficial. He contrasts the greatness of earlier epochs with the shallowness of the present: "What now grandiloquently assumes the title of 'German culture' is a sort of cosmopolitan aggregate, which bears the same relation to the German spirit as journalism does to Schiller, or Meyerbeer to Beethoven." He goes on to censure the dependence on the "thoroughly un-German civilization of France," which Germans slavishly imitate, resulting in "the society, the press, the art, and the literary style of Germany" acquiring a "hypocritical character" (BA II, KSA 1.690). The key notions are "cosmopolitan" and "un-German"; there was no need to emphasize Meyerbeer's cultural heritage, or the religious group that controlled the press, since Nietzsche's audience fully understood, as part of the Judeophobic cultural code, Jews as part of this foreign corruption of Germanness. In other passages Meyerbeer is juxtaposed directly with Wagner. Thus in *Richard Wagner in Bayreuth* (1876) he writes about Wagner's passion for grand opera as the most adequate mode of expression, but relates as well the resistances and disappointments he encounters.

> Another artist understood better what it took to become a master in this field, and now that we have gradually become aware of the extensive, artificially spun web of influences of every sort with which Meyerbeer prepared and achieved his victories and how meticulously he weighed even the succession of "effects" in an opera, we can understand the degree of humiliating bitterness that overcame Wagner when his eyes were opened to the "artistic devices" the artist was virtually obliged to employ in order to achieve success with the audience. (WB 8, KSA 1.473–74)

Wagner comes to understand the nature of modern art through the artificiality of Jewish art, which continues to dominate Germany and Europe in the early 1870s. In his notes for the Wagner essay, Meyerbeer again serves as a foil for the Meister. Wagner's art does not belong to the modern world; it is either far ahead of the times or above the times. By contrast Nietzsche mentions Meyerbeer, who is concerned primarily with commercial success in his own era (Nachlass 1875, 11[19], KSA 8.205). Nietzsche is following Wagner's thoughts on modernity, which becomes associated with the hegemony of journalism, the press, newspapers, and, of course Jews in art and in the stock market. The use of the well-known and successful Jewish composer Meyerbeer as a contrast to—and hindrance to—the more noble and

German cultural aspirations of Wagner is no coincidence. Rather, it is part of the discourse Wagner developed and Nietzsche mimicked to further the Wagnerian mission against the "Jewified" culture of the Second Empire.

Nietzsche, like Wagner, is somewhat more charitable toward Mendelssohn, perhaps because both mentor and acolyte recognized that he is the greater musical talent. Still Nietzsche's remarks on the celebrated composer bear the stamp of the Meister. Wagner makes two fundamental criticisms of Mendelssohn: first, that despite his talents and formal eloquence, he fails to produce a profound effect on his listeners; and second, that his orientation on Bach is an artificial imitation whose net achievement is a near perfection in form, but nugatory content. He pushes the current musical style in Germany to its utmost pitch, but it is ultimately a music characterized by dissolution and capriciousness. In his notebooks from 1878 Nietzsche writes similarly that Mendelssohn lacks "the power of elementary convulsion," and in an interesting parenthetical remark he comments "in passing" that it—presumably producing convulsions—is the "talent of the Jew in the Old Testament" (Nachlass 1878, 30[133], KSA 8.545–46). Mendelssohn is associated with Wagner's criticism and dissociated simultaneously from his religious heritage, although, as we will explore in chapter six, Nietzsche in later works at times distinguished sharply between the qualities of older forms of Judaism in the first part of the Old Testament and the priestly Judaism in the era of the Second Temple. In *Human, All Too Human* (1878–80) Mendelssohn's music is lauded for its good taste, but Nietzsche also notes that it "points back behind itself" and therefore has no future (WS 2 157, KSA 2.618).[16] These passages, written after Nietzsche's break with Wagner, still retain the general contours of Wagner's assessment, but his note from the end of 1874 places Mendelssohn squarely within the antithesis of Germans and non-Germans (or corrupters of Germans) that Wagner and Nietzsche frequently thematized. Nietzsche is expounding on the neglect of the German language and how it has become degraded by foreign and academic manners. In order to escape the disgust emanating from current language usage, Nietzsche maintains, one is forced to take refuge in artificiality. He continues: "just as I can no longer tolerate Mendelssohn's phrasings; I demand a stronger and more stimulating language" (Nachlass 1874, 37[7], KSA 7.833). In musical composition Mendelssohn represents the foreign and the academic path that has ruined the genuine German language and corrupted the German spirit. As Jew he is the "other" of Germanness.

A more curious sign of Nietzsche's complaisance toward Wagner's distaste for Mendelssohn, however, does not appear in a written document, but in an incident in 1872. In early February Gustav Schönberg, an economist

who was employed at Basel when Nietzsche arrived, but had since moved to
Freiburg, wrote to Nietzsche relating an offer to serve as a travel companion
to the Freiburg historian Karl Mendelssohn-Bartholdy, the son of the composer, who was contemplating a trip to Greece. Schönberg made it clear
that money was no object; Mendelssohn would bear all the costs and remain flexible with regard to travel plans as well (February 1, 1872, Nr. 278,
KGB II 2.530–31). Nietzsche's response does not survive, but from two short
letters written to him by Mendelssohn-Bartholdy, we know that he rejected
the offer, and that he sent Mendelssohn-Bartholdy a copy of *The Birth of
Tragedy* (1872) with his rejection on February 5. We can also surmise that
he declined with the excuse that he was committed to finishing his public
lectures on educational institutions, which were held in Basel in the late
winter months of 1872. The historian's first letter is extremely polite and
endeavors to persuade Nietzsche to change his mind (February 9, 1872, Nr.
283, KGB II 2.536–37). He was obviously unsuccessful, since in a second
letter he writes openly that he suspects Nietzsche's reasons are "personal"
and involve "your relationship to Wagner, mine to my father." He persists
in his efforts to persuade Nietzsche by disclosing that although he himself
prefers Bach's preludes and fugues, he considers Wagner's music to be
among the best in the nineteenth century. He does not know Wagner personally, but he is convinced that if he did, they could reach an amiable understanding. He obviously knows "Judaism in Music," but he is confident he
and Nietzsche could have a good discussion of its pros and cons on the boat
trip across the Ionian Sea. He then implores him again to reconsider (February 15, 1872, Nr. 287, KGB II 2.546–47). From Nietzsche we have only a
few indirect references to the offer in letters to other correspondents. He
writes to Gersdorff about the proposition he had received, identifying the
Freiburg historian only as "the son of Felix Mendelssohn-Bartholdi" [*sic*],
and adding with emphasis: "Of course I'll say no!" (February 4, 1872, Nr.
197, KSB 3.287). He also mentions the offer to his mother and sister without
initially revealing its source and then concludes with the following revealing remark: "Maybe you'll laugh when I tell you that this acquaintance is
the son of Felix Mendelssohn" [*sic*] (February 14, 1872, Nr. 200, KSB 3.292).
Later in 1872 Nietzsche returns to the invitation in an exchange with Hugo
von Senger, the composer and musical director in Geneva, and invents the
lame excuse that his view of Greece and that of the son of the composer of
Antigone (Op. 55 by Mendelssohn) are incompatible (September 23, 1872,
Nr. 254, KSB 4.50–51). Nietzsche was obviously uncomfortable with the
prospect of traveling with Mendelssohn-Bartholdy, and his stated reasons
for declining the invitation are transparently pretexts. The real issue had to

do with Jews, and whether Germans should associate so closely with them, and the Freiburg historian intimated it. The exact reason for Nietzsche's refusal—whether he feared Wagner would not approve of him traveling to Greece with the son of a despised rival Jewish composer, or whether he did not want to travel to Greece with a man of Jewish heritage—is worth considering, but probably impossible to determine with certainty. What we can ascertain is that at this point in his development Nietzsche was so deeply ensnarled in Wagnerian ideology that he would not do anything to violate the anti-Jewish sentiments he shared with the Meister.[17]

The added reflections in the 1869 version of "Judaism in Music" may have been even more important for establishing the mental state of the Wagnerian movement on the eve of the new German Empire. The tone and tenor of these remarks, whose length almost equals that of the original essay, is one of paranoia and persecution; like many anti-Semites who would come to the fore around 1880, Wagner regards himself and his supporters, as well as the entirety of German music, as victims of a cunning, malicious, and unified Jewish assault. Wagner reports that Franz Brendel, the publisher of the periodical in which the original essay appeared and a professor at the Leipzig conservatory, has gradually found that the number of "blond musicians" has dwindled among the student body, and that the natural sympathy for "local patriotism, which was otherwise so manifest in German cities, has disappeared." In short, Leipzig, in part owing to the influence of Felix Mendelssohn, founder of the Leipzig conservatory, had become exclusively a "world city for Jewish music" (*Judenmusikweltstadt*).[18] Far worse, however, is the persecution that Wagner and anyone allied with his musical tastes have had to suffer at the hands of the Jews. Wagner is convinced that he and his friends have been denied all access to the press since it is in the hands of his enemies. Indeed, like most anti-Semites of a later generation, he believes not only in Jewish control of the press and the economy but also that Jews belong to a unified and coordinated organization that threatens to gain complete hegemony over the Fatherland:

> I cannot judge how far this factual relationship [between Jews and the control of music] extends even into greater political affairs, although the stock exchange gives an indication about it with quite a degree of openness: in the area of music, abandoned to the most dishonest prattle, there is absolutely no doubt for those having any discernment that here everything has been subjected to a highly remarkable rule of a religious order, whose observance in the most widely diverse circles and with the most coordinated precision leads one to conclude the existence of a highly energetic organization and leadership.[19]

Jewish control of musical life and criticism means that Wagner is unable to defend his ideas and theories in Germany, France, or England; only in Saint Petersburg and Moscow has he found that "Jews have neglected the terrain of the musical press."[20] Fortunately, Jewish interference has not yet cost him his audience, in particular for his older operas, which were written and premiered prior to "Jewish agitation," although it has made matters more difficult, especially for his newer works. The Jewish press accuses him of composing according to his nonsensical theories, and his works are excluded from the stage. Wagner asks rhetorically: "In whose hands is the direction of our theaters, and what sort of trend does the theater follow?" The answer of course is that the persecution of Wagner in contemporary Germany is the result of the "insertion of a Jewish essence into our artistic state of affairs."[21] Responsible for this miserable situation are not only the Jews, who have taken control of musical life in Germany and most of Europe, but also the Germans, whose trusting complacency and quiescent inertia have allowed the deterioration of artistry and excellence. German influence in artistic life is reduced to a modest journal—the *New Journal for Music* in which Wagner's original essay on "Judaism in Music" appeared—and Wagner concedes "the complete victory of Judaism on all sides,"[22] a conclusion that would be echoed a decade later in the seminal anti-Semitic publication, Wilhelm Marr's *The Victory of Judaism over Germanism* (1879).[23] Like Marr, however, Wagner suggests that this victory is not quite as conclusive as it now appears; there are two alternatives for eliminating the pernicious Jewish occupation of the German artistic realm: "Whether the decline of our culture could be halted through the violent expulsion of the depraved foreign element, I cannot judge, because to do so would have to involve powers whose existence is unknown to me."[24] The other possibility Wagner mentions is assimilation, but it would have to be a special type of assimilation and quite obviously on terms compatible with Wagner's ideals. The difficulties with such a solution are apparent, not only because Wagner points to the necessity for "uncovering" rather than "hiding" them, but also because he, like many nineteenth-century anti-Jewish thinkers, apparently believes that conversion and even integration into a German community do not necessarily remove something essential and abhorrent in the Jewish character.[25]

NIETZSCHE IN BASEL

We will see that these comments from 1869 leave their mark on Nietzsche and his writings. We should not forget, however, that his acquaintance with

Wagner's inflammatory pamphlet occurred at almost the same time that he was settling into his position on the faculty at the University of Basel. Like many professors at the university, Nietzsche was also obliged to teach at the Pädagogium, an institution that provided the final three years of preparatory instruction for the university. He was therefore well integrated into the life of the city and familiar with the patrician strata, whose sons were the pupils Nietzsche taught at this advanced high school. In contrast to Berlin or Leipzig, Basel did not have a large Jewish population, and Nietzsche leaves no record of association with Jews during the decade he was a professor, or of chance encounters with Jews. Like cities in Germany, Basel had a checkered past with regard to race relations. On January 9, 1349, the Gentiles massacred nearly the entire Jewish population on account of the Black Plague. With few exceptions Jews were not given permission to reside in Basel until the establishment of the Helvetic Republic in 1798; the emancipation that came with the Napoleonic conquest was rapidly undone in 1814, when the city was "liberated" from the French. The number of Jewish residents in Basel was reduced by almost two-thirds from 1815 to 1837, when only thirteen families remained. The emancipation of Jews was notoriously protracted in Switzerland and occurred only under pressure from more liberal countries; unrestricted residence was finally granted in 1866, and in 1874 Jewish residents achieved full emancipation. The referendum in Basel regarding Jewish emancipation is indicative of the racial bias of the city; a significant number of citizens were opposed to extending civil rights to everyone, and the measure passed by less than five hundred votes. But Basel has another, more positive side in its relationship with contemporary Jewry, serving as a place of refuge for Jews fleeing pogroms in nearby Alsace in the wake of the revolutionary uprisings in 1789 and 1848. Its acceptance of Jewish refugees was no doubt one reason that Theodor Herzl selected it as the site for the first Zionist Congress in 1897.[26] What Nietzsche knew of this history is unknown, but he may well have been familiar with the synagogue, which was dedicated only a year and a half before he arrived in the city. It is fair to conclude, however, that his acquaintance with Jewish life in Basel from personal experiences during his employment as a professor at the university was minimal.

With the exception of Paul Rée, whom he met in Basel in 1873, Nietzsche probably had no students of Jewish heritage or Jewish colleagues at the university. We will have an opportunity later to examine the views of his closest friend on the Basel faculty, Franz Overbeck, since they are important for an understanding of Nietzsche's relationship to the anti-Semitic movement. The only other professor who merits our attention is the noted histo-

rian Jacob Burckhardt, an older colleague whom Nietzsche greatly respected
and to whom Nietzsche faithfully sent copies of his latest published writings.
The relationship with Burckhardt, as Overbeck describes it in retrospect,
was one-sided, but it was typical in this regard for Nietzsche's relationship
with other celebrated individuals.[27] Nietzsche often sent books and accompanying letters to famous persons in Germany or Europe and at times depicted to third parties—or even the reading public—a much more intimate
relationship than actually existed. In *Twilight of the Idols* (1888) he refers to
the historian as "my honored friend Jacob Burckhardt of Basel" (GD, Was
den Deutschen abgeht 5, KSA 6.107),[28] and it was this imagined closeness
that is probably responsible for two letters sent to Burckhardt immediately
after the outbreak of insanity in January of 1889 (Nr. 1245, 1256, KSB 8.574,
577–79). Considering Nietzsche's obvious admiration for Burckhardt, and
the absence of other individuals in Basel whom he similarly esteemed,
Burckhardt's views on Jews are probably relevant; at the very least they give
us an indication of the climate surrounding the Jewish Question at this
Swiss institution. Quite simply stated, Burckhardt was unequivocally opposed to Jewish emancipation, and we should recall that he would have experienced at first hand the debates surrounding the issue from the 1860s.
As a cultural heritage he considered Judaism inferior to Greek and Roman
antiquity, and he believed that anything of worth in the heritage of contemporary Europe was due to the latter, and not the former, tradition. Like
Richard Wagner and many of his contemporaries, Burckhardt came to regard Jews as responsible for the worst manifestations of modernity. As a
young professor in Basel he wrote to a friend that the sight of Jews in the
audience of a theater in Berlin destroys his enjoyment of the event, and that
he would rather skip the performance entirely if Jews are present.[29] This
sort of statement corresponds well with remarks Nietzsche and his friends
made about Jews in the late 1860s and early 1870s. In response to the anti-
Semitic agitation around 1880, Burckhardt confided to an acquaintance that
he would advise "the Semites" to exercise "great wisdom and restraint." He
predicts that National Liberalism, which has to that point protected the
Jews, will take the opportunity to discontinue its defense, especially since the
conservatives and Catholics "have the most popular trump card that exists"—
the aversion to Jews among the masses and will play it out against them.
He predicts that Jewish emancipation, which was secured only a little over
a decade earlier, will be eliminated by law, and that the "Semitic jurists" will
lose their positions. These changes will occur "as soon as it is safer for the
State to take action than it is for it to continue observing." He continues:
"Namely, the Semites will have to pay for their fully unwarranted interference

in everything possible, and newspapers will have to get rid of their Semitic editors and correspondents if they want to survive. Something like this can happen suddenly and spread rapidly from one day to the next."[30] We know that Nietzsche attended several of Burckhardt's lectures and engaged in private conversations with him, but we do not know what they discussed. If the legacy of Judaism in the ancient world or its relationship to the modern world were ever broached as topics, it is likely that the new Basel professor heard a confirmation of views to which he had been exposed prior to his appointment, and which Wagner and Wagnerians actively reinforced.

The anti-Jewish remarks in Nietzsche's letters and notebooks made prior to his relationship with Wagner fit seamlessly into the period of his visits to Tribschen and his engagement with the Wagnerian cause. They continue unabated in notes and in correspondence with his family from 1869 until the middle of the next decade. In November of 1869 he thanks his mother and sister for their help, and continues: "everything else, as the Jewish money-changers say, will be due on demand!" (Nr. 45, KSB 3.80); once again he associates Jews with financial dealings, especially the less savory type of business practices. His uncle, Oscar Oehler, receives a letter in which his nephew, recently appointed to a post in Basel, states that he saw, but did not speak to, a physician named Richard von Volkmann because he was dressed "fantastically tasteless like a theatrical Jew" (February 13, 1870, Nr. 63, KSB 3.103). Reporting on his experiences as an orderly in the Franco-Prussian War, he obviously feels compelled to describe individuals he encounters with racial referent: at one point he mentions that an innkeeper is a Jew, and later he divulges that he meets "two lecturers from Heidelberg and a Berlin Jew" (Nachlass 1870, 4[1, 3], KSA 7.89–90). In the fall of 1872 when touring in Switzerland he writes to his mother that he left early with fellow travelers in the morning on the mail run for the next stage of his trip and adds: "unfortunately there was a Jew among them" (October 1, 1872, Nr. 257, KSB 4.55). In his notes for the letter, he comments that he consoles himself knowing that he will disembark in Thusis, a Swiss town in the canton of Graubünden, and obviously will no longer have to bear the presence of the Jew (Nachlass 1872, 22[1], KSA 7.535). A dispute with his sister at Christmas in 1871 is revealing for Nietzsche's racism as well as his sister's relative innocence at this stage in her development. Nietzsche had purchased for her a book on art history, and Elisabeth must have assumed the shop where he bought it was a used bookstore owned by a Jewish proprietor. Nietzsche responds indignantly: "But how can you make the insulting assumption that I ordered a book from a scandalous Jewish antiquarian shop?" (Nr. 179, KSB 3.262). In her response Elisabeth asks her brother not to be upset; she had concluded that he bought it at that shop because it was so inexpensive (December 30, 1871, Nr. 253, KGB II 2.489). Indeed, the evidence here and throughout the 1870s suggests that Elisabeth, who, as we have seen in the first chapter, often shoulders the blame for fostering her brother's connection to anti-Semitic views, in many instances was actually exposed to racist remarks by her brother, first in his letters, but probably also in conversation with him and his friends, and then to a more elaborate anti-Jewish ideology when he introduced her into the circle of Wagnerians. In general, we should note again that letters written by family members normally do not contain any obvious racial slurs; at this point in time derogatory remarks about Jews emanate exclusively from Nietzsche.

There is a greater mutuality of racist proclivities in Nietzsche's correspondence with his friends. The letters Nietzsche exchanged with peers also provide an indication of the type of oral conversations in which Nietzsche undoubtedly engaged, and demonstrate how natural and accepted remarks were that portrayed Jews and Judaism in a negative light. Heinrich Romundt, for example, relates to Nietzsche from Leipzig that he has met David Ascher, the Schopenhauer enthusiast; in a catty aside indicating his disregard for his intellectual abilities he states that at least his work will contribute to the popularity of Schopenhauer among the Jews (May 4, 1869, Nr. 3, KGB II 2.10). A few months later he is more direct: "I've gotten to know people like Dr. Ascher etc. a bit better and lost all respect for their intellect. They are very mediocre minds and Jews *comme il faut*." He goes on to state that he knows book dealers and other Schopenhauerians who have never studied at a university, but who stand intellectually head and shoulders above "these Jews" (February 20, 1870, Nr. 78, KSB II 2.155–56). A few years later he returns to Ascher, who had evidently written a short review of Romundt's book and sent him his own volume on Schopenhauer, which Romundt characterizes as a "worthless potboiler": "and just imagine, the Jew impudently demanded as a *quid pro quo* that I review it in the *Augsburg General Newspaper*—That's what you get when you touch Jew's pitch" (October 12, 1872, Nr. 365, KGB II 4.85). Jews are identified with undesirable places or with inconvenience. Carl Fuchs reports to Nietzsche about a trip to the "Jew-city Breslau" (December 16, 1874, Nr. 614, KGB II 4.626) supplying this sobriquet because Breslau, like Fürth, was known to be hospitable to its Jewish residents, and because it was a center for Jewish scholarship and learning. Gersdorff calls "desolate, ice-cold Berlin" "the capital of the new Jewish Reich," probably because of its large Jewish population and the prominent Jewish leaders in the National Liberal Party (December 1872, Nr. 397, KGB II 4.160). Rohde announces that he will be in Leipzig "if the

Jews from the fair and other Jews do not take my place" (October 5, 1871, Nr. 226, KGB II 2.444–45). There are also the usual references to the desirability of avoiding any contact with Jews. Gersdorff relates an experience he had on a train, where he was seated in a car with two women and at first "smelled Jewishness" and fell into a bad mood, but he was relieved when he heard the women converse in Italian since it liberated him from his discomfort (July 1872, Nr. 341, KGB II 4.46). In another letter he encourages his friend to "climb confidently into the high mountain regions and find a place like our dear Waldhäuser, where there is fresh air and no Jews, that is, as Lagarde would say, a Jew-free boarding house" (July 10, 1874, Nr. 555, KGB II 4.512).[31] At one point Gersdorff, influenced by Schopenhauer's comments on animals and Wagner's antivivisectionist proclivities, proclaims himself a vegetarian and clarifies for his friend regarding the Indian aspect of his new lifestyle with a phrase lifted from the anti-Jewish writings of the pessimist philosopher: "A victory of India slowly makes a path for this way of life, and Christianity is liberated from the *foetor Judaicus*" (September 8, 1869, Nr. 20, KGB II 2.43). Nietzsche himself is not uncomfortable in the least spouting Judeophobic comments. Writing with exuberant enthusiasm to Gersdorff about the Franco-Prussian War, he claims that the "German mission" is not yet finished, and that he is more encouraged than ever: "for not everything is subsumed under French-Jewish decline and 'elegance', or has been destroyed by the greedy urges of modern times" (June 21, 1871, Nr. 140, KSB 3.203). And advising Carl Fuchs on how to get along in Berlin, he counsels: "you just have to desire very little and set yourself a goal, so that you are no longer tempted to look at the restless educated Jewish rabble and the whole accepted public sphere" (February/March 1874, Nr. 342, KSB 4.194–95). Neither Nietzsche nor his friends focus their attention on Jews and Judaism; they speak mostly of other matters in the vast correspondence. Unlike Wagner, they are not obsessed with Jewish influence over Germany. But they do not hesitate to freely employ slurs against the Jews, to indicate that Jews are personally offensive to them, and to assert that their very presence in the Fatherland is antithetical to a genuine German culture.

A LESSON WELL LEARNED

Against this background of antipathy toward the Jews and Judaism, and of Wagner's republished text excoriating the Jews, disqualifying them from any cultural relevance, and depicting them as the hegemonic force in German culture, Nietzsche developed his intellectual program of the early 1870s.

Initially he integrated that program into his classical studies, the results being the lectures in preparation for *The Birth of Tragedy* and *The Birth of Tragedy* itself. When he no longer believed that he could contribute effectively to the program of cultural rejuvenation, which in its Wagnerian manifestation always included a dimension of anti-Jewish rhetoric, with classical studies, he switched to commentaries on contemporary life in Germany, lecturing on the educational institutions and composing the "Untimely Meditations." Nietzsche delivered an inaugural lecture in May 1869, but it dealt with Homer and was unrelated to his first book. In January and February of 1870, however, he offered two public presentations on topics that would be central for *The Birth of Tragedy*. In the first, "The Greek Music Drama," Nietzsche's reliance on Wagner and his terminology is already evident. Indeed, the very title, which differentiates opera from music drama, derives from Wagnerian discussions in *Opera and Drama* from 1851. The brief exploration of the lost roots of drama in Germany and the deprecation of modern opera as a "distortion of ancient music drama" that "strains to achieve effects" (GMD, KSA 1.516) are reflections of Nietzsche's endeavor to integrate his classical studies into the Wagnerian enterprise. But Nietzsche was not content to follow Wagner in mere considerations of genre. In his second lecture, held on February 1, whose topic was "Socrates and Tragedy," Nietzsche allied himself with Wagnerian observations on the deleterious impact of Jews on contemporary art and culture. The main contours of the argument are well known since they would be repeated at the very end of 1871, when Nietzsche's *Birth of Tragedy* appeared in print.[32] True tragedy, by which Nietzsche means the Greek plays of Aeschylus and Sophocles, ends "tragically" through the machinations of Euripides, who caters to the lower segments of society by implementing a rationalist and realist aesthetic, destroying the mystery of genuine tragic art. Behind Euripides and united with him in this attack on tragedy is a phenomenon Nietzsche identifies as "Socratism," which eradicates "instinct and with it art" (ST, KSA 1.542) through the introduction of logic and the dialectic. Not only does Socratism annihilate Attic tragedy, it is also a more general force in history: "Viewed from the endless profound Germanic consciousness, this Socratism appears as a completely inverted world" (ST, KSA 1.541). It is an optimistic principle, as opposed to the pessimism inherent in the tragic worldview, and we will recall that Schopenhauer, from whom Wagner and Nietzsche draw inspiration, identified optimism with this-worldly Judaism. This optimistic principle, penetrating to the core of tragedy, causes it to perish. With this thought Nietzsche returns at the conclusion of his lecture to the present and to his Wagnerian program:

Should the Teuton have nothing else to place at the side of that vanished artwork of the past except the "grand opera," something akin to the ape appearing next to Hercules? This is the most serious question of our art: and anyone who, as a Teuton, does not understand the seriousness of this question, has fallen into the snares of the Socratism of our times, which, to be sure, is neither capable of producing martyrs, nor speaks the language of the wisest Hellene. This Socratism is the Jewish press: I'll say nothing more. (Drafts of ST, KGA III 5/1.670)[33]

It is impossible to determine how Nietzsche's audience reacted to this provocative anti-Jewish remark or, indeed, whether the newly appointed professor actually uttered it to his auditors on that Tuesday afternoon in Basel. We can conclude from Nietzsche's own reports that it was the source of unease for some of the attendees. In a letter to Rohde he writes: "I delivered a lecture here on Socrates and tragedy, which aroused alarm and misunderstanding" (February 15, 1870, Nr. 58, KSB 3.95). A few days later he corresponds with his friend Deussen: "I would like to send to you soon the lectures I delivered most recently, the second of which (Socrates and Tragedy) was understood as a series of paradoxes and aroused in part hate and anger." To justify the brashness of his ideological stance, he adds the following comment: "I have already unlearned being considerate: in connection with individuals, let us be compassionate and indulgent; in announcing our worldview as rigid as ancient Roman virtue" (February 1870, Nr. 60, KSB 3.98–99). We can be certain, however, that Nietzsche sent his lecture with the anti-Jewish conclusion to Richard Wagner and Cosima, since the latter mentions in her diary that they received "letters" from Nietzsche and that he had enclosed "his lecture on Socrates."[34] Both Richard and Cosima respond in letters on consecutive days, and each expresses trepidation about their young friend's temerity. Wagner's letter from February 4 is more evasive. He relates that he read the lecture to Cosima last night, and that she was concerned with the way Nietzsche had modernized the views of Athenian personages. Wagner appears to be referring obliquely to Nietzsche's final remarks, which in an almost unmediated fashion thrust the issue of Socratism into the present. For himself Wagner expresses alarm at Nietzsche's boldness in presenting new ideas to the public, which he believes will not have understood what he was saying, and he writes that even those familiar with his—Wagner's—ideas will experience a similar shock. Again Wagner is probably not confronting the issue directly, although he does recognize that Nietzsche is making a contribution consonant with his own writings. He encourages him by stating that he is in fundamental agreement with his thoughts—"I say to you: that's the way it is"—and has great expectations of him for the future. He then adds the cautionary note: "But I am concerned about you, and wish with my entire heart that you don't ruin yourself." He advises him not to place these "unbelievable views" in short treatises, but instead to compose a larger, more encompassing work that will allow him to explicate more fully the "divine errors of Socrates and Plato." He closes the letter with the following comment: "Above all I hope very much that you have no uncertainty with regard to *my* opinion with regard to your Socrates, since I have just told you what I think about it" (February 4, 1870, Nr. 71, KGB II 2.137–38). Wagner must have been aware that the most audacious and potentially troublesome part of the lecture was Nietzsche's intrepid association of Socrates with the Jewish press. But Wagner likely found himself confronted with a dilemma: he wanted to encourage Nietzsche to continue working with him on the program of cultural renaissance in Germany and wished to express his support. But he also saw potential danger in the way Nietzsche was modernizing his contribution to the cause and needed to express this caution. He solved this dilemma through circumlocution. Although he never directly supported Nietzsche's anti-Jewish remark, which, after all, was drawn as much from him as from any other source, his assurance that he agrees with Nietzsche's characterization of Socrates, and his encouragement for Nietzsche to expand on his thoughts in a longer monograph, appear to validate the closing statements in "Socrates and Tragedy"—despite the alarm that both he and Cosima experienced in reading it.

The issue must have weighed heavily on Richard and Cosima, and it festered for another day in Tribschen before further action was taken. When Cosima sent a letter to Nietzsche on February 6, she must have done so after conferring with her husband. The relationship between them was such that Cosima rarely ventured an opinion on important matters that did not coincide with Wagner's view. The part of the letter written on Saturday, February 5, repeats much of what Wagner had written the previous day except that it is composed from Cosima's perspective. She starts by citing Goethe: "Everything significant is uncomfortable," and goes on to assure him that while she agrees with his fundamental views, the "boldness" and "bluntness" in the presentation surprised her. She depended on "the Meister" to explain to her how correct Nietzsche was in his assertions and went through the entire lecture with him sentence by sentence. She repeats that she was upset not with what he had to say, but with the abruptness with which he felt he must explain "the most profound and far-reaching" problems. When she read the lecture again the following day, she was relieved and had the impression of grandeur and beauty. Like Wagner, she encourages Nietzsche to expand his thoughts into a book. She does not mention the anti-Jewish re-mark in this first installment of the letter, but returning to her correspon-dence on Sunday, she immediately speaks of the offensive passage. She has one request of him, and he should consider it something like a "maternal" admonition that will prevent him from getting into trouble, from "stirring up a hornet's nest":

> Do you really understand me? Don't mention the Jews, and especially not *en passant*; later, when you want to take up this gruesome fight, in the name of God, but not at the very outset, so that on your path you won't have all this confusion and upheaval. I hope you don't misunderstand me: you know that in the depths of my soul I agree with your utterance. But not now and not in this way. I see an army of misunderstandings that will whirl up around you.

On Sunday she and Wagner finally ceased dancing around the real issue: the openly Judeophobic climax to the lecture. They fear that Nietzsche's attack on the Jews, which they wholeheartedly endorse, will destroy his credibility and invalidate his contributions to the "program" and to the Wagnerian mission for German culture. "I fear great confusion as a result of your lec-ture," Cosima continues, "whose conception is much too magnificent and—namely with regard to your knowledge of the essence of music—much too new to be understood by the audience." She believes that no one except perhaps Burckhardt will be capable of grasping what Nietzsche is saying (Nr. 72, KGB II 2.138–40). The message to Nietzsche is to move forward with his parallel program, which provides academic legitimation for Wag-ner, but to stay away from inflammatory comments about Jews. Wagner himself writes a few days later, inviting Nietzsche to Tribschen for a visit, where they can chat further about the lecture (Nr. 73 KGB II 2.145–46). Nietzsche travels to the villa on February 12, and Cosima notes laconically in her diary: "Prof. Nietzsche arrives. Lengthy conversation about his lec-ture."[35] He returns to Basel the following day.

Nietzsche understood and obeyed. He appreciated the support of Wag-ner and Cosima, writing to Rohde that the lecture and the ensuing discus-sions about it had "strengthened the bond with his Tribschen friends" (Feb-ruary 15, 1870, Nr. 58, KSB 3.95).[36] In the version of the lecture he prepared for publication he dropped the reference to the Jewish press, eventually eliminating the entire paragraph in which it was originally contained. In his published writings of the Wagnerian period, from *The Birth of Tragedy* until the last *Untimely Meditation*, there is not one direct mention of Jews, Judaism, or Jewish activity in the contemporary world, although there are many passages that make indirect reference. Nietzsche becomes adept at using the "cultural code" for anti-Jewish statements.[37] He continues to expound on the evils of the press, newspapers, financial affairs, the stock exchange, modernity, urban life, and cosmopolitanism; he does so in such a manner that a Judeophobic audience will understand, but never in a fashion where he can be accused of a direct assault on Jews and Judaism. In his private correspondence, of course, he did not hesitate to formulate derogatory remarks. A few days after Cosima's admonishment, he writes about Volkmann as a "theatrical Jew," and in March of 1870, as we have seen, he comments to Gersdorff about the opposition to Wagner: "Our 'Jews'—and you know how widely I conceive this notion—despise Wagner's idealist manner, which is related most closely to Schiller" (Nr. 65, KSB 3.105). His contact with Wagner and Cosima taught Nietzsche a lesson, however, that extended beyond the art of indirect reference. He was also convinced that Jews, whom he, like Wagner, considered a unified and cohesive group, had real power to derail the cultural mission he came to associate with Wagner and Bayreuth. After the publication of "Judaism in Music," Tribschen was buzzing on an almost daily basis with news of the reaction to this Judeophobic diatribe. There were some letters and newspaper articles supporting Wagner's views, but there were many more public and private statements opposing these malicious racist sentiments. It must have been disconcerting for Wagner to read, for example, a notice in the *Karlsruhe Newspaper* expressing the opinion, as Cosima reports, that "by treating all his opponents contemptuously, R. is harming both himself and his cause!"[38] Wagner and Cosima may have even understood the reality of the self-inflicted damage, and certainly an observer of the situation, such as the young Basler professor, could determine that the publication of "Judaism in Music" had a definite downside. Wagner and Cosima were quick to blame Jews or Jewish machinations for most of the unfavorable comments, and Nietzsche was no doubt treated to these sorts of explanations when he visited the composer and his consort. Even more distressing for Wagner—and probably for his young academic observer—was that Jewish interference threatened the spread of Wagner's celebrity and therefore the viability of the entire project of cultural renewal. In the letter just cited to Gersdorff, Nietzsche sets up the antithesis that Wagner himself repeatedly asserted and now experienced: the Jews and their allies on the one side, Wagner and his faithful followers on the other. Indeed, Cosima's diaries from 1870 are replete with reports of Jews disrupting performances of Wagnerian operas or causing them to be canceled. *The Meistersinger* was particularly open to attack, since Beckmesser's arias were frequently considered Jewish. Cosima records an occurrence in Vienna on March 15, 1870: "Among other things the J[ews] are spreading a story around that 'Beckmesser's Song' is an old Jewish song which R. was trying to ridicule. In consequence, some hissing in the second act and calls of 'We don't want to hear any more,' but complete victory for the *Germans*."[39] Although it is possible that "the Germans" prevailed in this instance, the agitation surrounding Wagner increased noticeably in the wake of the publication of his old essay; Tribschen tried to spin the news to Wagner's advantage, or see it as a necessary action in the desperate cultural struggle, but it was quite evident that provoking "the Jews" in this fashion was tantamount to "stirring up a hornet's nest."

Nietzsche received firsthand reports about one set of disturbances from Gersdorff in Berlin. In March 1870 Nietzsche had asked Wagner whether he could procure a ticket for Gersdorff to the Berlin premiere of the *Meistersinger*, and he reports to his friend that the Meister had asked his colleague, the conductor and composer Karl Eckert, to arrange it for him. In turn, Eckert evidently forwarded the request to Botho von Hülsen, the theater manager in Berlin, but something went awry, either because Gersdorff had to report for a stint in the military or because von Hülsen simply did not think about the matter until the day of the performance. Gersdorff, in any event, did not receive the free ticket, but he was determined to attend anyway, which was not easy since, as he states with characteristic anti-Jewish overtones, "the house was sold out, no, *huckstered out*; seats were being scalped for 25 Thaler apiece at the stock exchange."[40] What occurred at the performance leaves Gersdorff fuming about the "baseness of Jewry." He tells Nietzsche that he has written to Wagner with details, and relates to his friend only that the difficulty of the opera will mean reduced attendance in the future unless there is a campaign to hiss the opera, as there obviously was for the premiere, in which case hundreds will be attracted to see the disturbance. He has heard that yesterday—he is writing several days after the premiere—the opera was subjected to hissing from the audience, and the announcement of illness on the part of one of the performers and the reopening of an abbreviated version later in the week have provoked "the anger of Jewry," presumably because many had already purchased tickets at the scalped price of 25 Thaler (April 4, 1870, Nr. 92, KGB II 2.188–92). This opposition between Jewry and Wagnerian opera, to which Gersdorff alludes in several passages in this letter to his friend, is the central point in his missive to Tribschen. After thanking Wagner for providing the ticket, he writes that "a half hour ago the decisive battle between Jewry and art was still burning heatedly" and then narrates a "report about the progress of this battle." The overture and the first act were uneventful; indeed, Walther's aria was greeted enthusiastically by everyone who did not have ulterior motives for attendance (suggesting that the Jews do); the acclaim it received was the result of pure enchantment, Gersdorff assures Wagner, not crazed opposition against the enemy. The second act, however, brought out the boos and cat-calls at Beckmesser's serenade: he had hardly sung the first strophe before "an artificial—in any case—well paid, and audacious laughter made itself heard" and the commotion lasted until the end of the act, drowning out the performance. In the third act there was again no disturbance—"here Jewry had to be silent"—so that Gersdorff predicts that reviewers will be com-pelled to proclaim an overall success.[41] Although the final result of the "bat-tle" was a "victory for the Germans" over the Jews, this report and the threats to future performances on the part of the Jews left its mark on Nietzsche. Conditioned, like Gersdorff, to regard Jewry as a unified entity organized against the Wagnerian mission, he experienced vicariously the power of the enemy to thwart true art and cultural renewal.

Nietzsche's experience in the early 1870s, while he was developing his program for support of the Wagnerian renaissance, thus had two essential elements. He learned first that he should not mention the Jews by name and certainly not attack them in print. Wagner, of course, had done so con-sciously and viciously in 1869, but he was an older man with more stature and legitimacy. Besides, it had become obvious that the republication of "Judaism and Music" had proved detrimental to his own cause. Second, Nietzsche became convinced that Jewry in Germany possessed considerable power and would not hesitate to exercise it against enemies. Under the spell of Wagnerian racist paranoia, Nietzsche believed that the abstract opposi-tion between Jews and Germans in Wagner's essay had become manifest in the events in 1869 and 1870. In preparation for his fourth *Untimely Medita-tion*, which deals with Wagner, his music, and his place in modern times, Nietzsche reflects on the composer's errors in two passages that do not wind up integrated into the final work. In the first Nietzsche develops the theme of Wagner as a tyrant who possesses a "false omnipotence"; not having any heirs, he seeks to spread his influence as widely as possible and achieve le-gitimacy. But the tyrant does not recognize the validity of anyone except his own most trusted associates. "The danger for Wagner is great when he does not recognize the validity of Brahms, etc.: or the Jews" (Nachlass 1874, 32[32], KSA 7.765). Nietzsche's comment summarizes something of what he learned through contact with Wagner in Tribschen. Certainly Wagner possessed a dominant personality and, like Nietzsche himself, had mono-maniacal tendencies. But he underestimated his adversaries, both the musical opposition Brahms represented and the social opposition of the Jews. This weakness, which Nietzsche imagined he witnessed firsthand in Tribschen,

brought his cultural project into peril. In the second passage Nietzsche re-
proves Wagner for concerning himself with politics. His involvement with
King Ludwig II of Bavaria, who first prohibited the performance of his operas, then ruined performances by having them staged prematurely, and
generally damaged his reputation by association, highlights the mistake of
mixing politics and art. Wagner's participation in the 1848 revolution is
also an error since he lost his patrons, aroused fear, and then appeared as an
apostate to his socialist peers: "all of this without any advantage for his art
and without any higher necessity." But his third political error is insulting
the Jews, "who now possess the most money and the press in Germany.
When he did it, he had no cause; later it was revenge" (Nachlass 1874, 32[37],
KSA 7.766). Attacking the Jews is part of a political miscalculation that
stems from a fundamental character flaw and has had only a deleterious
impact on the nobler mission of cultural excellence. Nietzsche's analysis of
the deficiencies in Wagner during his campaign for the opera house in
Bayreuth reveals that disregarding or assaulting Jewry hinders the possibilities for public success in contemporary Germany.

THE BIRTH OF TRAGEDY

Nietzsche was determined not to commit the same error, and even after he
broke with Wagner, he demonstrated that he had learned the dual lesson
well: do not attack the Jews publicly, and fear Jewish power and influence.
In the early 1870s he put this lesson into practice in supplying academic
legitimation for the Wagnerian cause by merging classical philology with
the cultural program he had acquired under Wagner's tutelage. One dimension of this program embraced anti-Jewish views, but Nietzsche was careful
to incorporate them into his writings without specific reference to modern
Jewry. Indeed, Nietzsche's first nonacademic work, *The Birth of Tragedy Out
of the Spirit of Music*, seeks to further the Wagnerian mission, including its
racist proclivities, without direct recourse to Judeophobic phrasing. It is
important to note that although the hypothesis concerning the Dionysian
and the Apollonian has attracted the most critical attention in recent times,
Nietzsche considered the advent of Socratism and its potential overcoming
in German music and philosophy of modern times to be the heart of the
text. When he had difficulty finding a publisher for the essay, he decided to
self-publish part of the work for his friends, as he had done with his inaugural
lecture on Homer. He chose for this publication a reworked version of the
lecture "Socrates and Tragedy"—without its overtly anti-Jewish conclusion—

and it consisted of material that was eventually incorporated into sections eight to fifteen of the finished book. Moreover, sections sixteen to twenty-five of *The Birth of Tragedy* envision a supersession of Socratism largely in a German movement culminating in the music dramas of Richard Wagner. As we have seen, in 1870 Nietzsche had associated Socratism with the "Jewish press," and although there is no open identification between Socratism and anything Jewish in subsequent publications, the term contains obvious references to items pertaining to Jewry in Schopenhauer's writings, Wagner's thought, or the general cultural code of Judeophobia in the late nineteenth century. We will recall, for example, that Schopenhauer consistently criticizes Judaism for its optimistic worldview, so we should not be surprised to find that in Nietzsche's philosophical ruminations Socrates brings about the demise of tragic art by promoting optimism, reason, logic, and dialectical thought: "for who could fail to recognize the *optimistic* element in the essence of the dialectic, which celebrates exultantly in each conclusion and needs the cool radiance of consciousness in order to breathe: the optimistic element which, once it has penetrated tragedy, gradually overgrows its Dionysian regions and must necessarily drive it to self-annihilation." The new "Socratic-optimistic stage-world" with its "optimistic dialectic" drives "*music* out of tragedy with the whip of its syllogisms: that is, it destroys the essence of tragedy" (GT 14, KSA 1.94–95).[42] The crucial antithetical tendencies that Nietzsche establishes in this text are not the Apollonian and the Dionysian, but the tragic and the Socratic, the world of the Greeks as manifested in the tragic worldview and the rational, logical world of "Socratism" that has dominated Western thought ever since. "I want to speak only of the most *illustrious opponent* of the tragic worldview, and by that I mean science [*Wissenschaft*], which is optimistic in its deepest essence, with its ancestor Socrates to the forefront" (GT 16, KSA 1.103). The German word "Wissenschaft," here translated as "science," includes far more than the natural sciences; it encompasses all branches of knowledge and could be rendered more accurately, albeit more awkwardly, as "systematic knowledge." But the point is simply that Nietzsche's term "Socratism," drawing on Schopenhauer and the criticism of Enlightenment traditions, still contains the association with Judaism that it did in Nietzsche's 1870 lecture.

Socratism is opposed to more than Greek tragedy; like Jewish intervention in Wagner's worldview, it is also antithetical to the essence of genuine German art and thought. Nietzsche is one in a long line of German philosophers who insist that Germany is the true heir to ancient Greece. At the beginning of section twenty he asks in which era, and in which individuals, had "the German spirit" learned most from the Greeks, and his answer is not surprising. He finds that German classicism has previously done the most to unite the Greeks with the German spirit, and specifically cites Johann Winckelmann, Johann Wolfgang Goethe, and Friedrich Schiller as the chief proponents of that movement. Nietzsche's point, however, is that German classicism did not go far enough and did not achieve a thorough and profound understanding of antiquity: "Should we, in order not to have to despair completely of the German spirit, not conclude that in some essential point or other those participants in the struggle might have failed to penetrate to the core of the Hellenic character and to establish a lasting bond of love between German and Greek culture?" (GT 20, KSA 1.129). What was lacking in that earlier era of the German Grecophilic tradition was an appreciation of the fundamental pessimism of pre-Socratic art. German classicism invariably presents ancient Greece in optimistic language, as the epitome of harmony, beauty, and serenity. These writers confuse the Apollonian appearance and the Socratic/Platonic philosophical tradition with the essence of Greek cultural achievement in the tragic art of Aeschylus and Sophocles. Nietzsche admires German classicism, but he argues that the true successors of Greece do not appear until the last half of the nineteenth century with Wagner's operas and Nietzsche's own insights into tragic art.[43] Even Schopenhauer was partially deceived by Greek optimism, or at least in need of Nietzsche's clarification and corrective: "Greek paganism and Islam," Schopenhauer wrote, "are entirely optimistic; therefore in the former the antithetical tendency to have to vent itself at least in tragedy."[44] For Schopenhauer tragedy is the exception in an essentially optimistic spirit that is shared by Judaism, Islam, and Greek pagan society; for Nietzsche it is fundamental for Greek art. Nietzsche's *Birth of Tragedy* can be understood in part as an extended comment on Schopenhauer's observation, as an endeavor to place tragedy at the center of Greek concerns and conceive the "entirely optimistic" and "Jewish"[45] spirit as foreign invaders supplanting a fundamentally correct worldview with something false and vapid.

The last ten sections of *The Birth of Tragedy* are devoted to the conflict between the Dionysian or tragic spirit and Socratism in all its manifestations. Philosophically Socratism is associated with logic and rationalism, and while these qualities are not specifically Jewish, they do form part of the traditional opposition between the romantic, metaphysical German and the clever, analytical Jew. Nietzsche attributes to Kant and Schopenhauer the great achievement of overcoming pure rationality and showing us its limitations. "The great audacity and wisdom of *Kant* and *Schopenhauer* succeeded in winning the most difficult victory, the victory over the optimism which lies hidden in the essence of logic, the optimism which is also the substratum of our culture." Kant receives credit for introducing a "tragic culture" based on wisdom rather than systems of knowledge (GT 18, KSA 1.118).[46] What we call culture, education, and civilization today, Nietzsche asserts, will eventually be brought before the "unimpeachable Dionysian judge," to which genuine German philosophy also pays its respects. Currently standing at a point of transition from Socratic scientism to Dionysian wisdom, we are proceeding toward another age of tragic art. The birth of a new tragic art, however, will be for the German spirit "a return to itself, a blissful rediscovery of the self, after a long period during which the previously helpless barbaric form of this spirit has been suppressed by tremendous encroaching powers and forced into a feudal subservience to outside form" (GT 19, KSA 1.128). Analogous to the Jewish hegemony over Germany in Wagner's "Judaism in Music," German philosophy must free itself from a foreign power that has enslaved it and prevented it from developing in an authentic manner. Fortunately Nietzsche is convinced that "the age of the Socratic man is over" (GT 20, KSA 1.132), and leading the charge against this foreign, debilitating, rationalist, and antiartistic force is German music, the "Dionysian ground of the German spirit." It represents a power "which has nothing in common with the original conditions of Socratic culture, a power which Socratic culture can neither explain nor excuse, but which it rather senses as something horrifically inexplicable, something overpoweringly hostile." "What," Nietzsche asks, "can the Socratic system of our time with its lust for knowledge even begin to do with this daemon rising from the unfathomable depths?" (GT 19, KSA 1.127). Socratic culture of the present, Nietzsche makes clear to his reader, thrives on the superficiality of the journalist, "the paper slave of the day," and in the "journalistic idiom" with its "frivolous elegance" (GT 20, KSA 1.130). It is the domain of the critic, by which Nietzsche does not mean the Kantian critique that sets limits to knowledge, but rather a way of confronting art that "has been artificial and no more than thinly coated with an appearance of life." The rebirth of tragedy will produce "the *aesthetic listener*," in contrast to the current public consisting of "the student, the schoolboy, indeed even the most harmless female creature ... prepared through education and newspapers for the same perception of a work of art" (GT 22, KSA 1.143). Characteristic for Socratic culture is therefore the debasement of genuine artistic achievement through various social agents, all of which have connections with anti-Jewish stereotypes: "While the critic had come to dominate the theater and culture, as the journalist had come to dominate the school, and the press had come to dominate society, art degenerated into an entertainment object of the lowest kind" (GT 22, KSA 1.144), Nietzsche writes, echoing Wagner's criticism of Jewish music culture. In the struggle between an authentic German culture and the alien culture that currently dominates the Fatherland, Nietzsche is convinced that the former will prevail: "We think so highly of the pure and strong core of the German character that we dare to expect it to excise the foreign elements which have been forcibly implanted and consider that the German spirit may well be in the process of returning to itself" (GT 23, KSA 1.149). Left unidentified are the "foreign elements" that must be removed, just as the nature of Socratism and scientific Socratism (*Sokratik*) is not associated with any specific collectivity. Similarly, in the penultimate section of his work Nietzsche refers to "the protracted disgrace in which the German genius, estranged from house and home, lives in the service of spiteful dwarves" (GT 24, KSA 1.154), an assertion that Wagnerians would immediately recognize as a theme from "Judaism in Music."[47] A tendency in modern German society that is optimistic, antiartistic, rationalist, and critical in a negative sense; that partakes in journalism, the press, and newspapers; and that debases genuine German art, promotes entertainment, and fuels degeneration would surely suggest to an audience in 1872, especially a Wagnerian readership, that Socratism was a foreign and powerful force intimately related to Wagner's view of contemporary Jewry.

Nietzsche's only specific reference to something resembling Judaism occurs in section nine, where he discusses myths, and in particular founding myths of two larger cultural traditions. The distinctions he draws juxtapose a "Jewish" with a "German" myth with the former depicted as inferior to the latter. After mentioning the "passive" myth of the "hapless Oedipus," Nietzsche turns to "the glory of activity" in Prometheus. In this myth "the Titanic artist found in himself the defiant belief in his capacity to create men and at least to destroy Olympian gods: and this through his higher wisdom which he was admittedly forced to expiate through eternal suffering." Nietzsche associates the story of Prometheus "from the very beginning" with "the entire Aryan community of peoples and is evidence of their gift for the profound and the tragic." This Aryan interpretation of Prometheus is contrasted with another myth of defiance of divine power and suffering as the punishment for the transgression: "It may not be beyond the bound of probability that this myth contains precisely the same characteristic meaning for the Aryan character which the myth of the Fall possesses for the Semitic character," Nietzsche hypothesizes, "and that these two myths are related to one another like brother and sister" (GT 9, KSA 1.65–69). Where did Nietzsche obtain this terminology and the notion of antithetical myths? He could have borrowed the term "Aryan" from a number of sources; its origins extend back into the eighteenth century, and during the Romantic era Friedrich Schlegel and Christian Lassen used it to designate the language family known as Indo-Germanic. He may have found it in several works dealing with the history of language. It is chronologically possible that he encountered both the Aryan and the Semitic in *An Essay on the Inequality of the Human Races* (1853–55) by Arthur de Gobineau, but Gobineau's name appears in neither Nietzsche's works nor his literary remains. Wagner knew Gobineau and published essays by him in his house journal, but his acquaintance with him postdated *The Birth of Tragedy*. Most likely, he had no specific source, since the opposition between Aryan and Semitic, according to Léon Poliakov, "was already a part of the intellectual baggage of all cultivated Europeans" by 1860.[48] Even if Poliakov is exaggerating, especially with regard to these precise terms "Aryan" and "Semitic,"[49] we can be certain that Nietzsche was not entirely original in his distinction. More important for Nietzsche's views on Jews and Judaism, he leaves no doubt which tradition is superior:

> The best and the highest blessing which humanity can receive is achieved through sacrilege, and its consequences must be accepted, namely the whole flood of suffering and troubles with which the insulted gods have no other choice but to afflict humanity as it strives nobly upward: a severe thought which, through the *dignity* ascribed to the sacrilege, stands in strange contrast to the Semitic myth of the Fall, in which curiosity, dissimulation, the susceptibility to be led astray, lasciviousness, in short, a series of eminently feminine feelings, are viewed as the origin of evil. (GT 9, KSA 1.69–70)

Prometheus commits an active, masculine offense; Eve commits a deceptive, feminine sin. At the origin of the two traditions are differing conceptions of the world, values, and meaningful action. The Aryan/Dionysian/German heritage is heroic, masculine, and courageous; the Semitic/Jewish paradigm is craven, feminine, and dissembling. Not coincidentally these stereotypes accord well with the anti-Jewish rhetoric of Wagner and, later, of anti-Semitism during the 1880s.

Wagner conceived of his cultural mission as a war against enemy forces, the most pernicious of which was Jewry. Although in "Judaism in Music" he claims that the Jews have achieved a victory, it is just as obvious that the true German will not surrender without a noble fight to the finish. The Manichaean portrayal of Jews and Germans in Wagner's essay and thinking recurs in Nietzsche's writings on tragedy, but the oppositions are sublimated into tragedy versus Socratism and the prototypical Aryan myth versus the prototypical Semitic myth. The academic audience may not have been sensitive to the antithetical foundations on which this essay was based, and certainly the general public might not have suspected that *The Birth of Tragedy* was in essence a programmatic piece of propaganda for Wagner with a philological veneer. But Wagner and his followers readily recognized what it represented. Wagner's copy arrived at Tribschen on January 3, 1872, and Wagner and Cosima's customary evening reading was devoted to it. They found it "splendid," and Cosima appropriately situates it in the context of Wagner's cultural struggles: "R. thinks of the people who at the moment set the tone in Germany and wonders what the fate of this book will be." It was unnecessary for her to specify what she meant by "the people who at the moment set the tone"; after their very first contact with the book, the Wagners have already situated it squarely in the struggle between the Meister and his dreaded Jewish adversaries. In the middle of January, after they have received the deluxe editions, Cosima writes: "We consider how to prevent his [Nietzsche's] books being killed by silence."[50] In Wagner's letter to Nietzsche thanking him for the book, he implicitly recognizes that it belongs to literature pertaining to Wagner and his cause (Nr. 256, KGB II 2.493), and that he and Nietzsche are allies in the same struggle. Thus when Nietzsche reports that on account of *The Birth of Tragedy* no students enrolled in his seminar, the Wagners try to figure out how to "send him students" or to force Bismarck to appoint him in Berlin. When Wagner's sister Ottilie reports gossip about Nietzsche from academic circles, an enraged Cosima writes in her diary that she should consider "that N. has jeopardized his whole career for the sake of her brother."[51] Nietzsche's Wagnerian friends, who likewise subscribed to a dichotomous view of the German culture wars, are more specific in naming the adversary to Tribschen and the Bayreuth plans for cultural renewal. We know that Nietzsche's book received no attention from any reputable classical scholar with the exception of Ulrich von Wilamowitz-Moellendorf, who, like Nietzsche, was a former pupil at Schulpforta. Wilamowitz's reasons for writing a review appear to have been motivated by a cabal of sorts on the part of a young classicist envious of Nietzsche receiving the position in Basel.[52] But his pamphlet, parodying Wagner's "Music of the Future,"[53] with its title *Philology of the Future! (Zukunftsphilologie!)* (1872), had a revealing reception from Nietzsche's closest friends. Gersdorff communicates his outrage:

> I have to express my regrets for the author, after I read it, not without agitation. I see this young individual, blessed with understanding and knowledge, on the easy path—no, already in the very middle of Berlin literary Jewry. I regret that a young man stemming from a good aristocratic family, who certainly devoted himself to scholarship out of a passion for knowledge, denying the advantages of

his class, straying from the usual path of a young nobleman, and allowing himself to be carried along at such an early age by the current that dominates our present educational system. Dialectic à la Lessing, the accumulation of learned materials, a lively language, apparent moral indignation toward your alleged ignorance and deficient love of truth—that is entirely the customary tone of reviewers and critics, as it manifests itself in the feuilletons of political newspapers and scholarly journals. The hastiness, the obsessive focus on details, the petty fault-finding, abusing, quarreling, and despite all the application of discernment and knowledge, no view of the totality and its interconnections. (31 May 1872, Nr. 326, KGB II 4.9–10)

Gersdorff provides a veritable inventory of traits associated with Jews by the academic Wagnerians: the use of dialectics, empty displays of learning, disingenuousness, journalistic language, critique, hastiness, quibbling, a proximity to the Judeophile Lessing. Writing two days later, Rohde is more succinct: "This is really a scandal in its most repulsive Jewish arrogance!" (Nr. 327, KGB II 4.11). Nietzsche gives credence to this theory of a Berlin plot inspired by Jewry when he responds to Rohde: "He [Wilamowitz] must be very immature—obviously someone has used, stimulated, and incited him—everything reeks of Berlin" (June 8, 1872, Nr. 227, KSB 4.7). A week later he fulminates against the "boundlessly impudent tone of that Berlin youngster" (Nr. 230, KSB 4.11), and to Ritschl he writes about eliciting a cry of rage from the Berliners (June 26, 1872, Nr. 235, KSB 4.17).[54] In a letter to Gustav Krug, a childhood friend in Naumburg, he too makes the purported Jewish connection explicit. After punning on Wilamowitz's name,[55] he exclaims: "What a presumptuous-Jewish infected fellow!" (July 24, 1872, Nr. 242, KSB 4.30). That Wilamowitz had nothing to do with a Berlin-Jewish conspiracy is obvious enough to us today and may even have become clear to Nietzsche at some later point. Significant in this episode, however, is not the mistaken facts, but the readiness of the young academic Wagnerians to conceive any opposition as part of a cultural war between urban, sophistic, journalistic Jews and noble, stalwart, superior Germans.

There is one additional Jewish dimension to the reception of *The Birth of Tragedy*, and it involves the Jewish scholar Jacob Bernays. As we have already seen, two decades before Nietzsche began his studies at Bonn, Bernays had been Friedrich Ritschl's star student, and in the 1860s Nietzsche even contemplated a trip to Breslau to study with Bernays, who was employed there at the Jewish Theological Seminary. As Ritschl's successor in Bonn, Bernays was a well-respected classical scholar, and when we consider that many of his interests overlapped with Nietzsche's, it is not surprising that Nietzsche consulted his writings in preparation for his reflections on the origins of Greek tragedy. Nietzsche's depiction of the "Dionysian phenomenon," comparing "the world-forming force to a child at play" (GT 24, KSA 1.153), is drawn from a study by Bernays, although we should note that the Dionysian was an important figure for German Romantics opposing their Enlightenment predecessors.[56] And in his description of the effects of tragedy, he follows suggestions from the older Jewish scholar, adopting occasionally identical expressions: the notion that tragedy is not only a stimulating and purifying force, but also a "discharging" force (*entladenden Gewalt*) for the life of the people (GT 21, KSA 1.134), and the reference to a "pathological discharge" (*pathologische Entladung*) (GT 22, KSA 1.142) in tragedy are both evidence of Nietzsche's direct reliance on Bernays's treatise from 1857.[57] It is not uncommon for an academician to recognize mainly his own thoughts in the writings of another scholar, and Bernays must have seen only Nietzsche's dependence on him when he remarked, as reported by Cosima Wagner in a letter, that *The Birth of Tragedy* "contained his views, only exaggerated" (December 4, 1872, Nr. 388, KGB II 4.143).[58] Nietzsche was obviously quite perturbed by this message, which not only questioned his originality but also cast him as dependent on a Jew. He writes to Rohde about the remark:

> The latest is that Jacob Bernays has declared that they are his views, only strongly exaggerated. I consider that divinely impudent from this educated and clever Jew, but at the same time an amusing sign that the "shrewd ones in the country" have already gotten a scent. Jews are everywhere—and here also—ahead of the game, while the good old Teuton Usener remains obliviously behind in a fog. (December 7, 1872, Nr. 277, KSB 4.97)[59]

The former admiration Nietzsche had shown for Bernays has all but disappeared under the pernicious mantle of typical anti-Jewish clichés. Bernays is impudent (*frech*) and clever, he belongs to a group known for shrewdness, and he has a good nose for the current and most promising ideas. Rohde supports his friend's bias, writing that Nietzsche's book will have an impact in the future, while in comparison "the Jew Bernays" has only the claim that he thought all of this already a long time ago (January 12, 1873, Nr. 400, KGB II 4.168). Again the discourse with which Nietzsche is comfortable fits in seamlessly with the Judeophobic tendencies of the Wagnerian circle.

USING THE CULTURAL CODE IN THE 1870S

While *The Birth of Tragedy* was not an anti-Jewish diatribe comparable to "Judaism in Music," it was nonetheless part of a larger project that accorded well with the Wagnerian enterprise and its Judeophobic tenor. The same can be said about Nietzsche's lecture series, "On the Future of Our Educational Institutions," which Nietzsche delivered in the early part of 1872, just after his first publication had appeared in print. The fictive framework for these lectures is that Nietzsche and his friend, both young students at the University of Bonn, are on an outing to shoot pistols when they happen upon an older philosopher and his companion. The philosopher is obviously modeled on Schopenhauer. A conversation on educational institutions in Germany ensues, and while the philosopher offers most of the opinions in the lectures, we can surely assume they express Nietzsche's views. Although Jews and Judaism are never mentioned by name, the cultural code antagonistic to Jewry is liberally employed, especially the cipher of journalism and newspapers, which become a major topic and are regarded as decisively pernicious forces, according to the philosopher, for undermining genuine culture and education. After identifying two harmful tendencies, the expansion and the diminution of education, the philosopher comments:

> It is precisely in journalism that the two tendencies combine and become one. The expansion and the diminution of education here join hands. The newspaper actually steps into the place of culture, and he who, even as a scholar, wishes to voice any claim for education must avail himself of this viscous stratum of communication, which cements the seams between all forms of life, all classes, all arts, and all sciences, and which is usually as firm and reliable as magazine paper is. In the newspaper the peculiar educational aims of the present culminate, just as the journalist, the servant of the moment, has stepped into the place of the genius, of the leader for all time, of the deliverer from the tyranny of the moment. (BA I, KSA 1.671)

In the anti-Jewish mentality of the late nineteenth century, journalism was the special province of the Jews. Among Judeophobes they were regarded as the owners of the major newspapers and journalistic organs, and the newspaper or magazine article, with its quick and mass appeal, its flashy and insubstantial language, and its superficial display of learning and virtuosity, became the paradigm for Jewish culture, which was antithetical to everything truly profound, serious, genial, and German. We will recall that when Nietzsche wanted to bring Socratism into modern times, he conceived of it as the "Jewish Press," and we often find Wagner excoriating journals and newspapers because they belong to "Israel." In 1870 Cosima accordingly bemoans the loss of a major newspaper to the Jews in her *Diaries*: "A Jew, Herr Strousberg, has bought the *A. A. Zeitung*, the only paper which was not hitherto in the hands of the Jews, having belonged to an old German firm!!"[60] In other passages in his lectures Nietzsche writes of "the repulsive signature of our aesthetic journalism" (BA II, KSA 1.678), and, when he broaches the topic of the German Gymnasium, he asserts that this institution currently unites "learnedness with barbarous taste, scholarship with journalism" (BA II, KSA 1.685). Although Nietzsche carefully obeys Cosima's prohibition on naming Jewry, in one passage we have examined above in connection with Meyerbeer, he makes the connection fairly obvious. German culture has become a debased "cosmopolitan aggregate," which relates to the genuine German spirit as "journalism does to Schiller or Meyerbeer to Beethoven" (BA II, KSA 1.690). Jewry, as the people without any national home, is often associated with internationalism or cosmopolitanism in anti-Jewish thought of the nineteenth century, and the parallel between journalism and Meyerbeer, Wagner's detested Jewish foe, makes the connection that Nietzsche included in his lecture "Socrates and Tragedy" almost explicit. In these lectures we once again encounter the familiar antithesis of the Wagnerian cultural project: a German realm of true artistry and genius opposed to, and at present thwarted by, a Jewish-dominated culture of journalism and kitsch.

Nietzsche was learning well how to vent his frustration at modern Jewry and its tyranny over German culture without specific references to Jews. Additional practice is provided later in 1872 when he composed "Five Prefaces to Five Unwritten Books," a work that he dedicated and sent to Cosima Wagner at Christmas in 1872 in lieu of his personal presence. Its content was probably directed as much at Wagner's approval as Cosima's.[61] Two of the prefaces deal with topics from Nietzsche's classical training: "The Greek City-State" and "Homer's Contest," the latter of which sought to establish an agonistic foundation for Greece. Two relate to current concerns: "On the Relationship of Schopenhauerian Philosophy to a German Culture," and "On the Future of Our Educational Institutions," which does not recapitulate the lectures he had delivered earlier in the year but tries to establish the ideal reader for a written version of his lectures. The fifth preface deals with more general philosophical considerations: "On the Pathos of Truth." Each of these prefaces contains its own interesting dimensions, but in the preface on the Greek City-State, which, if we follow Nietzsche's notebooks, was one of many book projects that never came to fruition, we find the most troubling passages. It begins by questioning the phrases "dignity of man," "dignity of work," "equal rights for everyone," and "basic rights of man" as modern expressions that reveal only that in our era we are ashamed of advocating slavery. Using Greece as his model, Nietzsche counters with the "brutal sounding truth" that "slavery belongs to the essence of a culture" (CV 3, KSA 1.764–67). He proceeds to denigrate the "liberal-optimistic worldview" derived from the French Enlightenment and the Revolution of 1789 as "an entirely un-German, genuinely Romanic-shallow and unmetaphysical philosophy." He then provides his analysis of the present state of European affairs:

> I cannot help seeing in the prevailing international movements of the present day, and the simultaneous promulgation of universal suffrage, the effects of the *fear of war* above everything else; yes, I behold behind these movements, as the really fearful, those truly international homeless money-hermits, who, with their natural deficiency of the state-instinct, have learned to abuse politics as a means of the exchange, and state and society as an apparatus for their own enrichment. Against the deviation of the state-tendency into a money-tendency, which should be feared from this side, the only remedy is war and once again war, in the emotions of which it at least becomes obvious that the state is not founded upon the fear of the war-demon, as a protective institution for egoistic individuals; but rather in love for fatherland and its monarch, it produces an ethical impulse, indicative of a much higher destiny. (CV 3, KSA 1.773–74)

These contentions are quite remarkable in their openness and serve as a contrast for Nietzsche's more guarded, public statements. Of greatest significance for our concerns is that the Jews, although never named, are cast as liberals, continuing an enlightenment and revolutionary tradition, and as manipulators of markets and politics to serve avaricious ends. To thwart Jewish liberalism and capitalist greed, the state must be harnessed for military combat. The flexibility of the Judeophobic mind is quite remarkable. We will recall that in 1866 Gersdorff accuses the Jews of promoting war for selfish reasons; here his friend Nietzsche maintains that the promotion of peace serves the cause of Jewish greed. Nietzsche continues his thoughts in the preface by holding the unnamed Jews responsible for all the ills he identifies with modern times:

> If I therefore designate as a dangerous and characteristic sign of the present political situation the application of revolutionary thought in the service of a selfish stateless money-aristocracy; if at the same time I conceive of the enormous dissemination of liberal optimism as the result of modern financial affairs fallen into strange hands; and if I imagine all evils of social conditions together with

the necessary decay of the arts to have either germinated from that root or grown together with it, one will have to pardon my occasionally chanting a Paean on war. (CV 3, KSA 1.774)

Cosima—and very likely her husband—was delighted to read these sentiments, which accorded so well with her and Wagner's thinking. Although Cosima did not get around to responding to Nietzsche until February, she suggests that Nietzsche write a book based on this preface and the sketch in "Homer's Contest" (Nr. 412, KGB II 4.207). As in the encouragement Cosima and Richard had shown for Nietzsche's *Birth of Tragedy*, here the Wagners are promoting the "academic" program of the Wagnerian mission, whose chief representative was the young classicist in Basel.

Nietzsche, however, did not follow this path. Instead, he turned away from his philological studies and sought to contribute directly to the Wagnerian cause with meditations on the current state of affairs in Germany.[62] He characterized his four essays written in this mode as *unzeitgemäß*, which usually translates as "untimely" but also has the connotation of "inopportune" and "unmodern." Opposition to the Jews, who are the "timely" and "modern" people par excellence, is thus built into this project. The only sense in which these essays were truly "untimely," however, is in opposing the manifestations of the modern era, which included basic human rights, constitutional guarantees and parliamentary actions, a capitalist economy, and a belief in progress. As we have seen, Wagner and his entourage at one point or another associated most of these features with Jewry as well. Nietzsche shared multiple aspects of his "untimeliness" then with many others in the Second Reich, including not only the Wagnerians but also conservative and reactionary parties and individuals as well as many Judeophobes. The *Untimely Meditations* are thus consistent with the worldview articulated in the preface to "The Greek City-State": antidemocratic, antiliberal, opposed to equal rights, critical of the manipulation of politics and finances in the modern state, concerned about the decline of genuine education and culture, censorious of the direction of contemporary art, and, of course, as a background for all the failings of modernity, anti-Jewish. The elitist underpinnings in the preface "The Greek City-State" recur with particular emphasis in the second and third *Meditations*, where Nietzsche asserts baldly that "the goal of humankind cannot possibly be found in its end stage, but only in its highest specimens" (HL 9, KSA 1.317), and that the life of the average citizen is best spent "living for the benefit of the rarest and most valuable specimens, and not for the benefit of the majority, that is, for the benefit of those who, taken as individuals, are the least valuable specimens" (SE 6, KSA

1.384–85). These foundational convictions, drawn largely from Schopenhauer's remarks on genius, in turn serve as the basis for Nietzsche's condemnation of modern society, which he continues to disparage in the *Meditations* in terms associated with Judeophobic platitudes. In *David Strauss, the Confessor and the Writer* (1873), for example, he denounces once again newspapers and popular magazines, displaying special pique for "the producers of these newspapers" since they are "most accustomed to the slime of this journalistic jargon." In case the reader has not figured out who these "producers" are, he then attacks Berthold Auerbach's un-German phrasings (DS 11, KSA 1.222), thereby connecting these journalists with the noted Jewish writer. In *On the Advantage and Disadvantage of History for Life* (1874) he writes of the weakened personality of the moderns and compares the present to the period of decline in Roman civilization, when Romans became un-Roman through "the influx of foreign influences and degenerate in the cosmopolitan carnival of gods, customs, and arts" (HL 5, KSA 1.279). Or we could turn to a passage from *Schopenhauer as Educator* (1874), where Nietzsche asserts that "journalism" has pervaded higher education under the guise of philosophy. This perversion of the university entails "a slick, showy delivery, constantly spouting quotations from *Faust* and *Nathan the Wise*, adhering to the language and opinions of our disgusting literary journals, more recently even with babble about our sacred German music" (SE 8, KSA 1.424–25). Again Nietzsche indicates the relationship to contemporary Jewry in German culture not only by the references to "slick" language, pretentiousness, and slimy journalism but also in the sole reference in his published writings to *Nathan the Wise* (1779), the exemplary German play advocating tolerance toward Jews.[63] In the *Untimely Meditations* the understood background to the ills of modernity remains the Jews and their inordinate influence over German culture. Nietzsche, paying heed to Cosima's admonition, nevertheless fulfills his obligations to the Wagnerian program by employing the extensive Judeophobic cultural code familiar in Wagnerian circles and throughout Wilhelmine society.

The final work of Nietzsche's Wagnerian period is the last of the *Untimely Meditations*, *Richard Wagner in Bayreuth* (1876). Many commentators have pointed out that if we read this work carefully, we will discern the beginnings of Nietzsche's criticism of Wagner, which will culminate over a decade later in *The Case of Wagner* (1888) and *Nietzsche contra Wagner* (1895). Nevertheless, this *Meditation* was written and understood by Wagner himself as an encomium,[64] and at various points the flattery seems so obsequious that we are left to wonder how Nietzsche, who was purportedly moving away from his quondam mentor, could publish a piece in which he would appear so servile. As appreciative as Wagner was of the praise, he must have also recognized that Nietzsche was still adhering closely to the program of Wagnerian cultural renewal. Several of the motifs we have identified as part of a Judaized modernity are conspicuous in the text: from a claim that our relationship to art has become a symbol for the "degeneration of life" (WB 4, KSA 1.448), or assertions about the "dullness and hastiness" of urban life (WB 5, KSA 1.461) to the recognition of the "entirely humiliating position in which art and artists find themselves" and of "a society without a soul or with a calloused soul," a society that "numbers arts and artists among its slavish retinue for the gratification of its *illusory needs*" (WB 8, KSA 1.475). But Nietzsche evidently wanted to make the Jewish connection clearer for the Meister and his readers. At the beginning of the sixth section he writes about two examples that demonstrate "how perverted feeling has become in our age and how the age itself has no awareness of this perversity." "Previously people were especially admonished not to take the day, not to take the moment, too seriously, and the *nil admirari* and concern for the matters of eternity were recommended; now there is only one form of seriousness left in the human soul, that concerned with the news conveyed by newspaper and telegraph." This illustration could be mistaken for a generic complaint, although we have seen how frequently Jews are associated with newspapers and the concern for the immediate and mundane. Nietzsche continues by noting that the sole virtue of contemporary times "is in truth more like the omnipresence of a filthy, insatiable greed and an all-intrusive curiosity that has taken possession of everyone." The other example makes the Jewish connection apparent: "Previously people looked down with honest superiority upon those who traffic in money, even though they were in need of them; it was admitted that every society has to have its bowels. Now they are the dominant power in the soul of modern humanity, the group most coveted" (WB 6, KSA 1.462). The allusion to Jews, the traditional usurers in Germany according to a long anti-Jewish tradition, is unmistakable, as well as their denigration as the "bowels" of the organic community, and their alleged domination in the present as the "soul" of modernity. In this tribute to Wagner Nietzsche once again pays homage by replicating the racist sentiments the composer had promulgated seven years before in his anti-Jewish pamphlet. Although he never mentions the Jews or Jewry by name in *Richard Wagner in Bayreuth* or in any of his works published from 1872 to 1876, Nietzsche repeatedly demonstrates his faithful adherence to a program that parallels and supports the Judeophobic animus of his friend and mentor.

CHAPTER FOUR

An Ambivalent Course

THE ANTI-WAGNERIAN

Nietzsche broke with Wagner at some point in the 1870s. It is difficult to provide a precise date for this break, but by the end of the decade, when Wagner had finished most of his final opera *Parsifal* (1882) and Nietzsche had published *Human, All Too Human* (1878–80), the two men were no longer friends, and Nietzsche was no longer one of the many followers in Wagner's entourage. The estrangement of the Meister from his quondam enthusiastic acolyte was experienced very differently in Bayreuth and Basel. For the Wagners there was consternation, anger, and disappointment. In 1877, however, Wagner did not yet seem to recognize that he and Nietzsche had drifted far apart. Through the latter part of the year Cosima continued to refer to the Basler professor as "friend Nietzsche" in her diary entries, and both the Wagners were solicitous of Nietzsche's chronically poor health. Their attitude changed rapidly with the publication of *Human, All Too Human*. Wagner evidently tried to treat the matter with a degree of levity, since Cosima reports that he "wanted to amuse himself by sending Prof. Nietzsche a telegram of congratulations on Voltaire's birthday," but his wife advised against it and recommended silence.[1] The Wagners appear to have been a bit confused on this point, since the book was dedicated to Voltaire on the occasion of the hundredth anniversary of his *death*. The dedication announced Nietzsche's sharp turn away from the Wagnerian cause, since Voltaire was both French and an enlightened rationalist, neither of which were particularly pleasing to the Francophobic, romantic composer and his bride. The content of the volume of aphorisms confirmed the worst for Bayreuth. Cosima notes that Wagner "feels he would be doing the author a favor, for which the latter would one day thank him, if he did not read it."[2] Although Cosima admits that they partake of only small glances into the book, they condemn its content as "strangely perverse" and its manner as "pretentious ordinariness."[3] The "feelings that gave rise to it," Wagner concludes are "evil," and it is the cause of much embarrassment for "our friends."[4] At the time of its appearance, Ernst Schmeitzner, Nietzsche's publisher, was also publishing Wagner's house journal, the *Bayreuther Blätter*, but Wagner informed him that he would no longer be using him for further issues. Schmeitzner knew that Wagner disliked the book, but he reasoned that a public dispute between Wagner and Nietzsche could only boost sales, so he advertised *Human, All Too Human* in one of the issues of the journal to spark controversy. The Wagners appear to have been upset by this association of Nietzsche's latest work with the journal, since Cosima reports that excerpts from the book were published as a supplement to an issue,[5] which, like many of Cosima's accounts, does not entirely accord with reality. The Jewish Question did not play a central role in the estrangement, although, as we shall see, in retrospect the Wagners did blame Nietzsche's Jewish friend Paul Rée for the changes they observed in Nietzsche's writing. In any case, for the Wagners the publication of a book that strayed significantly from Wagnerian ideology was the primary cause of alienation from Nietzsche. But we should not forget that Nietzsche was only a small part of Wagner's world. No matter how we evaluate the success of the Bayreuth opera house, it was a major cultural undertaking, and it attracted attention throughout Germany and Europe. Wagner was an acclaimed composer whose celebrity was enormous in comparison with the relative anonymity of his wayward disciple. Wagner and Cosima were certainly upset by Nietzsche's disloyalty, and they noted with dismay his apostasy, but Wagner had many other followers and supporters, a journal that he used effectively to propagate the Wagnerian message beyond Bayreuth, Wagner societies across Europe, and ambitious plans for a new opera, *Parsifal*.

For Nietzsche the break with Wagner was much more momentous and should be considered one of the major turning points in his intellectual development. Indeed, to a certain extent, as much as Nietzsche believed that he had severed connections with the composer, Wagner continued to be very much present in his thoughts and writings right up until the outbreak of insanity at the start of 1889. Wagner had been Nietzsche's world for the better part of the decade leading up to the publication of *Human, All Too Human*, and in the public eye, if he was noticed at all, he was still regarded very much as a participant in the Wagnerian movement. Unlike Wagner, he was relatively unknown, since he had experienced minimal exposure from his publications in the 1870s. His books did not sell very well, and the majority of interest in his writings came from Wagnerians. He had switched publishers in 1875, but Schmeitzner showed no greater success in creating excitement around his writings than had Ernst Wilhelm Fritzsch. Although he maintained a position on the faculty at Basel, the combination of poor health and lack of interest in philological studies made his chosen profession increasingly a burden he bore reluctantly. The break with Wagner effectively cut him loose from the only group of friends he knew; even many of his former university colleagues, whom he had introduced into the Wagnerian circle, evidenced greater ideological affinities with Wagner than with the latest views Nietzsche was espousing. Although Nietzsche had begun to acquire new friends at Basel, many had dual allegiance to him and to Wagner, and only a few, such as Paul Rée, stood largely outside Wagnerian influence. The break with Wagner allowed Nietzsche to rethink his own intellectual ties and proclivities; he rejected Schopenhauer's philosophy and began to fashion himself as an affirmer of life, rather than as a pessimist. But in the immediate aftermath of the break with Wagner, it is sometimes difficult to determine how much Nietzsche assumes positions because he has altered his views, and how much he is simply reacting against positions associated with Wagner. He firmly rejects the nationalist stance that Wagnerians embraced, emphasizing that he is a good European. But we often detect in this radical rejection of a narrow Germanness the endeavor to strike out at Wagner, from the selection of Voltaire as the dedicatee for *Human, All Too Human* in 1878 to the laudatory remarks about Bizet and Offenbach in 1888. We can certainly discern a rejection of many aspects of Wagner's palette of ideological tenets, but in some areas, in particular in his attitude toward Jews and Judaism, there are vestiges of Wagnerian (and pre-Wagnerian) positions mixed with an anti-Wagnerian perspective.

For our purposes it is therefore important to understand that Nietzsche's break with his former mentor was largely unrelated to Wagner's anti-Jewish thought. We have seen that Nietzsche associated with Wagner during a period when Judeophobia was rampant in his life and writings, and that Nietzsche never balked at this dimension of his discipleship, but rather sought to develop a program that complemented the cultural project of the Meister. Nietzsche rarely mentions Wagner's racism in connection with the disintegration of their relationship. Indeed, the reasons most frequently offered have nothing to do with Wagner's anti-Jewish convictions. If we give credence to Nietzsche's own explanation in 1888, he was disillusioned with the festivities surrounding the opening of the Bayreuth opera house. Contributing to his disillusionment in the summer of 1876 was his extremely ill health and the sultry weather, which combined to make his visit to the ceremonies extremely uncomfortable. Arriving on July 29, Nietzsche attended a few rehearsals but was forced to leave in early August because of persistent headaches and general fatigue. He did return on August 12, but the scene he encountered must have made him wonder whether Bayreuth would really contribute to the renaissance of German culture that he envisioned. In Bayreuth Nietzsche found the German kaiser, the archduke of Weimar, Ludwig II, and the emperor of Brazil, all of whom were in attendance at the official opening on August 13. Perhaps even more disturbing for Nietzsche was the general atmosphere, which was characterized by ostentatiousness and philistinism. The true believers, those who, like Nietzsche, had adopted Wagner as their cause, were obviously shunted to the side, while the rich bourgeoisie and the aristocratic patrons were courted. To make matters worse the performances were a general disappointment, to some degree because Wagner placed demands on the staging that simply could not be fulfilled. Nietzsche's letters from the late summer and fall of 1876 do not speak of his disappointment or of any affront he may have felt, but his almost complete silence about his Bayreuth experience is perhaps even more telling.[6] His most extensive description of Bayreuth occurs in sketches designed for *Ecce Homo* (1908):

> Even to those most intimately concerned, the "ideal" was not what mattered most.... Then there was the pathetic crowd of patrons ... all very spoilt, very bored and unmusical as yowling cats.... The whole idle riff-raff of Europe had been brought together, and any prince who pleased could go in and out of Wagner's house as if it were a sporting event. And fundamentally it was nothing more. (Kommentar, EH, KSA 14.489–90)[7]

Nietzsche's accounts in his autobiography are notoriously fictional, so we have no reason to believe that he is providing the genuine reason for his alienation from Wagner and his cultural enterprise. Noteworthy, however, is that Nietzsche does not describe his estrangement from Wagner in terms of ideological disagreement, and, in particular, that anti-Jewish attitudes play no role in this explanation of his disillusionment.

We have seen that Wagner did not approve of Nietzsche's book *Human, All Too Human* and the ideological direction it represented. Similarly, Nietzsche objected to Wagner's preoccupation with what he considered the composer's return to Christian piety in his opera *Parsifal*. The diverging perspectives of the two men might have been enough to drive them apart, but at one point Nietzsche mentions a much more personal reason for his break with Wagner, and again it has nothing to do with his views on Jews and Judaism. It involves a "mortal insult" and is mentioned in letters written on February 21 and February 22, 1883, to Malwida von Meysenbug and Franz

Overbeck, respectively, shortly after Wagner's death, which occurred on February 13. To Meysenbug he writes:

> It was difficult, very difficult to be the adversary for six years of someone whom I so respected and loved as I loved Wagner; and even as adversary to have to be condemned to silence—for the sake of the respect that the man deserved in general. W[agner] insulted me in a mortal fashion—I want to tell you about it!—his gradual retreat and creeping back into Christianity and to the church I experienced as a personal affront: my entire youth and its trajectory seemed to me soiled insofar as I paid homage to a spirit that was capable of this step. (Nr. 382, KSB 6.335)

It is not entirely clear what the "mortal insult" is; it could refer merely to Wagner's purportedly sudden embrace of Christianity, although it is difficult to reconcile Nietzsche's description of what appears to be a personal insult with Wagner's Christian leanings, which should have been evident to Nietzsche for a long time.[8] In the letter to Overbeck, Nietzsche repeats the message: "Wagner was by a great distance the most complete person I have known, and in *this* regard I have suffered a great privation during the past six years. But there was between the two of us something like a mortal insult, and it could have become terrible if he had lived longer" (Nr. 384, KSB 6.337). Although some scholars attributed this deadly insult to a presumed Wagner criticism of Nietzsche's musical composition, "Hymn to Friendship," that hypothesis appears unlikely, since it would place the date of alienation between the two men in 1874, when Nietzsche was still singing Wagner's praises in public pronouncements and private communications.

Somewhat more plausible is the notion that Nietzsche was offended by Wagner's interference with Nietzsche's medical condition as it pertained to the presumption of sexual deviance. In the summer of 1877 Nietzsche met a Frankfurt physician named Otto Eiser, who took great interest in his health, which had deteriorated so severely that he took leave from his teaching duties at Basel. He visited Frankfurt in October of 1877 and was examined by Eiser for eye problems and headaches. Eiser believed the illness originated in the nerve centers of the eyes and prescribed a prohibition on reading and writing for several years, avoidance of light stimulation by wearing blue sunglasses, and abstention from all somatic and psychic exertion. Eiser evidently told Nietzsche that he himself had suffered from similar nervous symptoms and depression and had fully recovered, whereupon Nietzsche responded: "Yes, but in your case it was rather different and did not cause any harm. But I *cannot* become ill, be ill, remain ill! The burden of determining and ordering the future is in my hands, not only for the nation, not only for humanity, not only for the world; no, for the entire universe and for all future times."⁹ Eiser was also the cofounder of the Frankfurt chapter of the Richard Wagner Society; he had published (evidently through Nietzsche's mediation) essays in the *Bayreuther Blätter*, and he had personal contact with Wagner. When Wagner learned he was treating Nietzsche, he expressed concern and did not hesitate to offer his own diagnosis, which differed from Eiser's:

> In judging Nietzsche's condition, for a long time I have carried around the memory of identical and very similar experiences, which I have observed in other young men of great intellectual abilities. I have seen similar symptoms have ruinous results and found out very definitely that they were the consequences of onanism. Since I have observed Nietzsche more closely, from this experience and from all of his temperamental traits and characteristic habits my suspicion has become conviction.... It was also very important for me to learn recently that the physician consulted by Nietzsche a short time ago in Naples, advised him above all to—get married.¹⁰

Whether Nietzsche visited Eiser again is uncertain, but he evidently did find out about the correspondence between Wagner and Eiser, although it is unclear whether Eiser showed him the letter, related its contents to him, or whether Nietzsche learned of the letter because Wagner confided in Nietzsche's sister, and she relayed the message to him. We do know that Nietzsche wrote the following to Köselitz in April 1883:

> Cosima spoke about me as if I were a spy who insinuates himself into the confidence of another and then retreats when he has what he wants. Wagner is full of evil ideas; but what do you say to the fact that he exchanged letters (and even with my physician) in order to express his conviction that my changed way of thinking is the result of unnatural excesses with an indication of pederasty. (Nr. 405, KSB 6.365)

We will probably never know precisely what the "mortal insult" was. But from the evidence we have, we can ascertain that Nietzsche was justifiably offended that Wagner was interfering in very personal matters related to his health and sexuality. If this incident was the cause or one of the causes of the break between the two men, we again see that Nietzsche's move away from Wagner had nothing to do with objections to anti-Jewish prejudices on the part of the Meister.

In the last two years of his sane life, Nietzsche did on several occasions associate Wagner with anti-Semitism, and he sometimes gives the impression that racist thought was a factor in his estrangement from him. But Nietzsche is clearly rewriting history when he proffers this sort of explanation. What is most peculiar about Nietzsche's "memory" is that he portrays Wagner as changing his views, and, by implication, he acts as if he himself had remained faithful to the ideals he and Wagner held in the early 1870s. He broaches this topic in one of his last published works, *Nietzsche contra Wagner*. In the section "How I Broke Away from Wagner," he relates from the perspective of 1888 his recollection of 1876: "By the summer of 1876 during the time of the first *Festspiele*, I took leave of Wagner in my heart. I suffer no ambiguity; since Wagner had moved to Germany, he had condescended step by step to everything I despise—even to anti-Semitism." Nietzsche continues by citing "proof" that his farewell to Wagner was justified even as Wagner was apparently at the high point of his life with the opening of the Bayreuth festival. "Richard Wagner, apparently most triumphant, but in truth a decaying and despairing decadent, suddenly sank down, helpless and broken, before the Christian cross" (NW, Wie ich von Wagner loskam 1, KSA 6.431–32).[11] Nietzsche is surely referring to the opera *Parsifal*, which he often cites as a sign of Wagner becoming piously religious. The sudden Christian piety and the embrace of anti-Semitism are two sides of the same coin from Nietzsche's later perspective, since anti-Semitism is frequently interpreted as a product of Christian rancor against the Jews.[12] In a similar vein he complains in a draft letter to his sister that almost all his friends have swerved into a most unfamiliar partisan camp, adding parenthetically "e.g. W[agner], whose last six years I experienced as a monstrous degeneration" (end of January 1888, Nr. 981, KSB 8.237). And in another draft for a letter to Elisabeth he writes of his "most painful and most surprising experience": "that the man I respected most changed, in the most disgusting degeneration, exactly into what I detested most, into the fraud of moral and Christian ideals" (end of December 1887, Nr. 968, KSB 8.218). In fact, however, Wagner had changed very little over the time he and Nietzsche were closely associated. With regard to anti-Jewish sentiments, as we have seen, he published his most venomous Judeophobic essay, "Judaism in Music," in 1869, shortly after he had met Nietzsche, and anti-Jewish remarks were frequent in his, in Nietzsche's, and in Nietzsche's friends' conversations. With regard to *Parsifal*, Wagner worked on the opera for over two decades, starting in the 1850s. It seems unlikely that it never came up as a topic of conversation between mentor and mentee during the eight years they were intimate. Indeed, Wagner had included a mention of *Parsifal* and its connection with Good Friday in his autobiography, which Nietzsche had proofread for him. And on Christmas Day in 1869, Cosima notes in her diary that she "read *Parzival* with Prof. Nietzsche," and adds: "renewed feelings of awe."[13] The attitudes that Nietzsche seems so astonished to have discovered in Wagner and that he claims were the result of a degenerate metamorphosis were firmly established from the beginning of their relationship. Nietzsche could not have been ignorant of Wagner's Judeophobia; he knew about it first-hand and partook in it as a disciple for the better part of eight years.[14] It is possible, of course, that Nietzsche came to object to Wagner's racism, religious views, and jingoism, but in presenting Wagner as someone whose views on these matters changed suddenly and radically, Nietzsche is distorting the past and his own role as part of the Wagnerian retinue.[15]

A TRIO OF JEWISH FRIENDS AND ADMIRERS

Paul Rée

It is quite possible that Nietzsche's break with Wagner had something to do with his friendship with Paul Rée, but it is unlikely that it was a primary cause of the estrangement between the two men. In the scholarship on Nietzsche, Rée is consistently regarded as Jewish, although both his parents converted to Protestantism shortly before their marriage in 1843. Since Rée was born in 1849, he was actually Protestant on both sides of his family, thus more accurately designated by religion as a Protestant of Jewish heritage. But conversion means as little to contemporary scholarship as it did to many in the nineteenth and twentieth centuries; most individuals who knew about his ancestry never hesitated to consider him Jewish and sometimes to attribute to him qualities stereotypically identified with Jewry. Rée is not only deemed Jewish, he has also been categorized as a special type of Jew; an idea that has gained credence without solid factual foundation is that Rée was extremely sensitive about his Jewish heritage, that he was ashamed of his Jewish background, and that he was therefore a prototypical "self-hating Jew." The chief proponent of this view was Theodor Lessing whose 1930 book on *Jewish Self-Hatred* contained an entire chapter on Rée.[16] This chapter, however, is replete with inaccuracies about Rée's relationship with Nietzsche and with Lou Salomé, and on the basis of these erroneous claims Lessing builds a narrative and provides a facile psychological analysis to establish Rée's self-loathing owing to his Jewish heritage.[17] If we consult the documentary evidence, with a single exception, there is no indication Rée was troubled by his parents' former religion. We have no letters or reported conversations from Rée that could lead to this conclusion, and Judaism is a topic absent from his writings. He was a nonobserving and nominal Protestant, thoroughly atheist in his spiritual life. The single piece of contemporary testimony that subsequent commentators have cited is found in a letter to Ferdinand Tönnies written by Lou Andreas-Salomé, who was close to Rée in the 1880s. She analyzed his personality in terms of his repressed Jewish heritage: "To be totally a Jew yet nonetheless to identify with something within himself which opposes this self in such a despicable and contemptuous manner—I never saw that in others to the degree I saw it in him."[18] This evaluation from 1904 was countered by Tönnies, who asserted that Rée had nothing or very little of what might strike us as unpleasant in educated Jews. Tönnies's further reflections on Rée provide additional insight into his personality. He was a "finely educated and ingenious human being," soft-spoken and characterized by a calm attitude, yet exuding authority. Although he was modest, he was self-assured of the correctness of his own thought. He engaged readily in conversation, but could be easily thrown off track.[19] Reports of his later life, when he became a physician, portray him as a dedicated loner, highly respected by the community in which he worked.[20] These remarks describe a quiet, polite, honest, self-assured individual. Nowhere does Rée appear haunted by his Jewish heritage. The notion that he was tortured by self-hate because he had Jewish ancestry would thus appear to be the result of overzealously applying a speculative psychological analysis to a peculiar and singular interpretation of Rée's personality and interactions.

Nietzsche was first introduced to Rée in the summer of 1873 by Heinrich Romundt, who at the time was living in the same house Nietzsche and Overbeck occupied in Basel. Nietzsche had first met Romundt as a student in Leipzig in 1866, and he was one of his closest friends during the next decade. Romundt had become acquainted with Rée through common friends in Berlin, and the latter, who had been a philosophy student in Leipzig before serving in the military during the Franco-Prussian War, attended Nietzsche's lecture course on pre-Platonic philosophers. The friendship between the two men was sealed when in 1875 Nietzsche, having discovered a copy of Rée's first book, *Psychological Observations* (1875), wrote to Rée, who was studying in Paris, praising the volume. Rée was delighted to receive this unexpected recognition from a professor he so admired, and on his return from France, he stopped in Basel to solidify the relationship. They agreed to spend time together in 1876 in Sorrento at the villa of Malwida von Meysenbug,[21] along with a student from Basel, Albert Brenner, and in this setting, without any other responsibilities, they were able to engage in conversation and a productive exchange of ideas.[22] Rée's Jewish background played no apparent role in this initial period; it is quite possible that Nietzsche did not even know about Rée's "Judaism" until sometime in 1876. Indeed, Rée was seamlessly integrated into Nietzsche's circle of friends, which consisted mostly of Wagnerians, many of whom harbored anti-Jewish views. Nietzsche even refers to Rée in a letter to Wagner himself in 1873 as part of a "small school" of friends in Basel dedicated to the celebration of Wagner's genius (May 20, 1873, Nr. 309, KSB 4.154). Nietzsche probably would not have mentioned Rée to Wagner if he had known about his Jewish ancestry. Nietzsche's friends appear to have accepted Rée without any reservations. We should recall that Romundt uttered slurs about Jewish Schopenhauer enthusiasts, and that Rohde and Gersdorff attributed Wilamowitz's critique of *The Birth of Tragedy* (1872) to a conspiracy of the Berlin Jewish establishment. Without stretching the facts too much, Rée could have been considered part of both these Jewish groups, yet his friendship with Nietzsche elicited no negative comments. For his own part Rée shared many of the same intellectual predilections that we find in other members of Nietzsche's inner circle. He writes to Nietzsche in 1876 that nothing can prevent him from going to Bayreuth for the opening of the opera house, and that he recognizes the "immeasurable significance" of Wagner for "the culture of the entire, great nation" (end of June/beginning of July and July 22, 1876, Nr. 788 and 802, KGB II 6/1.349, 368). In June of 1877 in an encounter with the Jewish writer Siegfried Lipiner, who evidently evidenced more visually detectable Jewish qualities, Rée writes to his friend that Lipiner is an "unappetizing person" (Nr. 915, KSB II 6/1.583), a view Rohde shared. We should also recall that Rée's enthusiasm for Nietzsche was sparked not by his aphoristic writings of 1878, which resembled Rée's own works, but by the books of the Wagnerian period, when Nietzsche was promoting a nationalist and somewhat furtive anti-Jewish program.[23] In the first several years of their relationship Rée was virtually indistinguishable from Nietzsche's other friends; his Jewishness appears to have never been an issue, and he was easily integrated into the ongoing cultural activity that Nietzsche at the time most cherished.

Rée's putative Jewishness became a topic only in November 1876, when the Wagners discovered his heritage. Although, as we have seen, Nietzsche mentioned Rée as early as 1873, and he accompanied Nietzsche to Bayreuth, the Wagners appeared not to have taken any special notice of the new friend of the Basler professor. In October 1876, while Nietzsche and Rée were lodged at Malwida's home, the Wagners came to Sorrento for a vacation, staying at the Victoria Hotel, which was five minutes away by foot. Nietzsche and Rée visited regularly with the Wagners, and at this point the Meister must have learned about Rée's background. In a diary entry on October 27, Cosima merely reports that "Malwida, Dr. Rée, and our friend Nietzsche" paid them a visit, but on the last day of the month, she pens a more ominous entry: "In the evening we are visited by Dr. Rée, whose cold and precise character does not appeal to us; on closer inspection we come to the conclusion that he must be an Israelite."[24] Although Cosima writes as if she and her husband were able to detect Rée's heritage owing to their keen powers of perception, it seems more likely that the Wagners were informed about Rée's Jewish origins by Hans von Wolzogen, a trusted follower and fervent anti-Semite, whom Wagner appointed as editor of the *Bayreuther Blätter* in 1877. Von Wolzogen had graduated from the Gymnasium Fridericianum in Schwerin one year ahead of Rée and knew him personally. According to Nietzsche's later accounts, Wagner warned Nietzsche about Rée at this time as well.[25] But Nietzsche was already set on a course that was moving him away from Wagner, who apparently let the matter drop and maintained an outwardly amiable relationship with his younger friend. With the publication of *Human, All Too Human*, as we have seen, Wagner recognized that Nietzsche's intellectual course had taken another turn. Since the Wagners tended to blame any misfortune in their lives on a Jewish conspiracy, Rée was now placed in the role of exercising a pernicious influence over Nietzsche. We are not privy to all the discussions in the Wagner household around Nietzsche and his intellectual "betrayal" of the Wagnerian cause, but Cosima does divulge how Wagner was affected by Nietzsche's preference for Rée. She reports his remark in June 1878 that he "can understand why Rée's company is more congenial to him than mine," and when Cosima observes that his earlier writings were "just reflections of something else, they did not come from within," Wagner retorts sardonically: "And now they are Rée-flections."[26] For the Wagners, Nietzsche was now in the opposing cultural camp, the one dominated by Jews and Jewish influence, as Wagner had analyzed the situation in "Judaism in Music." Wagner's ideological and racist schema determined their evaluation of the Nietzsche-Rée relationship, and Nietzsche's turn away from the cultural mission embodied in Bayreuth. Although Cosima insists that she has not read *Human, All Too Human*, her comments on the book in a letter to Marie von Schleinitz provide further evidence of the dogmatic framework in which the Wagners operated:

> The author has undergone a process that I saw coming for a long time, and that I struggled against with my meager powers. Many things came together to produce that deplorable book! Finally Israel intervened in the form of a Dr. Rée, very

sleek, very cool, at the same time as being captivated by Nietzsche and dominated by him, though actually outwitting him: the relationship of Judea and Germania in miniature. Malwida completely denies an evil influence from Rée.... She asks me not to give up on Nietzsche, but for every sentence I have read I have a commentary, and I know that here evil has been victorious.... Wagner himself asserts about Nietzsche that a flower could have come from this bulb. Now only the bulb remains, really a loathsome thing.[27]

A few days later on the occasion of a visit from Schmeitzner, the Wagners must have still had Nietzsche and Rée on their mind. Schmeitzner reports to Köselitz that Wagner had told him Nietzsche had a readership only as long as he belonged to the Wagnerians, and also uttered other "base thoughts about Nietzsche." Schmeitzner ducked the question he was posed about his views on Rée's latest book, but he also experienced in this context one of the most venomous statements by Wagner about Jews: "There are bugs, there are lice. Alright then, they exist! But you burn them out! People who don't do that are pigs!"[28] Rée's putative interference with Wagner's disciple had obviously exposed a raw nerve, and although Rée by almost all other accounts was never involved with his Jewish heritage and evidenced no interest at all in Jewry or Judaism, Wagner found it convincing to connect his hatred for Jews with his loss of a hitherto loyal follower. All the while Rée appears to have been oblivious to Wagner's vicious outbursts; Lou Salomé informs us that in 1882 she attended a performance of *Parsifal* in Bayreuth using Rée's patronage ticket.[29]

How did Nietzsche react to the fact that Rée was Jewish? It is quite possible that he learned of his friend's heritage only through Wagner, since nowhere do Nietzsche or any of his friends mention it prior to 1876. In a notebook from the summer of 1878, Nietzsche is again reflecting on Wagner's deficiencies, but he swerves slightly and speaks of Cosima as well: "With Wagner blind denial of the good (like Brahms); with the party (Fr[au] (W[agner]) sighted denial (Lipiner Rée)" (Nachlass 1878, 30[145], KSA 8.547–48). We will recall that in an earlier notebook Nietzsche had mentioned the danger in Wagner's not recognizing the validity of Brahms and the Jews (Nachlass 1874, 32[32], KSA 7.765); here, in a parallel thought, he identifies two Jewish acquaintances as Jews Cosima disregards. In 1885, thus after the break with Rée, we find Nietzsche sketching thoughts on the moral literature of Europe, and he includes a passage on "the German Jew Paul Rée" and his contributions to this topic (Nachlass 1885, 35[34], KSA 11.524–25). Why Nietzsche refers to Rée as a "Jew" in his notebooks is puzzling, since even in the introduction to the *Genealogy of Morals*, where he gives backhanded praise to his former friend (GM, Vorrede 4, 7, KSA 5.250–51, 254), he does not identify him with his religious or cultural heritage. A year later he returns to Rée's *The Origin of Moral Sensations* (1877) in what might have been an early draft for a new introduction to *Human, All Too Human*. He begins by simply discussing Rée's book, calling it a product of youth and berating his earlier consideration of the volume as belonging "perhaps really to my stupidities, at least to this point they were spoken in vain." He then adds parenthetically:

> I am recalling with vexation, as one can see, a deceived hope, of just the kind of hope that the talent of the Jews aroused in me on many occasions; as the kind of people who in contemporary Europe gain by inheritance an intelligence that is by far of the first order, but at the same time also a tempo of development that comes to *maturity* with ominous rapidity (and unfortunately also goes beyond it). (Nachlass 1886–87, 5[5], KSA 12.186)

Again it is difficult to understand the reason for raising the issue of Rée's Jewish origins in this note. But it is conspicuous that only after 1876 does Nietzsche begin to consider Jewishness as a feature of Rée's thought and to provide explanations that combine praise of Jewish intelligence with qualifications that denigrate this very quality. It is also worthy of note that he connects Rée with Judaism only in unpublished writings. Despite Nietzsche's distancing from Wagner, it appears that, in his more private reflections, he has not relinquished specific stereotypes and prejudices that extend from the pre-Wagnerian period to the 1880s.

How quickly more malicious anti-Jewish thoughts and language can emerge from Nietzsche is demonstrated by an incident that occurred shortly after he officially broke relations with Rée over Lou Salomé.[30] Angered and disgusted with what he assumed was Rée's suggestions of an impropriety on his part toward Lou, he wrote in July 1883 to Rée's brother Georg, who was managing the family estate in Stibbe. We have only the draft for the letter he sent, but if the final version resembled it, then it was highly inflammatory. He first makes it clear that he is breaking all relations with his brother: "any further intercourse between him and me is *beneath me*." Then he blames Rée for the insults he and his sister have suffered from Lou, and he spares no words when he claims that "behind my back" Rée "dealt with me like a sneaking, slanderous, mendacious fellow." "Your brother," he continues, "brings shame to me, as well as to you and your honorable mother." He concludes by heaping abuse on Lou. In a letter Rée wrote to Nietzsche, he had called Lou "his destiny." Nietzsche comments: "quel goût! This scrawny, dirty, foul-smelling monkey with her false breasts—a destiny!" (Nr. 435, KSB 6.400–402).

Rée's brother must have been shocked by this unexpected, abusive, and scurrilous missive. Georg Rée's return letter does not survive, but Nietzsche reports to Overbeck's wife Ida that the brother's response to the "fulminating letter" was the threat of a lawsuit for libel. Nietzsche suggests strongly to Frau Overbeck that he countered by challenging him to a duel: "I threatened him with *something else*" (August 14, 1883, Nr. 449, KSB 6.423).[31] Nothing comes of this angry exchange, and in August 1883 Nietzsche writes a letter to his sister containing four humorous poems summing up his experiences over the summer. It seems Nietzsche and Elisabeth were fond of inventing this sort of lighthearted verse, which contained some Saxon dialect, since in a letter to Köselitz in 1888 he includes a few new samples and informs his friend that he and his sister spent the time in transit from Rome to Genoa in the spring of 1883 creating such doggerel to amuse themselves on the journey (May 17, 1888, Nr. 1035, KSB 8.316). The letter from August 1883 must be an attempt to recreate the mood from earlier in the year. The third poem is titled "Libel Trial":

> Vor strömendem Geblüte
> Da förchtet sich der Jüde,
> Es macht ihn mißvergnügt.
> Viel lieber strömt er Gelder
> An seine Rechtsanwälter
> Bis *so*—"*die Ehre siegt.*" (Nr. 455, KSB 6.433)

> (The Jew is fearful of flowing blood; it displeases him. He would much rather let his money flow to his lawyers until *in this way*—"*honor is victorious*")

We might take into consideration the audience for these anti-Jewish slurs, Nietzsche's sister Elisabeth, who is typically viewed as an anti-Semite because of her marriage in 1885 to Bernhard Förster. We should recall, however, that when he was a true believer in the Wagnerian mission, Nietzsche introduced Elisabeth into the circle in Bayreuth, where she first met Förster, and that anti-Jewish statements are common in letters he wrote to her before and after she met Förster. We might also take into account that while Nietzsche was composing these verses he was still distraught over the situation with Rée and Lou, and that this Judeophobic outburst reflects his troubled state of mind.[32] While it is undoubtedly true that Nietzsche remained upset at Rée and Lou in August of 1883, the fact that he resorts to a stereotype of Jews as cowardly, wealthy, and quarrelsome continues a prejudicial proclivity Nietzsche had exhibited prior to 1883 and that would continue to surface on occasion until his last sane year in 1888. What this letter indicates is that even many years after his break with Wagner, Nietzsche still demonstrates ready access to the biases typical of many German Gentiles during the last decades of the nineteenth century. He is not virulently anti-Semitic, as were some of his contemporaries, and he did not reject association with Jews on principle, but in unpublished venues he did associate them with features that reveal a biased perspective.

Siegfried Lipiner

Wagner, of course, could also point to Jewish friends and acquaintances; as a general rule he accepted Jews as long as they were useful for him and his projects. Nietzsche acted in much the same fashion with a Jewish author who approached him with enthusiasm for his writings in 1877, Siegfried Lipiner. Lipiner was a member of the so-called Pernerstorfer Circle, a group of mostly Jewish students studying at the University of Vienna. Named for Engelbert Pernerstorfer, who later became a noted journalist and politician, the circle had already started as an association at the Schottengymnasium, and it continued as most of these highly assimilated Jewish preparatory-school students moved into higher education.[33] One member of the circle, Josef Ehrlich, had contacted Nietzsche in April 1876 with effusive praise of Nietzsche's *Untimely Meditations*, informing him of his popularity among a group of students attending the university in the Austro-Hungarian capital. Ehrlich provides a somewhat convoluted explanation of "untimeliness," includes with his letter a copy of *Fables and Aphorisms* (1876) he had just published, and exhorts Nietzsche to continue writing in the same vein: "I speak in the name of your enthusiastic admirers at the university here: with every literary news we receive from other countries we search with longing for your esteemed name, for a new book that bears your name" (Nr. 764, KGB II 6/1.314). Nietzsche was not accustomed to receiving fan letters; his celebrity to this point was restricted almost exclusively to the circle of Wagnerians he frequented. So it is not surprising that he responded favorably to Ehrlich, probably in June, and included his thoughts on Ehrlich's book. Nietzsche's letter does not survive, but Ehrlich's reply indicates Nietzsche praised the fables and recommended Rée's recently published *Psychological Observations*. After a few remarks on how he endeavored to combine philosophy and art in composing his fables, Ehrlich informs Nietzsche that he is baring his soul to him and sending a copy of the autobiographical account *The Path of My Life* (1874) (June 9, 1876, Nr. 784, KGB II 6/1.342–43). The subtitle of this book, *Memories of a Former Hasid*, identified Ehrlich quite explicitly as an erstwhile Orthodox Jew, just months before Wagner warned him about his continued association with his "Jewish" friend Paul Rée. Since there are no further letters in the correspondence, it is impossible to ascertain Nietzsche's reaction, and the autobiography, in contrast to the volume of fables, is not found in Nietzsche's library.[34] If Nietzsche was uncertain about whether he had an ardent group of Jewish followers in Vienna, those doubts were laid to rest on his birthday in 1877, when six members of the Pernerstorfer Circle, including Pernerstorfer himself and Victor Adler, who would later become a prominent socialist politician in Austria, sent Nietzsche best wishes along with lavish praise of his oeuvre.

> We believe we are acting in accord with your own wishes, when we endeavor to convey how much your writings have moved us, not just in employing words, but in giving you the assurance that this emotion has resulted in each of us—as far as we are able to do so—declaring the resolve to follow you, as our shining and inspiring example, with the strongest volition, selfless and sincere, just as you have done in striving toward the realization of the ideal that you have outlined in your works, especially in your *Schopenhauer as Educator*. (Nr. 1000, KGB II 6/2.737)

Nietzsche had his first fan club, and we have to assume that he recognized it consisted mostly of educated Jewish young men from Vienna.

Behind this birthday missive was most likely Lipiner, who was the first signatory and who also enclosed with it a personal letter to Nietzsche. A Galician Jew who was born in 1856 in Jarosław, Lipiner came alone and without means to Vienna in 1871, where he attended the Gymnasium and then studied philosophy at the university; he was integrated into the Pernerstorfer Circle in 1874 and soon thereafter became enthralled with Nietzsche's early writings. In June 1877, several months before the birthday greeting, he had endeavored to establish contact with Nietzsche. At the end of 1876 he had sent a copy of his epic poem *Prometheus Unbound* (1876) to Nietzsche in Naumburg, whence it was inadvertently sent back to Vienna and lost in transport.[35] As an industrious young man, Lipiner pursued the matter further, seeking personal contact with Nietzsche and finding instead his friend Rée in June 1877. As we have already seen, Rée characterized him rudely as an "unappetizing individual" and, protecting Nietzsche's ill health and desire for solitude, did not disclose his whereabouts, adding, however, in his letter to Nietzsche that he fears he will not escape his perseverance (Nr. 915, KGB II 6/1.583). Lipiner also encountered Erwin Rohde, who asks Nietzsche whether he has received Lipiner's book, and, if he has, to send a few lines of confirmation to Lipiner. In his report Rohde is even less flattering and more overtly racist than Rée, calling Lipiner "one of the most bandy-legged Jews I have ever seen." He mitigates by adding: "his vile Semitic face has certain not unsympathetic, shy and sensitive features," and continues with regard to *Prometheus Unbound*: "Please let me know soon [if you have received the book], and perhaps even make *pater patriae* Prometheus-Lipiner with a letter the happiest of all bandy-legged Jew-boys" (June 29, 1877, Nr. 925, KGB II 6/1.595–96). Rohde's remarks are oddly anti-Jewish considering that he invited Lipiner to accompany him to his wedding and seems to have established a fairly amiable relationship with him. Since Rohde also refused to disclose Nietzsche's current address, Lipiner traveled to Naumburg, where he met with Nietzsche's mother and finally obtained the information he desired, as well as a photograph of his object of admiration. Franziska Nietzsche must have given a detailed account of Lipiner's visit in a letter that we no longer possess, since her son writes on July 25, 1877, thanking her "for the detailed report on Lipiner" (Nr. 637, KSB 5.257–58). A few days later he receives a letter from Elisabeth and shortly thereafter one from his mother again. But significant about these communications for our purposes is that unlike Rée and Rohde there is no reference to Lipiner as a Jew or as an "unappetizing" person; both sister and mother comment only that Lipiner would be extremely jealous if he knew about Heinrich Köselitz, who had agreed to assist Nietzsche with corrections on his most recent manuscript. Indeed, Nietzsche's mother seems particularly well disposed toward Lipiner, expressing concern for his financial situation and even suggesting that Lipiner could stay at her home in Naumburg if Nietzsche wanted to visit and spend time with him. At this point, Nietzsche was certainly aware Lipiner was Jewish from Rohde's snide remarks, but his family is not the source of any anti-Jewish sentiments directed toward him.

Nietzsche's own views on Lipiner were already positively disposed when he finally received and read *Prometheus Unbound*, which Lipiner sent to him again on August 3, 1877, with a short note (Nr. 949, KGB II 6/1.663). He reacts to the epic poem with enthusiasm that is both unusual and genuine. It is unusual because of the enormous praise he accords to a work of literature that has left almost no mark in literary history. It is genuine because he praises the poem not only in his correspondence with Lipiner but also in letters to third parties. To his mother he writes of his *"indescribable* joy" in reading the poem, calling it a work of the *"first order"* and Lipiner a *"real* poet" (August 25, 1877, Nr. 653, KSB 5.275). He writes in a similar vein to Rohde: "Just recently I experienced a truly sacred day through *Prometheus Unbound*: if the poet is not a veritable 'genius,' then I don't know anymore what one is: everything is wonderful, and for me it is as if I met in it my elevated and apotheosized self" (August 28, 1877, Nr. 656, KSB 5.278). Puzzling is a remark in his response to Lipiner. Unfortunately, we have only the fragment of a draft of his letter, but in it, after praising him as a poet, he inquires: "Tell me then with complete candor if with regard to your ancestry you have any connection to Jews. I have recently had so many experiences that arouse in me *very great* expectations, especially from young men of this ancestry" (August 24, 1877, Nr. 652, KSB 5.274). We know that Nietzsche must have posed something very close to this question in his actual letter, since Lipiner responds laconically with the simple confirmation: "I am a Jew" (September 10, 1877, Nr. 975, KGB II 6/2.696). As we have seen, Nietzsche must have known about Lipiner's Jewish heritage from Rohde's letter, so the question was superfluous and slightly disingenuous. Most commentators have assumed that Nietzsche's reference in this letter to other Jews refers to Rée, about whose Jewish heritage Nietzsche knew at the latest when Wagner "warned" him about his friend the previous year. But Nietzsche could just as well be reflecting on the letters he had received from Ehrlich, which mention enthusiastic followers at the University of Vienna. At the very least Nietzsche's desire for confirmation of Lipiner's heritage points to a growing realization Nietzsche has about Jews as a group. From his experience with the Wagners he had learned that Jews should not be attacked in public documents, and that they allegedly have the power to affect negatively a Gentile's success in German culture. Now he was also beginning to recognize, as Wagner had as well, that there was significant advantage he could garner from Jews, who appeared to appreciate his writings as much as, or even more than, German Gentiles. We can think back to Nietzsche's comment on Bernays as a further indication that Nietzsche was drawing the conclusion that Jews are more perceptive and in tune with the zeitgeist, and therefore essential for the dissemination of his philosophy in the public sphere. As the years went on, he would receive further corroboration of his "insight" into Jewish Nietzscheans, most prominently in connection with the Danish critic Georg Brandes in 1887 and 1888.[36]

Nietzsche's enthusiasm for Lipiner cooled rather rapidly. The usual explanation given for his estrangement from his ardent disciple is a difference in views on important matters of art and culture. Like other members of the Pernerstorfer Circle, Lipiner was a pan-Germanist, and his initial interest in Nietzsche stemmed from his conviction that Nietzsche shared his values. We should recall that all of the Austrian Jews in this Nietzsche fan club knew only his early writings: *The Birth of Tragedy* and the *Untimely Meditations*. When they contacted Nietzsche with their letters of admiration and flattery in 1877 and 1878, they assumed that Nietzsche was still a German nationalist, that he supported a notion of *Bildung* that was meant to contribute to a recrudescence of the German spirit, and that he remained a loyal supporter of Richard Wagner and his cultural mission. They had no way of knowing about the strain in his relationship with Wagner, the recent influence of Paul Rée on Nietzsche's thought and perspective, and his work on a new volume, *Human, All Too Human*, that reflected a sharp deviation from his former intellectual path. Lipiner was himself a Wagnerian and quickly became a favorite of Malwida von Meysenbug, herself an ardent Wagnerian, although she also remained a friend to Nietzsche and Rée. There is little doubt that Lipiner and Nietzsche met at a crossroads of their respective development and continued along divergent paths. Still, Nietzsche stayed on good terms and in active correspondence with many individuals—Overbeck, Malwida, Otto Eiser, Reinhart von Seydlitz, and others—who had connections to Wagner, so his abrupt turn from Lipiner cannot be explained by ideology alone. The pivotal juncture in their relationship, which never included a personal meeting and was solely conducted through correspondence, appears to have come at the beginning of the year 1878. In November 1877 Nietzsche was still contemplating a trip to Vienna because there is now a "true nest of people there who have the dubious taste of appreciating my writings"; he calls them "competent," but Lipiner is regarded as a "genius" (to Paul Rée, November 19, 1877, Nr. 671, KSB 5.291). In January Nietzsche writes that Lipiner is "a good Wagnerian," which at this point in Nietzsche's life is probably not a compliment, and suggests ironically that he almost wishes Lipiner could rewrite the libretto to *Parsifal* (to Reinhart von Seydlitz, January 4, 1878, Nr. 678, KSB 5.300). In April 1878, Lipiner had signaled his differences from Nietzsche, informing him that the philosopher now has "a strong rival in my heart: Paul de Lagarde" (Nr. 1057, KGB II 6/2.838). Although Nietzsche himself had expressed approval of Lagarde in the early 1870s, he could hardly have been pleased to learn he was in competition with the ultranationalist, Judeophobic orientalist for Lipiner's affections. The following month we find Nietzsche asking Reinhart von Seydlitz, the president of the Munich Wagner association, about his impressions of Lipiner, since he complains that the Austrian poet is trying to "dispose over my life from a distance and to intervene in it through counsel and deed" (Nr. 721, KSB 5.327). Lipiner had obviously violated propriety   at least as conceived by Nietzsche—in trying to persuade the philosopher to tend to his health by spending time with him in a vacation area in Austria (April 20, 1878, Nr. 1057, KGB II 6/2.836–37).[37] By August of 1878 he informs his mother and sister that he has broken with Lipiner and his Austrian devotees, although we do not know exactly what this break entails since Nietzsche's correspondence with Lipiner does not survive: "From Lipiner a letter that significantly speaks for him, but is of incredible impertinence towards me. I am now rid of the 'admirer' and his circle—I breathe a sigh of relief" (Nr. 744, KSB 5.346). We do not possess the letter to which Nietzsche refers,[38] but from remarks in other letters we can gather that Lipiner criticized *Human, All Too Human* as well as Paul Rée's writings.[39] With Lipiner's criticism of his latest book he now saw clearly that his former acolyte was squarely located within the dreaded and adversarial Wagnerian camp.

Lipiner's Jewishness—or at least personality characteristics that Nietzsche associated with Jewry—also played a decisive role in his banishment from Nietzsche's discipleship. Although Nietzsche began his relationship with Lipiner stating that he had great expectations of Jews, his remarks about Lipiner as a Jew become increasingly critical. We have already seen that Nietzsche comments on Lipiner's impertinence, and in his letter to Seydlitz he calls him "shameless." Lipiner's putative pushiness and his deficiencies in decorum and social grace are features typically identified with Jews in Nietzsche's circles, and Seydlitz responds by first deflecting some of Lipiner's inappropriate behavior onto his own desire to convince Nietzsche to visit Austria, but then he continues by commenting: "You are right, it was a bit shameless, and you—and I—should remain separated from Lipiner by many miles in the future, and never have a constant telephone between you; for, like all Semites, he kills tender things." He goes on to compliment Lipiner for his candor, but qualifies, stating, "his book is the best thing about him." "To be sure he must first seek out people who can tolerate his restless, shrieking goodness, his offensive frankness, his 'natural' tactlessness" (May 18, 1878, Nr. 1069, KGB II 6/2.855). Nietzsche would appear to agree with the racial profiling Seydlitz has articulated, since he writes to his mother and sister that he is very concerned about Lipiner, and "does not confuse him with his Jewish characteristics, which he can't do anything about" (August 13, 1878, Nr. 744, KSB 5.346–47). Coincidentally, Wagner's relationship with Lipiner had the identical trajectory. Seydlitz reports that Wagner and Malwida reproached him for giving a negative report on Lipiner, since they harbored a higher opinion of him (October 15, 1878, Nr. 1120, KGB II 6/2.986), and Cosima indicates in September 1878 that Wagner and Lipiner are engaged in conversations of mutual benefit. But a few months later, Wagner is "completely disgusted" by an article Lipiner wrote on art and rejects out of hand a submission by Lipiner on Lagarde for the *Bayreuther Blätter*.[40] For his part, Nietzsche continues to associate Lipiner with negative qualities and with Judaism. He criticizes him for obscurantism and sentimentality, and in his late notebooks disqualifies him as a mere imitator of genuine art. Imitation is considered the "talent of the Jew," who is able to accommodate artistic production in a formal manner: "therefore actors, therefore poets like Heine and Lipiner" (Nachlass 1884, 25[282], KSA 11.84). The notion that Heine was an insincere copier of authentic verse and its attendant emotional states is a frequent claim in the anti-Semitic disqualification of him in the late nineteenth century. And in another passage from Nietzsche's notes he writes under the heading "Jew": "I emphasize with distinction Siegfried Lipiner, a Polish Jew, who understood how to imitate many forms of European lyric poetry in the most elegant fashion—'almost genuine,' as a goldsmith would say" (Nachlass 1885, 39[20], KSA 11.627).[41] These remarks reveal again that Nietzsche retained a good deal of his former anti-Jewish bias. We might note as well that Lipiner, as well as many in the Pernerstorfer Circle, was not entirely free from what we would call today "cultural anti-Semitism,"[42] and that in the 1880s Nietzsche reports Lipiner converted to Protestantism and became an anti-Semite himself (to Franz Overbeck, April 7, 1884, Nr. 504, KSB 6.494).[43] Many commentators have taken Nietzsche's association with Lipiner as a sign of his freedom from racial discrimination against Jews and Judaism, as proof that he had moved away from Wagner's allergic Judeophobia toward a position devoid of prejudice. The reality is clearly more complex, but at the very least Nietzsche's relationship with Lipiner indicates that the philosopher harbored a profound ambivalence toward Jews, at times believing they were supporters and promoters of his works, as well as potential allies in helping him achieve fame, while on other occasions applying to them the platitudes common to anti-Semites of his own era.[44]

Josef Paneth

Nietzsche was acquainted with one other Jewish intellectual who had studied at the University of Vienna, Josef Paneth. Like his peers, Paneth was integrated into the reading circle that discussed Nietzsche in the early 1870s, and, like Lipiner, at the time he was an enthusiastic pan-Germanist. By the time Nietzsche met him in late December 1883, however, he had moved significantly away from the original Pernerstorfer perspective and embraced a career in the natural sciences. Paneth was a physiologist who worked for a time in the laboratory of Ernst Wilhelm von Brücke. He was a close friend of Sigmund Freud, who was likewise one of Brücke's assistants while he was a student, and in scientific circles he is still known today for his description of "Paneth cells," which are found in the epithelium of the small intestine. Although he was thoroughly taken by a positivist and scientific worldview,

Paneth maintained an avid interest in philosophy, and when he traveled for his research to the zoological station at Villefranche, near Nice, he evidently took the opportunity to contact Nietzsche, who was spending his winter in the southern French city. Nietzsche must have been eager to meet with him, since, after receiving contact, he traveled to the laboratory in Villefranche. Paneth was not there, but he returned the visit to Nietzsche a few days later, only to find Nietzsche not in his apartment. Eventually they arranged a meeting for the day after Christmas in Nice. For the next three months they saw each other frequently and carried on lengthy conversations on a great variety of topics. We know about the content of these conversations only from the letters Paneth sent to his fiancée in Vienna. What Nietzsche knew about Paneth before they became personally acquainted is difficult to determine, but he certainly must have been aware that he was involved in Vienna with the same circle of Jewish students to which Ehrlich and Lipiner belonged. Since Paneth remained in Villefranche only until the end of March in 1884, their personal contact lasted just three months. A single letter written by Nietzsche in May 1884 survives from what must have been a short afterlife of correspondence. The name Paneth appears nowhere in Nietzsche's writings or notebooks, and the philosopher alludes to him only twice in letters to Overbeck, mentioning him by name only once. Why the relationship, which from Paneth's account appears to have been amiable and at times even intimate, did not survive the physical separation of the two men is impossible to ascertain.

Paneth had adopted science as his religion. As he tells Nietzsche, the fact that he worked in Brücke's laboratory is more important for him than his Judaism. Unlike Lipiner, he was not searching for some metaphysical truth and does not evidence any anti-Jewish tendencies; he was not a candidate for conversion to Christianity. Although he was not a practicing Jew and considered himself fully assimilated into the Austro-Hungarian scientific establishment, he did not abandon his co-religionists and, from the evidence we have, he was concerned about the rise of anti-Semitic movements in the German-speaking world in the 1880s. We will have an opportunity to return to parts of the conversations he had with Nietzsche regarding anti-Semitism in the next chapter; for now it is important to note only that Nietzsche told Paneth that he was resolutely against this virulently racist movement, and that his occasional association with anti-Semites in the mind of the public was the source of much distress for him. Paneth even reports Nietzsche stating that if he had committed suicide in the last few years, anti-Semitism would have been a major cause for his action. From Paneth's letters to his fiancée we would conclude that Nietzsche had never

been involved with any sort of anti-Jewish discourse, that he had never subscribed willingly to Wagner's Judeophobic predilections, and that he was
shocked when he learned the extent to which Wagner promoted racist
views. Paneth reports Nietzsche assuring him that "from his youth onwards
he held himself free from any prejudices regarding race and religion." We
have the suspicion that in these discussions Nietzsche is behaving much
as he did in his correspondence: he says what he suspects his interlocutor
wants to hear. For example, when Paneth asks him whether the Jews were
the cause of the venality of the press, he responds equivocally that "it is a
natural development that a market would form for public opinion." Paneth
writes that Nietzsche at first wanted to defend the influence of race, but in
the course of their conversation he abandoned this view and agreed with
Paneth that there are no pure races. Nietzsche obviously could not refrain
from posing some awkward and revealing questions. He asks what kinds of
hopes exist among the Jews and receives the response that Jews like Paneth
do not want to be considered as part of a separate race, but wish instead to
be regarded as individuals, and further that there was an ebb and flow to the
notion of a chosen people adhering to the Pentateuch, and that there is
nowhere a center or a unity for Judaism and Jewish opinions. When Nietzsche utters the thought that the Jews as a people have a specific ideal, Paneth
has to disappoint him by confessing to know nothing about it and to reject
the implication that Jews are somehow exceptional in this regard.[45] The
sense we get from the report of this conversation is therefore not only that
Nietzsche was seeking to please and sometimes placate his interlocutor, but
also that he still adheres to odd, prejudicial notions about Jewry as a unified
entity having a common goal and a coordinated plan or ideology.

There are other passages in Paneth's letters that should make us wonder
about how forthright Nietzsche really was in these conversations. For example, in discussing the influence of nationality, he asserts first that one cannot
deny it, but goes on to tell Paneth in no uncertain terms that he is not a
German, but a Pole: "his name is Niecki, the 'annihilator,' 'nihilist,' the 'spirit
that always negates,'"[46] which gives him great pleasure. Because of his facial
features he is still often addressed by Poles in Polish; just recently one of
them had told him "the race is still there, but your heart has turned away."[47]
In fact, however, as we saw in chapter two, we can trace Nietzsche's ancestors as Germans reaching back into the seventeenth century,[48] and we suspect that Nietzsche, despite his claim here and elsewhere, knew he was not
Polish or descended from Polish nobility, as he sometimes maintained.[49] In
another passage Nietzsche states accurately that he lives in an isolated fashion, but adds that he has a "silent community—but chosen ones, Gottfried

Keller, Burckhardt, Overbeck."[50] Here Nietzsche is boasting, trying to appear more prominent than he actually was by mentioning people with whom he is supposedly on intimate terms.[51] Of the three individuals, only Overbeck was actually a close friend. Nietzsche had spoken to Keller, and there was a brief correspondence, but, as Nietzsche's biographer confirms, the admiration was manifestly "one-sided."[52] And although Nietzsche had been a colleague of Burckhardt in Basel and continued to faithfully send him his publications, Burckhardt did not reciprocate in any fashion. Overbeck, who knew them both, states explicitly that their relationship was "one-sided," and that the older professor was increasingly horrified by the content of Nietzsche's works.[53] Nietzsche also prevaricates in the account of his relationship with Wagner; he tells Paneth that Christianity was mentioned only ironically while he was associated with him, and indicates that Wagner's anti-Semitism is a later development.[54] Since we know that Nietzsche was often in the Wagner household when the repercussions from the republication of "Judaism in Music" were at their height, we have to conclude that here too Nietzsche is being somewhat less than candid with Paneth, quite possibly in order to downplay his own anti-Jewish convictions, remarks, and associations. Taken as a whole, when we examine carefully the reports Paneth sends to his fiancée, we are apt to be suspicious of Nietzsche's motivation in pursuing contact with the Viennese scientist. Overbeck, who knew Nietzsche better than almost anyone else, supplies a rather cynical explanation: Paneth served, the Basler theologian claims, as a "helper in a time of emergency" in two respects: he assisted him in gaining "an orientation regarding his personal reputation with Viennese Jewry," and, since Paneth was a natural scientist and physiologist Nietzsche met at a time when he was extremely interested in these areas, he could provide him expert advice about matters of interest.[55]

Although Nietzsche evidently did not want to extend his personal relationship with any of his Jewish followers in Vienna, he appears to have been anxious about losing their fealty, especially through the appearance that he harbored anti-Jewish sentiments. Indirectly Paneth did supply Nietzsche with information regarding the views of his fellow Austrian Jews, although from his queries, Nietzsche seems to have continued to believe that they acted in a more coordinated fashion than was actually the case. But Nietzsche also received from Paneth something of what he needed in scientific knowledge. Paneth recognized on two occasions that natural science was a deficiency in Nietzsche's education and intellectual development,[56] but he also saw clearly that Nietzsche had a much different way of approaching knowledge than he did. While Paneth possesses a more conventional view of scientific knowledge, how to attain it, and its application, Nietzsche engages with science as part of questions of morality, or in connection with his visionary project for humankind. For this reason it is not surprising that their perspectives intersected in the figure of Frances Galton, Darwin's cousin and the originator of eugenics, who could appeal to both men for different reasons. Galton becomes a topic in their very first meeting,[57] and later Paneth loans Nietzsche one of Galton's books, most likely *Inquiries into Human Faculty and Its Development* (1883), a copy of which exists in Nietzsche's library with Paneth's name on the title page. When Nietzsche returns the book in March and indicates he has not finished with it, Paneth gives it to him as a memento of their relationship. Owing to his poor knowledge of English, Nietzsche would have probably had to engage someone to translate Galton for him, which is likely the reason that he was unable to return the borrowed volume to Paneth in a timely fashion. His lack of English did not prevent him from discussing Galton with Paneth, however. At issue first was Galton's assertion that certain mentally deficient individuals do not experience pain as we do,[58] and Nietzsche hypothesizes from this claim that we reach a place as we descend into the animal world where only the stimulus counts, not pain or pleasure. Paneth demurs, and Nietzsche turns to another topic Galton suggested: eugenics. Paneth reports that Nietzsche posits "a perspective and goals, according to which one would have to suppress one's good impulses and compassion for the sake of a higher purpose." Paneth objects to the implied notion of breeding "an improved human culture and race, that he [Nietzsche] calls 'supermen,'" stating that there is no one who could rule over human beings the way a cattle breeder does over his cattle, and that the higher purpose is impossible to define. Paneth recognizes a critical issue debated by others in the nineteenth century and essential for Nietzsche's eugenic thought: in the world of nature, selection attends to the disposal of weak and deficient specimens, but in human society we have established institutions that protect the bad and the weak exemplars and thus contribute to a deterioration of the race as a whole. Paneth adds parenthetically a humanistic response to his own dilemma, claiming that with human beings we are dealing with mental qualities more than somatic traits, and that humanity itself has so much value that the greater efficiency of the race should not be a consideration. But he had entered onto Nietzsche's terrain with these reflections, and the philosopher responds that the remnants of Christianity were responsible for the disdain for "everything useful and efficient." He adds: "perhaps one has to be cruel in order to create a few outstanding human beings and eras, perhaps suppressing everything else."[59] The discussion continues in this manner, Nietzsche defending a eugenic program that Paneth rejects for its harsh and redemptive assumptions, while Paneth takes the side of science and humanism in questioning the practicality and desirability of Nietzsche's vision.

Nietzsche was fascinated by eugenics in the 1880s, and we find numerous remarks in published and unpublished writings that deal with the subject.[60] He explored both the positive and negative dimension of social engineering, promoting in different passages procreation of preferable types and the elimination of undesirable individuals. Unlike the National Socialist regime of the twentieth century, however, he did not advocate a method of selection based on the Aryan race and its purification or the Jewish race and its eradication. In an odd fashion Jews figure prominently in his eugenic calculations. At times the improvement of the human race and the assimilation of the Jews into Europe appear to be part of the same eugenic project. Paneth reports Nietzsche's thoughts as follows:

> His personal wish was that the Jews should enter into unions with the best and most noble families in all countries and in this way transmit their good qualities; all nations should really do that. And then, as the only and best refutation, the Jews should produce a number of great men; for the examples that one could cite up until now—Heine, Lassalle—were not pure enough.[61]

The program Nietzsche seems to be proposing for a solution to the Jewish Question is assimilation through marriage—a solution advocated by many others, including, as we have seen, Schopenhauer—with an eye toward preserving the "positive" characteristics of the Jews, while integrating them into the upper classes of European society. Nietzsche is more suggestive and occasionally more explicit in other passages. For example, in a note written in the spring of 1885, he includes Jews as a necessary component of a German ruling elite: "The Germans should breed a ruling caste: I confess that the Jews possess inherent abilities that are essential ingredients for a race conducting world politics. The sense for money must be learned, inherited, and a thousand times inherited" (Nachlass 1885, 34[111], KSA 11.457). During the summer of 1885 he returns to this topic. After citing Jews as "the oldest and purest race" and as "actors," he turns to the "problem of the amalgamation of the European aristocracy or rather of the Prussian Junker with Jewesses." This passage may relate to a thought directly preceding it: that "the future of German culture depends on the sons of Prussian officers" (Nachlass 1885, 36[43, 44], KSA 11.569). What Nietzsche apparently envisions as desirable for Germany and Europe is a pairing of Prussian military with Jewish women to produce a new class of superior individuals. The former have the discipline necessary for a ruling class; the latter possess quick intelligence and financial acumen. In a note from the previous year reflecting on the

potential greatness of the German Reich he writes similarly of the intertwin-
ing of the German and the Slavic races and adds: "we also need the cleverest
people with money, the Jews, without question, in order to have dominance
over the earth" (Nachlass 1884, 26[335], KSA 11.238). His thoughts are less
concerned with Jewish assimilation in Europe than with producing a new
class for world dominance, a topic he broaches in aphorism 251 in *Beyond
Good and Evil* (1886). He again describes the Jews as "without doubt, the
strongest, toughest, and purest race now living in Europe," and he mentions
them along with the Russians as essential for any thoughts on the future of
the continent. In his closing reflections he turns to "the strongest and better-
established types of the new German (an aristocratic officer from the March
of Brandenburg, for example)," and then repeats the suggestion for his "*serious* concern, the 'European problem' as I understand it, the breeding of a
new caste to rule over Europe": "It might be of diverse interest to see whether
his [the aristocratic officer's] inherited skill in commanding and obeying ...
could be added to, bred together with their [the Jews'] genius for money
and patience (and especially some of their intellect and intellectuality)"
(JGB 251, KSA 5.194–95).[62] In his notes Nietzsche makes it clear what is
driving this odd eugenic fantasy: military officers and Jewish bankers represent for him the will to power (Nachlass 1888–89, 25[11], KSA 13.642).[63] In
essence the qualities Nietzsche associates with Jews are still the same stereotypes drawn from the long tradition of anti-Jewish thought, but he reverses
their valuation in his account, turning vices into virtues for his new ruling
class. In particular, the claim of Jewish power or Jewry's potential to dominate and subject "native" populations is an important part of most anti-
Semitic ideology in Germany in the last third of the century.[64] Once again
we find an underlying ambivalence in Nietzsche's dealings with contemporary Jews: they continue to be considered a unified type endowed with certain fixed characteristics that anti-Semites of his era also identify, but Nietzsche, in his transvaluation of values, supplies a positive assessment of these
qualities, considering them productive and necessary for the type of hierarchical social order he envisions.

A POSITIVE SPIN FOR THE PUBLIC

In Nietzsche's published and unpublished writings of the post-Wagnerian
period we witness a similar ambivalence toward Jews and Judaism. In many
cases he retains the clichés about Jews he had employed in the late 1860s
and the first half of the 1870s, but he alters the evaluation of these ascribed
attributes as he becomes less invested in Wagner and the Wagnerian project.

Thus the association of Jews with the press or with financial canniness remains very much alive in Nietzsche's thought, but he deals with this central theme of anti-Jewish thought in a very different manner from 1878 until his outbreak of insanity in January of 1889. As his various remarks about Jews possessing financial aptitude indicate, he now situates this putatively Jewish attribute in a vastly altered framework. In the early 1870s under the influence of the rising tide of criticism of Jews for their role in the financial crisis of 1873, the so-called Founders' Crash (*Gründerkrach*), German Judeophobes accused European Jewry of undermining German prosperity through dishonest manipulation of markets and fraudulent business dealings. We have seen Gersdorff and Wagner anticipate these accusations in their letters and works, but starting in 1874 the journalist Otto Glagau penned the most celebrated attacks on the Jewish world of finance. Since his series of articles appeared in the popular journal *Die Gartenlaube* before they were collected in book form, Glagau's claims received wide exposure in Germany during the latter part of the decade.[65] Nietzsche, in the period postdating his *Untimely Meditations*, now makes the truly provocative and "untimely" suggestion that Jewish success in business partakes in the will to power, and that Jews are therefore preferred genetic material for a new European ruling class. In these years Nietzsche also exhibits understanding and even some compassion for the Jewish plight in the diaspora, as well as for the discrimination and oppression they have borne for many centuries in German and European society. At the same time we continue to find comments in his works and correspondence that are a continuation of his earlier anti-Jewish attitudes. Writing to his family from Marienbad, he notes that the resort is teeming with foreigners, adding parenthetically: "by the way three-quarters are Jews" (July 27, 1880, Nr. 43, KSB 6.32). After meeting the spouse of his childhood friend, he comments to his mother about "Professor Deussen and his wife (somewhat Jewish)" (September 4, 1887, Nr. 901, KSB 8.141).[66] He writes to Köselitz about "the rich Jew" Bischoffsheim, an amateur astronomer who sponsored a conference in Nice, and remarks derisively: "Ecco! Jewish luxury in grand style!" (October 27, 1887, Nr. 940, KSB 8.180). And he expresses his preference for a French translation of Dostoevsky over the German rendition of "the dreadful Jew Goldschmidt (with his synagogue rhythm)" (March 17, 1887, Nr. 822, KSB 8.50).[67] It would be foolish not to recognize that Nietzsche modified significantly his evaluation of Jewry after his break with Wagner,[68] especially in what he wrote for public consumption, but it would also be foolish to ignore the continuity in stereotyping and "cultural anti-Semitic" slurs from the mid-1860s through his last written documents.

The change in the depiction of Jewry can be detected most easily in his very first published work after his Wagnerian period, *Human, All Too Human*. We should note first that this book contains the first public mention of Jews since the episode with Cosima, in which she admonished Nietzsche for identifying Socratism with the Jewish press. As we shall see, Nietzsche is more effusive in his positive comments on Jews in his published writings than in his notes, where more reservations arise; it is quite possible that he is simply putting into practice the lesson he had learned while he was closely associated with the Wagners about publishing negative remarks about Jews. In this book of aphorisms he is appropriately circumspect and differentiated in his discussion. In an early aphorism he observes a difference between the Greeks' relationship to their gods and the Jewish view of their divinity: "The Greeks did not see the Homeric gods as set above them as masters, or themselves set beneath the gods as servants, as the Jews did" (MA 114, KSA 2.117);[69] a relatively innocuous observation made in passing, unlike Nietzsche's comparison of the Semitic versus the Aryan myth in *The Birth of Tragedy*. In volume two Nietzsche even speaks of the "Jewish-heroic impulse that created the whole Reformation movement" (VM 171, KSA 2.450), a striking contrast to the nationalist interpretation of Luther he had embraced in earlier writings. His most extensive discussion of Jews occurs in aphorism 475, titled "European man and the abolition of nations." Nietzsche begins by reflecting on the current state of affairs in Europe, where an "artificial nationalism" is upheld for the benefit of a few princes and certain businessmen. National ties, he avers, are now under considerable strain owing to the expansion of trade and industry and, among other things, the "nomadic life now lived by all who do not own land." He therefore foresees "an abolition of nations" and the appearance of a "mixed race," presumably an amalgam of the various national strands, and the rise of the "good European," a notion post-Wagnerian Nietzsche frequently opposes to the nationalist ideologies of his contemporaries. The Jews, as the prototypical nomads not possessing a homeland or real estate in the various European countries, are perfectly suited for this postnational vision, and in a long aside Nietzsche deals with their history, their current status, and their potential contribution to a future Europe. Indeed, the Jewish problem exists only because of nation-states, "inasmuch as it is here that their energy and higher intelligence, their capital in will and spirit accumulated from generation to generation in a long school of suffering, must come to preponderate to a degree calculated to arouse envy and hatred." The result is that the Jews are scapegoated across Europe for anything that goes wrong. Here Nietzsche could very well be thinking about the assaults on Jews resulting from the economic difficulties in Europe in the 1870s. Because of their virtues, the Jews will be an essential ingredient for any future European race. Nietzsche recognizes that they possess "unpleasant, dangerous qualities," and that in the Jew "they may even be dangerous and repellent to an exceptional degree." Especially offensive is the "youthful stock-exchange Jew," which Nietzsche calls perhaps "the most repulsive invention of the entire human race." But the positive characteristics outweigh the negative, and Nietzsche points to the fact that in their "grief-laden history" the Jews have produced "the noblest human being (Christ), the purest sage (Spinoza), the mightiest book and the most efficacious moral code in the world." He goes on to credit Jewry with carrying the banner of enlightenment and of forging a firm connection with the ancient world: "it is thanks not least to their efforts that a more natural, rational and in any event unmythical elucidation of the world could at last again obtain victory and that the right of culture that now unites us with the enlightenment of Graeco-Roman antiquity remains unbroken." The passage as a whole is extraordinary in its praise of Jews; although Nietzsche does speak disparagingly about the clichéd notion of the "stock-exchange Jew," he reverses several other Judeophobic platitudes—the nomadic, landless Jew and the emphasis on intelligence—and expresses understanding for the plight of the Jews in the diaspora. Moreover, in most of Nietzsche's writings the Jews are viewed exclusively in opposition to the ancient world (as they are in the earlier passage in this book), especially to the Greeks. But here they are regarded as making "Europe's mission and history a *continuation of the Greek*" (MA 475, KSA 2.309–11). As Nietzsche's first extended public statement in which Jews are explicitly named, this passage represents an enormous modification of Wagnerian ideology, and it was perhaps conceived intentionally as an affront to Wagner's views.

We find a similar attitude toward Jews in *Dawn* (1881). At one point Nietzsche writes of "Jewish importunity" (D 192, KSA 3.165),[70] reviving a cliché employed in his association with Lipiner, and in another passage he points to the hypocrisy of the phrase "love your enemies," "invented by the Jews, the best haters there have ever been" (D 377, KSA 3.246), which anticipates the *Genealogy of Morals* (1887). In a further aphorism he deprecates the sincerity of Jewish philanthropy, claiming that the benefactor acts egotistically, satisfying "a need of his nature," and that when this need is strongest, he feels less for the object of his charity and often becomes "rough and, on occasion, offensive." He adds parenthetically the backhanded compliment: "This has been asserted of Jewish benefaction and charity, which, as is well known, is somewhat more effusive than that of other nations" (D 334, KSA 3.234–35). His protracted discussion of Jews in the aphorism titled "Of the People of Israel," however, is a long litany of praise. Since Nietzsche's topic is the "destiny of the Jews of Europe" in the coming century, the title is a bit odd; it is meant to emphasize a continuity between the ancient Hebrews and their modern descendants, a link that Nietzsche makes obvious at the beginning and close of his discussion. In some ways the substance of this aphorism represents an intensification of the passage in aphorism 475 in *Human, All Too Human*. The Jews are at a crossroads, Nietzsche claims, just as they were in Egypt long ago: they can either "become the masters of Europe" or "lose Europe." They have undergone eighteen centuries of "schooling," which has forged in every one of them "extraordinary" "psychological and intellectual resources":

> Every Jew possesses in the history of his fathers and grandfathers a great fund of examples of the coldest self-possession and endurance in fearful situations, of the subtlest outwitting and exploitation of chance and misfortune; their courage beneath the cloak of miserable submission, their heroism in *spernere se sperni*, surpasses the virtues of all the saints. For two millennia an attempt was made to render them contemptible by treating them with contempt, and by barring to them the way to all honors and all that was honorable, and in exchange thrusting them all the deeper into dirty trades—and it is true that they did not grow cleaner in the process.

Nietzsche confesses an admiration for Jewish perseverance in the face of centuries of persecution and presents a defense of less desirable attributes they may have acquired because of their oppression. Despite their historical plight they have retained a respect for the highest values; their marriage and family customs are laudable; and, perhaps most importantly, they have been able "to create for themselves a feeling of power and of eternal revenge out of the very occupations left to them." Yet they are also paragons of liberality, because they possess the "greatest experiences of human society." They are shrewd and intellectually supple; they have known how to avoid menial labor and still survived. Nietzsche interrupts his enumeration of virtues with a remark on Jewish deficiencies: "Their demeanor still reveals that their souls have never known chivalrous noble sentiments nor their bodies handsome armor: a certain importunity mingles with an often charming but almost always painful submissiveness." But he notes that since they will now unite with the aristocracy of Europe, they will soon shed these defects. In their present state, they know that they are not contemplating a mastery of Europe, but in the future Europe "may fall into their hands like a ripe fruit." In the meantime they will distinguish themselves throughout Europe and, on the basis of their onerous heritage, be the source of greatness: "And wither shall this assembled abundance of grand impressions, which for every Jewish family constitutes Jewish history, this abundance of passions, virtues, decisions, renunciations, struggles, victories of every kind—whither shall it stream out if not at last into great men and great works!" Then Jewry will be redeemed; it will have "transformed its vengeance into an eternal blessing for Europe," and just as God rejoiced on the seventh day of his creation, "let us all, all of us, rejoice with him" (D 205, KSA 3.180–83). The notion of the Jews as masters of Europe was not original with Nietzsche, of course; it was the stock-in-trade of anti-Jewish thought and occupied a prominent place in the anti-Semitic movement of the early 1880s, at precisely the time Nietzsche composed *Dawn*. What was new for Nietzsche and antithetical to his former Wagnerian perspective was the celebration of Jewish hegemony in Europe. The solution to the Jewish Question is not assimilation—although there is some suggestion of intermarriage with the upper classes—or the gradual disappearance of Jewish vices in favor of their virtues. Rather, at least in *Dawn*, the dilemma of Jewish existence in a hostile Europe will be resolved by Jewish dominance over the continent.

A somewhat different perspective on a similar issue is apparent in Nietzsche's notebooks from the summer of 1885, just four years after the publication of *Dawn*. Nietzsche asserts that if intellect, diligence, and aptitude were the sole criteria, Prussian Jews would have all governmental power in their hands. He adds, "as they already have it in the pocket," employing the hackneyed notion of Jewish dominance owing to financial prowess. The stage is somewhat smaller in that Nietzsche is considering only Prussia, but the assertion that Jews have superior abilities and could easily obtain a hegemonic position parallels the passage in *Dawn*. The reason the Jews do not already control Europe, according to the earlier aphorism, has to do with their unwillingness to claim it in a precipitous fashion. In his notebooks Nietzsche cites less seemly reasons for Jewry being unable to ascend to a ruling role in the Prussian state. In rapid succession Nietzsche maintains: Jews do not look you squarely in the eyes; they speak too quickly and clumsily; their anger is dishonest; they do not tolerate great quantities of food and cannot hold their liquor; their arms and feet do not give a noble impression; their hands quiver; "and even the manner in which a Jew mounts a horse (or a Jewish musician approaches a theme—'the Jewish leap'—) is not unobjectionable and allows us to understand that the Jews were never a *chivalric* race." He goes on to assert that Jews are uncertain in representing their morality and concludes that the Jews of Prussia must be a debased and stunted type of Jew. Nietzsche does supply a reason for this pitiful state of Prussian Jewry: the "degeneration" of the Jew is the result of the wrong climate and of an association in Prussia with "unattractive and oppressed Slavs, Hungarians, and Germans." Jews in Portugal or the Jews of the Old Testament are very different and even exemplary in their behavior and could even teach something to the Greeks. But what is remarkable is, in contrast to the published discussion of Jews, this is a very different kind of enumeration of Jewish characteristics, all of which are unflattering and often drawn from the immense arsenal of European Judeophobia. Nietzsche continues his derogatory account of Jews by delineating two "dangers of the Jewish psyche": "(1) they try to gain a foothold in a parasitic manner," and "(2) they know how to adapt themselves, as the natural scientists say." For that reason they have become actors, "just like the polyp that, as Theognis sings, borrows the color of the cliff on which they fasten themselves." These two Jewish tendencies have carved a "fateful rut" in the Jewish character. As a result, "even the most reputable wholesale merchant at the Jewish money market cannot resist, when the circumstances present themselves, from reaching out with his fingers in a coldblooded fashion to gain petty and paltry defraudations that would make a Prussian financier blush" (Nachlass 1885, 36[42], KSA 11.568–69). Again we easily recognize that Nietzsche ascribes to Jews the very qualities that are frequently found in the writings of the worst German anti-Semites, but here the reversal or revaluation is absent. It is difficult to reconcile passages such as this one with Nietzsche's published comments on Jews. Not all of the published comments, as we have seen, are unambiguously positive, but in his longer discussions he portrays Jewry as a positive force for Europe's future, not as an inherently dishonest, fraudulent, degenerate blight on the contemporary world.

Nietzsche's aphoristic writings contain one additional long passage dealing with the Jewish Question of his time. It occurs in *Beyond Good and Evil*, and we have already examined one portion of aphorism 251 in which Nietzsche deals with the prospective breeding of aristocratic officers with the daughters of Jewish financiers to form a new ruling caste in Europe. He begins his discussion by noting the various "becloudings of the German spirit," that is, the various nationalist tendencies to oppose the French, the Jews, and the Poles and to support the Wagnerian, the Teutonic, and the Prussian. In this context he offers his only public apology for his own flirtations with this ideology in the 1870s. "May I be forgiven that I too, during a short, hazardous stay in a very infected area, did not remain entirely spared by the disease." He then presents an intriguing analysis of the Jewish situation in Germany. He has never met a German who was well disposed toward the Jews, and he therefore expresses some understanding for policies that restrict immigration. Nietzsche knew, of course, that prohibition on permission

for Jews to enter Germany from the East was one of the central demands of
the Anti-Semites' Petition of 1880–81, a document promulgated and supported by his brother-in-law Bernhard Förster, signed by over a quarter of a
million people, including Nietzsche's publisher Ernst Schmeitzner, and then
presented to Bismarck, who refused any response. Nietzsche's explanation for
the German reaction to Jews employs an extended alimentary metaphor:

> That Germany has *more than enough* Jews, that German stomachs, German blood
> have found it difficult (and will continue to find it difficult) to deal with even this
> amount of "Jew" (which the Italian, the Frenchman, the Englishman have dealt
> with, thanks to their stronger digestions): a general instinct states this in clear
> language, and one must listen to that instinct and act accordingly.

In this passage Nietzsche may be referencing the mass deportation of Jews
the German foreign ministry undertook in 1885.[71] Significant is that Nietzsche regards Germany and Germans from an external perspective; he does
not identify himself with his birthplace, but he also seems to validate the
German need to exclude Jews as crucial for the health of the nation. He
continues with two sentences in quotation marks, and we have to presume
they are something he is imputing to a German, and possibly even to an
anti-Semite, responding to Jewish immigration: "Do not allow any new Jews
to enter! And bar especially those doors that face East (and also towards
Austria)!" This demand represents the instinct of a weaker people trying to
fend off a stronger people; the Jews, Nietzsche tells his reader, are "without
a doubt the strongest, toughest, and purest race living in Europe." They succeed because they employ certain virtues that are today considered vices;
Nietzsche is probably thinking of the alleged financial acumen of Jews. As
in the passage from *Dawn*, he claims that Jews could "gain the upper hand,
could in fact quite literally rule over Europe," but he believes that it is clear
"that they are *not* planning or working toward that end." Their desire, Nietzsche states without reference or evidence, but quite possibly relying on his
conversations with Paneth, is to be assimilated into Europe "to be established, legitimate, respected, somewhere at last, and to set an end to their
nomadic life as 'wandering Jews.'" This assimilation should be encouraged,
Nietzsche continues, but "with great caution, with selectivity, more or less
as the English nobility does." And he concludes his thoughts on the contemporary Jewish situation in Germany with the previously cited vision of
breeding the rulers of Europe (JGB 251, KSA 5.192–95).

Nietzsche's attitude toward contemporary Jewry is again ambivalent in
this passage. He certainly continues to recognize, as he did throughout the
late 1880s, that Jewish financial abilities were a necessary element for a new

ruling elite, and he rejects without reservation the ultranationalist political movements in Germany, including, as we shall see in more detail in the next chapter, the various strands of anti-Semitism. But he also continues to reproduce stereotyped depictions of German Jewry: they excel in matters of money, they have the potential to rule over other nations, they are nomads seeking to integrate themselves into "foreign" societies. There is a danger inherent in Jews, so they must be treated with care and assimilated on a selective basis; native populations should not accept every Jew. It is difficult to ascertain Nietzsche's feelings about Eastern European Jewry from this aphorism—the comments about restrictions are put into the mouth of a hypothetical speaker—but a note he composed at the time he was writing *Beyond Good and Evil* is revealing in this regard. He refers in this draft aphorism, as he does in the published book, to the "imperative of the German instinct" against new Jewish immigration: "No more *new* Jews! And keep the gates to the East closed!" In the note, however, Nietzsche maintains that these imperatives ought to be the mantra of German Jews, not simply anti-Semitic petitioners. If Jews are going to achieve their objective, "integration into the German essence," and if they are going to acquire a "more German type of expression and gestures," then they should consider themselves advocates of "border-regulation." Nietzsche propounds a theory whereby external behavior becomes internalized, where "appearance" becomes reality, and thus these outward forms of behavior will alter the Jewish psyche, making it more compatible with Germanness. Immigration is a hindrance to assimilation: The appointed task of the German Jews "should not be pushed back again and again into the realm of the insoluble by the horrible and despicable ugliness of the recently immigrated Polish and Russian, Hungarian and Galician Jews." This is the point, Nietzsche continues, "where Jews for their part must act and namely set limits." And he closes by observing that this is the single and last point where Jewish and German interests overlap, and then admonishing the former: "but really, it is time, it is high time!" (Nachlass 1885, 41[14], KSA 11.688). The parallels between this note and aphorism 251 suggest it may have been originally part of Nietzsche's plan for the text, but it obviously did not find its way into the manuscript. That Nietzsche's derogatory view of Eastern European Jewry was not an isolated instance, however, is demonstrated by a passage in *The Antichrist* (1895), where he writes: "One would no more choose to associate with 'first Christians' than one would with Polish Jews: not that one would need to prove so much as a single point against them.... Neither of them smells very pleasant" (AC 46, KSA 6.223).[72] Nietzsche's celebration of the Jews of finance evidently did not extend to co-religionists from the shtetls of Eastern Europe.

Nietzsche's record on Jews and Judaism after severing relations with Richard Wagner was thus one of mixed reactions and profound ambivalence. He establishes a friendship with Paul Rée, a man of Jewish heritage, and he has intercourse with two Viennese Jews, Siegfried Lipiner and Josef Paneth, but none of the three identified strongly with Judaism, evidencing a greater fealty to philosophy, art and metaphysics, and natural science, respectively. Nietzsche's dealings with them do not speak unequivocally of a changed attitude toward Jews, and retrospectively he identifies them with their faith and on occasion with unbecoming features associated with Jews. From the totality of these connections he appears to gain no understanding of European Jewry or of contemporary Judaism, but he does come to recognize the importance of Jews for promoting his works and thought. At best, he realizes that Jews are more intellectually aware and therefore more appreciative of what he has to offer; at worst, he sees that he must appease Jewish interests if he is going to achieve success. His post-Wagnerian comments on Jews likewise run the gamut from admiration to disdain. Remarks in letters throughout the period reveal a "cultural anti-Semitism" that represents a continuation from the 1860s. What changes most clearly are his published discussions. The three long aphorisms in collections spanning the years 1878 to 1886 evidence a good deal of high praise for Jews and a newly found appreciation for the persecution and discrimination they have suffered at the hands of Christians throughout Europe. But surrounding these aphorisms and sometimes contained in them are clichéd pronouncements on Jews and Judaism that are frequently less than flattering to Jewry. Perhaps most disturbing are some of Nietzsche's notes, which sometimes contain the types of anti-Jewish sentiments found in the writings of the nascent anti-Semitic political movement Nietzsche was at pains to reject. In published material we cannot help but recognize the enormous change from his Wagnerian period; the qualities associated with Jewry are sometimes retained, but they are given an antithetical valuation and regarded as a positive feature in a vision for Europe's future. But if we examine passages in the notebooks, we cannot escape the suspicion that Nietzsche was not always completely candid about his views on Jews in his published writings. He appears to have harbored considerably more Judeophobic animus than his publicly accessible works evidence. It is not easy to sort out Nietzsche's views on contemporary Jewry once he abandoned the Wagnerian sphere of influence. But it seems fair to say that there is considerably more continuity with his anti-Jewish attitudes from the 1860s and early 1870s than most commentators have been hitherto willing to admit.

CHAPTER FIVE

Anti-Semitic Confrontations

There is probably no aspect of Nietzsche's views on Jews and Judaism that is more misunderstood than his relationship to anti-Semitism. The reason for the misunderstanding has to do with confusion around the notion of anti-Semitism itself. The *Oxford English Dictionary* defines the term simply as "hostility and prejudice directed against Jewish people; (also) the theory, action, or practice resulting from this."[1] Certainly this definition captures the most common meaning of the word in the twentieth and twenty-first centuries, especially in the period since the Second World War in the Anglophone world. If we assume that this understanding prevailed at the time Nietzsche was writing, then we can construct a scenario very easily in which he was adamantly opposed to any "hostility or prejudice" against Jewry. For there is no question that he was unequivocally antagonistic toward what he understood as anti-Semitism and anti-Semites. In his published work in the 1880s Nietzsche consistently expresses his aversion toward them. The same holds true for remarks in his literary remains. We have seen that there are discrepancies between his published and unpublished attitude toward Jews and Judaism, and that in some passages in his notes we still find an irrational prejudice against Jews that does not surface in most writings that appeared in print. But there is absolute accord with regard to anti-Semitism. Similarly, he never validates anti-Semitism in any of his correspondence. For the most part he rejects individuals he finds closely associated with the anti-Semitic movement; he detests anti-Semitic journals once he becomes conscious of their existence; he frequently ridicules the absurdity of anti-Semitic theories and claims. We can therefore understand how it was possible for postwar scholars to extricate Nietzsche so cleanly from claims of hostility and prejudice toward Jews relying on his statements regarding anti-Semitism. Walter Kaufmann is the most prominent in a long line of postwar critics to cite Nietzsche's many hostile and unequivocal rejections of anti-Semitism as proof positive that his National Socialist and—during the Second World War—some of his Western interpreters were utterly mistaken about his enmity toward Jews. Any association with racist doctrine must be the result of a serious misreading, as Kaufmann demonstrates in a lengthy footnote criticizing Crane Brinton's account,[2] or the fault of others who interfered illicitly in his intellectual legacy:

> Anti-Semitic Teutonism—or proto-Nazism—was one of the major issues in Nietzsche's life, if only because his sister and Wagner, the two most important figures in his development, confronted him with this ideology. In both cases Nietzsche's attitude was uncompromising—and if his suggestion to "expel the anti-Semitic squallers out of the country" might seem a mere literary flourish, one may recall that this idea so possessed him that, when madness began to break down his inhibitions, he scrawled across the margin of his last letter to Burckhardt: "Abolished [Kaiser] Wilhelm, Bismarck, and all anti-Semites"—while the last note to Overbeck ends: "Just now I am having all anti-Semites shot."[3]

Even if we leave aside the fact that Nietzsche was a willing accomplice to Wagner's anti-Jewish campaign in the early 1870s, and that it was Nietzsche who introduced his sister to anti-Jewish thought and rhetoric for the better part of their early lives, Kaufmann's explanations—and those of the many critics who follow him, some of whom even label him "philo-Semitic"[4]—do not account for the many Judeophobic statements in Nietzsche's notebooks and correspondence, as well as clichés regarding Jews in his published writings during his post-Wagnerian period. Nietzsche's polemical attitude toward anti-Semitism obviously does not tell the whole story about Nietzsche and the Jewish Question, and the reason that so many critics go astray has to do with their neglect of the context in which the political anti-Semitic movement originated during the Second Reich.

As a word and as a political movement "anti-Semitism" does not make an appearance until late in the year 1879.[5] At that point "Semitic," which had been employed first by August Ludwig von Schlözer in 1771 and was used six years later by Johann Gottfried Eichhorn to designate a group of languages spoken in the Middle East, was barely a century old. "Semitic" was derived from Sem or Shem, who was the son of Noah and thought to be the ancestor of Assyrians, Arameans, and Hebrews. The term is inappropriate linguistically since the purported descendants of Sem do not match the speakers of Semitic languages, and the cultural unity ethnographers sometimes forced onto this group—for example, the purportedly nomadic nature of the Semitic people—turns out to be of questionable validity as well. Like many terms in the vocabulary of racism, "Semitic" migrated from historical linguistics into ethnography before becoming subject to "scientific" hypotheses about biologically based race in the latter part of the nineteenth century. Arthur de Gobineau, whose *Essay on the Inequality of the Human Races* (1853–55) marked a pivotal juncture in the history of racism, is usually credited with introducing the term "Semitic" as a designation for a racial type and opposing it to the Aryan, which again is a term borrowed from scholars originally studying language and language change. At this point "Semite" referred to more than Jews, but in the last third of the nineteenth century, it became a popular designation for only Jews, probably because it was felt to lend an aura of scholarly legitimacy to racist bias. Since it suggests a genealogy that extends back into the ancient world, "Semitic," as opposed to Jewish, referred implicitly to more than a religious affiliation, imputing fixed and timeless traits to those it designates. We will recall that Nietzsche uses the term in his *Birth of Tragedy* (1872) in connection with the founding myth of humankind's fall from grace in Genesis and in opposition to the Aryan Prometheus legend, and it also appears in various remarks in correspondence written to Nietzsche.[6] Already at a very early stage in the second half of the nineteenth century, the word "Semitic" became closely associated with Jews, to the exclusion of other Semitic peoples, and contained an implicit critique of "Jewish" modernity.[7] In a sense, by the late 1870s the appearance of the word "anti-Semitic," which would express an opposition to "Jewish" modernity, was long overdue. A confluence of events around 1880 surrounded the emergence of the word in the public sphere: the beginning of the anti-Jewish speeches of the court chaplain Adolf Stöcker in 1879; an article from 1879 composed by the noted Prussian historian Heinrich von Treitschke, "Our Views," which inaugurated a protracted debate known subsequently as the "Berlin Anti-Semitism Controversy";[8] and the publication of one of the seminal pamphlets in the incipient anti-Semitic movement, Wilhelm Marr's "The Victory of Judaism over Germanism Considered from a Non-Confessional Perspective."[9] Indeed, although Marr did not include the expression "anti-Semitism" or any derivatives in his anti-Jewish philippic, most scholars believe that the term originated in Marr's circles in connection with the foundation of the Anti-Semitic League and the announcement of the publication of an *Anti-Semitic Weekly*.[10] Once in the public domain, the word was quickly disseminated in the German-speaking world, and its usage then spread rapidly throughout the Western world.[11]

Anti-Semitism as a designation for anti-Judaism thus had an inherent appeal because of the implication that it was describing a people with inherent character traits, but also because it provides racial prejudice an academic veneer owing to its origins in linguistics and ethnography. In terms of ideological content, anti-Semitism is hardly new, since it appropriates many of the prejudices and distortions to which Jewry had been subjected for many centuries.[12] Novel in the 1880s was chiefly its incorporation into a more or less cohesive program as part of a political movement based on the historical circumstances of the Second Reich.[13] Many individuals nonetheless recognized that anti-Semitism, like "Semitic," was an inappropriate term, and it has not always been universally accepted as the apposite label for the political stance opposing the Jewish people. In Nietzsche's time Eugen Dühring, the socialist philosopher whom Nietzsche excoriated for his anti-Semitic invectives, argued that anti-Semitism is an inaccurate label for what it purports to describe: "It [the Jewish people] is a specific tribe, which has developed the characteristics of a race in the most marked opposition to other human beings, and not the entire Semitic race, that comes into question in our modern culture and society."[14] The author of the Anti-Semites' Petition of 1880–81 and Nietzsche's eventual brother-in-law, Bernhard Förster, was even reluctant to accept the word "Semitic," stating "if the terminus 'Semite' instead of the accurate designation 'Jew' has already been established and can no longer be eliminated, it will have the same fate as other termini that also have little justification for existing and must also always be interpreted correctly, for example, 'Gothic architecture' or 'Renaissance' and many others."[15] Even the National Socialists, seeking to distinguish between the Jews and the Arabs, rejected the use of "anti-Semitism" as a false label, "since this movement directs itself against Jewry, the corrupters of all peoples, but not against the other peoples speaking Semitic languages, who have likewise been anti-Jewish since ancient times."[16] In 1935 the Propaganda Ministry of the Third Reich advised its press organs to avoid its use and employ "anti-Jewish" in its stead.[17] Nietzsche, like any good philologist, was apparently also uncomfortable with the equation of anti-Semitic and anti-Jewish. Even after the emergence of the political movement that went by this appellation, he uses the neologism "Misojuden" (literally, "Haters of Jews," from the Greek μῖσος, hatred, and the German word for Jews) to designate people he would later call "anti-Semitic."[18] Although there existed some confusion about the new terminology and its appropriateness on the part of individuals during the early 1880s—as well as later racist ideologues—it is important to recognize that "anti-Semitism" at the time of its emergence, when Nietzsche encountered it, referred very specifically to a political movement reacting to Jewish emancipation and the perception of Jewish dominance in Germany through control of the financial system, the press, and the cultural world. The term was certainly directed against Jews, but opposition to anti-Semitism did not imply philo-Semitism or even a freedom from holding biased views about Jews and their collective character.

Anti-anti-Semitism meant quite simply a rejection of the main tenets of specific political tendencies that were embodied in ideologies throughout the nineteenth century, but that appeared in party platforms and periodicals starting in the early 1880s and persisted through the decade.[19] Only gradually in the twentieth century, when anti-Semitism as a political movement had long since passed from the scene, does the word become synonymous with anti-Judaism and acquire its current sense of hatred and prejudice against the Jewish people.[20]

Nietzsche's views on anti-Semitism therefore do not tell us everything we need to know about his opinions on Jews and Judaism. The two are closely connected: anti-Semitism obviously partakes of the long tradition of anti-Judaism, and earlier manifestations of anti-Judaism contain elements that would only become prominent with the appearance of anti-Semitism in the 1880s. But in Nietzsche's personal dealings with anti-Semitism narrowly defined, many additional factors come into play, and in many cases these factors are both extraneous to the Jewish Question and clearly unrelated to the reasons for which we have become accustomed to opposing racial prejudice. Nietzsche's repugnance for anti-Semitism was overdetermined and, as we shall see in more detail later in this chapter, had both personal and principled dimensions. Although it is not entirely accurate when Nietzsche claims that anti-Semitism destroyed his relationship with Richard Wagner and his sister, and prevented him from acquiring "pecuniary independence, disciples, new friends, and influence" (to Franz Overbeck, April 2, 1884, Nr. 503, KSB 6.493), we should not discount the adverse impact anti-Semitism had on his personal life. One of the reasons that it affected him so greatly is his own acquiescence to anti-Jewish thought when he was associated with Wagner, and his own early admiration for writers who developed into important anti-Semitic thinkers. In the inner circle of Wagnerians he became intimately acquainted with individuals who, following the lead of the Meister, turned into advocates of anti-Semitic causes.[21] The *Bayreuther Blätter*, to which Nietzsche subscribed along with other members of the Wagner society, contained frequent racist articles, including excerpts from Gobineau. Marr was a member of the extended Wagner circle, as was Bernhard Förster, Elisabeth's future husband and the founder of Nueva Germania in Paraguay, a colonial undertaking that was designed to allow him and other anti-Semites to flee a "Jewified" Europe.[22] We should not forget that Nietzsche was quite close to his sister, especially during the 1870s. Although their relationship cooled somewhat in the next decade, due in part to Nietzsche's affair with Lou Salomé, it is obvious that he harbored strong feelings for Elisabeth throughout his life, even after her marriage to

Förster. As we shall see below, part of his reaction against anti-Semitism can be explained by the role he attributed to Elisabeth's anti-Semitic husband, who took his "beloved llama" away from him[23] and indoctrinated her in an ideology he disdained. In this sense anti-Semitism did become a wedge between Nietzsche and Wagner, as well as between Nietzsche and Wagnerians, including his sister and brother-in-law. If we examine Nietzsche's readings during the early part of his career, we also find that he was positively inclined toward many writers who became anti-Semites. For example, he admired Heinrich von Treitschke's political tracts during the 1860s, and in Overbeck, who had known Treitschke well when the two studied together in Leipzig, he and Treitschke had a mutual close friend. Nietzsche was also an enthusiastic reader of Dühring's *The Value of Life* (1865) during the 1870s and read carefully many of his subsequent philosophical works.[24] In his early career at Basel, Nietzsche also knew and admired Johann Zöllner's book *On the Nature of the Comets* (1870); later Zöllner distinguished himself by being the sole academic to sign his name to the notorious Anti-Semites' Petition.[25] Paul de Lagarde was another future anti-Semite for whose writings Nietzsche expressed approval in the 1870s. Finally, Nietzsche's claim about anti-Semitism robbing him of financial independence, disciples, and influence has a grain of truth to it. As we shall see shortly, Nietzsche's publisher, Ernst Schmeitzner, became heavily involved with anti-Semitic literature and organization, and Nietzsche frequently blames his lack of success as an author on Schmeitzner's neglect in promoting his writings. Thus anti-Semites and anti-Semitic thought surrounded Nietzsche during his years as a Wagnerian and, in some cases, well into the 1880s. That he himself did not undergo a transformation into an anti-Semite is certainly to his credit. But we should remember that his strong reaction against anti-Semitism as a political movement had a significant basis in perceived personal misfortune; in his mind it had destroyed—or contributed to the destruction of—formerly solid relationships and was largely responsible for his isolation and relative lack of celebrity among his countrymen.

Nietzsche also had more general, ideological objections to anti-Semitism. Although we today commonly consider anti-Semitism, like other racist sentiments, to be part of a right-wing political profile, in the historical context in which it first appeared it had many associations that we would consider odd in the twenty-first century. Within the circle of Wagnerian beliefs, for example, anti-Semitism was part of a palette of ideological convictions held by the Meister that included vegetarianism and antivivisectionism. In Nietzsche's own thought and writings anti-Semitism was sometimes associated with the democratizing tendencies that he felt were leveling necessary hierarchies across Europe, as one of many "isms" that arise from *ressentiment*, including feminism and nationalism, which were likewise taking hold in contemporary Europe. In *Ecce Homo* (1908), referring to the Wagner circle in Bayreuth, Nietzsche notes that anti-Semitism flourished in an atmosphere of narrow German virtues (EH, Warum ich so gute Bücher schreibe, Menschliches, Allzumenschliches 2, KSA 6.323–24), and, indeed, anti-Semitism is most frequently regarded as an ally of *völkisch*, chauvinistic attitudes. But anti-Semitism is also viewed as part of a political context that includes socialism and anarchism. In a letter to Overbeck in 1887 Nietzsche marvels at his popularity among "radical parties" and clarifies parenthetically: "socialists, nihilists, anti-Semites, Christian orthodoxy, Wagnerians" (March 24, 1887, Nr. 820, KSB 8.48). In *The Genealogy of Morals* (1887) he observes that one can study rancor up close since it is a dominant trait in both anti-Semites and anarchists (GM, Zweite Abhandlung 11, KSA 5.309). Later in this work he reinforces this image when he calls Dühring an "apostle of revenge" and the "the foremost moral bigmouth at the moment that exists, even among his own kind, the anti-Semites" (GM, Dritte Abhandlung 14, KSA 5.370),[26] but he also considers Dühring the "most dreadful anarchist and calumniator" (to Franz Overbeck, December 1885, Nr. 649, KSB 7.117). And near the close of *The Genealogy* he writes: "Nor do I like these most recent speculators in idealism, the anti-Semites, who, rolling their eyes in a Christian-Aryan-Philistine way, seek to rouse all the bovine elements of the people through an exasperating abuse of the cheapest means of agitation and moral attitudes" (GM Dritte Abhandlung 26, KSA 5.407). What emerges from these passages is that Nietzsche opposed anti-Semitism not out of a belief in tolerance or equal civil rights for all people, or out of a particular respect for the Jews, the Jewish religion, or Jewish culture, but because he saw this movement as a further manifestation of an unhealthy moralism. Connected with anti-Semitism from Nietzsche's perspective was a quasi-socialist need to redeem the world through a political movement. Writing to his publisher Schmeitzner, he comments that all movements, "your anti-Jewish movement included," lead to "anarchies and earthquakes," and he continues: "From a distance 'anti-Semitism' appears to be exactly like the struggle against the rich and the means previously employed to become rich" (April 2, 1883, Nr. 399, KSB 6.356). This impression was no doubt reinforced by some of the anti-Semitic propaganda of his time. Dühring, we should recall, was widely known for his advocacy of socialism, and is perhaps best remembered today because of Friedrich Engels's polemic against him and his brand of socialism in 1878. Even Förster conceived of his colonial project in Paraguay as a German socialist venture. Nietzsche's response to and rejection of anti-Semitism, viewed from the perspective of the 1880s, is part and parcel of his assault on Christian ethics, narrow-minded nationalism, and redemptive socialism. It does not arise from philo-Semitic sentiments and is unrelated to the liberalism we normally identify with attitudes opposed to racism and supportive of civil liberties in an egalitarian society.

NIETZSCHE'S PUBLISHER, ERNST SCHMEITZNER

If we examine more closely Nietzsche's dealings with and objections to anti-Semitism, we can comprehend more accurately its locus in Nietzsche's ideological universe. Perhaps the best place to start is with Ernst Schmeitzner, who was the publisher of Nietzsche's writings from the third *Untimely Meditation* through the third book of *Thus Spoke Zarathustra* (1883–85). After Ernst Wilhelm Fritzsch announced to Nietzsche that due to adverse financial conditions his works no longer fit into his publishing program,[27] the philosopher was delighted to have Schmeitzner approach him and offer his services. Schmeitzner was the friend of a friend—Paul Heinrich Widemann, later editor of Schmeitzner's *International Monthly*, had studied with Heinrich Köselitz—and his attention was brought to the Basel professor through this connection. The relationship between Schmeitzner and Nietzsche was never without problems; Nietzsche was a demanding author, not so much in terms of remuneration, but with regard to the appearance of his books, the typeface, the quality of the paper, and especially the speed of publication once the manuscript was completed. For his part Schmeitzner appears to have expended considerable effort in promoting Nietzsche's reputation, but it bore no fruit, and only when Nietzsche began to self-publish, starting with the fourth book of *Zarathustra*, did he recognize that his publisher was not at fault for the poor sales and distribution of his oeuvre (to Heinrich Köselitz, June 8, 1887, Nr. 856, KSB 8.87). As Schmeitzner became more involved with anti-Semitic parties and congresses, as well as anti-Jewish journals and other printed material, he had less time to devote to Nietzsche and his books, and he often did not respond in a timely fashion to Nietzsche's requests. At various points we encounter bitter complaints from Nietzsche about how his writings have to take a back seat to other—often anti-Semitic—priorities Schmeitzner set. With regard to *Zarathustra* Nietzsche writes to Köselitz in July of 1883: "I just heard about *Zarathustra* that it is waiting 'unsent' in Leipzig: even the gratis copies. This is due to the 'very important negotiations' and continuous travels of the chief of the *alliance antijuive*, Mr. Schmeitzner: 'The publishing house must wait a bit,' he wrote"

(Nr. 428, KSB 6.388). Nietzsche sends the identical message to Overbeck a few days later and adds: "Bravo! But who will save me from a publisher who takes anti-Semitic agitation more seriously than *my* ideas?" (Nr. 431, KSB 6.393). The next month he again laments to Köselitz about the poor and prolonged production of his magnum opus, and tells him he suspects "that he [Schmeitzner] is not doing well as a result of this *antisemitica*" (Nr. 452, KSB 6.430). And finally, in a moment of despair about his fate being tied to anti-Semitism, he writes to Overbeck with a list of all the things that this racist movement has taken from him, including his potential celebrity (April 2, 1884, Nr. 503, KSB 6.493). Schmeitzner's anti-Semitism is beyond question, and Nietzsche undoubtedly had some basis for his accusations against him. From the late 1870s onward not only was Schmeitzner involved with publishing anti-Semitic works and journals, including a few issues of Marr's short-lived *Anti-Semitic Notebooks*, he was also one of the chief organizers of the anti-Semitic movement and instrumental in the coordination of international conferences.[28] It is worth remarking, however, that Nietzsche's objections to these anti-Semitic activities rarely include any reference to his rejection of Schmeitzner's racist politics. They are usually focused on how Schmeitzner has failed to devote the appropriate care and attention to Nietzsche's writings. Nietzsche may have disapproved of anti-Semitism because of its racist foundation, but he never communicates anything to his correspondents except anger that his books are being ignored.

With regard to the Jewish Question, there are two central issues in Nietzsche's relationship with Schmeitzner, and they are somewhat related. The first is how much Nietzsche knew about Schmeitzner's anti-Semitic activity, and when did he learn about it. A subsidiary question to this issue is why Nietzsche remained associated with the publisher when he discovered he was intimately involved with the anti-Semitic movement. The second issue concerns Nietzsche's publication of a series of poems, the "Idylls of Messina," in *Schmeitzner's International Monthly*. These two matters were a focal point in Nietzsche's discussion Josef Paneth reported. The Jewish scientist had asked Nietzsche how he could allow his poetry to appear in "a journal for the struggle against Jewry." Nietzsche responded that the journal was not dedicated to anti-Semitism when he published in it; in fact, it was conceived "in an exactly opposite sense of those who wanted to be good Europeans," and both the journal and its publisher "became anti-Semitic only later."[29] Nietzsche's response denies that Schmeitzner was an anti-Semite in 1882 when the first issue of the *International Monthly* appeared, or, alternatively, that his anti-Semitism was not known to Nietzsche at that time. But, as we have seen in our consideration of Nietzsche's relationship to Paneth in the previous chapter, Nietzsche tended toward prevarication in his conversations with the Viennese physiologist, and he surely was not completely candid with him in this case. It is not possible to date precisely Schmeitzner's initial involvement with anti-Jewish politics, but an indication of his sentiments is found at the end of 1879 in a letter he wrote to Heinrich Köselitz; he expresses relief that the liberal era of government is over and that "finally the liberal Jewish establishment is coming to an end."[30] At the very latest Nietzsche learned of Schmeitzner's anti-Semitic activity when he saw a letter Overbeck had written to Köselitz in May of 1880. Overbeck relates to Köselitz concerns about Schmeitzner's views and mentions specifically his involvement with an anti-Semitic journal.[31] A subsequent letter to Nietzsche also contains mention of the anti-Semitic journal Schmeitzner is publishing (Nr. 27, KGB III 2.71). To this news Nietzsche reacts with disdain: "Schmeitzner's latest undertaking about which you wrote disgusts me; I'm indignant that he didn't say a word to me about it" (June 22, 1880, Nr. 33KSB 6.24). In June 1881 Nietzsche writes to Schmeitzner directly when he suspects that his publisher is no longer interested in his books: "I presume that you have secretly sworn to yourself that this will be the last piece of writing from me that you will publish. Really I no longer fit in with your Wagner-Schopenhauer-Dühring-and-other-*party*-literature" (Nr. 117, KSB 6.93).[32] Then in September 1881 Schmeitzner boasts to Köselitz about being the "leader of a political party here that I myself created." It is neither liberal nor conservative, he tells Köselitz; it is involved with anti-Jewish agitation. He continues by touting Dühring's anti-Semitic book about the Jewish Question, which he is publishing, recommending that he purchase it and encouraging him to interest Nietzsche in it as well.[33] Because of Köselitz's close friendship with Nietzsche, we can be certain he heard about Schmeitzner's activities from him. By the end of 1881, therefore, well before the first issue of *Schmeitzner's International Monthly* appeared, Nietzsche was certainly aware that his publisher was directly involved with the promulgation of anti-Semitic writings and active in the emerging anti-Semitic political scene. In the early 1880s there is no indication whatsoever that Nietzsche considered Schmeitzner's anti-Semitism a barrier to their continued association—except insofar as his publisher had no time to devote to his writings. Indeed, after he learns of Schmeitzner's activities in 1880, he even enters into an agreement with him to assist him with financial difficulties by lending him part of his pension.[34] When he was discontent with Schmeitzner prior to 1884, it had to do primarily with issues of his business practices, not his ideology and politics.

Nietzsche's involvement with Schmeitzner's journal raises other, albeit related, questions. At some point in the early 1880s, while he was involved with the initial phases of anti-Semitic agitation, Schmeitzner came up with the idea to publish a journal. It seems that he conceived of the publication in order to accomplish multiple purposes; it was supposed to deal with current events, in which he was interested, but it is also obvious from the path the journal took that it was designed to contribute to the anti-Semitic propaganda with which he was involved. He writes to Nietzsche that he is seeking to bring together like-minded contributors and emphasizes that the journal is not designed to harm anyone (May 10, 1882, Nr. 121, KGB III 2.253). It was probably also motivated by the simple desire to profile his own authors and, in the case of Nietzsche, to spur the lagging sales of his books. When Nietzsche first heard about Schmeitzner's plans to publish a house journal, he was unenthusiastic. He writes to Köselitz, punning on the German word "Zeitschrift" ("journal," but literally "time writing") that he doesn't know the "times" anymore, that he takes his "time," and that he doesn't need any publicity. If he did need publicity, he would not think about a journal that has such a restricted circle of readers. Then he adds parenthetically his suspicion that his publisher is "speculating on anti-Jewish" readers (November 27, 1881, Nr. 171, KSB 6.144). Schmeitzner in the meantime was recruiting contributors and evidently let it be known that both Nietzsche and Overbeck had already agreed to participate in the venture. At that point he had approached neither man about writing for the publication, and Nietzsche is justifiably upset when he learns, through Paul Rée, of Schmeitzner's unprofessional actions, calling them "shameless." He indicates that he is "unspeakably far removed from participating in this journal" (to Franz Overbeck, December 12, 1881, Nr. 178, KSB 6.148). A few days later, however, Köselitz informs Nietzsche that he is preparing an article for the journal, which is being edited by his university friend Paul Widemann, but his reasons are hardly an earnest endorsement of the undertaking. In the first instance he is showing support for his friend, although he appears to be convinced that the editorship will not be to his ultimate benefit; he also writes that he is contributing because the project will go forward anyway with or without his participation (Nr. 93, KGB III 2.201–2). Nietzsche responds, perhaps tongue-in-cheek: "any journal that convinces *you* to write for it will be *dear* and *valuable* for me" (December 18, 1881, Nr. 180, KSB 6.150). Although Köselitz's essay never appears, Nietzsche is impressed with the direction he senses in the initial issue, since he believes that the opening editorial, composed by Bruno Bauer, corresponds closely to his own thought: "The new 'journal' *surprised* me in a not unpleasant fashion. Or am I deceiving myself? Is the fundamental idea of the introduction—*Europeanness* from the perspective of the destruction of nationalities—isn't this *my* idea? Tell me the truth about this: perhaps a cloud of vanity is leading me astray" (to Heinrich Köselitz, February 5, 1882, Nr. 195, KSB 6.167). Köselitz assures him that the thoughts in Schmeitzner's journal are similar to Nietzsche's, and that Bauer is reading his works, although Bauer expresses himself awkwardly to get his point across to the German public.[35] On the basis of his reading and the report from Köselitz, Nietzsche consents to contribute, and in May 1882 he sends Schmeitzner eight poems under the title "Idylls of Messina" with very specific instructions for how his poetry is to appear in the journal (Nr. 227, KSB 6.193). They are published as the first item in the May issue, which was released in the first week of June.

How do we evaluate Nietzsche's assertion to Paneth that he did not know of the character of *Schmeitzner's International Monthly* when he submitted his "Idylls of Messina" for publication? Some scholars have made a strong case supporting Nietzsche's statement based on a number of facts about the journal, its editorship, and its content. Although "international Jewry," a key notion in anti-Semitic vocabulary, is mentioned in an early article, in the issues Nietzsche could have seen prior to offering his poems, there were no overtly Judeophobic contributions. Some commentators claim that the nature of the journal changed after the sudden death of Bruno Bauer in April 1882, and certainly we do find a series of articles in the second half of 1882 with definite anti-Jewish content. Included among them was a piece by Eugen Dühring on the "Parties of the Jewish Question," and a series of anonymous contributions dealing with the Jewish Question in Russia, the Jewish Question in Algiers, Voltaire's views on the Jewish Question, and ritual murders. In its second and final year of publication, the journal changed both its editor and subtitle. Carl Heinrich Rittner, a man intimately connected with the anti-Semitic movement in Saxony, replaced Widemann, while the subtitle changed from "Journal for General and National Culture and Its Literature" to "Journal for the General Association Combating Judaism (*alliance antijuive universelle*)." These changes may appear to alter radically the direction of the journal, but in fact they did not necessarily have any significant effect. From the very outset the journal was conceived as part of Schmeitzner's anti-Semitic politics. In his correspondence the Judeophobic publisher never concealed his desire to have his house journal contribute to his racist political movement,[36] and Nietzsche, knowing about Schmeitzner's anti-Semitic proclivities, suspected as much in his letter to Köselitz in November 1881. Schmeitzner staffed the journal to ensure the promulgation of an anti-Semitic message; it is a mistake to believe that the original editor of the journal would have been inclined to reject the Judeophobic articles that appeared in the second half of 1882 and in 1883. Widemann, like Schmeitzner, was a confirmed anti-Semite, and it is hard to imagine that Nietzsche was not aware of his political persuasion since he was Köselitz's friend; Rittner was not selected to replace Widemann because the latter refused to cooperate with Schmeitzner's anti-Semitic tendencies. In 1885 Widemann writes to Köselitz, who remained in contact with him despite their very different views on the Jewish Question, and praises Dühring for his struggle against "obscurantism," but also for his assault on "the humanistic idiocy of Jewish sympathizers" and "the swindle regarding freedom on the part of Social Democracy and Jewified progress."[37] Indeed, it is quite possible that the anonymous articles in the *International Monthly* about the Jewish Question were penned by Widemann.[38]

Nor was Bruno Bauer, heralded as the guiding spirit for the new journal,[39] likely to have objected to anti-Semitic content in the *Monthly*. In 1882 Bauer had already enjoyed a much longer career than Schmeitzner or Widemann, but it was marked by anti-Jewish thought since the 1840s. Born in 1809, Bauer belonged to the generation of Karl Ludwig Nietzsche and Richard Wagner. He studied under Hegel in Berlin, moving from an initial right-wing stance to left-wing Hegalianism by the 1840s. A prolific writer, he produced, prior to the 1848 revolution, works on Hegelian philosophy and the critique of religion as well as books on more politic topics, but perhaps his most noted contribution occurred in 1842 when he examined *The Jewish Question*. Unlike most liberals and republicans in Germany, he opposed Jewish emancipation, arguing that the Jews must first liberate themselves from their outmoded religious views. His analysis was famously criticized by Karl Marx, whose response was also not free from anti-Jewish animus, but who relocated the issue from the realm of religion into the sphere of economics.[40] After the failed revolution of 1848, Bauer, like many radicals of the "pre-March" period, abandoned leftist political positions and migrated toward conservatism, rejecting Hegelian progress of history in any form and embracing positive science and empiricism. In the political realm he jettisoned his national republicanism and began to espouse a transnational imperialism in which Europe figured as one of the great powers. Here was the real meaning of the Europeanism that Nietzsche mistook for his own ideas. At the same time, however, Bauer intensified his anti-Jewish convictions. His biographer laments "the baleful influence of his later writings. After the failure of 1848, he promoted a virulent anti-Semitism in the antiliberal circles he came to frequent."[41] There is thus a continuity in Bauer's thought from the position against Jewish integration into Prussia in 1842 through his writings of the Second Reich: "It is clear ... that the anti-Semitism for which Bauer was taxed in the 1840s becomes a much more prominent feature of his later thought."[42] Nietzsche's connection with Bauer stems from his first *Untimely Meditation*, for which Bauer praised him in 1880 as the "German Montaigne, Pascal, and Diderot"; in the same work Bauer publicly admonished Treitschke to read Nietzsche and learn from him something about "historical life, the character of nations, and the psyche of old and new literature."[43] At first Nietzsche reacts disdainfully: "How little fineness in such praise: therefore, how little praise!" (to Heinrich Köselitz, March 20, 1881, Nr. 94, KSB 6.73), but over the next few years Bauer becomes one of the venerable writers he includes as his exclusive readership. His name appears, for example, in two draft letters from October 1886 alongside Burckhardt and Hippolyte Taine as illustrations of the small circle of appreciative proponents of his thought. In *Ecce Homo* he is included as one of the "elderly gentlemen" "unconditionally" on his side and an "attentive reader": "In his last years he liked to refer to me ... Heinrich von Treitschke, the Prussian historiographer, for a hint as to where he might find information about the concept 'culture', which he had lost hold of" (EH, Warum ich so gute Bücher schreibe, Die Unzeitgmässen 2, KSA 6. 317).[44] When Nietzsche submitted his poetry as a contribution to the *International Monthly*, he thus had a good sense of the cast of characters leading the journal and should have deduced very quickly what sort of publication they were going to produce. He had heard on numerous occasions that Schmeitzner was deeply involved in anti-Semitic publishing and political activity; he suspected the motivation for the journal was anti-Jewish; he knew that the editor of the journal, Paul Widemann, shared Schmeitzner's views on Jews and Judaism; and the leading intellectual force behind the journal, Bruno Bauer, exhibited a long history of anti-Jewish thought stretching back to the 1840s. The nature of the *International Monthly* may have shifted slightly in 1883, but Nietzsche would have had to ignore everything he knew about the men most intimately involved with the journal to believe that it was not a publication devoted to furthering anti-Semitic causes.

Nietzsche expressed no real surprise in late 1882 or in 1883, when a series of more openly anti-Semitic articles begins to appear in the *Monthly*. Perhaps one of the reasons he initially remained so sanguine about the journal was that he was a featured author and topic. In 1882 Rudolf Lehmann wrote a two-part study of his writings, noting dutifully, but not critically, the radical change Nietzsche's thought underwent after the *Untimely Meditations*. Indeed, *Human, All Too Human* (1878–80), the "book for free spirits" that marked Nietzsche's transformation, is called "the most significant work of the author" in both content and form.[45] Toward the end of the year we find a lengthy book review of Nietzsche's recently published collection of aphorisms, *The Gay Science* (1882, 1887). It was clearly conceived as a promotional piece: Nietzsche is lauded for his ability to synthesize philosophy and poetry, for being able to combine "clear expression and rigorous seriousness of his ideas" with "an artistically significant presentation." The only hint of criticism occurs around the Jewish Question: "His discussions on the significance of the Jewish people for our times evokes beneficence, but also ignorance of the real existing situation." The anonymous reviewer quickly adds, however: "whoever sees in the origins of Christianity from Jewish monotheism a cause for the multitude of imperfections in our morality cannot be an unqualified friend of Jewry."[46] Nietzsche was upset neither about this remark nor by the inclusion of a review in an openly anti-Semitic journal—the review follows a blatantly Judeophobic article on "The Jews in Algiers." Although he remarks that the journal "stinks of Dühring and Jew-hatred," he finds the review "not bad! For the first time in six years I read something about me *without disgust*" (to Heinrich Köselitz, January 10, 1883, Nr. 368, KSB 6.317). Only after Paneth relates to him that Nietzsche's circle of Jewish admirers in Vienna is concerned about his connections with an anti-Semitic publication does he begin to regret his association with Schmeitzner and the journal, and understand the damage to his reputation that can result from consorting with overt racists. In his conversation with Paneth, as we have seen, he invents a timeline that mitigates his involvement with the unsavory dimensions of his publisher and Schmeitzner's house journal, and it is probably not insignificant that his outburst to Overbeck about how damaging anti-Semitism has been for him personally occurs just a few days after Paneth returns to Austria.[47] In an obvious reference to Paneth's query to him about publishing in an anti-Semitic journal, Nietzsche explains the reason for his agitated state of mind: "I learned here [in Nice] how much I am being reproached in Vienna for having such a publisher" (April 2, 1884, Nr. 503, KSB 6.493). As Overbeck had indicated, in his encounters with Paneth Nietzsche obtained "an orientation regarding his personal reputation with Viennese Jewry,"[48] and his emotional reaction in the postcard to Overbeck, as well as his lack of candor in his conversations with Paneth, especially in matters relating to the Jewish Question, reflects his trepidation about upsetting a significant and potentially influential group of admirers. Even after this recognition, his relationship with Schmeitzner dragged on for two more years. Nietzsche ultimately sued Schmeitzner for the return of the sums he had lent him and eventually regained the money, but the court case combined with the frequent reproaches from Nietzsche's side that Schmeitzner was not competently promoting his books did irreparable damage to the relationship. The bankruptcy of Schmeitzner's publishing house in 1886 put an exclamation point on their break. Schmeitzner's anti-Semitism was perhaps a factor in Nietzsche's estrangement from his publisher, but from all the evidence we have, it was never a major objection for the philosopher. While Nietzsche continues to express disdain for this racist movement and carefully avoids (or regrets) direct and public involvement with it, his main complaints about his publisher were most frequently focused on the poor volume of sales and the belief that not enough was being done to promote his books.[49]

THE FÖRSTERS

Nietzsche's relationship to anti-Semitism was affected tremendously by his sister's involvement with this racist movement. We should not forget, however, that to a great extent Nietzsche was responsible for molding Elisabeth's ideology with regard to Jews and Judaism. In spite of the provincial atmosphere in which the siblings were raised, we do not find any evidence they were attracted to anti-Jewish thought in their childhood. Nietzsche's mother Franziska does not include anti-Jewish slurs in letters to her son, and, as we have seen, the notebooks from Nietzsche's earliest childhood years contain almost nothing that suggests hatred or prejudice against Jews and Judaism. Remarks that contain anti-Jewish sentiments begin only when Nietzsche moves away from Naumburg to attend the university, in particular in his letters from Leipzig, where he became friends with students who were apparently similarly inclined. His mother and sister made no comments about the anti-Jewish remarks in his letters home, and they did not reciprocate with similar utterances. As we have seen, Nietzsche persisted with anti-Jewish remarks in letters even after his break with Wagner, and gradually we find that Elisabeth begins to partake in the cultural racism she had meanwhile acquired.[50] At no point do we detect any discouragement on the part of her brother. Nietzsche was also responsible for introducing Elisabeth to Wagner and the inner circle of Wagnerians, who clearly held Judeophobic views. We assume that Elisabeth was also privy to many conversations Nietzsche conducted with his friends during his initial years in Basel; we have seen how they freely employ anti-Jewish remarks in their letters, and we have to believe that similar utterances were part of their oral exchanges as well. As the years progressed, however, and Nietzsche moved away from his former Wagnerian convictions, brother and sister drifted apart in many regards, one of which was their attitude towards Jews—or at least toward anti-Semitism. Although we find considerably more continuity in Nietzsche's sentiments toward Jewry than scholars usually admit, the aphorisms we have examined in chapter four demonstrate a belief that Jews had exercised a largely positive influence on Europe, and that they could continue to be a benefit for the continent if their positive traits could be bequeathed with appropriate selectivity to future generations. Elisabeth did not share in this departure from Wagnerian ideology; indeed, she had become more ensconced in the proto-anti-Semitism Wagner and his circle had been promoting since the 1860s. If Elisabeth had merely continued as part of the larger movement surrounding Wagner and Bayreuth, it is doubtful that her occasional anti-Jewish statements would have affected the sibling relationship very much. Nietzsche was perfectly capable of accepting individuals with various views on the Jews and Judaism, even if they did not coincide with his own. The estrangement of Nietzsche from his sister was thus not directly related to her anti-Jewish sentiments but to her intimate involvement with the anti-Semitic political movement he loathed so intensely.

The person responsible for her close association with political anti-Semitism was Bernhard Förster. Born in 1843, Förster, like Nietzsche, was the son of a Protestant pastor. He studied history, German, and ancient languages in Berlin and Göttingen, and after German unification in 1871 he became a teacher at a Gymnasium in the capital city. Förster's mother, like Nietzsche's, lived in Naumburg, and the two women were acquainted, which meant that news about the activity of family members was frequently shared. Förster was also similar to Nietzsche in his admiration for Wagner, except that his enthusiasm for the composer lasted well into the 1880s, long after Nietzsche's break with the Meister. Elisabeth had met Förster in Bayreuth in 1876, and the first mention of him in correspondence occurs in January 1877. Förster had paid Elisabeth a visit at Christmas, and she provides her brother with an enthusiastic report of their meeting. His mother accompanied Förster, and Elisabeth assures her brother that they are both admirers of his writings and his outlook.

For me it was a great pleasure to speak with someone who shares so completely your views, someone who feels in the most painful manner the decline of German style, who respects Jacob Burckhardt and Gottfried Keller as writers and stylists, who knows everyone, or almost everyone, whom we love: Burckhardt, Gersdorff, Overbeck, Rohde, and moreover many inhabitants of Basel; who finds

Basel to be an extraordinarily pleasant city with very noble sentiments and understands very well why you are happy to live there: in short, it was really a great pleasure for me to hear once again from one of our own. (Nr. 861, KGB II 6/1.480)

It is quite possible that Elisabeth was already attracted to the man who would later become her husband, but more likely her favorable impression comes from the similarities in experiences and views that Förster shares with her and with Nietzsche himself. We should recall that this meeting takes place in 1877 prior to the publication of *Human, All Too Human*, and before there was any reason for Förster—or Elisabeth—to suspect that Nietzsche's relationship with Wagner and Wagnerian ideology was rapidly deteriorating. Förster's enthusiasm for Nietzsche obviously survived Nietzsche's aphoristic period, since his next mention in Nietzsche's correspondence occurs in two communications with Overbeck from 1882, in which Nietzsche informs his friend that "Dr. Foerster" has spoken about him in a public lecture in exalting fashion (March 1882, Nr, 204, KSB 6.174): "In Berlin I have a strange apostle: just imagine, Dr. B. Förster presented me to his audience in his public lectures with very emphatic expressions" (March 17, 1884, Nr. 210, KSB 6.180). Noteworthy is that Nietzsche appears to be quite sanguine about the public exposure he is receiving from Förster. But by March 1882, Förster was no longer a mere family friend who visited his mother and sister for tea, but a well-known anti-Semitic agitator. The Anti-Semites' Petition that he composed had gained notoriety across Germany, and it had already been given to Bismarck for action. Förster had already founded the German People's Association along with Max Liebermann von Sonnenberg, another noted anti-Semitic demagogue. Förster had already been dismissed from his teaching position in 1880 for public rowdiness and roughhousing directed at Jewish citizens. His public lectures included such items as *The Relationship of Modern Judaism to German Art*, published in 1881; this presentation starts by lauding Wagner's "Judaism in Music" and proceeds to establish the absolute antagonism between Jewry and Germanness: "The Palestinians living among us do not have the slightest part [in German art]; they can't have any part in it because they are absolutely incapable of producing it."[51] He then demonstrates the deleterious effect of Jews on German cultural life, sometimes borrowing themes from the works of Nietzsche's Wagnerian period, such as the adverse impact of newspapers or German academics. Nietzsche certainly must have had knowledge of Förster's views by May 1882; indeed, his mother had already written to him in 1880, describing her future son-in-law as someone "inflamed with hatred of the Jews" (May 31, 1880, Nr. 28, KGB III 2.72). At this point, however, his association with a known anti-

Semite does not raise objections on his part; rather, he displays slight amusement that Förster is praising him, but appears generally delighted that he is receiving exposure in a public venue.

Nietzsche became concerned with Förster's anti-Semitism only once it became obvious he was romantically involved with his sister and planned to leave with her for a colony he was founding in Paraguay. Again we are dealing with events that postdate Nietzsche's fateful conversations with Paneth, when he recognized the damage his reputation was suffering by his association with racist thought. It is quite possible, however, that Nietzsche would have had mixed feelings about Elisabeth's marriage even if Förster had not been associated with a political movement he abhorred. Much scholarship has focused on the enmity that arose between Fritz and his beloved llama during the latter part of the 1880s, and on a few remarks in which Nietzsche lashes out at his sister, or else on Elisabeth's putative role in corrupting Nietzsche's writings with the inference that she made her brother and his thought more susceptible to anti-Semitic interpretation. In the haste to disqualify Elisabeth and make her responsible for any blemishes on Nietzsche's ideological surface, it is often forgotten how truly close the siblings really were. Growing up in the same household and being only two years his junior, Elisabeth had insights into areas of Nietzsche's upbringing and personality that no one else had, with the possible exception of Nietzsche's mother or his closest childhood friends. When he went to Pforta and then to the university in Bonn and Leipzig, Lisbeth and Fritz remained in frequent contact through correspondence and visits. After he received his professorship in Basel, Elisabeth became perhaps even more important for her brother since she spent a good deal of time living with him, running his household, and taking care of day-to-day business for him. Although her extended visits were not quite as long as she claimed they were, she still lived with him in Basel about half of the decade he was employed there.[52] At times she functioned in a manner that resembled more a wife than a sister; only in the summer of 1878 did they abandon for good their common household. In the 1880s, when Nietzsche led his itinerant existence, Elisabeth found her life suddenly changed, and she began to establish a more independent sort of existence. The correspondence between the two siblings indicates that their intimacy did not wane until the affair with Lou Salomé and Paul Rée, when Nietzsche for a time was convinced that Elisabeth was responsible for untoward actions and statements that precipitated the unfortunate outcome. After a few months, however, they again reestablished an amiable relationship. Nietzsche writes to his mother in October 1884 that he has reconciled with his sister (Nr. 545, KSB 6.543) and a few days later corresponds directly with Elisabeth, apologizing for not having sufficiently demonstrated his love for her when they were together in Zurich the first two weeks of the month. At the end of October he writes to Overbeck: "The most refreshing thing this autumn was the impression I had of my sister; she has gotten over the experiences of this past year and taken them to heart, and, what I respect in particular in everyone, without any spitefulness" (Nr. 551, KSB 6.551). At this point, even after Elisabeth was becoming more involved with Förster, the siblings appear to have renewed their former intimacy.

Elisabeth's closer association with Förster is in part the result of her recognition that the role she had played in her brother's life had altered significantly now that she was no longer his housekeeper and companion. Shortly after the Salomé affair Elisabeth's connection with Förster, which had consisted since the mid-1870s of an exchange of polite letters, became more openly romantic. It is understandable that her attention was turned toward marriage as a way of escaping the narrow confines of Naumburg. During the 1870s she had her brother and his career as her raison d'être, but after his departure from the university in 1879, she had lost her most important outlet to a more meaningful existence. Her acquaintances at the time consisted mostly of the extended Wagner circle into which Nietzsche had introduced her in the 1870s. But as a single woman approaching forty, she must have recognized that her chances for a husband and a family were quickly slipping away. The moment was propitious; in letters she began to encourage Förster to think of her as more than a friend, and in a missive written on May 15, 1884, from San Bernadino, Paraguay, Förster openly declared his love for her.[53] It is difficult to know what exactly Nietzsche thought of the romance and betrothal of his sister. Although Elisabeth's biographer maintains that "Nietzsche tried from the first to warn his sister of the dangers of associating with a man with such warped views,"[54] there is little evidence of this persuasion in his correspondence with her. He writes at the end of July in 1883 that he congratulates Förster on leaving Europe and the Jewish Question behind; he is obviously concerned primarily with the political activity in which Förster was engaged and cites the dangers of having to be associated with something akin to the Tiszaeszlár affair, where an accusation of blood libel in Hungary and its eventual acquittal caused uprisings of the local population. In part Nietzsche opposed anti-Semitic politics because it encouraged such unsavory activity. Nietzsche was mistaken, of course, about Förster leaving his Judeophobia behind; as he would come to learn, his anti-Semitism was one important rationale for establishing Nueva Germania, and he continued his participation in anti-Semitic publications from abroad. But when Nietzsche alludes to Förster's anti-Semitism in his letters, he most often does so with ironic resignation and humor; in the letters we know he sent—but not in some drafts for letters he may or may not have sent—he does not attack Förster for his racist attitudes and politics. Shortly after their marriage, for example, he expresses feigned surprise that "an old anti-Semite" would call her "Eli," which in Hebrew means "my God" "and perhaps in this special case 'my goddess'" (to Elisabeth Förster, July 5, 1885, Nr. 611, KSB 7.64). At the end of 1885 he writes to the newly-weds about a Leipzig council decision that "declared war on garlic," and he adds parenthetically, "the only form of anti-Semitism that smells good to your cosmopolitan rhinoceros" (Nr. 654, KSB 7.129). And in January 1886 he refers to himself lightheartedly as "the incorrigible European and anti-anti-Semite" in agreeing to purchase land in Paraguay (to Elisabeth Förster, Nr. 669, KSB 7.147). Indeed, Nietzsche often endeavors to find positive dimensions to Förster. Writing to Overbeck, he confesses to checking up on the reputation his new brother-in-law enjoys and is pleased by what he has learned: "What has relieved me is the unanimity in praise of his *character*" (October 6, 1885, Nr. 632, KSB 7.97). Once he meets Förster, as we saw in chapter one, he records his positive impression: he "was not unsympathetic," Nietzsche tells Overbeck, he has "something sincere and noble in his being" (to Franz Overbeck, October 17, 1885, Nr. 636, KSB 7.101–02). But more frequently in letters to friends and family Nietzsche emphasizes that his views and Förster's are incompatible or even antithetical. There is no question that Nietzsche rejected and detested Förster's political anti-Semitism. He reached a modus vivendi only by staying away from areas in which they violently disagreed, and he believes Förster does the same. To Köselitz he claims: "My brother-in-law also writes civilly enough to me; we both do our utmost to mitigate a somewhat extreme situation" (November 3, 1887, Nr. 944, KSB 8.184).

To a certain extent, Nietzsche was ready to tolerate Förster's anti-Semitism for the sake of his sister. Although Nietzsche was often combative and polemical in his published works, he is much more conciliatory when dealing with family members. Two days before her wedding he tells his sister that he recognizes that things will now be different, that she will have other concerns, and that "It is only natural that you will assume more and more your husband's way of thinking," but he adds in a strangely conciliatory gesture: "which is absolutely *not* mine, as much as I have to respect and praise it" (May 20, 1885, Nr. 602, KSB 7.51). Nietzsche could not refrain from criticizing publicly the anti-Semitism that was so central to Bernhard Förster's way of thinking, but at least in this letter he appears to pledge that he will control his censure and even embrace elements of thought with which he disagrees. In his wedding gift Nietzsche also appears to make a concession to Förster's anti-Semitism. Two weeks before their nuptials Nietzsche writes to Over-beck requesting that he send him a print he possesses of the copper engraving of Albrecht Dürer's *Knight, Death and the Devil* from 1513 (Nr. 599, KSB 7.46). Nietzsche informs his sister about the gift, which he considers "much too somber," adding that he will also give her a special edition of his *Zarathustra*, and that both can be displayed then "in some American primeval forest" (May 7, 1885, Nr. 600, KSB 7.47). Commentators have occasionally considered the Dürer print Nietzsche's ironic judgment of the marriage, but in fact it is more likely a reference to Förster's anti-Semitic lecture on Judaism and German art. In that presentation Förster begins by listing the greatest works of art over the past centuries, citing Bach's *St. Matthew Passion*, Beethoven's Fifth and Ninth Symphonies, Goethe's *Faust*, Schopenhauer's *The World as Will and Idea*, and Wagner's *Ring of the Nibelungen* as the high points of artistic excellence. But he adds Dürer's copper engraving, providing an interpretation that emphasizes the knight as noble and the "primeval image of the German": "He knows what he has to do, that the castle that we see at a considerable distance from him must be reached." He doesn't know whether he will succeed, but he is resolute and honest in his undertaking. In this lecture the knight becomes the symbol for Germany, similarly threatened, whose victory is similarly uncertain, and who must prevail at any cost. But the enemy of Germany and German art for Förster is not death, and certainly the Fatherland is currently menaced by a different kind of devil—namely, modern Jewry, which is a threat to the very survival of Aryan artistic endeavor.[55] Nietzsche's gift of the Dürer print may have been simply a reflection of his desire to please the couple; he does indicate to Overbeck that it was a request. But it was very likely also a present he recognized as an element of the anti-Semitic view of German history his future brother-in-law had developed in his Berlin lecture.

Nietzsche's objections to Förster certainly involved his worldview, but what appears to have upset Nietzsche most in his sister's wedding was that he was losing someone with whom he had an intimate relationship at a time in his life when friendships were few, and that Förster was taking her so far away from him in a risky colonial venture. If we follow Nietzsche's correspondence, especially his letters to Elisabeth, we obtain the distinct impression of the emotional turmoil her marriage caused. Although at one point he speculates that removing Elisabeth from his life might have a salutary effect[56]—she was someone with strong and sometimes dominating opinions—most of his communication reveals someone profoundly impacted by a prospective, and then an actual, loss. In a touching letter composed two days before the wedding, Nietzsche lays bare his soul in explaining to her why he will not attend the ceremony and give her away. He assures her that no one wishes her more happiness and prosperity than he does, but that the momentous day, which will decide her life's fate, is also a turning point for him, and that he must make "a life reckoning" about his own situation. He relates to her his disappointment that from his earliest years onward "I have found no one with whom I share the same needs of the heart and conscience." He believes that everyone thrives in the company of like-minded individuals, but to his disappointment he has no one who fits this description. He dismisses his time at the university and with Wagner as "an accommodation to a false milieu." All of his friendships—he lists Overbeck, Rée, Malwida, and Köselitz—were the result of fits of loneliness, and he intimates that the overlapping interests with these individuals were very minor, only "a small fleck of a little corner." He even considers his chronic ill health to be the consequence of his isolation: "because I lacked the proper milieu and always had to play the part in a comedy instead of strengthening myself with human contact." He has come to recognize that he is different from other people, that his words have a different meaning than the words of others, that his ways are "distant and foreign": "There are things of the most dangerous sort that I am dealing with" (May 20, 1885, Nr. 602, KSB 7.51–53). In this letter Nietzsche is making an excuse for not coming to the wedding, perhaps employing a pretext, but it is obvious that he is experiencing problems adjusting to the reality of his sister's betrothal. As he writes to his mother in June: "I confess that I am having difficulties coming to terms with the fact of the marriage and the immigration" (Nr. 606, KSB 7.56). And in a letter to his sister shortly before her departure abroad, he exclaims: "How stupid that I don't have anyone anymore to laugh with!," referring to their former happy times together. He continues lamenting their separation with the remark: "No one cares any longer about improving my existence; llama has 'better things to do' and in any case enough to do!" (December 20, 1885, Nr. 653, KSB 7.127). Elisabeth felt a similar regret regarding the demise of their former closeness, and she endeavors to reassure him of his continued importance for her:

> I certainly never had anything *better* to do in life than to care for you and your precious life; it was so infinitely important to make it easier and to clear away small obstacles; but now, as our diverging fates of the last years have unfolded, everything has become different. I do not have anything better to do now, but many, many other kinds of things. If I had taken care of you and could have been

useful to you in any way, then I would have done it for eternity; now I am doing it perhaps in another fashion. (December 26, 1885, Nr. 330, KGB III 4.102)

This exchange may strike us as a bit nostalgic and a trifle sentimental. But it is evident that the intimacy the siblings felt for each other in the 1870s had not disappeared even after the Lou Salomé affair and even with Elisabeth devoting herself to a husband whose anti-Semitic political activities Nietzsche despises.

Nietzsche was concerned that his sister was becoming involved with anti-Semitic politics, but he always appeared more worried about her physical and financial welfare in going to a foreign country so far from home. When he learned of the Försters' plan to emigrate, he began to gather as much information as he could obtain on colonial affairs in the New World. Writing to his sister shortly before her departure for Paraguay, he mentions that former Italian colonists from South America to whom he had spoken in Rapallo and Santa Margherita reported that they became wealthy and were able to return to Genoa with considerable profits (July 5, 1885, Nr. 611, KSB 7.64). He spoke with a Basel acquaintance in November 1885 about a failed Swiss colony that had settled in the La Plata region (November 23, 1885, Nr. 646, KSB 7.111),[57] and was informed that the chances of failure in such ventures are considerable owing to the mixing of nationalities (to Bernhard and Elisabeth Förster, January 2, 1886, Nr. 656, KSB 7.132). In Nice he attended lectures on South America held by a traveler who spent three and a half years abroad. And he evidently showed the book Förster had written on Paraguay to a pastor's wife in Nice, who related her experiences from a fifty-year stay in America. Once Förster and his sister arrived in Paraguay, he followed events closely, reading newspapers to gather information from the New World. The purpose of these activities was no doubt to gain knowledge concerning something he knew little about, but also to construct an argument against the South America venture. Indeed, in his very first letter to his sister in Paraguay he tries to talk her into returning to Europe. "I would send you everything I have," he tells her, "if it could help to make you return soon. Fundamentally everyone who knows and loves you is of the opinion that it would be three thousand times better if you were spared this experiment." He goes on to cite a pamphlet Förster has written on educational issues, asserting that her husband would be much better suited to the position of principal at a small provincial school than "agitator in a three-quarters bad and dirty movement." He then tells her: "I am pulling myself together as well as I can, but an incomparable melancholy comes over me every day and especially in the evenings: always because my llama ran away and gave up entirely her brother's tradition." Nietzsche clarifies what this tradition entails; she now thinks differently about his admirers and belittles those who are "merely Jews": "the same things no longer please us" (February 7, 1886, Nr. 669, KSB 7.147–49). Elisabeth responds that his letter moved her to tears: "So much love causes good feelings and pain in the one leaving," and she consoles him about her own welfare, telling him that she will be surrounded by practical individuals. She even discloses to him that she and her husband have written a will and made him their sole heir (February 9–10, 1886, Nr. 343, KGB III 4.124–25).[58] When Elisabeth married and moved to Paraguay, the tie with her brother loosened to an extent, and several incidents, not least of which was her marriage to Förster, put an unmistakable strain on their relationship. But even in this period, and despite Nietzsche's unswerving opposition to anti-Semitism, the siblings demonstrated obvious affection for each other. Nietzsche was concerned about his sister's welfare in foreign lands; she in turn was always solicitous of his health and his work. The closeness they exhibited in the 1860s and 1870s was never recaptured; they obviously drifted apart during the 1880s, and their correspondence became less frequent, but it is simply false to believe that the conflicts of these years, including Förster's anti-Semitism, destroyed the intimacy that had existed between them for three decades.[59]

We find a negative reaction to Förster's anti-Semitism and Elisabeth's association with it through her husband in two places: in a milder form mostly in remarks Nietzsche makes in correspondence we know he sent, and, in its most virulent manifestation, mainly in drafts of letters to his sister.[60] In the first category we could place his letter to Emily Fynn—an American admirer from Baltimore, whom Nietzsche met in Sils Maria—in which Nietzsche states that Förster's views are more foreign to him than Paraguay (February 1886, Nr. 671, KSB 7.150). In June 1887 he expresses self-pity and simultaneously reproaches his sister: "Everyone has left me, even llama has gone away and is now among the anti-Semites (which is probably the most radical means to finish me off)" (Nr. 855, KSB 8.83). And in his correspondence with Georg Brandes, Nietzsche refers to his "anti-Semitic brother-in-law" as someone disturbed by his attack on Richard Wagner in *The Case of Wagner* (1888) (October 20, 1888, Nr. 1134, KSB 8.456). Nietzsche's ambivalence toward the colonial adventure is directly related to the tension resulting from his concern for his sister's well-being and his disdain for her husband's anti-Semitism. As he writes to Elisabeth:

> I wish that I did not feel so entirely opposed to the tendencies and aspirations of my brother-in-law, so that I could sympathize with the success of his undertaking

in a more fundamental fashion. But as it stands, I have to keep separate in myself with some difficulty what I wish *personally* for both of you and what I *objectively* perhaps curse in it. (October 15, 1887, Nr. 925, KSB 8.166)

His most vitriolic attacks are contained in draft letters composed during the last year and a half of his sane life. In June 1887 Nietzsche sketches a response to his sister's request that he invest in Nueva Germania; he remarks sarcastically that he hopes Germany helps the Försters' colony by deporting all anti-Semites, forcing them to move to Paraguay. With regard to the Jews he expresses his oft-repeated desire for them to gain more power in Europe so that they lose the characteristics they have acquired in oppression. He concludes by commenting that a German who believes he is better than a Jew just because he is a German "belongs in a comedy" if not in an "insane asylum" (Nr. 854, KSB 8.81–82).[61] Six months later he composes a draft in which he informs Elisabeth that "a catalogue of the mentality that I regard as antipodal" can be found in her husband's book on *Parsifal*.[62] Later in this draft he communicates dismay about the mention of *Zarathustra* in the *Anti-Semitic Correspondence* and appears to hold Förster responsible:[63] "I am now against the party of your husband in a state of self-defense. These damned Anti-Semitic pusses should stay away from my ideal!" Ultimately Elisabeth is at fault for bringing him into association with racist politics: "That our name through your marriage is mixed together with this movement: what haven't I already suffered from it! In the last six years you have lost all reason and all considerateness" (December 1887, Nr. 968, KSB 8.218–19). Then, toward the end of his sane existence in November 1888 he drafts a letter in which he completely breaks relations with his sister (Nr. 1145, KSB 8.473)—although anti-Semitism is only implied as a reason for his action. It is unlikely that Nietzsche sent anything resembling these drafts; he is usually milder in tone and substance in his actual letters than in his sketches. These versions represent momentary outbursts, and once Nietzsche regained control of his emotions, he composed something more conciliatory. We can see from passages Nietzsche submitted for *Ecce Homo* that he was capable of tempestuous outpourings containing abuse of his sister,[64] especially for her association with anti-Semitism. But these moments are far outweighed by signs of intimacy, affection, and genuine concern. Even in the late 1880s he remained a loving, caring brother, and at times he blamed anti-Semitism, not always for its racist implications, but for taking his sister away from him.

ANTI-SEMITIC CORRESPONDENCE

Nietzsche had serious personal and psychic investments in his publisher and his sister that undoubtedly influenced his views on anti-Semitism. On the one hand, they contributed to his extreme dislike of the movement, since Nietzsche perceived anti-Semitism as contributing to the loss of livelihood, fame, and family. On the other hand, because Schmeitzner and Elisabeth were so intimately involved with the anti-Semitic cause, on occasion Nietzsche may have modified his direct assault or suppressed his feelings of extreme disdain. In his contact with the *Anti-Semitic Correspondence* and its editor Theodor Fritsch, Nietzsche knows no such restraint. We met Fritsch already at the beginning of the first chapter. He was an important initiator of the anti-Semitic movement in the 1880s and one of the few of this first generation to persevere along this racist path and achieve political success as a National Socialist.[65] His *Anti-Semitic Correspondence* began publication in 1885, and considering the average duration of anti-Semitic journals was very brief—we will recall that Marr's journal folded after three issues and that Schmeitzner's *International Monthly* lasted only two years—under its various names, editors, and publishers it was one of the longest-running Judeophobic publications in Germany, ceasing publication only in 1924. It was originally conceived as an internal party forum to discuss anti-Semitic politics, as the second part of its title indicated: "Discussion Room for Internal Party Affairs." The cover page also emphasized that the journal should be disseminated only among reliable "party comrades," and the third issue boldly features the word "Discretion" to reinforce this message. Eventually, however, the journal became available to the general public, a decision evidently aimed at promulgating anti-Semitic doctrine to a larger segment of the general population. In its initial year it appeared every other month, but by 1887 it was a monthly, and by the following year it was published every two weeks. The contributors consist of a familiar list of known anti-Semitic writers from the late nineteenth century. Fritsch wrote many of the pieces himself, using either his own name or one of several pseudonyms, and in the first issues its express purpose as a forum was taken very seriously, many of its contributions coming in the form of letters (some of which were perhaps not real letters) from anti-Semites around Germany. Wilhelm Marr wrote for the journal, as did Paul Förster, Bernhard's brother. Bernhard Förster was something of an honored contributor; his name appears in the very first issue, announcing his upcoming report on his two-year trip to the La Plata River region of South America and heralding him as the originator of the Anti-Semites' Petition from 1880–81. There is a repeated attempt to educate the readership on the most important writings of anti-Semites, and several of these listings contain names very familiar to Nietzsche: Wagner, Bruno Bauer, and Eugen Dühring. There was also a veritable obsession with impressing the readership about the nature of its supporters and soliciting new ones: one issue includes information on the status and occupation of the subscribers, which included five princes, forty-three dukes, sixty-two professors, and 156 members of the military. In another issue the editor asks for addresses of potential new subscribers by name; included are the eminent physiologist Emil du Bois-Reymond and the popular philosopher Eduard von Hartmann, whom Nietzsche had attacked in his second *Untimely Meditation*.

It was quite possibly in the context of this perennial membership drive that Fritsch contacted Nietzsche. It is uncertain who submitted Nietzsche's name to Fritsch. Förster may have been the mediator, but it is more likely that it was Otto Busse, who had carried on a rather one-sided correspondence with Nietzsche since the late 1870s. Busse was a strange and unstable character, but a fervent admirer of Nietzsche and his writings. He wrote to him first in January 1878 extolling his *Untimely Meditations* and *Birth of Tragedy* and assuring the philosopher that he had never learned more than he did from his work (Nr. 1027, KGB II 6/2.789–90). He writes again in October 1879, telling Nietzsche he had tried to visit him in Naumburg because he had heard he had resigned his professorship in Basel due to illness and wanted to check on his health. He mentions that he has now read *Human, All Too Human* with complete admiration, and he promises to do what he can to help disseminate Nietzsche's writings, which to his dismay seem to be relatively unknown (Nr. 1249, KGB II 6/2.1204–7). We know very little about Busse except what he records in his letters. He appears to have been relatively uneducated in a formal sense and had four sons, two of whom must have attended a Gymnasium in Jena, which allowed their father to travel easily to Naumburg. He himself lived in Berlin. At the beginning of 1880 Busse begins to send Nietzsche lengthy and confused manuscripts (February 20, 1880, Nr. 15, KGB III 2.31–46) that Busse obviously considers philosophical reflections. Nietzsche is at a loss with regard to how he should respond, especially since Busse claims to recognize references to himself in Nietzsche's works. Nietzsche dictates a reply to Busse through Köselitz clarifying the matter (Nachträge, Nr. 15a, KGB III 7/1.3–4)—Köselitz served as something like a secretary for Nietzsche at various points—but it does not deter Busse from sending a revised version of his treatise (March 11, 1880, Nr. 17, KGB III 2.49).[66] Busse's odd behavior is clarified for Nietzsche a year later in March 1881, when Busse's brother-in-law, Julius Wolff, writes to Nietzsche explaining that Busse suffers from an almost complete loss of hearing and a severe dose of megalomania: "He considers himself a prophet and the chosen reformer of the German nation." Wolff asks for Nietzsche's intervention and an evaluation of the "philosophy" Busse sent him (March 22, 1881, Nr. 64, KGB 3.2.149–51). Nietzsche responds that his relative's work is without scholarly merit and that he, Nietzsche, had discouraged him in his first and only communication with him (Nachträge, March 28, 1881, Nr. 96a, KGB III 7/1.4–5). Nietzsche does feel some compassion for this deranged soul, since he discovers a few very "delicate feelings" in his letter, and at one point he calls him with some irony "my entire 'publicum'" (to Heinrich Köselitz, November 27, 1881, Nr. 171, KSB 6.143). Busse also informs Nietzsche he will share with him his thoughts on the "Reproduction of Man," which will evidently include a suggestion drawn from the Spartan method of social engineering: killing children not fit for life (to Heinrich Köselitz, December 8, 1881, Nr. 177, KSB 6.147). But through Köselitz as a buffer Nietzsche manages to rid himself of Busse, at least for the time being. He resurfaces briefly, however, in early February 1887, having perhaps recovered from his struggles with mental illness. Recalling his promise to Nietzsche to work for the promotion of his writings, he acts in what he probably considered the spirit of the philosopher he so admires when he includes mention of *Zarathustra* in a letter to the *Anti-Semitic Correspondence*:

> In the 9th issue of the *Anti-Semitic Correspondence*, a journal that appears with Theodore Fritsch in Leipzig, has been printed a letter written to the aforementioned individual from 18 December of this year, in which your esteemed name and your works are mentioned. With this I intend to express my admiration and respect for you in a similar fashion as I have done at times before; I have even considered it my duty to do this, and if it would have been better for it not to be published, which you yourself can judge best, then I ask you most kindly to excuse it as a mistake. (Nr. 432, KGB III 6.17–18)

This letter was likely Nietzsche's first introduction to the *Anti-Semitic Correspondence* and its publisher.

Busse's letter in the ninth issue of the journal was not the first time Nietzsche's name had been mentioned in its pages. Indeed, Busse is merely responding to two previous letters in the seventh and eighth issues that cite Nietzsche's *Zarathustra* to bolster their arguments. The matter under discussion is one that often appeared in the first years of the *Anti-Semitic Correspondence*: how to conduct anti-Semitic agitation most effectively. The first correspondent, who is identified only as Dr. H-I, proposes two antithetical ways to approach the problem. Agitation can either be accomplished through enlightenment of the people or through a quiet reserve that does not seek to convince the masses. Preferring the second alternative, H-I remarks that the question of agitation is really unimportant since there are so many fragments and hints of anti-Semitism in the very air we breathe. Instead of placing his faith in the masses, who can easily be led astray by clever Jewish propaganda, he looks for a great personality to deal with the Jews, a great "improver and purifier." In choosing the second alternative, which advocates holding back, awaiting the great leader, and then having even friends of Jews recognize the error of their ways and undergo conversion to anti-Semitism, he points to the need to flee the "noise and cries of the masses and to go for a time, like Buddha, into the desert." He then cites from the first volume of *Zarathustra*: "Flee where the air is raw and strong. Thus spoke Zarathustra (see Nietzsche)" (Anhang, KGB III 7/3, 2.859–60).[67] The second letter, written by F. Roderich Stoltheim—which was one of several pseudonyms Fritsch employed—argues the antithetical position. "The question cannot be solved without the masses," Stoltheim asserts. Anti-Semitism is about more than solving the Jewish Question; it is a philosophy of wide purview that the masses need to embrace for themselves: "It raises humanity to a higher level of knowledge and moral maturity; it is a means of educating the nation" (Anhang, KGB III 7/3, 2.864–65). He too cites *Zarathustra*, but from early in the preface where the eponymous hero apostrophizes the sun, explaining that his years in isolation would have been wasted if he did not now distribute his surfeit of wisdom to the people: "Behold, I am weary of my wisdom, like a bee that has gathered too much honey; I need hands outstretched to receive it" (Z, Zarathustra's Vorrede 1, KSA 4.11).[68] Busse, having read these two opposing views, assumes a middle ground, siding first with the opinion that the masses are essential for agitation, and that leaders and "law-givers" will arise from them. But there may be an extraordinary circumstance, and we would then do well to listen to Nietzsche:

> Let us assume, however, that an exceptional case occurs ... so that an improver and purifier stemming from the people emerges of the stature of Zarathustra (and that is really Friedrich Nietzsche's magnificent idea on which I meditate so gladly—and who would not wish with him that it would happen?), who upholds purity in thought, speech and action; provides legitimacy for the Aryan people again; who distinguishes himself, like other great law-givers, in that he knows how to think and provide for not only the present, but, beyond the present, for coming generations; and to help us to achieve simple, that is, great laws. (Anhang, KGB III 7/3, 2.888)

In contrast to the initial contribution, Zarathustra is not the dictator, forcing enlightenment on an ignorant mob, but the leader of a triumphant Aryan national renewal. In a final conciliatory gesture Busse expresses appreciation for the stimulation of the first two letters and especially "the beautiful quotations" from his beloved teacher and mentor.

With Nietzsche featured in letters in three consecutive issues in the final months of 1886 and January of 1887, and very likely with the encouragement from the philosopher's misguided admirer Busse, Fritsch must have thought that recruiting him for the cause was a distinct possibility. We do not possess Fritsch's letter, which must have been sent in the third week of March in 1887, but we do have Nietzsche's rather sardonic response. Nietzsche's letter indicates that Fritsch sent him three sample copies of the *Anti-Semitic Correspondence*, and it is very likely that they were the issues in which he was cited. We also have to assume that Fritsch made it clear that he was trying to recruit him as a subscriber, perhaps even as a contributor, and Nietzsche opens his response by referring the anti-Semitic editor to the passage in *Dawn* that we examined in chapter four. We will recall that in aphorism 205, titled "Of the People of Israel," Nietzsche expresses an admiration for Jewry in persevering for so many centuries under persecution, and that he attributes their current characteristics, most of them laudable, to this long history of oppression. He also hopes that intermarriage with the noble classes of Europe will gradually remove any unfavorable character traits. In responding to Fritsch he writes that "the Jews are for me, stated objectively, more interesting than the Germans: their history contains many *more fundamental* problems." He then turns to his attitude toward the current "German mind," stating his impatience with its individual idiosyncrasies. "I consider in particular that anti-Semitism is one of them." He ridicules the list of "classical literature" recommended by the movement and contained in the journal, singling out Paul de Lagarde, whom he dubs a "pompous and sentimental crank." At one point in his letter Fritsch must have discussed Nietzsche's apparent change in worldview from his Wagnerian years. As we have seen, the anti-Jewish direction cedes partially in his aphoristic period to a more favorable public attitude toward modern Jewry and recognition of the long history of subjugation Jews have had to endure. Nietzsche quotes from Fritsch's letter the assumption or suspicion that he has been "led astray by some social consideration to his incorrect judgments" and later cites from Fritsch the supposition that "he has let his wings be trimmed." Although the Jewish Question is not explicitly stated, we can presume that Fritsch had remarked on Nietzsche's expressions of understanding and support for Jews. It is quite likely that Fritsch considered this change in Nietzsche's writings to be the result of Jewish pressure—such was the typical mindset of anti-Semites. Nietzsche informs him that he has been subjected to no such pressure to alter his views and assures Fritsch that although he counts no Jews among his friends, he also has no close association with anti-Semites. He closes the letter with the ironic suggestion that Fritsch publish "a list of German scholars, artists, poets, writers, actors and virtuosi of Jewish lineage or extraction! (It would be a worthwhile contribution to the history of *German culture* [and also to its criticism!])" (March 12, 1887, Nr. 817, KSB 8.45–46). The tone and the substance of Nietzsche's response clearly indicate his attempt to belittle Fritsch, his journal, and the movement to which he belongs.

Apparently Nietzsche was not content with sending only a single letter replete with ridicule and sarcasm. Five days later he writes to Fritsch again, returning to him the three issues of the *Anti-Semitic Correspondence* he had originally included in his first communication.[69] Nietzsche is more acerbic and direct in this letter, thanking him ironically for the insight he has gained into the "muddled principles" of his journal and its attendant movement. He requests a cessation of all communication with Fritsch and especially wants no more copies of the journal:

> I fear ultimately for my patience. Believe me: this revolting desire on the part of annoying dilettantes who want to speak about the *value* of human beings and races, this subjugation under "authorities" who are rejected with cold disdain by every more enlightened spirit, ... this constant and absurd falsification and propping up of the vague concepts "Teutonic," "Semitic," "Aryan," "Christian," "German"—all of that could in the long run make me seriously angry and take me out of the ironic beneficence with which I have observed up until now the virtuous whims and Pharisaisms of today's Germans.

We might note that in early writings Nietzsche had used several of the concepts he now derides, and that he was hardly immune from generalizations about races and peoples, as we have seen often in his remarks about Jews and Germans. When Nietzsche writes of the authorities to which anti-Semitic propagandists subject themselves he includes in parentheses a reference to several individuals and a commentary on their qualifications: "e.g. E. Dühring, R. Wagner, Ebrard, Wahrmund, P. de Lagarde—which one of them is in questions of morals and history the most unqualified, the most unjust?" Several commentators have assumed that Nietzsche's rogues' gallery of anti-Semites alludes to an article written by Bernhard Förster, "Our Work, Our Goals," which appeared in the same issue of the *Anti-Semitic Cor-*

respondence in which Busse's letter was printed. Förster does cite authors who have dealt with the question of anti-Semitism from "the highest ethical standpoint," and he specifically mentions the names, Wagner, Lagarde, Dühring, and Wahrmund, all of whom were well known and often referenced as trusted authorities in anti-Semitic periodicals.[70] In the middle of Nietzsche's list, however, is the name Ebrard, which must refer to the prolific, moderate Protestant theologian and professor at the University of Zurich, August Ebrard. His name appears nowhere in his brother-in-law's list for suggested reading because he was not known as a leading anti-Semite; indeed, he appears to have had no connection to anti-Semitic movements. Ebrard was an ardent supporter of German unification in the 1860s, and since in 1870 he, along with a Zurich professor of surgery, set up a special course for medics who wanted to participate in the Franco-Prussian War, it is quite possible that Nietzsche, who was one of the medics trained for the conflict, may have met him.[71] But Nietzsche is mistaken in including him in a list of noted anti-Semitic writers, and he certainly did not obtain his name from the article written by his brother-in-law.[72]

The reminder that Förster was writing for an anti-Semitic journal, however, came as a shock to Nietzsche. He recognized that Elisabeth's husband had not discarded his racist views when he left for Paraguay, but he appears to have hoped that he would no longer be an active participant in German discussions, and in that way his own name would not retain the association with anti-Semitism that it did through his sister's marriage. Nine months after his letters to Fritsch, Nietzsche erupts again and returns to the complex of issues surrounding the *Anti-Semitic Correspondence*, the fact that his name and Zarathustra's appeared in the journal, and the damage to his reputation caused by the Försters' association with this racist political movement. It is difficult to ascertain why he takes up these matters again after such a long period of time. It is quite possible that he was again reminded of the journal and his fate at the hands of the anti-Semitic press by a lengthy review of his book, *Beyond Good and Evil* (1876), written by Fritsch under the pseudonym of Thomas Frey, in the November and December issue of the *Correspondence* in 1887. We cannot determine with certainty that Fritsch sent him this issue, or whether he obtained it elsewhere. But if he did read this review or learn about its contents, he probably was not pleased to find his book and his philosophy mercilessly ridiculed in a protracted attack on his intelligence, an assertion of his ignorance of the real world, and a repudiation of his moral values. Fritsch had taken revenge on Nietzsche for the rude and dismissive treatment he experienced in the March letters. In the draft of a letter to his mother at the end of December Nietzsche states that after reading articles in the *Anti-Semitic Correspondence* he has lost all forbearance with the party and the movement. He is angry at being associated with such known anti-Semites as Dühring and will remain resolute in his defense against these character assassinations. He notes parenthetically that he is thankful that "this party" has now "declared war on me"—quite possibly a reference to Fritsch's scathing review of his book—but believes it has come ten years too late (Nr. 967, KSB 8.216–17).[73] In a draft meant for his sister, he asserts that his patience has now come to an end after he has read the name "Zarathustra" in the *Anti-Semitic Correspondence* (Nr. 968, KSB 8.218). This draft was composed at some point at the end of 1887, quite likely in late December; that Nietzsche after several months returns to the articles he had read in March indicates either that he was reminded of them by the recent review or that the incident from March had such a huge impact on his psyche that Nietzsche still had not recovered sufficiently from it in the intervening months. Significant evidence of Nietzsche's preoccupation with his reputation and the journal articles can also be found in a letter he purportedly composed on December 26, 1887, and sent to his sister in Paraguay.[74] He reproaches her for committing "one of the greatest stupidities" "for you and for me" by marrying into this racist movement, and he states to her unambiguously his opposition to anti-Semitism. He then refers back to the incident from March: "In recent times I have been afflicted with letters and *Anti-Semitic Correspondence* Journals; my aversion to this party (which only too gladly wants to gain advantage from my name!) is as definitive as possible, but the familial relationship with Förster, as well as the lasting effects of my former anti-Semitic publisher Schmeitzner, again and again bring the adherents of this unpleasant party to the supposition that I must belong with them. *How much it harms me and has harmed me* you can't imagine." He continues in a similar vein to the draft letter: "that I am able to do nothing against it, and that the name 'Zarathustra' is used in every *Anti-Semitic Correspondence* Journal has already nearly made me ill on several occasions" (Urabschriften, 7 [965a], KGB III 7/3, 1.26–27). In these outpourings of late 1887 there are three noteworthy features: anti-Semitism is repeatedly conceived as a party, that is, it is identified as a political movement, not as merely the hatred of, or prejudice against, Jews; Nietzsche repeatedly cites personal reasons for his antipathy toward anti-Semitism, stating explicitly that it has caused harm to him and his reputation; and nowhere does he mention any compassion for Jews, or express any sentiment resembling tolerance for diverse views and religions, or any conviction regarding protecting the rights and dignity of individuals from diverse cultural and religious heritages. His reactions to his brief involvement with the *Anti-Semitic Corre-*

spondence and its editor therefore remain consonant with his encounters with anti-Semitism from earlier in the decade.

ANTI-SEMITISM AND THE JEWISH QUESTION

During the four-day period between his two replies to Theodor Fritsch, Nietzsche composed communications to his two closest friends of the late 1880s, Franz Overbeck and Heinrich Köselitz. In the letter to Overbeck he mentions "a comical fact, of which I am becoming conscious more and more. I have gradually acquired an 'influence,' very subterranean, which is self-understood." In his presentation to Overbeck, Nietzsche appears more amused than annoyed or angered by his association with the anti-Semitic journal, but it is quite possible that he had not yet recognized the full ramifications at this point. He continues by boasting of a much broader "influence" than he has any right to claim: "In all radical parties (socialists, nihilists, anti-Semites, Christian orthodox, and Wagnerian) I enjoy a curious and almost mysterious reputation." He attributes this odd phenomenon to the pureness and clarity of his thought, contending that he can rail against these ideologically laden movements as much as he pleases, yet still be tolerated and cited: "they can't break free of me." To a certain extent Nietzsche is accurate—and prescient—in his observations on his influence, despite the scanty evidence he possesses; in his texts he quite often states clearly his opposition to socialism, anarchism, Wagnerian ideology of various stripes, Christianity, and anti-Semitism, but that has not prevented individuals identified with these various directions from considering him an intellectual ally. Interesting here is the field of association for Nietzsche; the various groups he considers "radical parties" are very different in character, and today we would hardly unite them under this rubric. Part of understanding what anti-Semitism meant for Nietzsche is related to where he situates it and other movements in their nineteenth-century context, which is very different from our own. Nietzsche continues with a remark familiar to us from correspondence at the end of the year: "In the *Anti-Semitic Correspondence* ... my name appears in almost every issue. Zarathustra, 'the divine man' has enthralled the anti-Semites; they have their own anti-Semitic interpretation of him, which made me laugh quite a bit." Again we note the exaggeration on Nietzsche's part concerning his reputation. As we have seen, there was no single, anti-Semitic interpretation of Zarathustra; passages from the book were used to support two antithetical propositions regarding agitation. And although Fritsch likely sent Nietzsche the three issues in which his name appears, we do not find him mentioned at all, and certainly not under the frequent lists of anti-Semitic authors, in previous or subsequent issues of the journal. Nietzsche concludes this passage in his letter by informing Overbeck of his advice to Fritsch about composing a list of Jewish contributors to German culture (March 24, 1887, Nr. 820, KSB 8.48). From his description to Overbeck we gain the impression that Nietzsche was not—or perhaps not yet—irritated by his inclusion in the anti-Semitic journal, that he was more entertained than outraged (and perhaps a bit surprised or even pleased regarding his influence), and that in his response to Fritsch, he was simply playing with him as a humorous diversion.

In the postcard he writes to Köselitz, he includes the short and dismissive statement we have already cited concerning the Dostoevsky translator, the "Jew Goldschmidt" and his "synagogue rhythms" (March 27, 1887, Nr. 822, KSB 8.50). We have seen that Nietzsche continued to make such comments even after he broke with Wagner, but the timing is curious. How could Nietzsche include in such a casual fashion an anti-Jewish remark when three days before—and two days after—he wrote this remark, he was excoriating the anti-Semite Fritsch for his journal, his movement, and his ideological convictions? We have to suspect that the answer lies in the dissociation of anti-Semitism from anti-Jewish sentiments in Nietzsche's mind and, to a degree, also in the minds of his contemporaries. Obviously Nietzsche recognized that anti-Semitic parties advocated measures against Jews, including the repudiation of legal emancipation and the introduction of measures that would eliminate Jewish influence in German society. At the same time he did not consider anti-Semitism to be an ideology that exhausted itself in anti-Jewish thought, and although he had some favorable views on modern Jewry, he did not regard bias toward the Jews as incompatible with an aversion to anti-Semitism. For this reason, Nietzsche can even postulate that anti-Semites resemble Jews. In one of his late notebooks Nietzsche differentiates between the two in a manner flattering to neither group: "What really separates a Jew from an anti-Semite: the Jew knows that he is lying when he lies: the anti-Semite does not know that he is always lying" (Nachlass 1888, 21[6], KSA 13.580). A bit later he defines the anti-Semite as "an envious, i.e. the most stupid Jew" (Nachlass 1888, 21[7], KSA 13.581). And, as we shall see, in the *Genealogy of Morals* anti-Semitism appears as a modern manifestation of values originating in priestly Judaism. Nor, as we have observed, does an individual's adherence to anti-Semitism disqualify that individual from possessing positive characteristics and even from securing Nietzsche's admiration. In drafts intended for *The Case of Wagner* Nietzsche speaks of the delightful and stimulating memories he has for Wagner and Cosima and then comments: "Even for anti-Semites, for whom, as is known, I am not fond at all, I would have to acknowledge, according to my not inconsiderable experience, many favorable things: this does not hinder me from declaring a merciless war against anti-Semitism, rather it is the condition for it" (Nachlass 1888, 24[1.6], KSA 13.622–23). The opposition to anti-Semitism was something very different for Nietzsche than for us; it did not necessarily entail the elimination of bias against Jewry, nor was it a fatal character flaw in friends. For Nietzsche, his aversion to anti-Semitism has numerous dimensions, many of them personal: (1) He blames it at times for destroying his friendship with Wagner and Cosima. (2) He considers it a decisive factor in his estrangement from his sister. (3) It caused, in his mind, his publisher Schmeitzner to lose focus on his writings, which resulted in (4) a lack of financial security and independence, (5) an insufficient dissemination of his ideas to the general public in Germany, and (6) the absence of followers and disciples of sufficient quality and quantity. (7) It also threatened to destroy his reputation with the one circle of admirers he had secured over the years, the Viennese Jews at the university. There were also philosophical and ideological objections, the most important of which were its origins in *ressentiment* and its close connection with German patriotism and Christianity. In none of these considerations does hatred of Jews or prejudice against Jewry play a decisive role.

Nietzsche recognized the compatibility of opposition to anti-Semitism and anti-Jewish sentiments in aphorism 251 of *Beyond Good and Evil*. After stating that he has not yet met a German favorably inclined toward the Jews, he draws a distinction between anti-Semitism and a more acceptable, less virulent anti-Jewish attitude: "and however unconditionally all careful and political people may repudiate real anti-Semitism [*Antisemiterei*], even this caution and politics is not directed against this class of feeling, but rather only against its dangerous immoderation, especially against the distasteful and ignominious expression of this immoderate feeling—we should not deceive ourselves about this" (JGB 251, KSA 5.193).[75] Nietzsche is making a quite remarkable claim in this passage, one that can easily be applied to him and his circle of friends. Individuals who are cautious and conscious of the political realities of the time are against anti-Semitism, which Nietzsche ridicules further by calling it *"Antisemiterei,"* clearly a derogative reference to this racist movement. At the same time the "class of feeling" that gives rise to anti-Semitism is not really at issue, and those who are "cautious and political" do not reject anti-Semitism because they also renounce sentiments directed against Jews but because the manner in which the anti-Semites conduct themselves is wholly distasteful to them. Anti-Semites and those who oppose anti-Semites share a common bond in their views on Jews and their effect in Germany, which appears to explain why Nietzsche claims to have met no German—anti-Semite or non-anti-Semite—who was well disposed toward Jews. Where they differ is in their solution to the German Question. Anti-Semites are "immoderate" and "distasteful" in the means they choose toward their goal. Presumably the more refined strata of German society adopt other paths to achieve a similar objective. As we have seen, Nietzsche can very well be included in this latter group; he is virulently opposed to anti-Semitism, but he too has developed a solution to the Jewish Question that would eliminate the baleful characteristic of modern Jewry. In the remainder of the aphorism Nietzsche juxtaposes the anti-Semitic perspective to a more "reasoned" alternative to the Jewish Question that closely resembles his own views. The anti-Semites, Nietzsche tells us, appear to want to force the Jews to assume dominance in Europe, a condition both Nietzsche and the anti-Semites should not welcome at the present time. The Jews themselves are strongly inclined toward assimilation, of which Nietzsche approves, and he states that they should be encouraged in this direction, since it represents "a softening of Jewish instincts," that is, German Jews are in the process of losing the characteristics they currently possess and becoming more suitable for the task of contributing to a ruling class for Europe. Because of their uncompromising and unreasonable political stance, Nietzsche makes the following ironic recommendation: "it might be useful and appropriate to banish the anti-Semitic loudmouths from the country" (JGB 251, KSA 5.194). With this suggestion Nietzsche turns the tables on anti-Semites, who advocate expelling Jews from Germany, but he does so not necessarily because he repudiates their views on the nature of modern Jewry but because he disagrees with their "immoderate" method for solving this problem. Nietzsche and the anti-Semites seek a resolution to the Jewish Question, but in aphorism 251 Nietzsche makes it clear that he opposes anti-Semitism because their activities threaten to undermine more reasonable and realistic proposals for dealing with Jews.

Because today we tend to identify anti-Semitism tout court as prejudice against the Jews, we may have difficulty appreciating the distinctions Nietzsche was drawing. Without the historical context, we can easily believe that Nietzsche's rejection of anti-Semitism says everything we need to know about his relationship to Jews and Judaism. But it does not. Nor was Nietzsche alone in espousing anti-Jewish views while at the same time expressing the conviction that anti-Semitism was a crude way to reduce or eliminate the influence of modern Jewry and therefore must be rejected. In our consideration of Ernst Schmeitzner, we reviewed a letter from 1880 that

Overbeck had sent to Köselitz as evidence for Nietzsche's knowledge of his publisher's anti-Semitism. Overbeck expresses concern about Schmeitzner's publication of anti-Semitic materials—Schmeitzner also published some of Overbeck's works, adding to his concern—and while he is on the topic of anti-Semitism, which was a very recent German phenomenon at that point, he broaches a discussion of the Jews with regard to this new political movement:

> Whatever grievances we have against the Jews, and whatever, as a rule, is repulsive about them: non-Jews as well as Germans can easily agree about this. But it seems to me that in today's whole public activity in Germany there is enough blindness, thoughtlessness, tactlessness, and narrow-mindedness, and that it would be increased even more by an agitation resting on the blindest instinct. It could be that Jews in Germany are a kind of state of emergency[76]—although in the torpor that has recently surfaced in our essence I can't see how we could do without our Jews—but we would certainly not be thinking about resisting them *in this fashion* if the shoe didn't pinch us in an entirely different place.

Overbeck represents a position with regard to Jews in 1880 that is quite similar to what Nietzsche would advocate six years later in *Beyond Good and Evil*. We can all agree on definite grievances against the Jews, as well as their repulsiveness, but we should not be dealing with the issue using the methods of the anti-Semites. He takes a neutral stance on the oft-cited anti-Semitic contention that the country is in a state of emergency owing to Jewish dominance of the press and the financial world, but he recognizes wistfully that Jews are presently so ensconced in German affairs that they are indispensible. In any case the sudden rise of anti-Semitism would not have been possible except for existing problems that have little to do with the Jewish presence or with an imagined Jewish dominance in Germany. Overbeck continues his reflections, referring to the National Liberals, the party with which Bismarck ruled Germany from 1871 to 1879, and its putative Jewish leanings. "Even if National Liberalism ever so loudly tells the Jew, now that he has provided his service, to leave, it will not be able to get rid of him, since I haven't really seen much else in it besides the Jew, and, to be sure, not the most pleasant sort. In short I consider the attempts to improve our public circumstances from *that* side to be driving out demons by Beelzebub." While it is true that several important members of the National Liberal Party were Jewish, Overbeck's remark about them not being "the most pleasant sort" evidences a gratuitous, anti-Jewish sentiment. Despite this unfavorable view of Jews, he indicates that anti-Semitism approaches the issue in the wrong manner and that to embrace the anti-Semites' position would only make a bad situation worse. Overbeck then makes specific reference to the beginnings of the "Berlin Anti-Semitism Controversy," which was started by his friend from his student years, Heinrich von Treitschke, the noted Prussian historian. Overbeck considers the legitimation of anti-Semitism by the Berlin academic to be wrongheaded and unseemly. "The endeavor of my friend Treitschke to turn a movement, whose sole effective rationale in the forms in which it has appeared hitherto has been admittedly base, into something wholesome through sanctimonious talk, and to give it the consecration of Christian Germanness—as if anyone, if it had to be, couldn't at present easily provide a shabby disguise for it—appears to me to be completely naïve." Overbeck, like Nietzsche, believed there was a problem with German Jewry and that Germans needed to find a solution to the Jewish Question, but he disapproves of anti-Semitic politics and is especially perturbed by their validation through otherwise respectable advocates. As we have seen, this letter was meant to be shown to Nietzsche, so it is appropriate that Overbeck concludes his remarks on Jews and anti-Semitism with the query: "What does Nietzsche say to this matter?"[77] The response appears in a letter Nietzsche writes to Overbeck's wife, Ida, a few weeks later. Nietzsche asks her to thank his friend for the letter he has now seen and states that he is delighted to know that from such a distance there is such a closeness of sentiments: "For example both of us do not need to waste another word with regard to our understanding of Jews and associates of Jews" (May 24, 1880, Nr. 28, KSB 6.20).

The harmony that exists between Overbeck and Nietzsche with regard to the Jewish Question and anti-Semitism contains a cautionary lesson for today's readers not to evaluate matters of race and racial bias without the relevant historical context. Nietzsche and Overbeck both recoil from the crude excesses of anti-Semitism, but they retain attitudes toward Jews we would categorize today as biased and perhaps even racist. The rejection of anti-Semitism entailed something quite different from an absence of anti-Jewish sentiments, and this distinction was obvious to writers of the late nineteenth century in a way that it is not to twentieth- and twenty-first-century observers. In his recollections of Nietzsche, Overbeck returns to the same constellations of issues we have been examining in this chapter and provides further confirmation for the necessity of historical contextualization. After discussing Nietzsche's relationship with Josef Paneth, Overbeck notes that although he and Nietzsche did not devote any special studies to Judaism, they came to appreciate the perseverance of the Jewish people in their native traditions; we may recall Nietzsche's respect for the "remarkableness of their tenacity" in his aphoristic writings. Overbeck then turns to the topic of anti-Semitism and draws a picture similar to the one contained in his letter to Köselitz:

> I believe that Nietzsche and I were very much in agreement in our thoughts with regard to anti-Semitism. Since fanaticism of any kind, nationalist hatred as well as religious hatred, was especially far from our thoughts—even though for different reasons that had to do with our divergent backgrounds—we had fundamentally no sympathy for anti-Semitism. Not that this closed attitude toward anti-Semitism made us so very different from other Europeans. This radically closed attitude was hardly anything other than what one would find in our contemporaries. In our era almost everyone—at least every educated person—had a certain antipathy toward the Jews, so much so that in our circles the Jews themselves had this attitude. In our social milieu this is inherent in practically everyone, only that almost everyone permits himself to express this antipathy in a great variety of nuances, while only a few conceal it completely, and not very many at all preach this antipathy out loud.

Overbeck continues by stating that he and Nietzsche did not pay much attention to anti-Semitism, considering it merely a passing sign of the times. However, he also comments that Nietzsche's writings exhibit a noticeable dose of "anti-Semitism" (Overbeck uses quotation marks here)[78] or at least only a slight love of Semites (by which he obviously means Jews), and that he suffered a great deal of personal frustration at the hands of anti-Semites. He wishes Nietzsche would have been spared all dealings with both Jews and anti-Semites since he recognizes from his last notebooks and letters how much these matters weighed on his thoughts. "Nietzsche was a heartfelt adversary of anti-Semitism," Overbeck states in summary, but he adds the caveat: "as he experienced it." Nonetheless, Overbeck comments that "when he spoke honestly, his remarks about Jews in his writings were much sharper than those of the anti-Semites themselves. His anti-Christianity was chiefly founded on anti-Semitism."[79] What Overbeck is observing in his friend is important for clarifying the historical specificity of Nietzsche's position toward the Jewish Question. An opponent of anti-Semitism, which he conceived in his time as a political party and vulgar racist movement, Nietzsche, like many of his contemporaries, could still harbor significant anti-Jewish sentiments and propound theories that could easily be judged a contribution to anti-Semitic thought by even a sympathetic readership.

CHAPTER SIX

Priests, Israelites, Chandalas

Up to this point we have examined primarily Nietzsche's remarks on European Jewry in the nineteenth century and his relationship to Jewish individuals or persons of Jewish heritage. A large part of his writing about Judaism, however, especially in the final two years of his sane existence, is devoted to topics that are more historical in nature and fall under the rubric of the history of religion. Nietzsche had been interested in this topic for quite a few years, but what changed in the latter half of the 1880s was Nietzsche's hypothesis—or the adoption of the hypotheses he found in recent scholarship—that there existed a strong continuity between Jewish values in the centuries prior to the birth of Jesus and the teachings that were ultimately incorporated into Christianity. Nietzsche's preoccupation with the Jewish tradition involved two interrelated themes that are of central importance for his thought in 1887 and 1888: the history of morals and the rise of Christianity. It is important to note, in addition, the increasing frequency with which Jews and Judaism are included in both his published writings and his notebooks. We have seen that after the admonition by Cosima, direct reference to Jewry disappeared from his works, but that he began to include references—many of them quite positive—in his aphoristic writings from *Human, All Too Human* (1878–80) to *Beyond Good and Evil* (1886). His published books and notes from the 1880s, especially from the last two sane years, contain a noticeable expansion in references to Jews, many of them alluding to historical Jewry and speculation on Jewish history during the time of the prophets. It is sometimes difficult to know precisely what period of Jewish history Nietzsche means, since he rarely includes dates or historical references. From his sources and occasional allusions we can assume that he was primarily concerned with the transition from the ancient Israelites, who possessed a nationalist God Yahweh, to the phase of Judaism in which their divinity becomes universal in character and morality enters strongly into religious practices and laws. Nietzsche's focus on Jews in his later works is extremely important for the concerns of this study, since most previous commentators who have associated him with anti-Semitic proclivities have relied on remarks made in writings from this period. Indeed, as we have seen in the first chapter, the fashioning of Nietzsche as an anti-Semite during the Third Reich is not dependent on the falsified letters in Elisabeth's edition or on any statements she made about his relationship with Jews or Judaism. Outside of the early period in the 1870s, when Nietzsche was part of the Wagnerian entourage, evidence for Judeophobia stems almost solely from his observations on morals and on religion in the late 1880s. Heinrich Römer succinctly summarizes the Nazi perspective when he notes that Nietzsche "is the most ruthless revealer of the pernicious role that Judaism played in the intellectual development of Europe, which it played above all as Christianity."[1] And, as we have just seen, even those close to him and disinclined toward virulent anti-Semitism, such as Franz Overbeck, concede that his anti-Christian perspective is founded on anti-Semitism. If we are going to understand Nietzsche's "anti-Semitism," we will have to examine more closely and critically the many passages in which historical Jewry is cited as the basis for modern morality and the life-negating values of Christianity.

THE GENEALOGY OF JEWISH SLAVE MORALITY

Jewry occupies a central position in Nietzsche's ruminations about the origins of our moral values, the topic of the first essay in *The Genealogy of Morals* (1887). In the first six sections of the essay, however, there is no hint of Jews or Judaism. After some cursory remarks about English psychologists and their naive reflections on the history of moral sentiments, Nietzsche outlines the two moral systems that are captured in the title of the essay: "good and evil" and "good and bad." The latter system of values predates the former and is characterized by a notion of "good" that is posited by noble individuals and their actions: "The 'good' themselves—that is, the noble, the powerful, the superior, and the high-minded—were the ones who felt themselves and their actions to be good—that is, as of the first rank—and posited them as such, in contrast to everything low, low-minded, common, and plebeian." The nobility of former times, distanced from the lower classes of society, is the creative source for an aristocratic or master morality. These noble souls are credited with the ability to name, to designate, and to label, and it is they who then call their own actions "good." The label "bad" is the designation for actions of those who stand outside of their circles, those who are subjected to them, their vassals or slaves or serfs. Thus Nietzsche clearly locates the origins of aristocratic morality in a defined social situation: "The pathos of nobility and distance, the enduring, dominating, and fundamental overall feeling of a higher ruling kind in relation to a lower kind, to a 'below'—*that* is the origin of the opposition between 'good' and 'bad'" (GM, Erste Abhandlung 2, KSA 5.259).[2] The aristocratic caste is also defined in vaguely racial terms as Aryan and fair-haired. The reason for the demise of the value system based on good versus bad seems to proceed organically from the constellation of the quasi-historical characters Nietzsche presents. Nietzsche introduces a new and central figure on the mythologized historical stage: the priest, who at first enforces a new dichotomy, pure and impure. The priests appear to form a caste alongside but separate from the noble warriors, and in contrast to the aristocrats by blood, they advocate an antisensual metaphysics, a denial of pleasure and life that would seem to oppose the class out of which they arose. They are ultimately responsible for the value system of good versus evil, but Nietzsche supplies no real explanation for how or why a ruling caste betrays its own peers. He notes only that we can readily understand "how easily the priestly mode of evaluation may diverge from the knightly-aristocratic mode and then develop into its opposite." But he leaves no doubt about his preference for the aristocrats, who exhibit "a powerful physicality, a rich, burgeoning, even overflowing health, as well as all those things which help to preserve it—war, adventure, hunting, dancing, competitive games, and everything that involves strong, free, high-spirited activity." The priests, by contrast, are portrayed as impotent and spiteful, as individuals whose "hatred grows to take on a monstrous and sinister shape" (GM, Erste Abhandlung 7, KSA 5.266–67). They do introduce intelligence into the human species, but the overwhelming impression is that they contribute to the destruction of something glorious and worthwhile.

Nietzsche shifts gears abruptly in section seven, and the Jews are suddenly thrust into this semihistorical narrative. They represent "the most important example" of the morals that overturn aristocratic values:

> Nothing that anyone else has perpetrated against the "noble," the "powerful," the "masters," the "rulers" merits discussion in comparison with the deeds of the Jews—the Jews, that priestly people who ultimately knew no other way of exacting satisfaction from their enemies and conquerors than through a radical transvaluation of their values, through an art of *the most intelligent revenge*. (GM, Erste Abhandlung 7, KSA 5.267)

In this initial mention of the Jews there are three features worth noting. First they are portrayed as aggressively opposing the value system that has subjugated them; Jews are directly antithetical to "aristocratic" social orders that Nietzsche has previously identified with the "master race," with "Aryans," and with blond and fair-haired peoples. This juxtaposition, even if Nietzsche did not intend it to be read as a concession toward anti-Semitic doctrines, resembles the opposition between Jews and Germans that was so prominent in racist propaganda from Richard Wagner to Wilhelm Marr. Second, the Jews are identified closely with intelligence; they extract revenge on their despised enemies through their mental prowess. Here Nietzsche is employing one of the favorite stereotypes of Jews in the modern world as clever and conniving, as well as seeking to gain advantage over the unsuspecting Gentile population through manipulation rather than direct confrontation. Third, Nietzsche changes completely the dynamics that he had established before the introduction of the Jews. While Nietzsche portrays the priests as part of the noble order that takes on an independence from, and then an opposition to, the aristocratic "warriors," the Jews are a people or race that is "priestly" and in which there is no differentiation among "Jewish aristocrats" or between priests and warriors. We are not dealing here with "Jewish priests"; the phrase appears nowhere in the *Genealogy*, although it does gain prominence in discussions in 1888, especially in the posthumously published work *The Antichrist* (1895). Nietzsche is rather referring to Jewry in its entirety or essence as priestly. He continues in this passage from section seven with uncomplimentary remarks about Jews and their reversal of noble values:

> This was only as befitted a priestly people, the people of the most downtrodden priestly vindictiveness. It has been the Jews who have, with terrifying consistency, dared to undertake the reversal of the aristocratic value equation (good = noble = powerful = beautiful = happy = blessed) and have held on to it tenaciously by the teeth of the most unfathomable hatred (the hatred of the powerless). It is they who have declared: "The miserable alone are the good; the poor, the powerless, the low alone are the good. The suffering, the deprived, the sick, the ugly are the only pious ones, the only blessed, for them alone is there salvation. You, on the other hand, the noble and the powerful, you are for all eternity the evil, the cruel, the lascivious, the insatiable, the godless ones. You will be without salvation, accursed and damned to all eternity." (GM, Erste Abhandlung 7, KSA 5.267)

Nietzsche adds between ellipses: "There is no doubt as to *who* inherited this Jewish transvaluation," and readers can easily discern the fundamental premises of Christian doctrine in the Jewish opposition to their masters. Nietzsche's obvious disdain for Christianity in his late writings has led many commentators to believe that his remarks are not infused with Judeophobia because his "real" target lies elsewhere. But this conclusion is odd because Christians are not the originator of the fundamental and deleterious transvaluation; they are merely the vehicle that propagates "Jewish values" in the centuries following the establishment of the church. Without Jews, there would be no Christians. Nietzsche's anti-Christian sentiments, as well as his diatribes against Paul and the official church, which we will have occasion to examine shortly in discussing *The Antichrist*, can more readily be judged as stemming from anti-Jewish stereotypes and prejudices. We should recall that Overbeck understood Nietzsche in this manner, as did many others, not all of whom were proto-National Socialists. Indeed, it is not the Christians who undertook "the monstrous initiative, disastrous beyond all bounds," but the Jews, who have issued, as it were, "the most fundamental of all declarations of war" (GM, Erste Abhandlung 7, KSA 5.267–68). And Nietzsche reminds us proudly that he had noted Jewish responsibility for the demise of aristocratic values in a previous publication, adverting to aphorism 195 in *Beyond Good and Evil*, where he had written "that with the Jews *the slave revolt in morals* begins" (JGB 195, KSA 5,117). This revolt has a history of two millennia, Nietzsche informs us, and the reason today we have lost sight of it is because it has been "victorious" (GM, Erste Abhandlung 7, KSA 5.268). Nietzsche, the opponent of political anti-Semitism in his own era, infuses his text with another motif from his adversaries by proclaiming, as Wagner had done in his "Judaism and Music" and Marr had claimed in his *Victory of Judaism over Germanness* (1879), the ultimate victory of Jewry over peoples closely resembling Germans.

Nietzsche's discussion of Christianity in section eight supplies further evidence that he conceives of the "slave revolt" in morals as primarily an instrument for Jewish domination, and that Christianity is a mere vehicle for this vengeful, decadent, Jewish activity. He begins with two questions to his readers that refer directly to his last assertion in section seven. "But you are finding this hard to follow? You have no eyes for something that took two thousand years to triumph?" We should not be deceived into thinking that Nietzsche's use of the round number "two thousand" means that he is referring to Christianity alone. In the first place, when Nietzsche was writing, the history of Christianity was less than two thousand years old. But more importantly the triumphal phase of Jewish animus against aristocratic morals receives its greatest impetus only in the transition from Judaism to Christianity, and in Christianity's spread across Europe over the centuries. If Nietzsche had wanted to attack primarily Christianity or the Christian tradition and to regard Judaism as a prelude to something more momentous, he could have easily done so. But instead his formulations make it apparent that his principal target is the Jewish heritage:

> all things whose *history stretches out far* behind them are difficult to see, to see in their entirety. But *this* is indeed what happened: from the trunk of that tree of revenge and hatred, Jewish hatred—the deepest and most sublime hatred, that is, the kind of hatred that creates ideals and changes the meaning of values, a hatred the like of which has never been on earth—from this tree grew forth something equally incomparable, *a new love*, the deepest and most sublime of all the kinds of love—and from what other trunk could it have grown? (GM, Erste Abhandlung 8, KSA 5.268)

Nietzsche is providing an explanation for the emergence of Christian love, but it was important for him not to claim that it was a departure from an initial and more fundamental Jewish impulse, as Christian theologians might assert. At the origin of doctrines that appear to contradict Judaism are roots that are identified with Jewish values. While much of the Christian tradition had sought to differentiate itself from its Jewish roots by citing the reversal of values, Nietzsche is at pains to associate the two religions, while always giving primacy and ultimate responsibility to Judaism. It is true that Nietzsche's discussion therefore contradicts the Christian anti-Semitism of his era, which was based on a strict distinction between Christianity and Judaism. But Nietzsche does so only by implicating Jews and Judaism for the degeneracy and mediocrity of the modern world at a more profound level. Nietzsche anticipates the objection that would emanate from Christian advocates:

> But let no one think that it [the new love] somehow grew up as the genuine negation of that thirst for revenge, as the antithesis of Jewish hatred! No, the opposite is the case! Love grew forth from this hatred, as its crown, as its triumphant crown, spreading itself ever wider in the purest brightness and fullness of the sun, as a crown that pursued in the lofted realm of light the goals of hatred—victory, spoils, seduction—driven there by the same impulse with which the roots of that hatred sank down ever further and more lasciviously into everything deep and evil. (GM, Erste Abhandlung 8, KSA 5.268)

Christian values are derivative. Jesus Christ, who embodies the doctrine of love, who promises redemption and salvation, represents "the most sinister and irresistible form of the very same temptation, the indirect temptation to accept those self-same *Jewish* values and new versions of the ideal" (GM, Erste Abhandlung 8, KSA 5.268–69). Christ is thus not the rebel against

Jewish values, the divinity who announces a new religious order, but the continuator of a moral regime that is essentially Jewish, the agent, as it were, of Judaism in the Roman world. Appearances and tradition are deceptive about Christ's role in the ancient world, since they have obscured the part Jewry plays in this historical drama:

> Has Israel not reached the ultimate goal of its sublime vindictiveness through the detour of this very "redeemer," who appeared to oppose and announce the dissolution of Israel? Is it not characteristic of the secret black art of a truly *great* policy of revenge, of a far-sighted, subterranean revenge which unfolds itself slowly and thinks ahead, that Israel itself was obliged to deny the very instrument of this revenge as a mortal enemy and crucify him before the whole world, so that the "whole world," all the opponents of Israel, might unthinkingly bite on just this very bait? And on the other hand, would it be possible, with the most refined ingenuity, to devise a *more dangerous* bait? (GM, Erste Abhandlung 8, KSA 5.269)

Far from undermining Judaism and redressing its shortcomings, Christianity becomes in Nietzsche's presentation a means to further the cause of "Israel" with activities and persons designed to mislead observers and interpreters. "Israel" employs Christ for its own ends, deceiving the world into believing that he opposes his Jewish persecutors. The advent of Christ and of the Christian Church is in reality an invention of Jewish interests bent on extracting revenge on their enemies and ultimately conquering the world under the repressive and life-negating regime of slave morality. It is a dangerous gambit because of the enigma involved with having a God die such a gruesome death for the sake of humankind, out of love for his fellow human beings. But it is under this sign, Nietzsche writes, alluding to Constantine's *"in hoc signo vinces"* ("in this sign you will conquer"), that Jewry celebrates its victory; in this radical reinterpretation of Christian iconography the cross symbolizes, not Christianity and the passion of Christ, but "Israel's revenge and transvaluation of all values" (GM, Erste Abhandlung 8, KSA 5.269), its defeat of all noble ideals.

Although Nietzsche is clear enough about the role of Jews and Judaism in his grand view of adversarial moral systems, commentators have consistently read the *Genealogy* as an indictment of Christianity and downplayed the world-historical mission attributed to Jewry.[3] Some attribute Jewish reaction to the "experience of exile and slavery,"[4] thus making the historical markers more specific, but Nietzsche mentions neither exile nor slavery, but only "enemies" and "conquerors," and he does not offer Jewish experience or history as a causal explanation for Jewish vindictiveness in this essay. Many other scholars who deal with the *Genealogy* ignore the potentially anti-Jewish passages entirely, or mention them only in passing.[5] But scholars concerned with demonstrating Nietzsche's positive relationship to Jews provide explanations that range from asserting Nietzsche's opposition to political anti-Semitism of the Second Empire and Nietzsche's categorization of anti-Semitism as a product of *ressentiment* to providing a tripartite schema in which Nietzsche writes supportively of ancient Hebrews and modern Jews and only criticizes Jews in the postexile period or the time of the Second Temple.[6] There is some evidence for Nietzsche's appreciation of the ancient Hebrews, if we consider, for example, his praise of the Old Testament in aphorism 52 of *Beyond Good and Evil* and the simultaneous belittling of the New Testament and its values (JGB 52, KSA 5.72).[7] And we have already witnessed passages in which Nietzsche expresses admiration for certain attributes of diaspora Jewry. But these observations are isolated and play no real role in Nietzsche's discussions of moral values in 1887 and 1888.[8] Almost all commentators, however, eschew a close and accurate reading of Nietzsche's provocative remarks in sections seven and eight of the *Genealogy*, where Nietzsche is making a claim for the significance of Jewry as the originator and propagator of the most debilitating moral system in human history. Nietzsche had already stated in *Beyond Good and Evil* that the "significance of the Jewish people" was that it inaugurated the slave revolt in morals, but in the *Genealogy*, which was composed specifically to clarify certain claims made in his earlier book, "Israel" is not only the inaugurator, but the clandestine power behind the transvaluation that Nietzsche deplores and that now dominates the modern world. It is difficult to miss the parallels to the anti-Semitic ideologies of Nietzsche's era, which similarly place the Jews in the role of furtive manipulators, taking advantage of honest and guileless Gentiles, and eventually achieving complete hegemony over their adversaries. The writings previously cited by Wagner and Marr are replete with such passages. The difference is that Nietzsche's view of Jewish dominance is more pervasive, more pernicious, and less recognized even by those who are disinclined toward the Jews. It would certainly make sense if Nietzsche's remarks in these sections were directed at a description of Jewry living in a specific historical period, and it would be plausible that this historical period would be associated loosely with the time of the prophets or the Second Temple. As we shall see, Nietzsche presents a slightly more differentiated view of Jewish history in *The Antichrist*, composed the very next year. But in the *Genealogy* these historical markers, which Nietzsche could have easily inserted for clarification, are entirely absent. Christianity is certainly the outgrowth of Judaism, but Nietzsche makes it clear that Christianity is an instrument of Jewish rancor. It is difficult to escape the conclusion that in the *Genealogy* Nietzsche sought to single out Jewry as such for promoting a life-negating, anti-Aryan, antiaristocratic value system that has gained world dominance. There is no textual basis for asserting that Nietzsche is referring to Jewry in one specific period of its historical development and excluding Jewry in other epochs.

As suddenly as Jews appear in the historical mythology of the *Genealogy* to assume responsibility for a degenerative morality, they disappear just as quickly. From section nine through section fifteen there is no further discussion of the Jewish conspiracy to displace noble morals and to impose a value system on the world. But Nietzsche does return to Jewry when he contemplates the long perspective on history and delineates the antagonism that has undergirded the fundamental struggle through the centuries. Nietzsche grants that the conflict may even be conceived as internalized in "higher natures," so that antithetical value systems coexist and fight for supremacy:

> The symbol for this struggle, written in a script that has remained legible throughout the whole of human history up until now, is called "Rome against Judaea, Judaea against Rome"—so far, there has been no greater event than *this* struggle, *this* questioning, *this* mortal enmity and contradiction. Rome felt the Jew to be something like the incarnation of the unnatural, its monstrous opposite, as it were: in Rome, the Jew "*stood convicted* of hatred towards the whole of mankind":[9] rightly, in so far as one is entitled to associate the salvation and future of mankind with the absolute supremacy of the aristocratic values, the Roman values. (GM, Erste Abhandlung 16, KSA 5.286)

In more traditional accounts Christianity is viewed as the adversary to Rome in this battle of value systems, but Nietzsche again indicates, by his use of the word "Judaea," that he is less concerned with Christianity as a continuation and logical conclusion to Jewish values than he is with Judaism as the historical force that manipulates Christianity. His citation from Tacitus provides further evidence for his primary focus on Jewry. In the *Annals*, from which Nietzsche's internal quotation is taken, Tacitus refers specifically to the Christians, not to the Jews, who were tortured by Nero not for their attack on the city of Rome but for their hatred of mankind. Nietzsche surely knew that Tacitus discusses Christians, but since his argument in the *Genealogy* has been that Christians are merely emissaries of Jewish values, his substitution of "Jew" for "Christian" is consonant with his assertion that Jews are the real agents of the new morality. The Jewish response to the Roman disdain for them is reflected in "a thousand signs," but Nietzsche invites the reader to examine *The Apocalypse of Saint John* (*The Book of Revelation*) in which the "deep logic of the Christian instinct" inscribes "this book of hatred with the name of the apostle of love" (GM, Erste Abhandlung 16, KSA 5.286). Again the confounding of Jewish and Christian, as well as the attribution of a book of the New Testament to Jews, reinforces Nietzsche's hypothesis concerning Jewish priority in the introduction and persistence of slave morality.

Nietzsche thus defines the greatest world-historical conflict as one between Romans and Jews, the former because they were "the strong and noble men, stronger and nobler than there had ever been on earth, or even dreamt of." The Jews, for their part, are the archetypal "priestly people of *ressentiment par excellence*," a people known for geniality in matters of slave morals. In case there is any question about who has been victorious in the epic battle of moral systems, Nietzsche informs his reader about the current state of affairs:

> Which of these is in the ascendant at the moment, Rome or Judaea? But there is no room for doubt: consider before whom one bows today in Rome as before the epitome of all the highest values—and not only in Rome, but over almost half the world, wherever man has been tamed or wants to be tamed—before *three Jews*, as one knows, and *one Jewess* (before Jesus of Nazareth, the fisherman Peter, the carpet-maker Paul, and the mother of the aforementioned Jesus, Mary). This is most remarkable: there is no doubt that Rome has been defeated. (GM, Erste Abhandlung 16, KSA 5.286–87)

Nietzsche's characterization of the most notable figures in Christianity as Jews is once again meant to emphasize the consistently Jewish nature of slave morality, and that Jewry, through Christianity, has come to dominate the Western world. The struggle, however, continues, and from time to time in the course of history noble values attempt to reassert themselves only to be thwarted by the Jews.

> Admittedly, during the Renaissance there was a simultaneously glittering and sinister reawakening of the classical ideal, of the noble mode of evaluation; beneath the weight of the new Judaicized Rome, which assumed the appearance of an ecumenical synagogue and called itself the "Church," the old Rome itself moved like someone reawakened from apparent death: but Judaea triumphed again immediately, thanks to a fundamentally plebeian (German and English) movement of *ressentiment*, known as the Reformation, as well as what necessarily arose from it, the restoration of the Church and the restoration also of the old, grave-like peace of classical Rome. (GM, Erste Abhandlung 16, KSA 5.287)

This passage represents a quite remarkable reinterpretation of history as well as a significant revision of Nietzsche's worldview under Wagnerian discipleship. Jewish dominance, interrupted by a resurgence of noble values in the Renaissance, is secured again by a movement that apparently opposes the Catholic Church but in reality (or at least Nietzsche's reality) restores the values of an institution, the Church, that is likened to an "ecumenical synagogue," a place where Jewish values under various religious guises are dispensed to the corners of the earth. The anti-Catholic, as well as the anti-Jewish, tirades of Martin Luther are presumably of the same deceptive character as the early Christian opposition to traditional Judaism; they give the impression of a new departure, of opposition to the old church associated with the Catholics, as well as to the ideals of the even older beliefs of the Jews, but in fact reinforce the slave morality attributed to Jewry. Judaea remains in firm control even as it is subject to disdain and Judeophobic invectives. The reach of Jewry extends even further. Nietzsche alludes to its social dimension when he calls the Reformation a "fundamentally plebian movement of *ressentiment*," but he augments this thought in implicating Jewry in the French Revolution:

> In an even more decisive and profound sense than previously, Judaea triumphed once more over the classical ideal with the French Revolution: the last political nobility in Europe, that of *France* in the seventeenth and eighteenth centuries, collapsed under the instincts of popular *ressentiment*—never before had a greater celebration, a noisier excitement been heard on earth! (GM, Erste Abhandlung 16, KSA 5.287)

Although Napoleon appears "like a last gesture in the *other* direction" (GM, Erste Abhandlung 16, KSA 5.287), there is no doubt that Jewry has reinstated its control over European affairs. We can see that Judaean dominance encompasses much more than a new moral or religious set of values; it entails hegemonic structures in the social and political spheres as well.

We can now understand better why Nietzsche was so dissatisfied with the anti-Semitic political movements of his own era and what his friend Overbeck meant when he maintained that his anti-Christianity was based on anti-Semitism. In Nietzsche's much larger framework anti-Semites of the 1880s were petty and crude ideologues; they partake of the very same *ressentiment* against the Jews that derives from Jewish values. Anti-Semites are similar to the early Christians or to Luther in the Reformation; in opposing Jews, they still remain caught up in moral valuations that are essentially Jewish. In the *Genealogy* Nietzsche makes the case that these instances of opposition are in reality a ploy the Jews designed to secure their supremacy. Anti-Semites are therefore not opposed to the Jews; they are in reality tools of the Jewish spirit that has become pervasive in nineteenth-century Europe. For this reason Nietzsche can equate Jews and anti-Semites, noting only that the former know when they are lying, while the latter, being dupes of the former, are ignorant of their actual status in propagating and reinforcing Jewish values (Nachlass 1888, 21[6], KSA 13.580). Anti-Semites despise modern Jews for their wealth and for their influence over politics and culture. They disdain, in short, the very qualities that demonstrate to Nietzsche that diaspora Jews are exercising a will to power. From the remarks we have examined in previous chapters, we understand that Nietzsche did not want to strip Jews of the qualities that had made them successful in the modern world; instead, he wanted to have these traits bred into a European race that would exercise hegemony over the entire world. Presumably this hegemony would entail something other than the dominance he associates with the current European state of affairs, which is still under the authority of Jewish values of *ressentiment* and life-negating morality. The anti-Semites, therefore, fail to grasp the real power that the Jews represent in world history, as well as the tremendous potential that they harbor in the contemporary world for overcoming the social order of mediocrity and degeneration. In the first essay of the *Genealogy* Nietzsche was thus more consistently and unrelentingly anti-Jewish than his anti-Semitic adversaries. He recognized, of course, that Jewish values were not completely without benefit for humankind. "Human history," he concedes just prior to his introduction of the Jews in section seven, "would be a much too stupid affair were it not for the intelligence introduced by the powerless" (GM, Erste Abhandlung 7, KSA 5.267). And he admires the tenacity of the Jews in contriving a way to survive; they exhibit an "innate genius in matters of popular morality": "one need only compare those people with related gifts, say, the Chinese or the Germans, with the Jews in order to appreciate the difference between first- and fifth-rate" (GM, Erste Abhandlung 16, KSA 5.286). Despite these concessions to the positive dimensions of slave morality and its Jewish propagators, the overall message of the initial essay in the *Genealogy of Morals* is Judeophobic. Rhetorically and substantively Nietzsche makes it clear that the introduction of "good and evil" has been detrimental to almost everything of value. He ultimately postulates an anti-Jewish historical trajectory that resembles anti-Semitic propaganda, but on a grander scale. Jewry displaces and defeats noble morality, associated with Aryans and fair-haired races, substituting for it life-negating and degenerate valuations, and, through deception or direct confrontation, manages well into the nineteenth century to retain its dominance over the peoples it has conquered.

NIETZSCHE'S SOURCES

It is difficult to locate Nietzsche's sources for his grand view of world history. It appears very likely that his hypothesis of Jewish hegemony over
quondam master races, accomplished through the clever insinuation of a
life-negating morality, was his own invention. This theory was probably influenced negatively by anti-Semitic propaganda. Nietzsche was presenting
his own more sophisticated, encompassing, and accurate account of Jewish
power in the modern world. But one pivotal piece of his historical outlook,
the continuity of the Jewish and the Christian tradition, was an issue that
he undoubtedly found in the writings of several contemporaries. Nietzsche
would have been familiar with some of the central theories about Judaism
and early Christianity from his theological background, and we should not
forget that he originally intended to become a Protestant minister like his
father and grandfather. But we should also recall that his closest friend at
the University of Basel was Franz Overbeck, the professor of New Testament
Exegesis and Old Church History, who arrived at the Swiss university one
year after Nietzsche was appointed. In his inaugural address Nietzsche
could have heard his colleague's plea for a broader historical understanding
of early Christianity and noted his depiction of the Apostle Paul and "his
train of thought deeply rooted in the religious ideas of Judaism" as well as
his assertion concerning the failure to appreciate "the profound connection
of Paulus's views with those of the Old Testament and Judaism of his era."[10]
Overbeck was also responsible for introducing Nietzsche to the theological
writings of Paul de Lagarde, in particular to his piece *On the Relationship
of the German State to Theology*, which Overbeck tells Lagarde in a letter
from February 1, 1873, he has shared with his colleague, "the philologist
Nietzsche."[11] We have already encountered Lagarde in previous chapters; in
Nietzsche's letter to the anti-Semitic publisher Theodor Fritsch he ridicules
Lagarde as a "pompous and sentimental crank" (March 23, 1887, Nr. 819,
KSB 8.46). Siegfried Lipiner wrote to Nietzsche that Lagarde had become a
"strong rival in my heart" (April 20, 1878, Nr. 1057, KGB II 6/2.838), and it
is worthwhile noting that during the 1870s Lipiner's judgment of the similarity between Lagarde and Nietzsche would not have been unusual. Both
men were somewhat querulous academics, supportive of Germanness but
skeptical about the trajectory of the Second Reich. Despite his disdain for
Lagarde as an anti-Semitic propagandist in 1887, Nietzsche appears to have
occupied himself with his writings on several occasions during the 1870s
and 1880s, and Richard Reuter reports that Nietzsche had recommended to
him a Lagarde pamphlet in 1876.[12] Nietzsche introduced Lagarde's thought

to Richard Wagner,[13] who recognized that he and Lagarde had similar ideas. And although Wagner and the Wagnerians were at first unsuccessful in attracting Lagarde to active support for their enterprise and for their house journal—it seems Lagarde intensely disliked the "music of the future"—he later became a favorite of the *Bayreuther Blätter*, which devoted an entire memorial issue to him in June 1892.[14]

Important for our concerns in this chapter is that Lagarde was very likely one of the initial sources for Nietzsche's more differentiated view of early Christianity, in particular the divergence between the values of Jesus and Paul. Although Nietzsche's presentation in the *Genealogy* tends to conflate all early Christians, just as it draws no distinction between the early Hebrews and later developments in Judaism, in *The Antichrist*, as we shall see, Nietzsche recasts his views, obviously influenced by several contemporary accounts of this pivotal period in religious and moral history. Lagarde was likely among the writers who impacted Nietzsche's extremely negative view of the Apostle Paul and his deviation from Jesus.[15] In Lagarde's writings from the 1870s Jesus is portrayed as someone who was in fundamental opposition to the dominant Judaism of his times and whose teachings emanate from his practical activities; his "evangelium" is inseparable from his person.[16] Paul, by contrast, had never met Jesus, and was not even acquainted with most of his disciples. He is not called upon by Jesus to spread his gospel; he assumes the task with impertinence. Unlike Jesus, Paul—and by extension the Christian Church—remains obligated to the Jewish traditions of the first century. Paul himself remains a Pharisee even after his dramatic conversion on the road to Damascus. Lagarde comments that although his conversion may have been sincere, he cannot understand why historically educated men have given such weight to his pronouncements: "How does it happen that we have to do with a Church that is built on such a foundation? Misunderstanding, lack of understanding, a hybrid of Pharisaism and fantasticalness are the foundations of a community that wants to harken back to an historical occurrence?" While Jesus broke with the laws of the Jewish religion, Paul brings them into the Christian religion, thus contaminating the message of Christ and distorting his teachings:

> Paulus brought the Old Testament into the Church on whose influence the *evangelium*, as much as this is possible, has been ruined: Paulus has bequeathed to us the pharisaic exegesis, which proves everything from everything, which brings with it in its pocket already finished the content that should be found in the text, and then boasts of merely following the word itself: Paulus brought into the house the Jewish theory of sacrifice and everything connected with it: the whole

> Jewish view ... has been imposed upon us. He did this in active contradiction to
> the original community, which, as Jewish as it was, thought less Jewishly than
> Paulus, and which at least did not consider crafty Israelism to be the *evangelium*
> sent by God.[17]

The assimilation of Paul to Judaism and his separation from Jesus are two
important points that Nietzsche did not consider in the *Genealogy* but that
become a central part of his presentation of early Christianity in *The Antichrist*. His reliance on Lagarde is demonstrated by the very language he se-
lects: Lagarde invented the expression "Judaine" to signify a pure, dogmatic
Judaism opposed by Jesus, but important for Paul. In *The Antichrist* Nietzsche refers to the Bible as "a foul-smelling Judaine of rabbinism and superstition" (AC 56, KSA 6.240), and in notes from 1888 he adverts to the initial
"degeneration of Christianity" as the "impact of Judaine" (Nachlass 1887–88,
11[384], KSA 13. 182).[18] Here we find Nietzsche following the anti-Jewish
interpretation of early Christianity in Lagarde's writings.[19]

More influential than Lagarde for Nietzsche's later writings on religion
and morals was Ernest Renan. One of the most renowned French intellectuals of the second half of the nineteenth century, Renan was most familiar
to Nietzsche from his *Life of Jesus* (1863) and other volumes in the *History
of the Origins of Christianity* (1866–81). Nietzsche had read Renan's works at
a relatively early date. In notebooks written in preparation for his first *Untimely Meditation*, he suggests Renan's biography of Jesus was greater and
more elegant that David Strauß's work on the same topic from 1835 to 1836
(Nachlass 1873, 27[1] and 1874, 34[37], KSA 7.587, 804). The respect he had
for Renan at this point in his development is indicated by his sending the
Wagners the German version of Renan's *Paulus* (1869)[20] along with Overbeck's book on Christian theology and the aforementioned treatise by
Lagarde (to Richard Wagner, April 18, 1873, Nr. 304, KSB 4.145). It is evident that he read Renan again in the mid-1870s in preparation for *Human,
All Too Human*.[21] Most of his preoccupation with Renan, however, occurs in
the 1880s, and his attitude toward the French philologist at that point is
extremely critical. Indeed, one commentator has suggested that Nietzsche's
view of history, at least as it has to do with early Christianity, can be read as
"a critique and parody of Renan's *History of the Origins of Christianity*."[22]
Renan has had a mixed reputation in the history of anti-Jewish thought.[23]
Although he considered Judaism to be an inferior religion in comparison
with Christianity and employed terms later associated with racism, such as
"Semitic" and "Aryan," as descriptors for both linguistic and ethnic entities,
he was not an anti-Semite in the sense in which Germans came to use this

term in the early 1880s. He believed that Semites belonged to the larger linguistic and ethnographical group identified as Indo-European and did not distinguish them physiologically from other peoples associated with the term "Caucasian." Moreover, Renan was concerned that his views not be confused with those of anti-Semites; he spoke of Semites as members of an ethnic group who spoke an ancient language and exhibited certain religious practices, not as a synonym for contemporary Jewry. Thus in the printed version of a talk concerning "Judaism as Race and as Religion" (1883),[24] published at the height of anti-Semitic political agitation in Germany, he states at the outset "it is clear" that "Judaism is a great religion" (2). Like many other religions it originated as a national religion, but with the advent of the prophets it became universal in character and no longer belonged solely to one people; indeed, Isaiah is the "first foundation" of Christianity 725 years before the birth of Jesus (9). The universalization of Judaism meant that the ethnic unity of Judaism gradually disappeared, so that "the word Judaism no longer possesses a great ethnographic signification" (20). Renan is thus at pains to distance himself from contemporary racist theory regarding Jewry:

> Without a doubt Judaism represents in its origins the traditions of a particular race. Without a doubt there was also in the phenomenon of the formation of the actual Israeli race a contribution of primitive Palestinian blood; but at the same time, I am convinced that in the entire Jewish population, as it exists in our times, there is a considerable contribution of non-Semitic blood.... [T]he signification of the word, from the perspective of ethnography, has become highly dubious. (24)

In his many comments on Renan and on anti-Semitism, Nietzsche implicitly recognizes Renan's opposition to anti-Semitism and never associates him with this racist political movement.[25] His interest in the French scholar, especially in his final sane years, appears to have been focused almost exclusively on his portrayal of Jesus and on his work dealing with the origins and early years of Christianity.

Nietzsche's later relationship to Renan is largely one of derisive disagreement with the views and attitudes the French professor of Semitic languages espoused. In Nietzsche's published writings he portrays Renan as a pious and pampered historian of Christianity who possesses no understanding for the psychological profundity of the phenomena he chronicles. In *Beyond Good and Evil* Nietzsche claims that "Renan, in whom some ephemeral religious tension disrupts at every moment the balance of his comfortable and (in the finer sense) voluptuous soul," is unintelligible to harsher, German spirits. After citing a passage from the essay "On the Religious Future of Modern Societies," in which Renan argues that religion is "natural" for human beings,[26] Nietzsche comments: "So *antipodal* to my own ears and habits are these sentences, that when I found them, my first fury had me write alongside them '*la niaiserie religieuse par excellence*'" (JGB 48, KSA 5.69–70). In the *Genealogy of Morals* Nietzsche writes of the "'objective' armchair scholar, a scented little historical hedonist, half-Pope, half-satyr, with his perfume by Renan" (GM, Dritte Abhandlung 26, KSA 5.406). In *Twilight of the Idols* (1889) Nietzsche devotes an aphorism to Renan, who, he avers, unsuccessfully seeks to reconcile aristocracy of the intellect with science and democracy; the result is "an *enervating* spirit," "one fatality more for poor, sick, feeble-willed France" (GD, Streifzüge eines Unzeitgemässen 2, KSA 6.111–12).[27] And in *The Antichrist* the French philologist is dubbed "the buffoon in *psychologicis*" (AC 29, KSA 6.199) for his utter failure to comprehend Jesus and his practice of good tidings. Despite the criticism of Renan as blinded by his own involvement with Catholicism and too naive in his psychological pronouncements to provide cogent insights into the initial period of Christianity, Renan does supply, as we shall see, a schema on which Nietzsche draws for the trajectory of religious history in *The Antichrist*. The notion that we can discern a fundamental break in the Jewish religion as it transitions from a national faith to a universalist doctrine, and that this period corresponds with a definite type of prophecy, forms the basis for Nietzsche's hypothesis of a continuity between Judaism and Christianity.[28] Where Nietzsche differs from his French colleague is in the ultimate constitution of Christianity, which Renan believes represents a marked departure from its Jewish origins: "I persist in thinking," Renan wrote in the article from the *Revue des deux mondes* that Nietzsche cites in *Beyond Good and Evil*, "despite some lively rejoinders, that Christianity is not the continuation of Judaism, but rather a reaction against the dominant spirit of Judaism operating at the heart of Judaism itself." For Renan, Judaism is the "yeast" for the fermentation that is Christianity.[29] For Nietzsche, as he will articulate it in his published and unpublished writings in 1888, Christianity is the fulfillment and logical conclusion of the Jewish spirit.

A final source for Nietzsche's hypotheses on the continuity between Judaism and Christianity—and perhaps the most important writer for his thoughts on religious history in *The Antichrist*—was Julius Wellhausen. Nietzsche purchased Wellhausen's *Prolegomena to the History of Ancient Israel* and his *Sketch of the History of Israel and Judah* in 1883 and 1884, respectively, but it appears that he did not read either text until a few years later. We find excerpts from the former volume in notebooks from early 1888 in preparation for *The Antichrist*, but there is some evidence that Nietzsche began read-

ing Wellhausen in 1887 and perhaps as early as 1886, in which case his acquaintance with him would have predated his composition of *The Genealogy*
and perhaps even sections of *Beyond Good and Evil*.[30] If he did begin his
preoccupation with the writings of the celebrated biblical scholar and orientalist in this earlier period, we find scant manifestation of it in his writings. As we have noted in the discussion of the passages on Jewry in *The
Genealogy*, Nietzsche fails to distinguish any development or change in Judaism over the centuries, relying instead on an essentialist view of "Jewish"
morality and its deleterious ramifications for the ancient world and for contemporary Europe. Only in his writings of 1888, most importantly in *The
Antichrist*, does he introduce a crude periodization of Jewish history, and
although he could have garnered this historical differentiation from Renan,
it appears that he relied primarily on Wellhausen, perhaps because he held
him in higher esteem than the Frenchman. Although today Wellhausen
is known chiefly for the "documentary hypothesis" that postulated four different and independent sources for the Old Testament, his importance for
Nietzsche lay in his portrayal of a bifurcation in Jewish history and in his
claims of a continuity of Jewish traditions in the early centuries of Christianity. The transition in the Jewish religion is described most succinctly as a
development from nationalism to universalism, from a god, Jehovah, who
belonged to one particular nation, to a divinity whose laws were valid for all
human beings. "In earlier times the national state as it had existed under
David was the goal of all wishes," Wellhausen writes. "Now a universal world
empire was erected in the imagination, which was to lift up its head at Jeru-
salem over the ruins of the heathen powers. Prophecy was no longer tied to
history, nor supported by it."[31] Both Wellhausen and Nietzsche view this
history as a decline, although the sense of nobility and grandeur in the Old
Testament is more emphatic in Nietzsche's writings prior to his preoccupation with Wellhausen.[32] For Wellhausen, however, Christianity, although it
proceeds from Judaism and evidences some tendencies of the Jewish religion, is antithetical to the "ethical monotheism" of the Jews. "Self-denial,"
Wellhausen states bluntly, "is the chief demand of the Gospel." And he observes that "the Christians found themselves in a position with regard to the
Roman Empire precisely similar to that which the Jews had occupied with
regard to the Persians; and so they founded, after the Jewish pattern, in the
midst of the state which was foreign and hostile to them and in which they
could not free themselves at home, a religious community as their true fatherland." But while "the Gospel develops hidden impulses of the Old Testament" and therefore a continuity with Judaism, "it is a protest against the
ruling tendency of Judaism." Christianity overcomes Jewish law and rituals.

Jesus "is most distinctly opposed to Judaism in His view of the kingdom of heaven, not as merely the future reward of the worker, but as the present goal of effort, it being the supreme duty of man to help it to realise itself on earth, from the individual outwards."[33] Wellhausen was therefore not any more anti-Jewish or anti-Semitic than Renan; he exhibits respect for Judaism and the Jewish people, but, like most Christian theologians, is convinced that Christianity represents the supersession of superannuated religious practices and dogma.[34]

Just as important as the more encompassing contours of religious history were specific aspects of Jewish experience that Wellhausen discusses and that Nietzsche appropriates in his writings of 1888. Since Wellhausen devoted multiple volumes to Jewish topics, culminating in his *Israeli and Jewish History* in 1894,[35] his accounts are much more detailed and differentiated than Nietzsche's borrowings, which include a few pages of notes, probably composed in early 1888 (11[377], KSA 13.169–74), and some extended passages in *The Antichrist*. Nonetheless, we can detect several important themes that Nietzsche adopted and adapted for his own purposes: (1) Nietzsche had characterized the Jews as a priestly people in the *Genealogy*, but Wellhausen adds a new dimension to his description. Wellhausen demonstrates that priests were not always dominant in Jewish society or in religious practice, but rather that hierocracy was a development that gains strength as Judaism becomes universalist in scope. Priestly influence is not restricted to the postexilic societies; it exists already under the kings. But its most important manifestation occurs when the legal structure, formerly an oral tradition of the Torah, becomes "the Priestly Torah," supported by pure moral suasion. "The priests thus formed a kind of supreme court, which, however, rested on a voluntary recognition of its moral authority, and could not support its decisions by force."[36] Wellhausen also indicates that the ascendancy of the priests in Jewry is correlated with the decline of political autonomy. The greatest changes were "wrought by the destruction of the political existence first of Samaria, then of Judah.... There arose a material, external antithesis of a sacred and a profane; men's minds came to be full of this, and it was their great endeavor to draw the line as sharply as possible and to repress the natural sphere more and more." In this historical situation the "Priestly Code" comes to predominate.[37] (2) A second important feature Wellhausen discusses in connection with the transition in Jewish belief is the denaturalization of religion and religious practices. Jehovah was originally a "natural," as well as a national, divinity, associated with the cycle of seasons and relating directly to his chosen people. Under more priestly and universalist circumstances, however, he cedes his connections to nature, and the bond between him and the nation is altered considerably. Wellhausen summarizes this change as follows:

> The relation of Jehovah to Israel was in its nature and origin a natural one; there was no interval between Him and His people to call for thought or question. Only when the existence of Israel had come to be threatened by the Syrians and Assyrians, did such prophets as Elijah and Amos raise the Deity high above the people, sever the natural bond between them, and put in its place a relation depending on conditions, conditions of a moral character. To them Jehovah was the God of righteousness in the first place, and the God of Israel in the second place, and even that only so far as Israel came up to the righteous demands which in His grace He had revealed to him.[38]

As the Jewish religion proceeds toward universalism, the natural bond, which Wellhausen likens to a relation "of son to father" is severed;[39] and although the prophets did not intend to introduce a new notion of divinity, "they none the less were the founders of what has been called 'ethical monotheism.'"[40] (3) In this transition from natural god to universalist divinity, therefore, we find Wellhausen emphasizing the drastically altered character of Jehovah. He points out on numerous occasions that Jehovah was originally conceived as a helper: "'God' was equivalent to 'helper'; that was the meaning of the word. 'Help,' assistance in all occasions of life."[41] But the new conception of god produced moral mandates for his people[42] and was concerned with such matters as sin, salvation, and redemption. "The centre of gravity of the cultus was ... transferred," Wellhausen observes, "to another field, that of morality. The consequence was that sacrifices and gifts gave way to ascetic exercises, which were more strictly and more simply connected with morality." And the results "led by the straightest road towards the theocratic ideal of holiness and of universal priesthood."[43] This account therefore accords well with Nietzsche's presentation of the rise of "slave morality" in the *Genealogy*, although we should recall that in that text from 1887 Nietzsche never presents Jewish history as progressing in stages or transitioning from an older, noble form of worship to a religion concerned with morality and dominated by priestly, ascetic ideals. The impact of Wellhausen's theories on Jewish history appears to manifest itself only in 1888, when Nietzsche focuses on how Judaism came to exert hegemony over Europe through Christianity.

JEWISH HISTORY IN *THE ANTICHRIST*

Nietzsche uses his sources in an unusual fashion. We can be quite certain that he read Lagarde, Renan, and Wellhausen, and it is likely that each of them, along with Overbeck and several other writers, including Tolstoy and Dostoevsky, influenced his views on either the history of the Jewish people or early Christianity and its psychological constitution. But he includes direct mention of the sources of his ideas on these matters very rarely in his writings—although references appear with somewhat more frequency in his notebooks and correspondence. Moreover, when Nietzsche does mention a source in his published volumes, it is usually a person of considerable renown, and frequently someone with whom Nietzsche disagrees. Thus although Nietzsche surely drew as much from Wellhausen as he did from Renan for his theoretical reflections in 1888, Wellhausen's name appears only in the notebooks, where Nietzsche excerpts extensively from the *Prolegomena*, while he mentions Renan a number of times in *Twilight of the Idols* and *The Antichrist*, usually as an object of contempt. In the latter work, for example, on the occasion of the first specific reference to Jewish history, Nietzsche writes that "one will understand without further indication at what moment of history the dual fiction of a good and an evil God first becomes possible." He had already hinted at the answer to this implicit question in the first sentence of section seventeen, when he referred to the decline in the will to power accompanying a "physiological regression, a *décadence*." Now, however, he supplies a more specific historical referent: "How can one today still defer so far to the simplicity of Christian theologians as to join them in proclaiming that the evolution of the concept of God from 'God of Israel,' the national God, to the Christian God, the epitome of everything good, is an *advance*?" The transition Nietzsche describes is a prominent feature, as we have seen, in both Renan and Wellhausen, when the natural and national bond between Jehovah and his chosen people is severed and universalism begins to take hold of Jewish belief. Although it may be true that Wellhausen considered this modification in the religion of the Jews to be a decline, both he and Renan do not consider the advent of Christianity to be anything but an "advance" over Judaism. Nietzsche, however, chooses to attack only Renan for his "simplicity" (AC 17, KSA 6.183–84). We can probably assume that Nietzsche selected the Frenchman because Wellhausen was too academic and had little exposure outside of scholarly circles, while Renan had acquired a European reputation. Nietzsche inclines toward promulgating the image that he is engaged in debates with the most eminent European intellectuals, not simply with German university professors. Finally, we should note that Nietzsche's sources often serve more as confirmation or inspiration for Nietzsche's own ideas than as material with their own validity and integrity. Nietzsche deviates from the accounts of both Renan and Wellhausen in developing the notion of the "good God," which seems to be his own invention; he conflates in his sketchy narrative the prophetic and the priestly contributions to Jewish history; he simplifies the vast amount of material from the sources discussed above to schemas that serve his notion of psychological correctness. In this regard Nietzsche was not "faithful" to his sources; they provide a framework that he feels free to alter when it suits him and that either confirms his insights into human psychology or serves as a straw man for his anti-Judeo-Christian polemics.

Nietzsche's readings in Jewish history and early Christianity in the second half of the 1880s did not produce any remarkable change in his attitude toward Jewry during the last year of his sane life. We have seen that Renan and Wellhausen have occasionally been accused of anti-Jewish proclivities, but that these accusations are based almost entirely on their preference for Christianity over Judaism, which they consider to some degree an outmoded system of belief. Lagarde was a bona fide anti-Semite, of course, but by 1887 we know that Nietzsche considered him little more than a "pompous and sentimental crank" (to Theodor Fritsch, March 23, 1887, Nr. 819, KSB 8.46). The differentiated notion of Jewry and its lengthy complicated history left no apparent marks in Nietzsche's attitudes. *Twilight of the Idols* is a case in point. In the section dealing with Socrates, Nietzsche has recourse to the stereotype of Jews as using argumentation and dialectical methods only because they lack the power to assert themselves without their mental faculties. "Dialectics can be only a *last-ditch weapon* in the hands of those who have no other weapon left. One must have to *enforce* one's rights: otherwise one makes no use of it. That is why the Jews were dialecticians" (GD, Das Problem des Sokrates 6, KSA 6.70). A few pages later, anticipating one of the main themes in *The Antichrist*, Nietzsche remarks on the place of Judaism in the epic struggle among value systems: "Christianity, growing from Jewish roots and comprehensible only as a product of this soil, represents the *reaction* against that morality of breeding, of race, of privilege—it is the *anti-Aryan* religion *par excellence*" (GD, Die "Verbesserer" der Menschheit 4, KSA 6.101). Here we observe that Nietzsche revives the opposition he had championed in *The Birth of Tragedy*, where he contrasted the Semitic and the Aryan myths concerning disobedience of the divinity. Christianity takes the lead in this discussion, but as in the *Genealogy*, it is conceived as an outgrowth of a more fundamental Jewish tendency, which are its roots. Toward the end of the volume Nietzsche writes abstractly about philosophers infusing their writings with their emotion, including love. He adds: "A woman who loves sacrifices her honor; a man of knowledge who loves sacrifices perhaps his humanity; a god who loved became a Jew" (GD, Streifzüge eines Unzeitgemässen 46, KSA 6.148). Nietzsche again adverts to the historic change in Jewish belief that we found in section seventeen of *The Antichrist*. But surely it is significant that the word "Jew" occupies a position parallel to the loss of honor and the sacrifice of humanity in Nietzsche's rhetorical observation. Finally, in returning to observations on Greek culture in the final section of *Twilight of the Idols*, Nietzsche remarks on Plato, whom he associates with the "higher swindle" of idealism, that he learned philosophically from the Egyptians, but he adds parenthetically "(—or with the Jews in Egypt?)," thus suggesting that Jews were not only at the "root" of Christianity, but also of Platonic thought (GD Was ich den Alten verdanke 2, KSA 6.156). In Nietzsche's late works, Plato, we should observe, had come to occupy a position in philosophical history analogous to Paul in religious history; he is the illicit, dogmatic systematizer and falsifier of the practice of Socrates and participates in the demise of master morality. Jews are again placed at the foundation of the most pernicious trends in Western history; they are dishonorable, antihumanitarian, anti-Aryan elements who contribute mightily to the revaluation of noble value systems.

The Jewish presence in *The Antichrist* contains some nuances that Nietzsche derives from his various sources, but in essence he reinforces the tendencies found in the *Genealogy* and *Twilight of the Idols*. Sections twenty-four through twenty-eight contain the main material pertaining to Jewish history and its foundational position for the development of Christianity. To this point in the text Nietzsche has been exploring the reasons for decadence and antinaturalness in modern life. Christianity is marked as the chief cause of the miserable state of humankind in contemporary Europe, but section twenty-four makes clear for the reader that Christianity is only the derivative of a more original "Jewish instinct"; indeed, Christianity "is *not* a counter-movement against the Jewish instinct, it is actually its logical consequence, one further conclusion of its fear-inspiring logic."[44] He continues with a discussion that contains apparent—or perhaps reluctant—admiration for ancient Jewry; they were faced, Nietzsche claims with an existential crisis, threatened with extinction, and chose the only viable means for survival. The price the Jews paid for their survival was extremely detrimental for them and for the modern world. It entailed:

the radical *falsification* of all nature, all naturalness, all reality, the entire inner world as well as the outer. They defined themselves *counter* to all those conditions under which a nation was previously able to live, was *permitted* to live; they made of themselves an antithesis to *natural* conditions—they inverted religion, religious worship, morality, history, psychology one after the other in an irreparable way into the *contradiction of their natural values*. (AC 24, KSA 6.191–92)

Almost all of these claims have their source in Wellhausen; some may have been borrowings from other writers as well. The notion that the Jews chose survival "at any price" may have multiple origins in literature familiar to Nietzsche, but it is noteworthy that the indestructible nature of Jewry, its perseverance in the face of extreme hardships and hostility, is also an integral part of anti-Semitic discourse about Jewry in the 1880s.[45] The departure from norms associated with national religious practices was emphasized in both Renan and Wellhausen, and Nietzsche had broached this topic already in section sixteen, where gods may either be "national" and an embodiment of the will to power or else a sign of impotence, in which case they metamorphose into "good" gods (AC 16, KSA 6.183). The notion of a transformation of values in opposition to nature and naturalness is directly derived from passages in Wellhausen, but Wellhausen appears to mean something quite different when he speaks of "nature"; the departure from nature for him implies a shift from what is natural for the relationship between a people and their divinity, while for Nietzsche this transformation in the godhead is clearly connected with a perversion of natural life. Nietzsche is primarily concerned with the introduction of life-negating values and a degenerate system of morality when he introduces the concept of a god who inverts nature; Wellhausen's focus is the "natural" or traditional or customary religious circumstances of ancient peoples.

There is a further twist in Nietzsche's narrative of ancient Judaism, remarkable because it appears in none of his known sources, but revealing for his attitude toward Jews and the connection with anti-Jewish thought of his era. We will recall that in the *Genealogy* the Jews as a people were considered responsible for the introduction of slave morality; Christianity was merely a continuation or tool of original Jewish impulses, and Nietzsche repeats this theme in *The Antichrist* in calling the Christian church "only a copy" of Jewish values "in unutterably vaster proportions"; Nietzsche does not make it clear whether the "vaster proportions" of which he speaks pertain to the violation of naturalness or simply to the larger reach of the Christian religion in comparison with the essentially local influence of Judaism. He leaves no doubt, however, that this revaluation makes the Jews "the most *fateful* nation in world history." Indeed, their impact has been so pervasive that today's Christians do not even recognize they are participating in an original Jewish transvaluation when they "feel anti-Jewish." Nietzsche himself makes reference to his thesis from the *Genealogy* and cites again the antithetical value systems of *"noble* morality" and *"ressentiment* morality." But in the *Genealogy* we have the impression that the Jews embraced the value system they introduced, propagating it with sincerity and conviction. In *The Antichrist* the Jews are likewise considered the proponents of slave morality, but they employ it deviously in the service of self-preservation. Nietzsche appears to compliment Jewry when he calls the Jewish nation "a nation of the toughest vital energy." But when faced with "impossible circumstances," the Jews channel this vital energy into a herd morality to which they do not themselves subscribe. The Jews, in short, are duplicitous in opposing master morality; they act out of "the profoundest shrewdness in self-preservation." Jewry endorses *"décadence* instincts," but it does so *"not* as being dominated by them but because it divined in them a power by means of which one can prevail *against* 'the world.'" In *The Antichrist* the slave morality of the *Genealogy* becomes just another mechanism by which Jews assure their own survival and their dominance over the rest of humankind: "The Jews are the counterparts of all *décadents*: they have been compelled to *act as decadents* to the point of illusion, they have known, with a *non plus ultra* of histrionic genius, how to place themselves at the head of all *décadence* movements (—as the Christianity of *Paul*—) so as to make of them something stronger than any party *affirmative* of life" (AC 24, KSA 6.192–93). *Décadence* is for them "only a *means*" to attain and maintain power, whether it be through Judaism or its "imitator" Christianity. To secure their own survival and enhance their power, the Jews have perverted all noble values and set humankind on the path toward sickness. The strength of Judaism, its "vital energy," as well as the "shrewdness" of the Jewish people translates into enslavement in a morality of *ressentiment* and self-abnegation for the entire Christianized world.

This passage is quite remarkable. Although it has frequently been regarded as a validation of Jewry, or at most, a condemnation of only a specific period of Jewish history—the postexilic years in which the religion was transformed from a national to a universal religion—it is actually quite consonant with a larger anti-Jewish sentiment that is foundational for Nietzsche's later thought.

(1) Nietzsche's primary target in this volume is undoubtedly Christianity; the very title of the book, which can mean both "the Antichrist"

and "the anti-Christian," clearly identifies the adversary in Nietzsche's polemic, as does the subtitle: "A Curse on Christianity." But Nietzsche consistently reminds his reader that Christianity, as the religion of the sick, the feeble, and the ill constituted, is the continuation and copy of an original Jewish impulse or instinct. Perhaps the most important individual in the early Christian era and the author of over half the books of the New Testament, the apostle Paul is frequently considered a Jew by Nietzsche; his advocacy for Jesus as the son of God and his conversion from Judaism to Christianity are unimportant for Nietzsche, since Paul, more than Jesus himself, represents the continuity between the Jewish antinatural tradition and its widespread dissemination in Christianity. Nietzsche's association between Paul and the Jews can be found early in the 1880s, for example, in *The Gay Science*, where they are contrasted with the Greeks in their consideration of passions (FW 3, 189, KSA 3.488–89), and it continues through Nietzsche's final works, where, as in the passage just cited, the Jews are regarded as the driving force behind "Paul's Christianity." The Christian religion may be the current enemy of everything Nietzsche deems noble and worthwhile, but it is merely the bearer of a more original and pernicious Jewish tendency. As Overbeck correctly noted in his discussion of Nietzsche's "anti-Semitism," his anti-Christian attitude is based on anti-Jewish thought.

(2) In the language that Nietzsche employs in section twenty-four to characterize the Jews and Judaism he resorts to notions that closely resemble the stereotypical character traits associated with Jews by the anti-Semitic movement of his era. The Jews are a people seeking to preserve itself at any price; they are not concerned with the welfare of their adopted nations or with the fate of humankind, but only with their own egotistical interests. They are physically inferior and unable to survive on the basis of somatic attributes, but they use their overdeveloped mental acuity, their cleverness and shrewdness, to devise a path for their own salvation. Their plan is inherently dishonest; they are hypocritical and do not believe the values they espouse and promote among an innocent and gullible populace. They are therefore a paradigm for deceit and duplicity in their dealings with others. If we comb the anti-Semitic tracts and periodicals written during the early 1880s, these features would fit seamlessly with those of European Judeophobes. While Nietzsche does show admiration for Jewish tenacity and a recognition of the historical difficulties the Jewish nation faced, his description of Jewish actions and attributes is frequently proximate to the anti-Semites he disdains.

(3) This passage confirms and intensifies anti-Jewish sentiments we have identified in earlier utterances. In his years as a Wagnerian acolyte

Nietzsche had become convinced by his mentor's paranoid world-view that Jewry wielded tremendous power. Here he recognizes that this power derives not just from their positions in the journalistic, financial, and cultural sphere, but from their more pervasive and malevolent propagation of the will to power as life negation, which ultimately forms the foundation for their hegemony in contemporary Europe. His explanation of the domination achieved by the Jewish instinct also reaffirms his opposition to the anti-Semitism of his era. As he makes clear in section twenty-four and later in section fifty-five (AC 55, KSA 6.238), the anti-Semites have adopted Jewish values. Their hatred for the Jews is narrow and petty; it takes superficial features, such as Jewish finance, and misses the real power Jewish interests exercise: the power stemming from the reversal of noble values. Anti-Semitism occupies a space within Jewish values; Nietzsche's anti-Judaism is more encompassing and contains more far-reaching implications for humankind.

The continuation of the discussion of Jewish history in sections twenty-five through twenty-seven indicates how Nietzsche used Wellhausen as a source but biased his presentation of the material to emphasize concerns sometimes very different from those of the biblical scholar. His description of the "*denaturalizing* of natural values" draws heavily on passages from Wellhausen. Israel's relationship to its divinity during the period of the Kingdom was "*correct*" and natural; it follows the logic of national self-affirmation. Even the "anarchy within" and "the Assyrians from without" did not alter the values associated with the Kingdom. But when God could no longer supply his people with the required assistance, his nature changed: "One altered the conception of him: at this price one retained him. Yaweh the God of 'justice'—*no longer* at one with Israel, an expression of national self-confidence: now only a God bound by conditions." The new priestly regime introduces sin as the cause of misfortune and develops an antinatural (in Nietzsche's sense of the word) system of values: "*Morality* [is] no longer the expression of the conditions under which a nation lives and grows, no longer a nation's deepest instinct of life, but become[s] abstract, become[s] the antithesis of life" (AC 25, KSA 6.193–94). Nietzsche summarizes Wellhausen in section twenty-five, simplifying a more complex narration of the interplay of prophets and priests, and emphasizing more than his source the role of morality as a life-negating force, which was a marginal concern for Wellhausen. Returning to his selective recapitulation of Wellhausen in section twenty-six, Nietzsche provides a version of Wellhausen's philological hypothesis concerning the composition of the Old Testament. Wellhausen was part of a nineteenth-century tradition of historical criticism of the Bible that disputed the authorship and unity of the Old Testament. Although he was not the originator of the contention that various authors composed different sections of the Old Testament, as we have seen, he became the most important authority for the "Grafian" or "developmental" hypothesis.[46] An important aspect of this hypothesis is that several sections of the Old Testament were written later and projected backward, lending these sections the appearance that they had been part of a more original Judaism. While Wellhausen provides an explanation for this procedure that considers historical circumstances, Nietzsche's "translation" of Wellhausen contains the direct accusation of the falsification and rewriting of history to serve the interests of a priestly regime. Nietzsche follows the general framework of the developmental hypothesis but distorts the careful historical account Wellhausen provided to portray Judaism of the postexilic period as manipulative and dishonest. For Nietzsche the notion of later authorship becomes the "most shameful act of historical falsification," which propagates "the *lie* of a 'moral world-order'" "with cold-blooded cynicism." Responsible for this situation is the priest, "a parasitic kind of human being who prospers only at the expense of every healthy form of life": "every natural custom, every natural institution … every requirement presented by the instinct for life, in short everything valuable *in itself*, becomes utterly valueless, *inimical* to value through the parasitism of the priest" (AC 26, KSA 6.194–97). While the change from a "natural" religion to one focused on morality can be found in Wellhausen, the sole ascription of this change to the "priest" and the enormity of the violation of historical fact are Nietzschean elaborations. Particularly troubling is Nietzsche's repeated accusation of priestly "parasitism," found nowhere in his source, especially since the notion of the Jew as a parasite is a recurring motif in the anti-Semitic literature of the era. The initial passages in section twenty-seven also exhibit anti-Jewish sentiments, here in connection with the advent of Christianity. Nietzsche emphasizes that Christianity could only arise "on a soil *falsified* in this way, where all nature, all natural value, all *reality* had the profoundest instincts of the ruling class against it." We will recall that Wellhausen admitted some continuity between Christianity and Judaism, but in Nietzsche's presentation the former is merely an intensification of the latter. It negates "the last remaining form of reality, the 'holy people,' the 'chosen people,' the *Jewish* reality itself," but it does so paradoxically "*once more*" in accord with the "Jewish instinct," "the priestly instinct" (AC 27, KSA 6.197). Wellhausen's text serves as the basis for these remarks, in particular Nietzsche's contention that "Christianity *negates* the Church"—by which he means "the Jewish Church"—

but the scholar's careful exposition contrasts sharply with the philosopher's polemic tirade. Wellhausen was indeed the most important source for Nietzsche's expanded remarks on Jewish history, but everywhere the appropriation in *The Antichrist* injects into the historiographical account a heavy dose of anti-Jewish sentiment.

Some scholars have sought to excuse Nietzsche's anti-Jewish supplements by recalling that his chief target in *The Antichrist* is Christianity. Insisting that Nietzsche's anti-Jewish statements are aimed solely at the Jews of a particular historical period associated with the Second Temple, they often cite aphorism 52 in *Beyond Good and Evil*, where Nietzsche extols the "grand style" of the Old Testament, even in comparison to Greek and Indian writing, and comments on the "fear and awe" we experience in the presence of "these tremendous remnants of what man used to be" (JGB 52, KSA 5.72). They point also to Nietzsche's various positive remarks about modern Jewry as part of Europe's future, which are consonant as well with the views expressed in *The Antichrist* regarding Jewish tenacity in the face of adversity. From this evidence they conclude that Nietzsche admired the ancient tribes of Israel and the Jews of the modern diaspora scattered across the globe.[47] But in *The Antichrist* Nietzsche has obviously assumed a slightly different view regarding the Old Testament. The passage in *Beyond Good and Evil* appears to predate his acquaintance with Wellhausen; at the very least there are no positive evaluations of the ancient Hebrews in the later text, where the Old Testament is considered a falsification perpetrated by Jewish priests, and Christianity becomes the heir to the pernicious value system of the Jews and their laws. At most we can discern a contrast between the age of a natural religion with its rites and rituals and the universalist religion dominated by a slave morality, but Nietzsche describes very little of the original state of affairs, which is apt to impress his contemporary reader as merely primitive and traditional. In the same vein there are no noteworthy complimentary passages regarding modern Jewry, such as we found in *Dawn*. One of the only references to Jews of the diaspora occurs in section forty-six, which offers a startling comparison: "One would no more choose to associate with 'first Christians' than one would with Polish Jews: not that one would need to prove so much as a single point against them.... Neither of them smell very pleasant" (AC 46, KSA 6.223). We encountered this passage earlier, commenting that it could be an oblique reference to Siegfried Lipiner, but that in any case it underscores that Nietzsche, like many of the anti-Semites (and some Jews) of his era, harbored disdain for Eastern European Jewry. Its significance in *The Antichrist* is threefold: (1) It reinforces the indissoluble bond between Jews and Christians in earlier sections of the text; (2) it relativizes earlier statements that appear to commend the Jewish people, calling into question these apparently positive valuations; and (3) it indicates that Nietzsche's regard for diaspora Jewry was at the very least not uniformly laudatory; he may have admired some segments of modern German, or perhaps even Western European Jews and viewed them as suitable genetic material for a master race in Europe. But as in other passages from his late writings pertaining to Jews, as well as in his correspondence, Nietzsche retains many of the prejudices he had acquired in the 1860s and 1870s well into the final years of his sane existence. His extensive readings in the history of Judaism apparently did not lead to any wholesale "transvaluation" of these anti-Jewish values.

THE TRADITION OF MANU AND THE ORIGIN OF THE JEWS

The sources Nietzsche used for most of his discussions of ancient Jewry were standard works whose authors were recognized scholars in their respective disciplines. Nietzsche was not always careful to choose reputable sources, however, when he was exploring the history of ancient civilizations and religions. In 1888 we encounter one further and extremely revealing instance of Nietzsche's complex relationship to the anti-Semitic tendencies of his era based on a highly questionable source. It involves a translation with footnotes, one whose validity he appears not to have questioned and to have adopted wholesale, even though its negligible scholarly worth was known even when Nietzsche consulted it. In *The Antichrist* and in the chapter "The 'Improvers' of Mankind" in *Twilight of the Idols*, as well as in his notebooks from 1888, Nietzsche mentions with much fascination and approval an Indian book, "The Law of Manu," contrasting it favorably to the Christian Bible. Nietzsche is referring to *Manu-smriti*, or, more officially, *Manava-dharma-shastra*, which may be translated in English more literally as "The Tradition or Institutions of Manu." Written in Sanskrit, "The Tradition of Manu," is one of the most authoritative of the books in the Hindu code (*Dharmashastra*). Although the work that comes down to us was probably composed between the first century BC and the first century AD, the original texts on which it is based likely extend back into the fifth or sixth century BC. Nietzsche uses the German title "Gesetzbuch," which has led his translators to render it the "Law of Manu" or "Law Book of Manu." But the actual text is less a legal code in the strict sense of the word than a treatise that describes customs, traditions, or behavior. In short, it is a work of what we might call practical morality, and it is precisely the contrast with

196 • Chapter Six

Judeo-Christian morality that occasioned Nietzsche's interest in it and ultimately his admiration for it. The "Tradition of Manu" prescribes to the
Hindu believer his *dharma*, or set of obligations as a member of a certain
caste (*varna*) and at a certain stage of life (*asramas*). Composed in verse form
and consisting of twelve chapters with 2,694 stanzas, the work ranges over a
wide variety of subjects, not distinguishing between what we would today
classify as secular and religious spheres. Among the topics it discusses are
dietary restrictions, marriage, donations, rites, the soul, and hell. Its actual
author is unknown, but authorship has been attributed to the mythologi-
cal figure Manu, who is an amalgamation of both Adam and Noah in the
Indian heritage. This attribution of authorship bestows on the code an authority that is immense, and in fact the document possesses tremendous
importance in the Hindu tradition.[48]

There were several publications of "The Tradition of Manu" in French
and German that would have provided Nietzsche with a reliable rendition
of the Sanskrit original.[49] Nietzsche, however, used a version translated and
annotated by Louis Jacolliot in 1876 under the title *Les législateurs religieux:
Manou, Moïse, Mahomet*,[50] a copy of which is found in his library. Although
it is possible that Nietzsche selected this edition because, in contrast to the
others available to him, it contained more extensive annotation,[51] it seems
just as likely that the book fell into his hands serendipitously. We may
consider it unfortunate that Nietzsche came across a version that contains
so many inaccuracies and dubious commentaries, but, as we have seen in
Nietzsche's use of bona fide source material, his major concern was not necessarily scholarly precision but rather how books he consulted either confirmed or contradicted positions he believed were justified psychologically
and genealogically. In dealing with a volume translated by Jacolliot, he was
encountering a writer who was unabashed in inventing and inserting material found nowhere in authentic texts and in providing footnotes that were
often pure fabrications rather than documentation. Jacolliot is a rather shad-
owy figure in French letters of the late nineteenth century. He was born in
Charolles in 1837, but we know little about his youth. He studied law, receiving his diploma toward the end of 1861, and worked in this profession
in France from 1862 to 1865, but his interest in foreign climes led him to
seek and obtain the post of deputy judge in Pondicherry in southern India.
He arrived in December 1865 and left on October 15, 1867, coincidentally
the date of Nietzsche's twenty-third birthday. He resided for an additional
four months in the French colony Chandernagor; thus the total amount of
time he lived on the Indian subcontinent amounted to only a little over two
years. Thereafter he spent a few years in Tahiti before returning to France,

where he participated in intellectual life with various contributions, including a lecture on whether the ancient Jews believed in the immortality of the soul. The remainder of his life—he died in 1890—appears to have been devoted to writing and occasional lecturing. He published his initial book on India in 1868, *The Bible in India*, the first of many volumes dealing with comparative religion. Jacolliot was a prolific writer, composing more than fifty books over a period of two decades, but his scholarly works have long been revealed as unreliable; he aimed at a popular audience and never achieved any acceptance in the academic realm.[52] Among his publications we find sixteen volumes devoted to India, eighteen travel books, and seventeen novels. In the writings on India, Jacolliot emphasizes the importance of India as the cradle of multiple civilizations, which were in his view merely imitators of Brahminism, and that the authentic texts in the Indian tradition are located in South India, where he spent most of his time, since these texts were undistorted by invasions experienced in northern provinces. Indeed, Jacolliot would have us believe that his edition of "The Law Book of Manu" is more authentic than other versions because he was able to collect unadulterated source materials during his time in Pondicherry.[53] There are no reputable scholars today who accept this claim.

Nietzsche was oblivious to the defects in Jacolliot's translation and commentary. Fascinated by his discovery of an alternative moral system to the Judeo-Christian heritage, Nietzsche cites it frequently during the last few months before his breakdown. Although in most instances he praises the ancient Indian code, Nietzsche also offers mild criticism of it in some of his notes (Nachlass 1888, 14[203] and 15[45], KSA 13.385, 439). His criticism stems from its status as a sacerdotal moral system, which, although perhaps superior in its overall social vision to Judeo-Christian morality, still operates with the priestly vocabulary of sin, punishment, and redemption. It is therefore called "a school of stultification" based on "the holy lie" of being able to "improve" humankind by obeying the dictates of priests.[54] But Nietzsche is obviously impressed with the way in which Manu deals with topics that can be found in Judeo-Christian morality, and nowhere do his reservations in the notebooks become part of his published writings. From his correspondence it appears that Nietzsche first discovered the work in May 1888. Writing to Heinrich Köselitz, Nietzsche describes in glowing terms his initial impressions of this Sanskrit text and its importance for him:

> The last few weeks have provided me an essential *education*: I found the Law Book of *Manu* in a French translation that was done in India under the strict supervision of the most eminent priests and scholars. This absolutely *Aryan*

product, a priestly codex of morality based on the Vedas, the idea of caste, and very ancient tradition—*not* pessimistic, albeit very sacerdotal—expands my views about religion in the most remarkable fashion. I freely confess that everything else that we possess about great moral legislation appears to me to be an imitation and even a caricature of this book: above all Egyptianism; but even Plato appears to me in all his main points to be simply well educated by a Brahmin. The Jews appear to be a chandala race that learned from their *masters* the principles according to which a *priestly caste* becomes master and organizes a people.... The Chinese also appear to have produced their Confucius and Lao-Tse under the influence of this *ancient classical law book*. Medieval organization seems like a strange and halting attempt to regain the notions that formed the basis of the ancient Indian-Aryan society—but with pessimistic values that have their origin in the soil of race *décadence*.—Here too the Jews appear to be merely "mediators"— they invent nothing. (Nr. 1041, KSB 8.325)

We note in the first instance that Nietzsche has adopted Jacolliot's preposterous contention concerning the Indian origins of all other civilized moralities. This uncritical reading characterizes his general interaction with this text. But there are two items that attracted particular interest from Nietzsche, and both have relevance for his views on the Jewish Question: the hierarchical structuring of society and the chandala caste. The description of four castes, which Nietzsche takes to be different races that are to breed simultaneously—the priest (*Brahmana*), the warrior (*Ksatriya*), the farmer and merchant (*Vaisya*), and the servant (*Sudra*)—served as a confirmation of the type of social ordering that Nietzsche felt was natural and just.[55] In *Twilight of the Idols* in the section "The 'Improvers' of Mankind," he expresses wholehearted approval for the attempt to distinguish, maintain, and even propagate classes of people by social function:

> Here the task set is to breed no less than four races at once: one priestly, one warlike, one for trade and agriculture, and finally a race of servants, the Sudras. Obviously, we are here no longer among animal tamers: a kind of man that is a hundred times milder and more reasonable is the condition for even conceiving such a plan of breeding. One heaves a sigh of relief at leaving the Christian atmosphere of disease and dungeons for this healthier, higher, and wider world. How wretched is the New Testament compared to Manu, how foul it smells! (GD, Die "Verbesserer" der Menschheit 3, KSA 6.100)

In *The Antichrist* Nietzsche again introduces Manu as a foil to the Bible and the Judeo-Christian heritage. In the Western tradition he finds only "bad ends": "poisoning, slandering, negation of life, contempt for the body, the degradation and self-violation of man through the concept of sin." The Hindu tradition is a welcome relief for him. "It is with an opposite feeling that I read the Law Book of Manu, an incomparably spiritual and superior work: even to mention it in the same breath with the Bible would be a sin against the *intellect*." In Manu he finds a real philosophy, in contrast to the "foul-smelling Judaine of rabbinism and superstition." We have noted previously that "Judaine" is the term employed by the anti-Semite Lagarde to refer to certain pure strands of Judaism, and the foul stench associated with rabbinism recalls the offensive odor of the Polish Jews a few pages earlier in *The Antichrist*. The specifically anti-Jewish element in Manu is identified with strict social differentiation such as we encounter in the *Genealogy*: "Not to forget the main point, the basic difference from every kind of Bible: here the noble classes, the philosophers and the warriors, stand above the masses; noble values everywhere, a feeling of perfection, an affirmation of life, a triumphant delight in oneself and in life" (AC 56, KSA 6.240). But races are also involved; in both the letter to Köselitz and *Twilight of the Idols*, as well as in Jacolliot, Manu upholds an order associated specifically with Aryan values: "These regulations are instructive enough: in them we find for once *Aryan* humanity, quite pure, quite primordial." Contrasted to this Aryan codex is a Judeo-Christian order in which Nietzsche again emphasizes the primacy of the Jewish foundation; in comparison to Manu, Christianity, understood as the continuation of "Jewish roots," is the very antithesis of everything the Indian code prescribes in terms of breeding, race, and privilege (GD, Die "Verbesserer" der Menschheit 4, KSA 6.101). The fateful contrast between a pernicious and inferior Semitic race and a noble master race of Aryans insinuates its way into Nietzsche's thought through his willing reception of Jacolliot's hypotheses.

In Manu Nietzsche also encountered a key term that he would frequently employ in his published and unpublished writings in the second half of 1888. The notion of the chandala, a lowest caste composed of products of mixed marriages, struck Nietzsche as the perfect label for the despicable, the despised, the discontent, the wretched, the lowly, the miserable—in short, for everything that opposes a hierarchical social order. Actually Jacolliot refers more specifically to the chandala as the offspring of a male Sudra with a Brahmin woman, thus the son or daughter from the combination of the lowest and the highest of the castes. In his late work, however, Nietzsche appears either to have ignored these details or not to have recalled what the details actually are. Although chandala is most frequently associated with the Judeo-Christian tradition, at times Nietzsche uses the term to designate any group that is excluded and despised. In his notebooks we even find statements such as "the concept chandala refers to the degenerates of all castes: the ones permanently discarded that procreate among themselves" (Nachlass 1888, 14[224], KSA 13.397). And in *The Antichrist* Nietzsche regards the free spirits, or at least the men of science who have opposed religious belief, to be chandala as well:

> Let us not undervalue this: *we ourselves*, we free spirits, are already a "revaluation of all values," an *incarnate* declaration of war and victory over all ancient conceptions of "true" and "untrue." The most valuable insights are the last to be discovered: but the most valuable insights are *methods*. *All* the methods, *all* the prerequisites of our present-day scientificality have for millennia been the objects of the profoundest contempt: on their account one was excluded from associating with "honest" men—one was considered an "enemy of God," a despiser of truth, a man "possessed." As a practitioner of science one was Chandala. (AC 13, KSA 6.179)

This usage, however, is exceptional; in most cases Nietzsche reserves the term for the prophets of *ressentiment*, and in many instances, as we have seen from his letter to Köselitz above, he applies it directly to the Jews. Indeed, Nietzsche at times conceives of Jewish social structure in terms of only priests and chandala: "The Jews endeavor to assert themselves after they have lost two castes, the warriors and the farmers. " And he continues: "in this sense they are the 'ones cut off'" (German: *Verschnittenen*, "cut off," "trimmed," or "castrated"), an obvious allusion on Nietzsche's part to the rite of circumcision. "They have the priest—and then immediately the chandala" (Nachlass 1777 14[223], KSA 13.396). In the summer of 1888 Nietzsche increasingly comes to mention the Jews as chandalas, who now occupy the position of social dominance. On occasion he includes the Jews as part of a former chandala grouping that will come to power when the order of rank is reversed: "The chandala from former times is now on top: leading the way the blasphemers, the *immoralists*, the liberated of all kinds, the Jews, the street musicians—in essence all *disreputable* classes of men" (Nachlass 1888, 15[44], KSA 13.438). But in the most expansive passage identifying Jews and chandalas, they are the present rulers of Europe: "The chandala are on top; leading the way the Jews. The Jews are in an unstable Europe the strongest race, for they are superior to the rest owing to the duration of their development." In this unusual note Nietzsche drifts from the Jews as chandalas, which normally implies a negative valuation, to Jewry as a special cultural entity, one endowed with intelligence and tenacity, and because of their special role, a people able to resist the "rabies" of nationalism, "the last illness of European reason" (Nachlass 1888, 18[3], KSA 13.532–33).

In his published writings Nietzsche sticks more closely to the negative features of the chandala and to the associations with Jewry suggested in the commentary supplied by Jacolliot. The term is employed frequently in hyphenated compounds: chandala-hatred, chandala-revenge, and chandala-morality, all of which place it in association with the slave values Nietzsche ascribed to the Jews in the *Genealogy* and in section twenty-four of *The Antichrist*. The most important passage pertaining to the chandala in its Jewish incarnation occurs in *Twilight of the Idols*. The "gentle and rational" order described by Manu contrasts sharply with the "ill-smelling" New Testament populated by "the non-bred human being, the hotchpotch human being, the chandala." Nietzsche continues by selecting passages that relate to salient features and restrictions on the chandala. He draws directly from Jacolliot's commentary, which cites a fictitious Indian source; significant is that Nietzsche never questions this source, and that he chooses items that bring the chandala into close proximity to Jewish stereotypes. Nietzsche's presentation assumes that the fabricated edicts he cites were introduced to protect Indian morality, in contrast to what occurred in the Judeo-Christian world, where "the Jewish instinct" succeeded in making humankind sick and degenerate:

> The third edict, for example (Avandana-Shastra I), that "concerning unclean vegetables," ordains that the only nourishment permitted the chandala shall be garlic and onions, in view of the fact that holy scripture forbids one to give them corn or seed-bearing fruits or *water* or fire. The same edict lays it down that the water they need must not be taken from rivers or springs or pools, but only from the entrances to swamps and holes made by the feet of animals. They are likewise forbidden to wash their clothes or to *wash themselves*, since the water allowed them as an act of charity must be used only for quenching the thirst.... The harvest of such hygienic regulations did not fail to appear: murderous epidemics, hideous venereal diseases and, as a consequence, "the law of the knife" once more, ordaining circumcision for the male and removal of the *labia minora* for the female children.—Manu himself says: "The Chandala are the fruit of adultery, incest and crime" ... "They shall have for clothing only rags from corpses, for utensils broken pots, for ornaments old iron, for worship only evil spirits; they shall wander from place to place without rest. They are forbidden to write from left to right and to use the right hand for writing: the employment of the right hand and of the left-to-right motion is reserved for the *virtuous*, for people of *race*." (GD, Die "Verbesserer" der Menschheit 3, KSA 6.100–01)

This passage is a faithful rendition of commentary Nietzsche found in Jacolliot, but the *Avadana-Shastra* from which Nietzsche draws secondhand does not exist in "The Tradition of Manu" or in any other Indian text. It is quite obvious, however, that the characteristics associated with the chandala in Jacolliot, and then taken over by Nietzsche, relate to stereotypical traits of Jews: from the eating of garlic and onions and the uncleanliness (to which Nietzsche refers in the reference to foul-smelling Polish Jews) to the eternal wandering, circumcision, and the Hebrew language, which is written from right to left.

Nietzsche's fascination with the chandala is revealing for his relationship to his source and ultimately for his views on Jews and Judaism. From Jacolliot he adopts passages and ideas that confirm his own opinions, in this case about Jews and their traditions. Jacolliot himself participates in the ethnographic and linguistic anti-Semitism that was so prevalent during the nineteenth century. His anti-Jewish thought is significantly different from the criticism of Judaism found in Renan and Wellhausen, who, as Christian theologians, simply believed that Christianity had overcome a superannuated religion with which it was at one point intertwined. By contrast, Jacolliot seeks to establish a fundamental inequality in races and peoples derived ultimately from social differentiation in ancient India. Indeed, so important is the origin and development of the chandala to Jacolliot that he devotes a twenty-three-page footnote to the topic,[56] although there is no discussion of the chandala in the Tradition of Manu itself. As we have already seen, much of what Jacolliot includes is fabricated. According to his account—which has no scholarly merit—the chandalas were a group of outcasts and lawless people who gradually developed into their own nation. In approximately 8000 BC the edicts that Nietzsche cites in *Twilight of the Idols* were promulgated with the consequence that the number of chandalas was reduced by about one-half. Four thousand years later they were forced to emigrate because of struggles between Brahmins and Buddhists.[57] They migrated into central Asia but also to Persia and settled on the banks of the Tigris and Euphrates Rivers. Thus Jacolliot claims that the descendants of the chandalas constituted various tribes that come from that region of the world, including the Assyrians, the Babylonians, the Syrians, the Phoenicians, and the Arabs. Among the descendants of the chandalas are the Chaldeans, who, in a further migration established themselves elsewhere in the Middle East and became known as the Hebrews. All of these Semitic tribes can be distinguished because they prefer eating with their left hand and because they submit to circumcision. They are all ultimately examples of an original slave-like attitude, which accounts for their servile demeanor and customs. The Europeans, by contrast, as well as the peoples of ancient Egypt, were descendants of a Hindu migration from the higher castes. These people eat and write with the right hand. The general conclusion Jacolliot draws is that the descendants of the chandalas are inferior; they can never raise themselves above the vulgarities that are in their bloodline, and they can never become as intellectually accomplished as the pure Europeans. Thus Jacolliot establishes the very antithesis between Aryans and Semites that had played an intermittent role in Nietzsche's thought.[58] There is, of course, some irony in Nietzsche's uncritical acceptance of the nonsense contained in Jacolliot's extended footnote. At the same time that he was declaring his disdain for the political anti-Semites in Germany, he accepts apparently without reservation a crude and incredible historical account that serves to bolster the racist foundations of Judeophobic movements. We have observed, however, that Nietzsche was perfectly capable of condemning anti-Semitism and retaining anti-Jewish views. Indeed, we have noted that his ability to simultaneously hold these two positions is the defining feature of his relationship to the Jewish Question throughout the 1880s.

Conclusion

From the foregoing chapters what can we conclude about Nietzsche's relationship to Jews and Judaism? In the first instance we can see that the issues surrounding this topic are complex, and to achieve an understanding of Nietzsche's intentions and motivation in making specific pronouncements we need to have knowledge that extends well beyond his writings. In dealing with the Jewish Question, Nietzsche was responding to several conflicting discourses of the late nineteenth century; he was appropriating at various moments traditions about Jewry and the Jewish religion that had come down to him from multiple sources; he was using various scholarly and nonscholarly studies and, more often than has been recognized, clichés from his own era. At times he followed the lead of others in formulating his thoughts, but often he struck out on his own, developing views that diverge slightly from anything found in the writings of contemporaries. Previous scholarship has often not done a very good job of separating Nietzsche's original opinions from those he borrowed, and it has frequently not situated his views in the rich context that allows them to be fully comprehended. This study, by contrast, has not only used all pertinent materials from Nietzsche—from published and unpublished writings to correspondence— to arrive at conclusions, but also carefully placed the comments Nietzsche made regarding Jews and Judaism among the source material Nietzsche confronted and the discourses that were important for the nineteenth-century understanding of the Jewish Question, in particular in Germany. From this sedulous consideration of texts, sources, and contexts this study arrived at a series of conclusions that deviate significantly from previous accounts. These conclusions can be summarized as follows:

(1) Nietzsche's reputation as an anti-Semite underwent several changes from the 1880s until the present, but only after World War II was there a significant attempt to purge him from any traces of Judeophobia (chapter one).

(2) Although commonly held responsible for Nietzsche's reputation as an anti-Semite during the Third Reich, Nietzsche's sister Elisabeth in

fact consistently maintained Nietzsche was not an anti-Semite. Her manipulation of his letters and writings did nothing to lend Nietzsche an anti-Semitic profile (chapter one).

(3) We find scant evidence that Nietzsche was attracted to anti-Jewish sentiments in his childhood and youth. Neither his letters nor his juvenilia contain statements we would associate with negative attitudes toward Jews and Judaism (chapter two).

(4) The first indication we have for Nietzsche's anti-Jewish thought comes when he transfers from the University of Bonn to the University of Leipzig in 1865. In the Saxon city he encountered Jewish traders who frequented the fairs; he and his fellow philology students expressed stereotypical attitudes toward these Jewish merchants and generally exhibited a "cultural" racism common even among educated Germans of the late nineteenth century (chapter two).

(5) Nietzsche was thus not infected with anti-Jewish thought by Richard Wagner, whom he met first in November of 1868; the association with Wagner, Cosima, and other Wagnerians validated and intensified anti-Jewish sentiments he already harbored (chapters three and four).

(6) From his association with Wagner and from the aftermath of the republication of "Judaism in Music" in 1869 Nietzsche came to believe that Jews held tremendous power in the cultural sphere, that they represented a unified group that would take concerted action against their enemies, and that they could cause considerable difficulties for even someone as eminent as Wagner (chapter three).

(7) A pivotal moment in Nietzsche's public attitude toward Jews and Judaism came when he sent the Wagners a copy of a lecture he delivered in February 1870. Nietzsche openly attacked Jewish control of the press and was rebuked by the Wagners for expressing himself so directly. As a consequence direct references to Jews disappear almost entirely from Nietzsche's published writings during his association with Wagner. He resorts to a "cultural code" that expresses anti-Jewish ideas while avoiding specific reference to Jewry (chapter three).

(8) Nietzsche's break with Wagner had nothing to do with Wagner's attitude toward Jews; indeed, Nietzsche knew about and participated in anti-Jewish sentiments as a Wagnerian in the early 1870s (chapter four).

(9) Nietzsche's association with Jewish admirers—notably Paul Rée, Siegfried Lipiner, and Joseph Paneth—during the later 1870s and early 1880s does not necessarily indicate a growing tolerance for Jews. At various points in these relationships we can detect either anti-Jewish stereotypes that Nietzsche continued to harbor or calculated attempts on Nietzsche's part to curry favor with Jews, whom he still felt to be powerful in the cultural sphere (chapter four).

(10) Although Nietzsche's occasional public pronouncements about Jews became more favorable during his so-called aphoristic period, his letters and his notebooks contain remarks that continue to indicate anti-Jewish bias. His "favorable" remarks often amount to a validation of existing stereotypes with a positive reevaluation of something formerly considered negative (chapter four).

(11) Anti-Semitism meant something different for Nietzsche and his contemporaries than it does for us today. It refers not merely to anti-Jewish attitudes and to hatred of the Jews, but to a specific political movement that arose around 1880 and to which Nietzsche had several personal ties (chapter five).

(12) Nietzsche could thus fervently oppose the political anti-Semitic movement of the 1880s for a number of personal and philosophical reasons, and still not relinquish long-held anti-Jewish sentiments (chapter five).

(13) The three most pronounced confrontations Nietzsche had with German anti-Semitism—with his publisher Ernst Schmeitzner, his sister and brother-in-law, and the publisher and agitator Theodor Fritsch—indicate that initially he did not take much notice of anti-Semitism and did not comment negatively about it, but from about 1884 onward, perhaps recognizing that the anti-Semites were in part responsible for his lack of popularity and for various personal misfortunes, he became vehemently opposed to anti-Semitism (chapter five).

(14) There is evidence that Nietzsche and some of his contemporaries recognized the seriousness of the Jewish Question and the necessity for coming to a resolution to this pressing social issue, but that they simultaneously regarded the solutions of the anti-Semitic movement to be both too crude and ultimately inefficacious (chapter five).

(15) Nietzsche's introduction of the Jews in *The Genealogy of Morals* (1887) as the originators of a slave morality that has now gained hegemony throughout Europe uses questionable racist notions: Jews are opposed to Aryans and fair-haired peoples, they insinuate themselves into powerful positions through shrewdness since they lack physical strength, and they oppose things "noble" with a value system that debases humanity (chapter six).

(16) Nietzsche's presentation of Jewish history in *The Antichrist* (1895) continues the narrative he started in the *Genealogy*, but here the Jews do not even believe in the values they propagate; they preserve their integrity as a people by ushering in a regime of decadence for everyone else. Nietzsche follows scholarly materials closely in much of his writing about historical Judaism in 1888, but in this accusation of duplicity he departs from his sources (chapter six).

(17) Nietzsche's uncritical adoption of the "Law Book of Manu" demonstrates an important instance where Nietzsche buys into anti-Semitic

ethnography, linguistics, and history, even while maintaining his opposition to contemporary anti-Semitism (chapter six).

Almost all of these conclusions are new to Nietzsche research, or at least not
common in the literature; certainly none has gained widespread attention
in the Anglophone world and its scholarship. In much of postwar criticism
Nietzsche's remarks against anti-Semitism have been taken as the decisive
indication of his sentiments regarding Jews and Judaism, and observers
have been content to support this image of Nietzsche as a resolute anti-anti-
Semite with assertions drawn from misunderstood relationships Nietzsche
had with friends and acquaintances of Jewish heritage, and from remarks
that are far more complex and ambiguous than they appear at first glance.

To understand a bit better Nietzsche's views with regard to anti-Judaism
and anti-Semitism, we might want to consider once again where he stood
in comparison to some of his prominent contemporaries on issues related
to Jews and Jewish influence. As we have seen, he most definitely rejected
the anti-Semitic movement of his times. But this movement was comprised
of various branches and ideologies that were not always in agreement about
anything except the undesirability of Jews in German society. Nietzsche's
fiercest statements were directed against crude anti-Semites like Theodor
Fritsch or his own brother-in-law Bernhard Förster, who exhibited a deep
ideological commitment to Judeophobia and put their prejudices into action. Fritsch, of course, turned to journalism and agitational literature as
well as to political activity. Förster drew the consequences from living in a
Germany he considered infected by Jews and Jewish values and left for Paraguay, where he wanted to establish a pure German colony that would be
in accord with his racist ideals. But Nietzsche had equal contempt for the
Christian anti-Semites, represented perhaps best by the Prussian court chaplain Adolf Stöcker, the founder of the Christian Socialist Party. Indeed,
Nietzsche's associations with anti-Semitism often included both German
nationalism and a redemptive socialism. While from our perspective today
we may consider efforts of Stöcker and others of his ilk to be an attempt to
counter the socialism inspired by cosmopolitan views and international sol-
idarity, such as we find in the works of Marx and Engels or in the Social
Democratic Workers' Party in Germany, Nietzsche considered chauvinistic
attitudes and the collectivism of socialism to be part and parcel of the anti-
Semitic program. Wagner, after all, as well as members of the extended Wagnerian circle like Förster or even Wilhelm Marr, openly subscribed to a
vague version of socialism as an alternative to the "Jewish" capitalism and
exploitation that prevailed in German and European affairs. Fitting in

seamlessly with this connection was Eugen Dühring, who enjoyed a popularity among many socialists during the 1870s that inspired Friedrich Engels
to compose an assault on his version of socialist theory. Dühring's rapid turn
to anti-Semitic writings in the early 1880s must have seemed like a quite
expected association from Nietzsche's vantage point. But Nietzsche also
opposed more academic anti-Semites, such as Heinrich Treitschke, who
instigated perhaps the largest public debate about the Jewish Question in
Nietzsche's lifetime: the Berlin anti-Semitism controversy. Treitschke had
no relationship to the socialism Nietzsche so despised, but he did represent
a nationalist sentiment that Nietzsche repeatedly ridiculed and attacked in
his later writings. Nietzsche was thus unlike any of these notorious anti-
Semites both in the vehemence of his anti-Judaism and in his motivation
for adhering to anti-Jewish clichés and stereotypes. In this regard we might
say that Nietzsche fits in well with a large segment of the German intelli-
gentsia, whose views were neither virulently anti-Jewish nor free from prejudice. Nietzsche mentions opinions on Jews and Judaism perhaps more frequently that others, and, as we have seen, he has opinions on the "solution"
to the Jewish Question and theories about a wider and more pernicious
Jewish influence on the Western world. But if we had to situate him among
his contemporaries, we would bring him into the proximity of many individuals, like his friend Overbeck, who freely express anti-Jewish sentiments
but are not obsessed with the Jewish presence or alleged dominance in German financial or cultural affairs.[1]

The conclusions that can be gathered from the discussions in the preceding chapters are apt to be controversial, but they will also leave some readers
dissatisfied. There is often a tendency to want to arrive at a bottom line,
especially when the topic involves race and racism. But the answer to the
simple question "Was Nietzsche an anti-Semite?" is anything but straightforward. We can easily determine that Nietzsche did not regard himself as
an anti-Semite, and anyone who reads his published writings, notebooks,
and correspondence will readily observe, especially in the years after 1884,
that he was violently antagonistic to anti-Semitism. But the argument in this
book has been that the verification of Nietzsche's anti-anti-Semitism does
not tell us as much as it seems, since in Nietzsche's case anti-anti-Semitism
does not carry the same meaning as opposition to anti-Semitism in the twentieth or twenty-first centuries. For Nietzsche and many of his contemporaries, anti-Semitism was a specific historical movement that arose to deal with
what many believed to be a pressing question of the era, and although part
of this movement was certainly involved with prejudices against and hatred
of Jewry, Nietzsche's hostility does not always relate specifically and invari-

ably to this racist dimension. As we have seen, the anti-Semitic movement of the 1880s inherits dimensions of earlier forms of prejudice,[2] and these earlier forms of racist thought occasionally contain aspects that become prominent only in the later, political atmosphere of the Second Reich. Nonetheless, Nietzsche was reacting to a definite historical situation when he vehemently denounced anti-Semitism. The question of whether Nietzsche was Judeophobic—a term I employ synonymously with anti-Jewish to refer to a more general realm of prejudice against Jews—has many dimensions. If I were compelled to give a summary statement I would note that he was more anti-Jewish in his early adulthood than has commonly been understood, and that he never completely relinquished anti-Jewish attitudes even when he opposed anti-Semitism. As we have seen, he is not obsessed with Jewish hegemony in Germany as were Theodor Fritsch, Eugen Dühring, his brother-in-law Bernhard Förster, or Richard and Cosima Wagner,[3] but he should not be mistaken for a Judeophile or philo-Semite either. Above all, he never expresses a principled attitude of tolerance toward Jews—or, for that matter, any religious or ethnic grouping—for their cultural and religious differences. He was not a liberal in the sense we use that word today, and even when he is ranting against anti-Semitism or extolling some feature of modern Jewry, he is doing so for reasons that are entirely dissimilar to most antiracist attitudes from the eighteenth through the twenty-first centuries.

An important consideration for anyone interested in Nietzsche is, what do his views on Jews and Judaism have to do with his philosophy? If we conclude that he harbored more anti-Jewish sentiments than most postwar commentators have previously detected, are his philosophical insights and speculations then somehow "contaminated by racism"? Should we proscribe the reading of Nietzsche based on his Judeophobic attitudes? Or severely restrict our reading of him with cautionary notes and warnings? There are several dimensions to this issue, but I think from the outset we should recognize that a great deal of Nietzsche's thought has little or no obvious relationship to the Jewish Question. His interrogation of the value of truth, for example, or his notion of "Eternal Recurrence" are, as far as I can ascertain, not directly affected by his views on Jews and Judaism, and any attempt to connect them would be strained and ill-conceived. We should note as well that Nietzsche was hardly alone in the German tradition in harboring anti-Jewish convictions, or expressing them in his writings. Kant, Fichte, Hegel, Schopenhauer, Frege, and Heidegger—to name only a few philosophers in the German heritage—all expressed disparaging views about Jews at one point or another, some of them more extreme than others. But there is scant connection between these anti-Jewish utterances and the notions that have established these individuals as important voices in the history of philosophical thought. A small minority of commentators may find these Judeophobic sentiments significant in evaluating their overall thought, but most professional philosophers do not.

In the foregoing study we have seen that Nietzsche's involvement with Jews and Judaism has the greatest implications for his published writings at two points in time: in his earliest published works during the years 1872–76, when he was part of the Wagnerian movement; and in the last two years of his sane life, when he speculated on the history of religion and morality. Jews and Judaism are mentioned sporadically in aphorisms in the intervening decade but are only one of many concerns and play a diminished role during the years 1878–86. Even in the two periods when Jewish concerns are more prominent, however, there were many other influences on, and dimensions to, Nietzsche's thought. Unlike the doctrinaire anti-Semites of his time, Nietzsche was never consumed by the Jewish Question. It impacted his perspective on modern German life when he fashioned himself a cultural commentator in the 1870s, and historical Judaism became a key element in his reflections on slave morality and its many ramifications in 1887 and 1888. But despite its significance for Nietzsche's early and late writings, it remains even during these periods one of many factors influencing him. From these considerations scholars might be tempted to argue that Nietzsche's views on Jews and Judaism should be merely a minor consideration in our understanding of his philosophy, just as we might find his attitude toward women to be an incidental concern, or his understanding of German nationalism, or his opinions on the working class and socialism. The Jewish Question will be more centrally important if we are examining Nietzsche's discourse on contemporary social issues or race or the Judeo-Christian heritage or the history of morality; it will be of less import if we are concerned primarily with epistemological and ontological reflections.

On the other hand, we would certainly be justified in asking ourselves what it means that a philosopher such as Nietzsche could hold the dubious views that he did about Jews and Judaism. Nietzsche is often seen as a thinker who constantly questions conventions and norms, who undermines foundational statements, and who never tires of assuming a stance that is contrary to the values of his contemporaries. Yet we find him at various points in his mature life spouting clichés about Jews and Judaism that appear to have been unreflected borrowings from a long tradition of prejudice. Moreover, we have seen that he is frequently less than candid when he reports to others his convictions regarding contemporary Jewry and even anti-Semitism. I do not believe we can simply reject the various utterances that contain anti-Jewish dimensions as insignificant for his thinking, as something extraordinary that has nothing to do with his "genuine" philosophical outlook. They must in some fashion diminish our regard for other aspects of his thought. We encounter a similar case in recent times with one of the most enthusiastic commentators on Nietzsche in the twentieth century, Martin Heidegger.[4] Although a careful reading of Heidegger's writings in the early years of the Third Reich, especially his official statements as rector of the University of Freiburg after Hitler came to power, as well as his actions as an academic leader, indicate a reprehensible adherence to anti-Jewish views, the recent publication of his "Black Notebooks" demonstrates beyond a doubt that he regurgitated some of the worst platitudes regarding Jewry and its role in his contemporary world. What is disturbing about certain passages in these writings from the 1930s and early 1940s is that these Judeophobic remarks do not occur in political speeches or personal commentary but as part of his philosophical reflections on Western metaphysics. We have seen that some of Nietzsche's observations on Jews and Judaism similarly occur in passages—published or unpublished—that are concerned with issues of philosophical import. The connection is fairly obvious in the early writings, where Nietzsche, as a Wagnerian acolyte, was expounding on the deficiencies of modernity, part of which related directly to the Jews as prototypes for the social and cultural ills of contemporary Germany. But we also encounter a heavy dependence on Jewry in Nietzsche's late moral theory and his comments on decadence and degeneration. We may be unable to find any immediate relationship of Jews and Judaism to specific notions traditionally advanced as important for Nietzsche's "genuine" philosophy, such as Eternal Recurrence or the Will to Power. But his habit of mind, as we have seen it manifested in his dealings with Jews and Judaism, and his lack of self-reflection on his own prejudices surely leave a mark on other aspects of his thought. We should be wary of trusting a thinker who was unable to escape in this instance—as well as in other instances, such as his obvious misogyny—the heritage he is often credited with overcoming.

These issues have produced and will continue to generate considerable debate among Nietzsche enthusiasts, and the response will no doubt vary considerably. The extreme positions appear wholly untenable. The image of Nietzsche as entirely free from anti-Jewish sentiments ignores too much: his willingness to participate in the Wagnerian ideological enterprise as a young man, the clichés about Jews found throughout his letters and notebooks, and the anti-Jewish foundation of his polemic against Christianity in his final two years. At the same time the contention that Nietzsche's anti-Jewish proclivities invalidate everything he professed ignores the fascination he has exerted over major thinkers since the late nineteenth century and his genuine contributions in modern philosophical thought. Moreover, the assertion of either extreme view places the individual taking this position in an extremely precarious position with regard to peers; a scholar who finds no anti-Jewish dimension, or who trivializes Nietzsche's anti-Jewish statements, can be easily accused of apologizing for racist thought, while someone who believes Nietzsche's statements on Jews and Judaism depreciate everything he wrote will undoubtedly be condemned as philosophically naive and reductionist. Advocating for ground in the middle, therefore, must not be understood as equivocation, as craven vacillation without a willingness to take a stand. Rather, it should be seen as the only position that does justice to the complexity and historical situatedness of Nietzsche's utterances and to Nietzsche's philosophy. It would be just as foolish to ignore Nietzsche's anti-Jewishness as it would be to consider it the sole determinate of his worth. For most commentators Nietzsche will remain, as he should, a stimulating, provocative thinker and writer, but, in light of his position on the Jewish Question, students of his thought would be well advised to approach him more warily, more critically, and more skeptically than they have in the recent past.

A final question that often arises when speaking of Nietzsche's "anti-Semitism" is whether Nietzsche should be categorized as a Nazi or a forerunner of National Socialism. This question is usually asked with considerable provocation. In the June 8, 1981, edition of the German news magazine *Der Spiegel*, for example, the cover displays a portrait of Hitler attached to Nietzsche as if they were conjoined twins connected from the back of their necks to the top of their heads. Hitler is waving a revolver menacingly with his hand on the trigger; Nietzsche is leaning on his elbow in a pose resembling Auguste Rodin's statue *Le Penseur*; the headline on the page translates as follows: "Return of a Philosopher: Perpetrator Hitler, Thinker Nietzsche."[5] The same desire to spark controversy can be detected in the more scholarly realm, for example, in the essay collection *Nietzsche: Godfather of Fascism?*, which appeared in 2002.[6] But the issue of Nietzsche's fascist affiliation cannot be adjudicated by appeals to his writings, which are inconclusive on this topic. Certainly we can find considerable evidence that Nietzsche supported strong, aggressive, and even dictatorial leaders—he speaks admiringly of Napoleon and Cesare Borgia; he ranted against democracy and parliamentary deliberations; he praised war and conflict; he opposed equal rights and feminism; and there are fairly substantial indications that Nietzsche had a great interest in eugenics[7] (which today we associate with right-wing politics, but in Nietzsche's time had adherents of various political persuasions). In addition, some of his terminology, including the notion of the "superman" or "the will to power," appears to fit seamlessly into National Socialist ideology; moreover, these concepts could also be used to justify anti-Jewish sentiments and to establish Nietzsche's credentials as a Judeophobe. But we can also make counterarguments based on textual evidence that is just as solid. As many other commentators have noted, he was adamant in his opposition to the two main pillars of National Socialist ideology: ultranationalism and anti-Semitism—although there is some oversimplification in assessing this latter pillar, as this study has been at pains to demonstrate. We have seen in chapter one how right-wing Nietzscheans managed to circumvent these issues and eventually claimed him as one of their own, but there was a considerable anti-Nietzschean sentiment even during the Third Reich. On the basis of his writings and the ideas he expressed in them we can construct various arguments, each amounting to little more than futile speculation on whether he belongs in the fascist camp.

We can aver that Nietzsche was a forerunner of fascism only to the extent that fascists believed he was a forerunner. But this judgment means little, since it is based on a partial view of Nietzsche, in both senses of the word "partial." Movements, whether they are political, cultural, or philosophical, create their own precursors, and if the precursor is no longer alive, he has no opportunity to confirm or deny the often-erroneous understanding of his thought. As we observed in the first chapter in citing Kurt Tulcholsky's comment about the malleability of his writings for disparate and even contradictory causes, Nietzsche lends himself to appropriation by different camps because of substantive ambiguities, changes in his perspective, and stylistic qualities that open his statements to interpretation. It is therefore not surprising that Nietzsche could be claimed by fascists, but also viewed in other circles as someone influential for socialism, anarchism, and liberal democracy. Nietzsche was not a political chameleon in his own lifetime; after a phase of National Liberalism in the 1860s, he was rather consistent. He abhorred democracy and socialism and disliked parliamentary forms of government as pandering to equal rights and the fiction that "all men are created equal." These views are close to conservative positions of his times, but he was never an adherent of any political party, since the very notion of political parties was something he believed was part of the problem. The nature of his writings, and the eagerness of generations after his death to venerate him as one of their own, cast him into rivaling political, cultural, and philosophical groupings. Since his death there has been no shortage of arguments concerning where Nietzsche should be properly placed as a thinker.

Let us return to the question at hand: Was Nietzsche a fascist or a precursor of fascism? Do his remarks on Jews, some of which reveal racist proclivities, qualify him for a specific political affiliation? If Nietzsche had been confronted with National Socialism, he might have rejected it decisively, as he did the anti-Semitism of his own era. He could have abhorred the ideology of Aryan superiority and the notion of a "national community" (*Volksgemeinschaft*). Or he might have welcomed Germany's seizing control of its own destiny, acquiring a strong leader, and ridding itself of the nonsense of equal rights, parliamentary deliberations, and academic freedom. When Martin Heidegger was faced with the reality of National Socialism, he chose—initially at least—to cast his lot with the fascists despite their crudeness and aggression against intellectual endeavors. For Nietzsche, the issue is ultimately nugatory, however. Indeed, the assumption underlying this study of Nietzsche's "Jewish Problem" has been that we cannot properly understand Nietzsche's relationship to Jews and Judaism outside of his historical context. We cannot place him with or against National Socialism; we can only make prudent judgments about his reactions to actual discourses, events, and movements of the late nineteenth century. It is, of course, impossible for us to remove ourselves entirely from our own times, and something of our era necessarily inheres in the assessments we make. We will always view and evaluate Nietzsche through a lens that was not entirely his own. But we will do him and ourselves an injustice if we unhistorically make him part of our time or see his value only as a precursor to notions we hold dear. Our best hope for understanding him, his writings, and, in particular, his complex relationship to the Jewish Question, will result from the most rigorous endeavor to envelop him in the discourses to which he responded and in the nineteenth-century context in which he formulated his controversial views.

Notes

PREFACE

1. Robert C. Holub, "Nietzsche and the Jewish Question," *New German Critique* 22, no. 3 (1995): 94–121.

2. A partial exception to this trend exists in several works in German, in particular in two books written by Thomas Mittmann: *Friedrich Nietzsche: Judengegner und Antisemitenfeind* (Erfurt: Sutton, 2001); and *Vom "Günstling" zum "Urfeind" der Juden: Die antisemitische Nietzsche-Rezeption in Deutschland bis zum Ende des Nationalsozialismus* (Würzburg: Königshausen und Neumann, 2006). Also useful as a correction to the one-sided postwar image of Nietzsche as the principled adversary of anti-Semitism is Domenico Losurdo's two-volume study *Nietzsche, der aristokratische Rebell: Intellektuelle Biographie und kritische Bilanz* (Berlin: Argument, 2012), which is translated from the original Italian.

3. Holub, "Nietzsche and the Jewish Question," 120.

4. Several preliminary essays that will contribute to this project have appeared in print: "Nietzsche and the Women's Question," *German Quarterly* 68, no. 1 (1995): 67–71; "Nietzsche's Colonialist Imagination: Nueva Germania, Good Europeanism, and Great Politics," in *The Imperialist Imagination: German Colonialism and Its Legacy*, ed. Sara Friedrichsmeyer, Sara Lennox, and Susanne Zantop (Ann Arbor: University of Michigan Press, 1998), 33–49; "The Birth of Psychoanalysis from the Spirit of Enmity: Nietzsche and Psychology in the Nineteenth Century," in *Nietzsche and Depth Psychology*, ed. Jacob Golomb, Weaver Santaniello, and Ronald Lehrer (Albany: State University of New York Press, 1999), 149–69; "The Elisabeth Legend or Sibling Scapegoating: The Cleansing of Friedrich Nietzsche and the Sullying of His Sister," in *Nietzsche: Godfather of Fascism?: On the Uses and Abuses of Philosophy*, ed. Jacob Golomb and Robert S. Wistrich (Princeton, NJ: Princeton University Press, 2002), 215–34; and "Dialectic of the Biological Enlightenment: Nietzsche, Degeneration, and Eugenics," in *Practicing Progress: The Promise and Limitations of Enlightenment*, Festschrift for John McCarthy, ed. Richard Schade and Dieter Sevin (Amsterdam: Rodopi, 2007), 173–85.

5. Robert C. Holub, *Friedrich Nietzsche*, Twayne World Author Series 857 (New York: Twayne Publishers, 1995).

6. Four of the most impressive books in this trend toward situating Nietzsche in his times are Christian J. Emden, *Friedrich Nietzsche and the Politics of History* (Cambridge: Cambridge University Press, 2008); Gregory Moore, *Nietzsche, Biology, and Metaphor* (Cambridge: Cambridge University Press, 2002); Robin Small, *Nietzsche in*

Context (Burlington, VT: Ashgate, 2001); and Christian J. Emden, *Nietzsche's Natu-ralism: Philosophy and the Life Sciences in the Nineteenth Century* (Cambridge: Cam-bridge University Press, 2014).

CHAPTER ONE

1. The *Anti-Semitic Correspondence* was first published in October of 1885 and was originally meant as an internal organ for "party affairs." At the top of the issues discretion was called for and the readers were cautioned that the periodical "was sent only to reliable party comrades." Nonetheless, recruitment was often a theme, and frequently Fritsch requested ways to contact individuals whose views might be sympathetic to his. Among the contributors to the *Anti-Semitic Correspondence* were both Bernhard Förster and his brother Paul.

2. Overbeck arrived in 1870, one year after Nietzsche was appointed to his position.

3. During the 1870s Meysenbug (1816–1903) served as an unsuccessful match-maker for Nietzsche. In 1876–77 she invited Nietzsche to spend time in her villa in Sorrento, where he worked on *Human, All Too Human*.

4. The journal appeared in 1882. The original subtitle was changed in 1883 from the more neutral *Monatsschrift für allgemeine und nationale Kultur und deren Litteratur* (*Monthly for General and National Culture and Its Literature*), but the anti-Semitic content was evident even in the initial year of publication. It is true that after the sudden and unexpected death of Bruno Bauer, who was the leading contrib-utor to the journal, the anti-Jewish tenor increased. The periodical was published for just two years. See Malcolm B. Brown, *Friedrich Nietzsche und sein Verleger Ernst Schmeitzner: Eine Darstellung ihrer Beziehung* (Frankfurt: Buchhändler-Vereinigung, 1987), 255–62; and Massimo Ferrari Zumbini, "'Ich lasse eben alle Anti-Semiten erschiessen': Anmerkungen zum Thema: Nietzsche und der real existierende Anti-Semitismus," in *Untergänge und Morgenröten: Nietzsche—Spengler—Anti-Semitismus* (Würzburg: Königshausen und Neumann, 1999), 135–50. Brown and Ferrari Zum-bini argue that Nietzsche knew nothing about the anti-Semitic direction of the jour-nal when he offered his contribution, the poems "Idylls of Messina," which appeared in May of 1882, and that he censures the journal once he discovered the true nature of the enterprise. But Mittmann points out that Nietzsche was well aware of the anti-Semitic profile of the journal, and that from the very beginning there was anti-Semitic content. Indeed, even a review of Nietzsche's *Gay Science*, which appeared in the journal in the November issue of 1882, contains remarks that link Nietzsche with anti-Jewish sentiments. Nietzsche approved of this review, although he does add that the journal otherwise "stinks of Dühring and Jew-hatred" (to Heinrich Köselitz, January 10, 1883, Nr. 368, KSB 6.317). See Thomas Mittmann, *Vom "Günst-ling" zum "Urfeind" der Juden: Die antisemitische Nietzsche-Rezeption in Deutschland bis zum Ende des Nationalsozialismus* (Würzburg: Königshausen und Neumann, 2006), 61–62. I take up this matter in more detail in chapter five.

5. Robert Misch, *Kinder: Eine Gymnasiasten Komödie* (Berlin: Harmonie, 1906), 12.

6. Robert C. Holub, "Nietzsche: Socialist, Anarchist, Feminist," in *German Cul-ture in Nineteenth-Century America: Reception, Adaptation, Transformation*, ed. Lynne

Tatlock and Matt Erlin (Rochester, NY: Camden House, 2005), 129–49. For Nietz-sche's general reception in the United States, see Jennifer Ratner-Rosenhagen, *American Nietzsche: A History of an Icon and His Ideas* (Chicago: University of Chicago Press, 2012).

7. For Nietzsche's German reception see Steven E. Aschheim, *The Nietzsche Legacy in Germany, 1890–1990* (Berkeley: University of California Press, 1992).

8. Max Nordau, *Degeneration* (Lincoln: University of Nebraska Press, 1993). The original German version appeared in 1892.

9. Bernard Lazare, *Anti-Semitism: Its History and Causes* (London: Britons, 1967); the original was (Paris: Léon Chailley, 1894).

10. Another Jewish writer who deals directly with Jewish and anti-Semitic aspects of Nietzsche's work was Caesar Seligmann, who points out the ambivalence in Nietzsche's attitude toward the Jews, but ultimately views Nietzsche's worldview and the Jewish worldview as adversarial. See Caesar Seligmann, "Nietzsche und das Judentum," in *Judentum und moderne Weltanschauung: Fünf Vorträge* (Frankfurt: Kauffmann, 1905), 69–89.

11. Ernst Jünemann, *Dühring und Nietzsche* (Leipzig: Reisland, 1931).

12. Heinrich Mann, "Zum Verständnisse Nietzsches," cited from *Nietzsche und die deutsche Literatur*, ed. Bruno Hillebrand, vol. 1, *Texte zur Nietzsche-Rezeption, 1873–1963* (Tübingen: Niemeyer, 1978), 106.

13. Tönnies himself admired Nietzsche's early work, especially *The Birth of Tragedy*, where he sensed a communitarian attitude, but criticized the later work as pseudoliberationist. Tönnies is most noted for the problematic distinction between community (*Gemeinschaft*) and society (*Gesellschaft*). The two texts by Tönnies on Nietzsche are collected in *Der Nietzsche-Kultus: Eine Kritik* (Berlin: Akademie-Verlag, 1990).

14. –t –n [Ernst Jünemann], "Friedrich Nietzsche, ein Stück Juden- und Irrenfrage," *Der Moderne Völkergeist: Organ des Socialitären Bundes* 3, no. 9 (1896): 65. Mittmann in *Vom "Günstling" zum "Urfeind" der Juden* points out that the notion that Nietzsche's popularity was achieved because of the Jewish press was widespread among anti-Semites in the Second Empire (82).

15. Jünemann, "Friedrich Nietzsche, ein Stück Juden- und Irrenfrage," *Der Moderne Völkergeist: Organ des Socialitären Bundes* 3, no. 12 (mid-June 1896): 94.

16. Ibid., 3, no. 10 (mid-May 1896): 73–74.

17. Ibid., 3, no. 13 (mid-July 1896): 102.

18. Ibid., 3, no. 11 (beginning June 1896): 83.

19. Ibid., 3, no. 13 (mid-July 1896): 102.

20. For a discussion of the persistent attacks from the Dühring camp see Mittmann, *Vom "Günstling" zum "Urfeind" der Juden*, 77–82.

21. All citations from Adolf Bartels, "Friedrich Nietzsche und das Deutschtum," *Deutsche Monatsschrift für das gesamte Leben der Gegenwart* 2 (1902): 81–91.

22. Kurt Tucholsky, "Fräulein Nietzsche," *Gesammelte Werke* (Hamburg: Rowohlt, 1960), 10: 14.

23. The fourth book was originally published in a private edition and did not appear in a public edition until 1892.

24. See Aschheim, *Nietzsche Legacy in Germany*, 135. Although I have had trouble verifying the frequent claim that *Zarathustra* was distributed to the troops, there

is little doubt that the outbreak of the war altered both the internal and external perception of Nietzsche. For the next three decades he was seen largely as a proponent of German nationalism.

25. Oswald Spengler, *The Decline of the West*, vol. 1, *Form and Actuality* (New York: Knopf, 1926), xiv. The original German text was published in two volumes in 1918 and 1922.

26. We should note, however, that during Elisabeth's lifetime Mussolini's Italy did not persecute its Jewish citizens. They were stripped of citizenship under German pressure in 1938 and transported to concentration and death camps after the German occupation of Italy in 1943. After Denmark and Bulgaria, Jews in Italy had the highest rate of survival among European nations.

27. The "Rosenberg Office" (*Amt Rosenberg*) was the official office for cultural policy and surveillance in the Nazi Party.

28. Arno Schickedanz, *Sozialparasitismus im Völkerleben* (Leipzig: Lotus-Verlag, 1927), 177. Schickedanz cites from an early Nietzsche text, "Five Prefaces to Five Unwritten Books": "But you are the fools of all centuries! History will make only the confessions to you that you deserve." Schickedanz substitues "times" (*Zeiten*) for "centuries" (*Jahrhunderte*), leaves out the word "only" (*nur*), and alters the punctuation.

29. Franz Haiser, *Die Judenfrage vom Standpunkt der Herrenmoral* (Leipzig: Theodor Weicher, 1926), 86–92.

30. Friedrich Nietzsche, "Rom gegen Judäa, Judäa gegen Rom," in *Klärung: 12 Autoren Politiker über die Judenfrage* (Berlin: Wilhelm Kolk, 1932), 57–65.

31. Ernst Johannsen, "Über den Anti-Semitismus als gegebene Tatsache," *Klärung*, 9–29, here, 15–17.

32. See Yvonne Sherratt, *Hitler's Philosophers* (New Haven, CT: Yale University Press, 2013), 70–72.

33. See, for example, his "Nietzsche" (244–80) and "Nietzsche und der Nationalsozialismus" (281–94), in Alfred Baeumler, *Studien zur deutschen Geistesgeschichte* (Berlin: Dünnhaupt, 1937). The first essay appeared as the introduction to Nietzsche's writings in 1930; the second was an essay in the *Nationalsozialistische Monatshefte* 5 (1934): 289–98.

34. For a more detailed view of Baeumler's writings on Nietzsche, as well as the National Socialist controversies around Nietzsche, see Max Whyte, "The Uses and Abuses of Nietzsche in the Third Reich: Alfred Baeumler's 'Heroic Realism,'" *Journal of Contemporary History* 43, no. 2 (2008): 171–94.

35. Baeumler, *Studien zur deutschen Geistesgeschichte*, 158–59.

36. There was a significant endeavor on the part of Bayreuth to discredit Nietzsche and to highlight his partiality for the Jews, his alleged Slavic origins, and his opposition to anti-Semitism. See Massimo Ferrari Zumbini, "Nietzsche in Bayreuth: Nietzsches Herausforderung, die Wagnerianer und die antisemitische Gegenoffensive," in *Untergänge und Morgenröte: Nietzsche—Spengler—Antisemitismus*, 87–133.

37. Gottlieb Scheuffler, *Friedrich Nietzsche im Dritten Reich: Bestätigung und Aufgabe* ([Erfurt-Melchendorf, E. Scheuffler], 1933), 35. Scheuffler, like many National Socialists, considers Lou Salomé to be Jewish, although she was not.

38. Heinrich Härtle, *Nietzsche und der Nationalsozialismus* (Munich: Zentralverlag der NSDAP, 1937), 44–54.

39. Heinrich Römer, "Nietzsche und das Rassenproblem," *Rasse: Monatsschrift der nordischen Gedanken* 7 (1940): 59–65.

40. See Rudolf E. Kuenzli, "The Nazi Appropriation of Nietzsche," *Nietzsche-Studien* 12 (1983): 428–35. We should refrain from seeing the National Socialist appropriation of Nietzsche only as one of "massive abuse" (428). The richness and contradictoriness of Nietzsche's writings, as well as his development over the years, requires many interpreters to be selective and to cite at times out of context. Indeed, the notion "out of context" is itself worthy of further examination, since context is not exclusively textual; Nietzsche's remarks about Jews, Judaism, and anti-Semitism relate to specific political, social, and historical contexts that are too frequently ignored, or inadequately explored. Although the Nazis are more offensive because of the worldwide scope of their criminality, their Nietzsche interpretation is no more egregious than many others.

41. Crane Brinton, *Nietzsche* (New York: Harper Torchbook, 1965). Brinton republished the original study from 1941, which appeared from Harvard University Press, with a new preface that disavows many of the earlier views.

42. I cite here the quotation as it appears in Brinton's book (*Nietzsche*, 214). But the parenthetical remark should surely be rendered by something like the following: "although between the old Teutons and us modern Germans there exists scarcely a conceptual, let alone a blood, relationship" (obwohl zwischen alten Germanen und uns Deutschen kaum eine Begriffs-, geschweige eine Blutverwandtschaft besteht") (GM I/11, KSA 5.276).

43. Citations are from Brinton's discussion of these issues on 214–16.

44. Henning Ottmann, *Philosophie und Politik bei Nietzsche*, 2nd expanded ed. (Berlin: de Gruyter, 1999), 249–50.

45. Bernd Magnus and Kathleen M. Higgins, "Nietzsche's Works and Their Themes," in *The Cambridge Companion to Nietzsche*, ed. Bernd Magnus and Kathleen M. Higgins (Cambridge: Cambridge University Press, 1996), 21–68, here, 57. The original editions of *The Will to Power* appeared well over a decade before there was a National Socialist party.

46. R. J. Hollingdale, "The Hero as Outsider," in *The Cambridge Companion to Nietzsche*, ed. Bernd Magnus and Kathleen M. Higgins (Cambridge: Cambridge University Press, 1996), 71–89, here, 86–87.

47. Weaver Santaniello, "A Post-Holocaust Re-Examination of Nietzsche and the Jews: Vis-à-vis Christendom and Nazism," in *Nietzsche and Jewish Culture*, ed. Jacob Golomb (London: Routledge, 1997), 21–54, here, 21.

48. Santaniello, "A Post-Holocaust Re-Examination of Nietzsche and the Jews," 23 and 43.

49. Paul Strathern, *Nietzsche in 90 Minutes* (Chicago: Ivan R. Dee, 1996), 42.

50. Simon Romero, "German Outpost Born of Racism in 1887 Blends into Paraguay," *New York Times*, May 6, 2013, A4

51. It is worth noting that the right-wing members of the Nietzsche Archive's board of directors were as upset about the homage paid to Mussolini as were the left-liberals. The nationalists, who favored an expansionist foreign policy, objected to anti-German measures in South Tirol. Thus Elisabeth's enthusiasm for Mussolini was not even consonant with nationalist sentiments, an indication that she was

thinking more about her brother's fame than about the politics of the persons who supported the Archives. See Roswitha Wollkopf, "Die Gremien des Nietzsche-Archivs und ihre Beziehung zum Faschismus bis 1933," in *Im Vorfeld der Literatur: Vom Wert archivalischer Überlieferung für das Verständnis von Literatur und ihrer Geschichte*, ed. Karl-Heinz Hahn (Weimar: Verlag Hermann Böhlaus Nachfolger, 1991), 227–41, here, 236–37.

52. The story of Elisabeth Förster-Nietzsche has been told on several occasions, but never with much sympathy. The most extensive studies are Carol Diethe's *Nietzsche's Sister and the Will to Power: A Biography of Elisabeth Förster-Nietzsche* (Urbana: University of Illinois Press, 2003); and H. F. Peters, *Zarathustra's Sister: The Case of Elisabeth and Friedrich Nietzsche* (New York: Crown, 1977). Erich F. Podach's sketch of "Bernhard and Eli Förster" in his *Gestalten um Nietzsche* (Weimar: Erich Lichtenstein Verlag, 1932), 125–76, focuses mostly on the colonial enterprise in Paraguay. See also Klaus Goch, "Elisabeth Förster-Nietzsche 1846–1935: Ein biographisches Portrait," in *Schwestern berühmter Männer*, ed. Luise F. Pusch (Frankfurt: Insel, 1985), 361–413; and Karl S. Guthke: "Zarathustras Tante," *Neue Deutsche Hefte* 29, no. 3 (1982): 470–83.

53. See Robert C. Holub, "The Elisabeth Legend or Sibling Scapegoating: The Cleansing of Friedrich Nietzsche and the Sullying of His Sister," in *Nietzsche: Godfather of Fascism?: On the Uses and Abuses of Philosophy*, ed. Jacob Golomb and Robert S. Wistrich (Princeton, NJ: Princeton University Press, 2002), 215–34.

54. Friedrich Nietzsche, *Friedrich Nietzsches Gesammelte Briefe*, vol. 5, *Friedrich Nietzsches Briefe an Mutter und Schwester*, ed. Elisabeth Förster-Nietzsche (Leipzig: Insel, 1909), 757–58.

55. A thorough discussion of the letters is found in Curt Paul Janz, *Die Briefe Friedrich Nietzsches: Textprobleme und ihre Bedeutung für Biographie und Doxographie* (Zurich: Editio Academica, 1972). Janz is on the whole fairer to Elisabeth than many postwar commentators, probably because he has taken the time to examine the evidence thoroughly. He concedes that Elisabeth may have been the only choice as an editor for Nietzsche's writings since no one else would have been able to do the job or would have wanted to undertake it (50–53). He includes a thorough discussion of the various distortions in Elisabeth's edition of the letters written to her and her mother (63–101). He lists eighty items that Elisabeth did not include in her original edition. However, of these eighty items, the vast majority are postcards of a paragraph or less; other "suppressed" items are telegraphs, short letters, drafts, and letter fragments. Only a half dozen items are substantial letters. More significant is that none of the excluded items alter anything significant in the ideological views of Nietzsche.

56. "You have committed one of the greatest stupidities, my dear llama—for yourself and for me! Your connection with the chief anti-Semite is totally foreign to my nature and fills me again and again with anger and melancholy. You have said that you married the colonizer Förster and not the anti-Semite, and this is true; but in the eyes of the world Förster will remain until his death the head anti-Semite." *Gesammelte Briefe*, 733–34.

57. Nietzsche, *Friedrich Nietzsches Gesammelte Briefe*, 801–2. An indication that the thoughts in this letter are not invented is that Nietzsche expresses a similar view in a letter to Franz Overbeck in September 1888 (Nr. 1115, KSB 8.433). He soon

corrects himself and places Wilhelm II in the anti-Semitic camp and, in his last letter in a state of mental deterioration, orders him to be eliminated along with all anti-Semites (to Jacob Burckhardt, January 6, 1889, Nr. 1256, KSB 8.579). It is unlikely, however, that Nietzsche would have thought the Kaiser capable of understanding his philosophy of the will to power. See my article in *Nietzsche-Studien*, "Placing Elisabeth Förster-Nietzsche in the Crosshairs," 43 (2014): 132–51, which discusses this letter and other alleged falsifications by Elisabeth.

58. Here Elisabeth is playing with the title and first line of the popular song "Deutschland, Deutschland, über alles," written by Hoffmann von Fallersleben in the early 1840s. At this time it was not the German national anthem; it became the national anthem during the early years of the Weimar Republic.

59. Elisabeth Förster-Nietzsche, *Das Leben Friedrich Nietzsche's* (Leipzig: Naumann, 1897), 2.1: 208.

60. Elisabeth Förster-Nietzsche, *Wagner und Nietzsche zur Zeit ihrer Freundschaft* (Munich: Georg Müller, 1915), 211. The two Nietzsche letters to Wagner with negative statements about Jews cited by Elisabeth are genuine.

61. See David Marc Hoffmann, "Chronik," in *Zur Geschichte des Nietzsche-Archivs: Chronik, Studien und Dokumente* (Berlin: de Gruyter, 1991), 98–99. It is interesting that Rolland broke his association with the Nietzsche Archives only after Hitler had come to power, and that he used as his reason the Archive's championing of Mussolini, which can be traced to the mid-1920s.

62. Wollkopf, "Die Gremien des Nietzsche-Archivs," 231.

63. Mittmann argues that Thiel's support of the Archives was the reason that Elisabeth disavowed her own anti-Semitism and emphasized Nietzsche's favorable attitude toward the Jews and opposition to anti-Semitism (*Vom "Günstling" zum "Urfeind" der Juden*, 97–99). But Mittmann places Thiel's support for the Archives in the years starting with 1906. By that time Elisabeth had already completed the two-volume biography of her brother in which she makes pronouncements denying her own connection to anti-Semitism and supporting her brother's pro-Jewish utterances and anti-anti-Semitism. Mittmann is surely correct in noting the anti-Semitic attitudes of the Archives, and in particular of the Oehlers, but he fails to make a convincing argument regarding Elisabeth's advocacy for an anti-Semitic interpretation of her brother's writings.

64. Paul Cohn, *Um Nietzsches Untergang: Beiträge zum Verständnis des Genies*, mit einem Anhang von Elisabeth Förster-Nietzsche: Die Zeit von Nietzsches Erkrankung bis zu seinem Tode (Hanover: Morris-Verlag, 1931).

65. Förster-Nietzsche, *Das Leben Friedrich Nietzsche's*, 2.2: 469.

66. Both citations are taken from Richard Roos, "Elisabeth Förster-Nietzsche ou la sœur abusive," *Études Germanique* 11, no. 4 (1956): 321–41, here, 340. See also Peters, who reports on her correspondence to Thiel: "Since she was the widow of one of the first German anti-Semites, many people thought that she was anti-Semitic herself, but that was quite untrue. Indeed, a number of her good friends were Jewish. On the other hand, she understood why there was so much anti-Semitic feeling in Germany at present. The reason was that in some professions, notably in medicine, law, and banking, Jews predominated while non-Jews were unemployed. She added that it still was not right to persecute them and that some of her Jewish friends had turned to her for help, hoping that she would bring this problem to Hitler's personal

attention" (220–21). Elisabeth was certainly naive to think that Hitler was not anti-Semitic and that he had adopted this ideology simply to achieve political advantage. But the evidence we possess indicates she apparently believed Hitler would drop the anti-Semitic plank of his party platform after his appointment as chancellor.

67. Erich F. Podach, "Anhang," in *Friedrich Nietzsches Werke des Zusammenbruchs* (Heidelberg: Wolfgang Rothe Verlag, 1961), 414. Podach claims that there is documentary evidence for his assertions, but cites nothing specifically.

68. Janz, who again is hardly an apologist for Elisabeth, states that she spoke "sharply and unambiguously against the persecution of the Jews" in 1933 after Hitler came to power. Curt Paul Janz, *Friedrich Nietzsche: Biographie*, 3 vols. (Munich: Hanser, 1978), 3: 203. It is worth noting for the record that Elisabeth was never a member of the National Socialist party, even after January of 1933. There are, of course, various statements, especially in correspondence, that indicate she found that Jews and Germans are different, although the differences do not seem to be attributable to race. See Sandro Barbera, "'Eine schreckliche Prophezeiung Nietzsches': Nationalismus und Antisemitismus im Briefwechsel zwischen Elisabeth Förster-Nietzsche und Hans Vaihinger," in *Friedrich Nietzsche: Rezeption und Kultus*, ed. Sandro Barbera et al. (Pisa: Edizioni ETS, 2004), 259–99. Some of her statements indicate that she harbors the same clichéd views that existed in her brother's writing, for example, that Jews have monopolized the press and have an inordinate amount of ill-gotten wealth. She also attributes to Jews, as well as to other nations, certain fairly fixed characteristics. But at the same time she writes to a friend who was more solidly in the anti-Semitic camp: "The enmity towards Judaism seems to me from all the experiences I have had not to be right. The Jews bear the same burdens that we do and are for better or for worse tied to the future of Germany just as we are.... Really anti-Semitism is not necessary and is based on a false understanding that we have of Jews and that Jews have of us, since we both demand the same views and characteristics of each other. The mistake on our side is that we regard the Jews as foreign interlopers; the mistake of the Jews is their super-sensitivity, which is really not necessary since they have such great power in their hands" (272–73). And in another letter: "I cannot agree at all that when the Jews judge the great German thinkers that these are always false interpretations. That was what always infuriated my brother: that the truth must be conceived nationally and that one does not allow another people a different opinion.... I believe that the relationship between Germans and Jews must be a reasoned marriage. In every marriage there are many differences and here and there antithetical views; but when you amiably respect and recognize the difference of opinion, then you can have an entirely bearable relationship; sometimes it can even develop into a love relationship, and this is what I wish for" (275). It is difficult to reconcile these statements with Barbera's conclusion that Elisabeth retains the same views on the Jewish Question that her former husband, Bernhard Förster, had (291).

69. Franz Mehring, the most influential cultural theorist in the German Socialist Party from 1890 through the First World War, considered Nietzsche to be the philosopher of advanced capitalism. He reprimands him for his ignorance of the history of his own times, but in particular for his complete misunderstanding of the ascendant working-class movement. Nietzsche represents "subjectively a desperate delirium of

the mind," but his philosophy is "objectively a glorification of capitalism." Franz Mehring, *Gesammelte Schriften* (Berlin: Dietz Verlag, 1961), 11: 219.

70. For the orthodox communist view see Hans Günther, *Der Herren eigner Geist* (Moscow-Leningrad: Verlagsgenossenschaft ausländischer Arbeiter in der UdSSR, 1935); and Günther's essay "Der Fall Nietzsche," *Unter dem Banner des Marxismus* 9 (1935): 541.

71. See Jeffrey Herf, *Divided Memory: The Nazi Past in Two Germanys* (Cambridge, MA: Harvard University Press, 1997), 106–61.

72. During the Third Reich Lukács had published two essays about Nietzsche that form the basis for much of what becomes the chapter in *The Destruction of Reason*: "Nietzsche als Vorläufer der faschistischen Ästhetik," *Internationale Literatur* 5, no. 8 (1935): 76–92; "Der deutsche Faschismus und Nietzsche," *Internationale Literatur* 13, no. 12 (1943): 55–64.

73. Georg Lukács, *Die Zerstörung der Vernunft* (Berlin: Aufbau, 1954), 244–317, esp. 283–84.

74. Karl Schlechta, "Philologischer Nachbericht," in volume 3 of Friedrich Nietzsche, *Werke in drei Bänden* (Munich: Hanser, 1956), 1409.

75. Karl Schlechta, *Der Fall Nietzsche* (Munich: Hanser, 1958), 78.

76. These exclusions were already noted by H. J. Mette in his introduction to the fragmentary critical edition started in 1933.

77. Richard Roos, "Les derniers écrits de Nietzsche el leur publication," *Revue philosophique* 146 (1956): 262–87.

78. Roos, "Elisabeth Förster-Nietzsche," 322.

79. Ibid., 339.

80. Walter Kaufmann, *Nietzsche: Philosopher, Psychologist, Antichrist*, 4th ed. (Princeton, NJ: Princeton University Press, 1974). His monograph was translated into German by the noted Nietzsche scholar Jörg Salaquarda, appearing in the prestigious publishing house Wissenschaftliche Buchgesellschaft (Darmstadt, 1982). We should also be aware that Kaufmann was not shy about pushing his views about Nietzsche in his editorial comments and notes to the English translations he published.

81. Roos also employs the notion of a "legend" about Nietzsche propagated by Elisabeth, but he does not fill in the content of this legend. Since it is mentioned directly after passages in Elisabeth's correspondence relating to her enthusiasm for Hitler, he leads the reader to believe that the legend she propagated has to do with chauvinism and anti-Semitism. Roos, "Elisabeth Förster-Nietzsche," 341.

82. Kaufmann does not make explicit what these "repudiations" entail, but there is nothing in *Ecce Homo* relating to race and anti-Semitism that clarifies or elaborates what appears in other published writings.

83. Walter Kaufmann, "Editor's Introduction" to Friedrich Nietzsche, *The Will to Power*, trans. Walter Kaufmann and R. J. Hollingdale, ed. Walter Kaufmann (New York: Vintage, 1967), xx.

84. Included in Kaufmann's introduction is a searing critique of Schlechta's handling of *The Will to Power*. Schlechta, in an attempt to move as far away from Elisabeth's practices as possible, had simply placed the notes included in *The Will to Power* in chronological order (although not entirely successfully, as Kaufmann points out) and labeled them "Literary Remains of the 1880s." In a certain sense, this

is exactly what they were, and in the authoritative Colli-Montinari edition, the editors simply reproduce the notebooks without any concessions to *The Will to Power*. Kaufmann considers Schlechta's arrangement "utterly pointless" and an "over-reaction" to previous editions; it "represents an attempt to render *The Will to Power* all but unreadable" (xiv), something we might have supposed Kaufmann would have welcomed as a correction to the "Nietzsche legend" the book implicitly advances. Kaufmann's inconsistency goes beyond the publication of Elisabeth's arrangement and into mercantile considerations. He criticizes Elisabeth's publishing practices as attempts to maximize the money she would receive from her brother's works, but Kaufmann himself appears to have followed the very same principles in publishing *The Will to Power* under its original title. One of the ironies of the postwar period is that Elisabeth is often criticized for milking her brother's works in order to procure a good living by precisely those scholars, translators, and editors who are doing exactly the same thing.

85. Kaufmann, *Nietzsche*, 8.

86. Kaufmann, "Editor's Introduction," *Will to Power*, xix.

87. Kaufmann, *Nietzsche*, 45.

88. Ibid., 42.

89. Ibid., 46.

90. Ibid., 486.

CHAPTER TWO

1. See Hans von Müller, "Nietzsches Vorfahren," *Nietzsche-Studien* 31 (2002): 253–75.

2. Siegfried Mandel, *Nietzsche and the Jews: Exaltation and Denigration* (Amherst, NY: Prometheus Books, 1998), 32–33.

3. Jacob Katz, *From Prejudice to Destruction: Anti-Semitism, 1700–1933* (Cambridge, MA: Harvard University Press, 1980), 195.

4. Stefi Jersch-Wenzel, "Legal Status and Emancipation," in *German-Jewish History in Modern Times*, ed. Michael A. Meyer, vol. 2 (New York: Columbia University Press, 1997), 31. In 1938 the Nazi historian Volkmar Eichstädt listed more than three thousand titles dealing with the Jewish Question between 1750 and 1848. See Volkmar Eichstädt, *Bibliographie zur Geschichte der Judenfrage I, 1750–1848* (Hamburg: Hanseatische Verlagsanstalt, 1938).

5. Michael Brenner, "Between Revolution and Legal Equality," in *German-Jewish History in Modern Times*, 291–92.

6. See Thomas Mittmann, *Vom "Günstling" zum "Urfeind" der Juden: Die antisemitische Nietzsche-Rezeption in Deutschland bis zum Ende des Nationalsozialismus* (Würzburg: Königshausen und Neumann, 2006), 25.

7. See Martin Onnasch, "Naumburg," in *Wegweiser durch das jüdische Sachsen-Anhalt* (Potsdam: Verlag für Berlin-Brandenburg, 1998), 142–49; and Jacqueline E. Jung, "The Passion, the Jews, and the Crisis of the Individual on the Naumburg West Choir Screen," in *Beyond the Yellow Badge: Anti-Judaism and Antisemitism in Medieval and Early Modern Visual Culture*, ed. Mitchell Merback (Leiden: Brill, 2008), 145–77.

8. Elisabeth Förster-Nietzsche, *Der einsame Nietzsche* (Leipzig: Kröner, 1914), 348–49.

9. "Pogrom in Neustettin (1881)," in *Ereignisse, Dekrete, Kontroversen* (Berlin: de Gruyter, 2011), 288.

10. *Der "Berliner Antisemitismusstreit," 1879–1881: Eine Kontroverse um die Zugehörigkeit der deutschen Juden zur Nation*, ed. Karsten Krieger, vol. 2 (Munich: K. G. Saur, 2003), 774–81. Originally in *Die Tribüne*, Nr. 298 (December 19, 1880).

11. "Kasperl und Abraham," in *Kasper Putschenelle: Historisches über die Handpuppen und althamburgische Kasperszenen*, ed. Johs. E. Rabe (Hamburg: C. Boysen, 1912), 178–86.

12. There were forty-one Jewish students from 1,177 matriculants in 1886–87. See "Universities," in *The Jewish Encyclopedia*, ed. Isidore Singer (New York: Funk and Wagnalls, 1901–6), 12: 379.

13. See "Bonn," in *Jewish Encyclopedia*, 3: 308–9.

14. See Jens Rybak, "Ernst Moritz Arndts Judenbilder: Ein unbekanntes Kapitel," *Hefte der Ernst-Moritz-Arndt-Gesellschaft* 6 (1997): 102–37.

15. See Sigrid Nieberle, "'Und Gott im Himmel Lieder singt': Zur prekären Rezeption von Ernst Mortiz Arndts 'Des Deutschen Vaterland'," in *Ernst Moritz Arndt (1769–1860): Deutscher Nationalismus—Europa—Transatlantische Perspektiven*, ed. Walter Erhart and Arne Koch (Tübingen: Niemeyer, 2007), 121–36.

16. Kuno Fischer, *Nathan der Weise: Die Idee und die Charaktere der Dichtung* (Stuttgart: Cotta, 1864), esp. 32, 102–5.

17. David Friedrich Strauß, *Nathan der Weise* (Bonn: Emil Strauß, 1877), 3. The lecture was originally published in 1866.

18. See Curt Paul Janz, *Friedrich Nietzsche: Biographie*, 2nd rev. ed. (Munich: Hanser, 1993), 3: 212–13.

19. Carl Albrecht Bernoulli, *Franz Overbeck und Friedrich Nietzsche: Eine Freundschaft* (Jena: Eugen Diederich, 1908), 1: 135–37.

20. Stirner viewed Jews as lacking spirituality in comparison with Christians. He contributed as well to the controversies around Jewish emancipation in left Hegelian circles in the 1840s.

21. Robert Allen Willingham II, "Jews in Leipzig: Nationality and Community in the 20th Century" (PhD diss. University of Texas 2005), 15–17. The Leipzig Jewish community increased rapidly during the nineteenth century, from 162 in 1838, to 1,739 in 1871, to 3,179 in 1880.

22. Mandel, *Nietzsche and the Jews*, 16.

23. In 1864 Pinder studied law in Heidelberg, but the friends exchanged letters frequently through the mid-1860s. Pinder visited Nietzsche in Basel, but they ceased all contact in the early 1870s.

24. Deussen later married a woman of Jewish heritage.

25. At the beginning of the nineteenth century every fourth citizen of Fürth was Jewish, and Jews enjoyed rights of citizenship in Fürth that they possessed nowhere else in Germany.

26. The last opera of Giacomo Meyerbeer, a Jewish composer who was important for Wagner's view on Jews in the musical world of the nineteenth century.

27. See Aldo Venturelli, "Asketismus und Wille zur Macht: Nietzsches Auseinandersetzung mit Eugen Dühring," *Nietzsche-Studien* 15 (1986): 107–39.

28. See Walter Boehlich, ed., *Der Berliner Antisemitismusstreit* (Frankfurt: Insel, 1965); and Karsten Krieger, ed., *Der "Berliner Antisemitismusstreit" 1879–1881: Eine*

Kontroverse um die Zugehörigkeit der deutschen Juden zur Nation, 2 vols. (Munich: Sauer, 2003).

29. His philological efforts are collected in volume 2, part 1 of his complete works.

30. See Johann Figl, "Nietzsches Begegnung mit Schopenhauers Hauptwerk: Unter Heranzeihung eines frühen veröffentlichten Exzerptes," in *Schopenhauer, Nietzsche und die Kunst*, ed. Wolfgang Schirmacher (Vienna: Passagen Verlag, 1991), 89–100.

31. Moshe Zimmermann, *Wilhelm Marr: The Patriarch of Anti-Semitism* (New York: Oxford University Press, 1986), 13.

32. An exception is chapter 48 in the fourth book of *The World as Will and Representation*. See Arthur Schopenhauer, *Zürcher Ausgabe, Werke in zehn Bänden: Die Welt als Wille und Vorstellung*, ed. Arthur Hübscher (Zurich: Diogenes, 1977), 2.2: 706–43.

33. David E. Cartwright, *Schopenhauer: A Biography* (Cambridge: Cambridge University Press, 2010), 542–43.

34. Maria Groener, *Schopenhauer und die Juden* (Munich: Deutscher Volksverlag, 1920).

35. See Henry Walter Brann, *Schopenhauer und das Judentum* (Bonn: Bouvier, 1975).

36. Arthur Schopenhauer, *Zürcher Ausgabe, Werke in zehn Bänden: Parerga und Paralipomena II*, ed. Arthur Hübscher (Zurich: Diogenes, 1977), 2.2: 417.

37. Schopenhauer, *Zürcher Ausgabe, Werke in zehn Bänden*, 1.1: 143–45.

38. Ibid., 1.2: 393–94. Wolfgang Weimer in "Der Philosoph und der Diktator: Arthur Schopenhauer und Adolf Hitler," *Schopenhauer-Jahrbuch* 84 (2003): 157–67, points out that Hitler was fond of citing Schopenhauer's contention that the Jews were the "great masters in lying." It is odd that Weimer states that he could not find the phrase anywhere in Schopenhauer's writings and therefore maintains that Hitler's citation of Schopenhauer is a "mystification" (163).

39. This concern with Jewish mistreatment of animals would become a central motif in National Socialist propaganda against the Jews, in particular in discussions relating to the kosher slaughter of animals. A large section of Fritz Hippler's propaganda film *The Eternal Jew* (1940) is devoted to a condemnation of kosher slaughtering, or "shechita."

40. Schopenhauer, *Zürcher Ausgabe, Werke in zehn Bänden*, 2.2: 409–15.

41. Ibid., 2.1: 284–87.

CHAPTER THREE

1. When Nietzsche first met Wagner, Cosima was still married to the conductor Hans von Bülow, although she had left him in 1868 and already given birth to two daughters fathered by Wagner. Cosima and Richard married August 25, 1870, in Lucerne.

2. See Joachim Köhler, *Nietzsche and Wagner: A Lesson in Subjugation* (New Haven, CT: Yale University Press, 1998).

3. See, for example, Robert S. Wistrich, "The Cross and the Swastika: A Nietzschean Perspective," in *Nietzsche, Godfather of Fascism? On the Uses and Abuses of a*

Philosophy, ed. Jacob Golomb and Robert S. Wistrich (Princeton, NJ: Princeton University Press, 2002), 144–69, here, 149. To a certain extent Elisabeth also argues this position.

4. See Yirmiyahu Yovel, "Nietzsche contra Wagner on the Jews," in *Nietzsche, Godfather of Fascism?*, 126–43, esp. 126. The irony is that Wagner and Cosima, after glancing at *Human, All Too Human*, claimed that Paul Rée captured Nietzsche in a similarly hypnotic fashion, removing him from his genuine identity and making him a tool of "Israel." See the excerpt from Cosima's letter in "Chronik zu Nietzsches Leben" (KSA 15.84).

5. The piano score was published well before the opening of the opera.

6. They did retain the formal level of address, however. Nietzsche's usual salutations in letters are "Geliebter Meister" or "Verehrtester Meister," and he addresses Cosima with "Verehrte or Verehrteste Frau," although before her marriage to Wagner he writes "Verehrteste Frau Baronin" (June 19, 1870, Nr. 81, KSB 3.125).

7. Tribschen is approximately 100 kilometers from Basel.

8. Cosima Wagner, *Diaries*, vol. 1, *1869–1877* (New York: Harcourt Brace Jovanovich, 1978), 28.

9. Cosima Wagner, *Diaries*, 1: 43.

10. In this general tendency Wagner is very much like Wilhelm Marr, one of the foremost anti-Semitic agitators of the early 1880s. See Moshe Zimmermann, *Wilhelm Marr: The Patriarch of Anti-Semitism* (New York: Oxford University Press, 1986).

11. Richard Wagner, *Das Judenthum in der Musik* (Leipzig: J. J. Weber, 1869), 9–32.

12. Auerbach joined the troops in the Franco-Prussian War in the headquarters of the grand duke of Baden. The poem in question supports the annexation of the Alsace region. This sort of comment and the following remark from her diary are typical of the Wagners' knee-jerk condemnation of almost anything that stems from a Jew.

13. Cosima Wagner, *Diaries*, 1: 224.

14. Karl Gutzkow was a writer and journalist associated in the 1830s with the Young Germans. Because two writers of Jewish heritage, Heinrich Heine and Ludwig Börne, were associated with Young Germany, Gutzkow was often assumed falsely to be Jewish himself. For translations from "On the Future of Our Educational Institutions" I have consulted the English rendition of J. M. Kennedy (Edinburgh: T. N. Foulis, 1910).

15. I have used the translations by Richard T. Gray in the volume *Unfashionable Observations*, The Complete Works of Friedrich Nietzsche, vol. 2 (Stanford, CA: Stanford University Press, 1995) for all citations from *Untimely Meditations* in this chapter.

16. English translation by R. J. Hollingdale from *Human, All Too Human: A Book for Free Spirits* (Cambridge: Cambridge University Press, 1986), 346.

17. The irony is that Wagner himself did not hesitate to associate with Jews and to employ them for his own purposes when he could reap a benefit. But from Wagner's later reaction against Paul Rée it is safe to conclude that he did not extend the same latitude to his disciples.

18. Wagner, *Das Judenthum in der Musik*, 33–34.

19. Ibid., 42.

20. Ibid., 43.

21. Ibid., 44–45.

22. Ibid., 52–54.

23. W. Marr, *Der Sieg des Judenthums über das Germanenthum* (Bern: Rudolph Costenoble, 1879).

24. Wagner, *Das Judenthum in der Musik*, 57.

25. Thus Mendelssohn or the poet and critic Heinrich Heine remain essentially "Jewish" for Wagner despite their conversion. Wagner did not have a fully developed biologically based racist theory of Judaism, but his views went beyond a simple religious notion. Conversion was not a definitive solution to the Jewish Question.

26. See Lionel Gossman, *Basel in the Age of Burckhardt* (Chicago: University of Chicago Press, 2000), 29, 463.

27. Franz Overbeck, *Erinnerungen an Friedrich Nietzsche* (Berlin: Berenberg, 2011), 89–90.

28. Translation from *Twilight of the Idols* based on R. J. Hollingdale in Friedrich Nietzsche, *Twilight of the Idols / The Anti-Christ* (London: Penguin, 1968), here, 75. Translation copyright © R. J. Hollingdale. Reproduced by permission of Penguin Books Ltd.

29. Hans Liebesschütz, "Das Judentum und die Kontinuität der abendländischen Kultur: Jacob Burckhardt," in *Das Judentum im deutschen Geschichtsbild von Hegel bis Max Weber* (Tübingen: Mohr, 1967), 220–44; see also Gossman, *Basel in the Age of Burckhardt*, 244–45.

30. Jacob Burckhardt, "Jacob Burckhardt an Friedrich von Preen," in *Der "Berliner Antisemitismusstreit," 1879–1881: Eine Kontroverse um die Zugehörigkeit der deutschen Juden zur Nation*, ed. Karsten Krieger (Munich: Sauer, 2003), 1: 251.

31. Gersdorff is referring here to Paul de Lagarde, a professor of oriental languages (which meant the languages of the Middle East), who was one of the sources of National Socialist anti-Semitism. The word "judainfrei," translated here as "Jew-free," is derived from Lagarde. The difference between "jüdisch" and "judain" is not made clear in Lagarde's writing, and there is probably only an academic distinction. Nietzsche used a form of "judaine" twice in his late writings. We know that Nietzsche was familiar with several of Lagarde's writings by the early 1870s. His initial admiration turned into disdain in the 1880s.

32. With a copyright date of 1872, however.

33. I am citing from the version that must have been close to what Nietzsche actually delivered in his lecture on February 1, 1870. The text in KSA 1.533–49 does not contain the final sentence and parts of the penultimate sentence. It is also difficult to determine with absolute certainty whether this passage was the final one in the lecture.

34. Cosima Wagner, *Diaries*, 1: 186.

35. Ibid., 189.

36. Nietzsche wrote these remarks shortly after he had returned from his visit to Tribschen.

37. See Shulamith Volkov, "Antisemitismus als kultureller Code," in *Antisemitismus als kultureller Code* (Munich: Beck, 1990), 13–36.

38. Cosima Wagner, *Diaries*, 1: 73.

39. Ibid., 199.

40. It is difficult to translate Gersdorff's sentence, since it uses German slang to slur the Jews. The verb "ausgeschachert," which I rendered as "huckstered out" refers to haggling and is often employed in connection with Jews. "Vermauschelt," which I have rendered simply as "scalped," refers to German speech by Jews that is influenced by Yiddish as well as to dishonest dealings of Jews. Gersdorff's point is obvious to the German reader: the Jews control not only the stock market, where they do their illicit dealings, but also the theater life, where they profit on the black market from tickets to Wagner's premiere.

41. The letter from Gersdorff to Wagner is printed in "Anhang: Briefe, Erinnerungen und andere Materialien" (Nr. 18, KGB II 7/1.615–17).

42. Translations from *The Birth of Tragedy* are based on Friedrich Nietzsche, *The Birth of Tragedy*, trans. Douglas Smith (Oxford: Oxford University Press, 2000).

43. Nietzsche rejected the traditional Grecophilic view of Greece throughout his sane life. He ridicules the notions of Greek harmony, simplicity, and serenity as a *"niaiserie allemande"* in 1888 in *Twilight of the Idols* (GD, Was ich den Alten verdanke 3, KSA 6.157).

44. Schopenhauer, *Zürcher Ausgabe, Werke in zehn Bänden, Die Welt als Wille und Vorstellung*, ed. Arthur Hübscher (Zurich: Diogenes, 1977), 2.12: 709.

45. Schopenhauer again notes the optimism of Judaism in passages that precede the citation from his magnum opus.

46. This view of Kant is clearly influenced by Schopenhauer; most historians of philosophy would not consider Kant to be a pessimist or to be opposed to enlightenment. With regard to the views of Enlightenment philosophers on Jews, we should note that their rationalism and "optimism" did not necessarily lead them to overcome their traditional and cultural Judeophobia. See Michael Mack, *German Idealism and the Jew: The Inner Anti-Semitism of Philosophy and German Jewish Responses* (Chicago: University of Chicago Press, 2003).

47. In a manner typical of Nietzsche's disingenuous attitude toward his earlier anti-Jewish statements, he writes the following about this passage in *Ecce Homo*: "In one place the Christian priests are alluded to as a 'malicious species of dwarves,' as 'subterraneans'" (EH, Warum ich so gute Bücher schreibe, Die Geburt der Tragödie 1, KSA 6.310). See Christian Niemeyer, "Nietzsches rhetorischer Antisemitismus," *Nietzsche-Studien* 26 (1997): 139–62, esp. 141.

48. Léon Poliakov, *The Aryan Myth: A History of Racist and Nationalistic Ideas in Europe* (New York: Barnes and Noble, 1996), 255.

49. Since the two terms originate in speculation about historical linguistics, it is likely that Nietzsche had encountered them in his reading. Certainly he was acquainted with the antithesis between things that were German or Germanic and those that were Jewish.

50. Cosima Wagner, *Diaries*, 1: 445–46, 450.

51. Ibid., 555, 681.

52. The conspiracy was probably related to the Bonn "battle of philologists" (*Philologenstreit*), a conflict that originated in the animosity between Nietzsche's dissertation director, Friedrich Ritschl, and his colleague Otto Jahn. The details of the academic politics that form a background to the Nietzsche-Wilamowitz controversy

are explicated best in William Musgrave Calder III, "The Wilamowitz-Nietzsche Struggle: New Documents and a Reappraisal," *Nietzsche-Studien* 121 (1983): 214–54.

53. Wagner's enemies used the term "Music of the Future" (*Zukunftsmusik*) to ridicule him.

54. The Wagnerians associated Berlin with the Jews for many reasons, but we should also recall Nietzsche's initial visit to the city and his encounter with Eduard Mushacke discussed in chapter two.

55. He calls him "Wilamo-Wisch" (literally, "Wilamo Rag") and "Wilam Ohne witz" (literally, "Wilam without Wit").

56. See Max L. Baeumer, *Dionysos und das Dionysische in der antiken und deutschen Literatur* (Darmstadt: Wissenschaftliche Buchgesellschaft, 2006); Manfred Frank, *Der kommende Gott* (Frankfurt: Suhrkamp, 1982); and Jürgen Habermas, "The Entry into Postmodernity: Nietzsche," in *The Philosophical Discourse of Modernity: Twelve Lectures* (Cambridge, MA: MIT Press, 1987), 83–105.

57. *Grundzüge der verlorenen Abhandlung des Aristoteles über Wirkung der Tragödie* (Breslau: E. Trewendt, 1857). See Jochen Schmidt, *Kommentar zu Nietzsches* Die Geburt der Tragödie (Berlin: de Gruyter, 2012), 47.

58. Cosima may have heard about Bernays's remark from Marie, Princess of Weid. See Hans I. Bach, *Jacob Bernays: Ein Beitrag zur Emanzipationsgeschichte der Juden und zur Geschichte des deutschen Geistes im neunzehnten Jahrhundert* (Tübingen: Mohr, 1974), 182.

59. Usener is Hermann Usener, like Bernays, a philologist in Bonn, who had made derogatory remarks about the book.

60. Cosima Wagner, *Diaries*, 1: 228. Cosima is referring to Bethel Henry Strousberg, the railroad magnate, who had formerly been a journalist and publisher in England. As is the case for so many other Jewish slurs, Cosima's claim is false: Strousberg never owned the *Augsburg Allgemeine Zeitung*.

61. In a letter to Gersdorff from December 23, 1872, he mentions the title as "Five Prefaces to Five Unwritten and Not-to-Be Written Books" (Nr. 284, KSB 4.108).

62. He also tries to contribute directly to propaganda for the Bayreuth project, as we see in his "Admonition to the Germans" (*Mahnruf an die Deutschen*) (KSA 1.891–97). Wagner rejected his efforts, probably because his piece was too academic in tone.

63. It may seem strange that Nietzsche mentions Goethe's *Faust* along with *Nathan*. But Goethe was a favorite of the assimilated Jewish community throughout the nineteenth century. See Klaus L. Berghahn and Jost Hermand, eds., *Goethe in German-Jewish Culture* (Rochester, NY: Camden House, 2001), esp. the essays by Barbara Hahn, "Demarcations and Projections: Goethe in the Berlin Salons" (31–43), and Jost Hermand, "A View from Below: H. Heine's Relationship to Johann Wolfgang von Goethe" (44–62). Indeed, Cosima mentions in her diary in 1876 that Michael Bernays, the brother of the classicist Jacob Bernays, is "the greatest living authority on Goethe" (901). Michael Bernays, like many persons of German Jewish heritage, abandoned Judaism for Protestantism in his early life. See also Nietzsche's own comment in *The Case of Wagner*: "One knows Goethe's fate in moraline-sour, old-maidish Germany. He always seemed offensive to Germans; he had honest admirers only among Jewesses" (KSA 6.18). For many German Jews and persons of

German Jewish heritage it was precisely Goethe's cosmopolitanism and lack of a rigid nationalism that made him so cherished.

64. Wagner wrote to Nietzsche: "Your book is tremendous! How did you acquire so much knowledge about me?" (July 13, 1876, Nr. 797, KGB II 6/1.362).

CHAPTER FOUR

1. Cosima Wagner, *Diaries*, vol. 2, *1878–1883* (New York: Harcourt Brace Jovanovich, 1980), 79.

2. Cosima Wagner, *Diaries*, 2: 65.

3. Ibid., 66, 100.

4. Ibid., 80, 90.

5. Ibid., 105.

6. His sister reports that he remarked as he left her: "Ach, Lisabeth, that was Bayreuth," but as Louis Kelterborn reports, Nietzsche hardly spoke about Wagner or the festival performances upon his return to Basel. Perhaps Nietzsche's silence was due to the fact that almost all his friends and correspondents were Wagner enthusiasts. See Sander L. Gilman, ed., *Begegnungen mit Nietzsche* (Bonn: Bouvier, 1981), 298–301.

7. Translations from *Ecce Homo* are taken from Friedrich Nietzsche, *Ecce Homo*, trans. R. J. Hollingdale (London: Penguin, 1979).

8. The latest defender of the theory that Nietzsche is referring to Wagner's embrace of Christianity as the "moral insult" is Reto Winteler, "Nietzsches Bruch mit Wagner: Zur Plausibilität seiner späteren Stilisierung," *Nietzsche-Studien* 40 (2011): 256–72. It is certainly the most plausible theory from the evidence we possess.

9. See Sander L. Gilman, "Otto Eiser and Nietzsche's Illness: A Hitherto Unpublished Text," *Nietzsche-Studien* 38 (2009): 396–409, here, 406.

10. See Curt Paul Janz, "Die 'tödliche Beleidigung': Ein Beitrag zur Wagner-Entfremdung Nietzsches," *Nietzsche-Studien* 4 (1975): 263–78. Janz quotes from Wagner's letter on pp. 270–71.

11. Translation by Walter Kaufmann in his *The Portable Nietzsche* (New York: Viking, 1968), 676.

12. It is necessary to draw the distinction between anti-Jewish thought, which Nietzsche did not find offensive and in which he continued to participate, and anti-Semitic thought, which Nietzsche rejected as part of *ressentiment* and often associated with Christian—and originally, Jewish—rancor. This distinction will be discussed in greater detail in chapter five.

13. Cosima Wagner, *Diaries*, 1: 176. What they read was likely a draft of the 1865 sketch of the opera.

14. See Christian Niemeyer, "Nietzsches rhetorischer Antisemitismus," *Nietzsche-Studien* 26 (1997): 139–62.

15. In his late correspondence Nietzsche is also disingenuous in writing to others about his relationship with Wagner. When he presents his "vita" to Georg Brandes, he emphasizes the "intimacy" he enjoyed with Wagner and Cosima but never mentions the adversarial role he has now assumed (April 10, 1888, Nr. 1014, KSB 8.289). To the German American author Karl Knortz he writes that the years

with "Richard Wagner and Frau Cosima Wagner" belong to the "most valuable of my life," again emphasizing their closeness. He does mention that he is now a Wagner adversary, but encourages Knortz to read Wagner's letter to him, praising *The Birth of Tragedy*, when it was under attack by Wilamowitz (June 21, 1888, Nr. 1050, KSB 8.340). In a letter to the French author Jean Bourdeau he assumes a similar tone: "in Richard Wagner and his wife, who at that time lived in Tribschen near Lucerne, I had such an intimacy that I cannot imagine one more valuable for me" (December 17, 1888, Nr. 1196, KSB 8.533). Again there is no mention that the two men had any subsequent disagreement. When corresponding with individuals of international repute, it seems that Nietzsche wanted to highlight his proximity to celebrity rather than his differences with Wagner. It is also noticeable that despite the many derogatory statements about Wagner following their estrangement, Nietzsche continues to value him greatly. A decade after their break, Nietzsche even writes the following to Overbeck, with whom he is usually quite candid: "It is amazing how faithfully all these followers of Wagner remain attached to me; I believe they know that even today as well as formerly I still believe in the ideal that Wagner believed" (October 27, 1886, Nr. 769, KSB 7.273). What that ideal consists of in Nietzsche's mind in 1886, and whether it includes any elements of Wagner's anti-Jewish sentiment, is difficult to determine with any precision.

16. Theodor Lessing, *Der jüdische Selbsthaß* (Berlin: Jüdischer Verlag, 1930), 55–79. Lessing meant something a bit different by the epithet "self-hating," but commentators have continued to employ it in its most obvious meaning.

17. See Robin Small, *Nietzsche and Rée: A Star Friendship* (Oxford: Clarendon Press, 2005), which is the best study of the Nietzsche-Rée relationship: "Theodor Lessing's account of Rée's relationship with Nietzsche is an imaginary construction which inspires little confidence in his psychological assessment" (50). Among the most egregious errors, Lessing has Lou Salomé accompanying Nietzsche to Sorrento as a secretary in 1876. In 1876 Salomé was fifteen and living in Russia; she met both Rée and Nietzsche in 1882.

18. Cited in the supplementary materials to Lou Andreas-Salomé, *Lebensrückblick: Grundriß einiger Lebenserinnerungen* (Zurich: Mas Niehans, 1951), 301. It is noteworthy that her description of Rée in the actual memoir does not even mention his Jewish heritage. She does mention that he was a "melancholic" and a "pessimist" who overcame these traits of his youth and became a "confident, cheerful man," and that therefore his "neurotic substratum remained for me undiscovered" (113). How she finally discovered the key to Rée, and why she assumed he was a self-hating Jew, are certainly not evident from her portrayal of him in her memoirs proper.

19. Tönnies's remarks are taken from notes Lessing used for his book on *Jewish Self-Hatred* (56–67).

20. Curt Paul Janz, *Friedrich Nietzsche: Biographie*, 3 vols. (Munich: Hanser, 1978), 1: 643–44.

21. Malwida von Meysenbug made the transition from revolutionary in 1848 to Wagnerian in the 1870s. She was inspirational for the first wave of feminism in the last three decades of the nineteenth century and something like a mother figure for Nietzsche.

22. Many of Rée's writings are now available in Paul Rée, *Basic Writings*, trans. and ed. Robin Small (Urbana: University of Illinois Press, 2003). Small also provides

an excellent introduction focusing on Rée's life and his intellectual relationship with Nietzsche.

23. Although Rée expressed admiration for Nietzsche, there is no evidence that he noticed or rejected the implicit anti-Jewish allusions in Nietzsche's writings or the anti-Semitism of the Wagner circle. He appears to have been simply uninterested in these matters and focused on more philosophical issues.

24. Cosima Wagner, *Diaries*, 1: 930 and 931.

25. In the draft of a letter to Rée in July 1883 he writes: "R[ichard] W[agner] once warned me about you and said: 'one day he will treat you badly; he has nothing good in mind for you'" (Nr. 434, KSB 6.399).

26. Cosima Wagner, *Diaries*, 2: 100.

27. Cited in KSA 15.83–84.

28. Cited in KGW IV 4.47.

29. Lou Salomé, *Lebensrückblick*, 101.

30. What actually occurred among the main actors in this drama will probably never be known exactly. We can say with certainty only that the plan for Rée, Lou, and Nietzsche to spend an extended period of time together in Paris never happened, and that Nietzsche was left alone while Rée and Lou were for a time together in Berlin. We know that Nietzsche had exceedingly bitter feelings toward Lou and then toward Rée. What role Elisabeth Nietzsche played is not entirely clear, although it is evident that she did everything possible to prevent the proposed *ménage à trois*. The best account in English can be found in chapters 8 and 9 of Small's book, *Nietzsche and Rée* (130–62).

31. In his draft for the letter to Paul Rée, Nietzsche writes: "How I would treat a man who speaks this way about me to my sister, there can be no doubt. I am a soldier and will always be one; I understand how to use a weapon" (beginning of December 1882, Nr. 339, KSB 6.285). Nietzsche had engaged in a duel as a student in Bonn and received the obligatory scar to prove his manliness.

32. Small in *Nietzsche and Rée* uses this line of argument for Nietzsche's "loss of self-control" (150).

33. For a comprehensive history of the Pernerstorfer circle, see William J. McGrath, *Dionysian Art and Populist Politics in Austria* (New Haven, CT: Yale University Press, 1974).

34. It is impossible to know why their correspondence ceased at this point. But we have to assume that Nietzsche was responsible for this cessation of contact, since Ehrlich initiated the contact and was so pleased that Nietzsche responded. Whether Ehrlich's Judaism had anything to do with the brevity of their exchange is open to speculation. Ehrlich is mentioned nowhere in Nietzsche's works or letters, except in the outline of a letter to be written to Cosima Wagner in May of 1876, where his name simply appears as one in a list of topics Nietzsche intended to write to her about (Nr. 527a, KSB 8.594).

35. The Prometheus figure appeared on the cover of Nietzsche's *Birth of Tragedy*, so that this epic poem already pays tribute to the philosopher Lipiner so admired.

36. See also Nietzsche's remarks about Helen Zimmern, an English enthusiast and early translator of Nietzsche: "Naturally a Jewess:—it is amazing how much this race now has the 'intellectuality' in Europe in its hands" (to Heinrich Köselitz, July 20, 1886, Nr. 724, KSB 7.214).

37. Lipiner also wanted him to consult with physicians in Vienna, especially Josef Breuer, who played such a significant role in the development of psychoanalysis by developing the "talking cure."

38. In a card written to Rée on August 10, 1878, Nietzsche indicates that Lipiner's letter was directed "entirely against you" (Nr. 743, KSB 5.346). Martin Liebscher, "'Lauter ausgesuchte Intelligenzen': Admiration for Nietzsche in 1870s Vienna," *Austrian Studies* 16 (2008): 32–50, speculates that Lipiner's remarks were "partly anti-Semitic in nature" (41), which contains a certain irony when we consider that Rée's initial remarks about Lipiner could also be considered as a slur motivated by anti-Jewish sentiments. The letter must have emulated the Wagner circle's reaction against the book *Human, All Too Human*, which had recently appeared. In October, Seydlitz, informing Nietzsche of the displeasure his book caused in Bayreuth, suggests strongly that the letter Lipiner had written to Nietzsche was thirty-two pages in length (Nr. 1120, KGB II 6/2.986). Lipiner wrote to Malwida in August about his thirty-two-page letter to Nietzsche. Part of the letter is reprinted in Renate Müller-Buck, "'Ach dass doch alle Schranken zwischen uns fielen': Sigfried Lipiner und der Nietzsche-Kult in Wien," in *Friedrich Nietzsche: Rezeption und Kultus*, ed. Sandro Barbera et al. (Pisa: Edizioni ETS, 2004), 33–75, here, 61.

39. See Müller-Buck, "Ach dass doch alle Schranken zwischen uns fielen," who includes a letter to Malwida, in which Lipiner calls Rée "unspeakably shallow": "It would be desirable for him to lose a large part of his ingenuity—then something decent could be made out of him" (61).

40. Cosima Wagner, *Diaries*, 2: 147, 152–26, 194, 254.

41. Nietzsche may have been thinking of Lipiner when he wrote in the *The Antichrist*: "One would no more choose to associate with 'first Christians' than one would with Polish Jews: not that one would need to prove so much as a single point against them.... Neither of them smells very pleasant" (AC 46, KSA 6.223).

42. See Aldo Venturelli, "Nietzsche in der Berggasse 19: Über die erste Nietzsche-Rezeption in Wien," *Nietzsche-Studien* 13 (1984): 448–80, here, 453.

43. Lipiner had converted to Protestantism in 1881. Nietzsche heard about Lipiner from Josef Paneth. See Richard Frank Krummel, "Dokumentation: Josef Paneth über seine Begegnung mit Nietzsche in der Zarathustra-Zeit," *Nietzsche-Studien* 17 (1988): 478–95, here, 480. See also Venturelli, "Nietzsche in der Berggasse 19," 475.

44. Müller-Buck includes a good overview of Lipiner's relationship with Nietzsche, including some of his correspondence with Köselitz and Malwida, as well as a brief account of his life after Nietzsche, when he was the director of the Library of the Austrian Imperial Council, the translator of Adam Michiewicz, and a close friend of Gustav Mahler.

45. Krummel, "Dokumentation," 484–85.

46. The reference here is to Mephistopheles's self-characterization in Goethe's *Faust*.

47. Krummel, "Dokumentation," 484. Nietzsche mentions this meeting with Poles who mistake him for a countryman in a letter to Köselitz (August 20, 1880, Nr. 49, KSB 6.37).

48. The most thorough investigation of the Polish issue is found in Hans von Müller, "Nietzsches Vorfahren," *Nietzsche-Studien* 31 (2002): 253–75.

49. Overbeck writes: "Nietzsche was in reality nothing else than a German; he was a Slav only in his fantasy. Nietzsche's interest for Slavism was vain sport and

games" (76). Franz Overbeck, *Erinnerungen an Friedrich Nietzsche* (Berlin: Berenberg, 2011). If Overbeck recognized the bogus nature of Nietzsche's Polish heritage, we have to conclude Nietzsche did as well.

50. Krummel, "Dokumentation," 490.

51. Nietzsche frequently tried to impress a correspondent with a list of famous readers, who in reality were just persons to whom he sent his writings. For example, in a letter to Hippolyte Taine he confesses he is a hermit who doesn't care about readers or being read—which is not at all true—and then cites Wagner, Bruno Bauer, Burckhardt, and Keller as readers who are "very devoted" to him (July 4, 1887, Nr. 872, KSB 8.107).

52. Janz, *Friedrich Nietzsche: Biographie*, 2: 343.

53. Overbeck, *Erinnerungen an Friedrich Nietzsche*, 89.

54. Krummel, "Dokumentation," 492–93.

55. Overbeck, *Erinnerungen an Friedrich Nietzsche*, 77.

56. Krummel, "Dokumentation," 481, 495.

57. Ibid., 480.

58. We recognize a reflection of this comment to Paneth a few years later in the second essay of the *Genealogy of Morals*. Nietzsche claims that pain is not the same phenomenon today that it was in former times. Categorizing Africans as human beings at a more primitive stage of development, an interpretation of evolutionary theory not uncommon in the nineteenth century, Nietzsche claims that they are able to withstand greater pain than even the most stoic European (GM, Zweite Abhandlung 6, KSA 5.303).

59. Krummel, "Dokumentation," 490–91.

60. See my "Dialectic of the Biological Enlightenment: Nietzsche, Degeneration, and Eugenics," in *Practicing Progress: The Promise and Limitations of Enlightenment*, Festschrift for John McCarthy, ed. Richard Schade and Dieter Sevin (Amsterdam: Rodopi, 2007), 173–85.

61. Krummel, "Dokumentation," 484. It is especially odd that Nietzsche would mention Ferdinand Lassalle, the socialist and political activist, in such a positive fashion, although Schmeitzner did publish part of his correspondence with Sophie Solutzeff.

62. I have rendered "Geist und Geistigkeit" as "intellect and intellectuality," although many translations prefer "spirit and spirituality." I believe Nietzsche is referring specifically to the intelligence of the Jews, a topic to which he often refers, not to their "spiritual" qualities. Otherwise here and later in this chapter the translation is taken from Friedrich Nietzsche, *Beyond Good and Evil*, trans. Marion Faber (Oxford: Oxford University Press, 1998).

63. See also Domenico Losurdo, *Nietzsche der aristokratische Rebell: Intellektuelle Biographie und kritische Bilanz*, trans. Erdmute Brielmayer, ed. Jan Rehmann, vol. 1, *Die Kritik der Revolution von den jüdischen Propheten bis zum Sozialismus* (Berlin: Argument, 2012), 541–45, 563, 572–73.

64. See Robert Nola, "Nietzsche as Anti-Semitic Jewish Conspiracy Theorist," *Croatian Journal of Philosophy* 3, no. 7 (2003): 35–62, esp. 44–45.

65. Otto Glagau, *Der Börsen- und Gründungs-Schwindel in Deutschland*, 2 vols. (Leipzig: Frohberg, 1876–77).

66. Paul Deussen was married to Marie Volkmar, the daughter of Jewish parents. Her father, Leopold Moritz Levy had converted in 1837 and taken the name Volkmar.

See Heiner Feldhoff, *Nietzsches Freund: Die Lebensgeschichte des Paul Deussen* (Cologne: Böhlau, 2009), 127.

67. Nietzsche is very likely referring to Wilhelm Goldschmidt's translation of Dostoevsky stories, *Erzählungen von F[edor] M[ichajlovič] Dostojewskij* (Leipzig: Reclam, 1886).

68. Thomas Mittmann, *Friedrich Nietzsche: Judengegner und Antisemitenfeind* (Erfurt: Sutton, 2001), argues unconvincingly that Nietzsche's views remained the same after his break with Wagner.

69. English renditions from *Human, All Too Human* are based on the translations by R. J. Hollingdale (Cambridge: Cambridge University Press, 1986).

70. English translations are taken from Friedrich Nietzsche, *Daybreak: Thoughts on the Prejudices of Morality*, trans. R. J. Hollingdale (Cambridge: Cambridge University Press, 1997).

71. Mittmann, *Friedrich Nietzsche: Judengegner und Antisemitenfeind*, 61–62.

72. Jacques Le Rider, "Les intellectuels juifs viennois et Nietzsche: Autour de Sigmund Freud," *De Sils-Maria à Jérusalem: Nietzsche et le judaïsme: Les intellectuels juifs et Nietzsche* (Paris: Les Éditions du Cerf, 1991), 181–200, advances the claim (186) that Nietzsche's reference to Polish Jews in *The Antichrist* is an allusion to Lipiner. Translation from Friedrich Nietzsche, *Twilight of the Idols / The Anti-Christ*, trans. R. J. Hollingdale (London: Penguin, 1968), 173. Translation copyright © R. J. Hollingdale. Reproduced by permission of Penguin Books Ltd.

CHAPTER FIVE

1. "anti-Semitism, n.," *OED Online*, December 2013, Oxford University Press, http://www.oed.com.proxy.lib.ohio-state.edu/view/Entry/8854?redirectedFrom=anti-Semitism (accessed December 22, 2013).

2. Walter Kaufmann, *Nietzsche: Philosopher, Psychologist, Antichrist*, 4th ed. (Princeton, NJ: Princeton University Press, 1974), 291–92.

3. Ibid., 45–46. The quote from Nietzsche's work stems from *Beyond Good and Evil* (JGB 251, KSA 5.194). The citations from letters are found in KSB 8.575, 579 (to Franz Overbeck, January 4, 1889, Nr. 1249, and to Jacob Burckhardt, January 6, 1889, Nr. 1256). We will return to the citation from *Beyond Good and Evil* at the end of this chapter and see that Kaufmann has not provided the appropriate context for understanding what Nietzsche truly means.

4. See Adam Sutcliffe and Jonathan Karp, "Introduction: A Brief History of Philosemitism," in their *Philosemitism in History* (Cambridge: Cambridge University Press, 2011), 1–26, esp. 14–15.

5. Paul Lawrence Rose, in "Renan versus Gobineau: Semitism and Antisemitism, Ancient Races and Modern Liberal Nations," *History of European Ideas* 39, no. 4 (2013): 528–40, points out that the noted Jewish scholar Moritz Steinschneider used the term "anti-Semitism" in 1860, but at that point he was responding to the writings of Ernest Renan, which had nothing to do with the Judeophobic political movement that would emerge in Germany around 1880: "Steinschneider's charge of 'anti-Semitic prejudices,' referred to Renan's prejudice concerning the historical and intellectual superiority of Aryan religion and 'race' over their Semitic counterparts, rather than to any anti-Jewish position as such, that is 'antisemitism' as it became known in the 1870s in Germany" (533).

6. Nietzsche did not use it in any of his letters, however.

7. In *Anti-Semitism: A Historical Encyclopedia of Prejudice and Persecution* (Santa Barbara, CA: ABC-CLIO, 2005), Richard Levy writes: "Although there are those who claim that the term initially had a fairly neutral connotation, this was no longer the case by midcentury, when it had come to signify a body of uniformly negative traits supposedly clinging to Jews" (1: 24). Most commentators have failed to regard Nietzsche's use of the term in *The Birth of Tragedy* as part of his anti-Jewish sentiments in his Wagnerian period.

8. Walter Boehlich, ed., *Der Berliner Antisemitismusstreit* (Frankfurt: Insel, 1965); and Karsten Krieger, ed., *Der "Berliner Antisemitismusstreit," 1879–1881: Eine Kontroverse um die Zugehörigkeit der deutschen Juden zur Nation*, 2 vols. (Munich: Saur, 2003).

9. W. Marr, *Der Sieg des Judenthums über das Germanenthum* (Bern: Rudolph Costenoble, 1879).

10. Moshe Zimmermann, *Wilhelm Marr: The Patriarch of Anti-Semitism* (New York: Oxford University Press, 1986), 90–95.

11. See Thomas Nipperdey and Reinhard Rürup, "Antisemitismus," in *Geschichtliche Grundbegriffe: Historisches Lexikon zur politisch-sozialen Sprache in Deutschland*, ed. Otto Brunner et al. (Stuttgart: Klett, 1972), 129–53; and Georges Roux, *Ancient Iraq* (London: Penguin, 1992), 123–35.

12. Michael Mack's study *German Idealism and the Jew: The Inner Anti-Semitism of Philosophy and German Jewish Responses* (Chicago: University of Chicago Press, 2003) is particularly interesting in this regard since it argues that the "anti-Semitism" in the German philosophical tradition should be traced back to German idealism. Anti-Semitism, which in his study is equated with anti-Judaism, was not an irrational romantic reaction against the Enlightenment, but itself a manifestation of Enlightenment philosophy.

13. For an overview of the anti-Semitic movement in Germany and Austria, see Richard S. Levy, "Political Anti-Semitism in Germany and Austria, 1848–1914," in *Antisemitism: A History*, ed. Albert S. Lindemann and Richard S. Levy (Oxford: Oxford University Press, 2010), 121–35.

14. Cited in Christoph Cobet, *Der Wortschatz des Anti-Semitismus in der Bismarckzeit* (Munich: Fink, 1973), 140. Dühring evidently later gave up on this objection to the word and used it rather liberally.

15. Bernhard Förster, *Das Verhältnis des modernen Judenthums zur deutschen Kunst* (Berlin: Schulze, 1881), 11.

16. Cited in Alex Bein, *Die Judenfrage: Biographie eines Weltproblems* (Stuttgart: Deutsche Verlags-Anstalt, 1980), 2: 168.

17. Nipperdey and Rürup, "Antisemitismus," 151.

18. The term "Misojuden" appears in his notebooks in the fall of 1881, shortly after the term "anti-Semitism" had become popular. See Nachlass 1881, 12[116] and 15[43], KSA 9.597 and 649.

19. See Peter Pulzer, *The Rise of Political Anti-Semitism in Germany and Austria*, rev. ed. (Cambridge, MA: Harvard University Press, 1988).

20. The heuristic distinction I draw here and throughout this study regarding anti-Judaism and anti-Semitism is thus not directly related to the anti-Judaism posited by David Nirenberg in his excellent study of a few years ago: *Anti-Judaism: The Western Tradition* (New York: Norton, 2013). Nirenberg focuses his attention on imaginary Jews or the image of Jews in the writings of non-Jews and the function of

that image. It is of course possible that Nietzsche partook of this sort of anti-Judaism himself in some of his writings. But essential for my purposes in understanding Nietzsche's various pronouncements on Jews and Judaism is the distinction between anti-Semitism, which refers to a political anti-Jewish movement that arises in 1880, and the bias against Jews and Jewry, which I refer to as anti-Judaism or Judeophobia.

21. Massimo Ferrari Zumbini, *Die Wurzeln des Bösen: Gründerjahre des Antisemitismus: Von der Bismarckzeit zu Hitler* (Frankfurt: Klostermann, 2003), notes that because of his early connection with Wagner and his circles Nietzsche was "one of the most knowledgeable individuals about the emerging organized anti-Semitism" (425).

22. The story of Förster's colony has been told most recently in a journalistic tone by Ben MacIntyre in *Forgotten Fatherland: The Search for Elisabeth Nietzsche* (New York: Farrar Straus Giroux, 1992).

23. "Llama" was Nietzsche's pet name for his sister.

24. See Aldo Venturelli, "Asketismus und Wille zur Macht: Nietzsches Auseinandersetzung mit Eugen Dühring," *Nietzsche-Studien* 15 (1986): 107–39.

25. See Dieter B. Herrmann, *Karl Friedrich Zöllner* (Leipzig: Teubner, 1982); and Robin Small, "Nietzsche, Zöllner, and the Fourth Dimension," *Archiv für Geschichte der Philosophie* 76 (1994): 278–301.

26. English rendition here and below from the Douglas Smith translation of *On the Genealogy of Morals* (Oxford: Oxford University Press, 1996). Used by permission of Oxford University Press.

27. Fritzsch was Wagner's publisher, and his firm specialized in music-related texts and musical scores. The publication of *The Birth of Tragedy* was therefore something of a stretch for him. The *Untimely Meditations* simply were items that stood outside his usual program.

28. See Malcolm B. Brown, "Friedrich Nietzsche und sein Verleger Ernst Schmeitzner: Eine Darstellung ihrer Beziehung," *Archiv für Geschichte des Buchwesens* 28 (1987): 213–90.

29. Richard Frank Krummel, "Josef Paneth über seine Begegnung mit Nietzsche in der Zarathustra-Zeit," *Nietzsche-Studien* 17 (1988): 478–95, here, 483–44.

30. Schmeitzner's letter is printed in Brown, "Friedrich Nietzsche und sein Verleger," 284. Schmeitzner is referring to the end of Bismarck's rule with the National Liberal Party, which was often identified with Jewish interests by anti-Semites because of prominent Jewish members.

31. Franz Overbeck and Heinrich Köselitz, *Briefwechsel*, ed. David M. Hoffmann et al. (Berlin: de Gruyter, 1998), 47. Although Overbeck does not mention the journal by name, he is referring to Wilhelm Marr's *Anti-Semitic Notebooks*, which was supposed to appear bimonthly but ceased publication after three issues because of the lack of interest.

32. The book to which Nietzsche is referring is *Dawn*, which was published in the summer of 1881. Nietzsche continues in his postcard: "But we need not be mean to each other! I remain with heartfelt wishes *always* your F. N." (Nr., 117, KSB 6.93–94). Quite obviously "party literature," in combination with the mention of Wagner, Schopenhauer, and Dühring, indicates Nietzsche had knowledge of Schmeitzner's anti-Semitic proclivities and publications.

33. The letter is reprinted in KGB III 7/1.856–57. Köselitz must have responded sharply and included the phrase "imbecilic race hatred," since in a later letter Schmeitz-

ner defends himself against this phrase by telling Köselitz that he must be misinformed about the realities in Germany through foreign newspapers (KGB III 7/1.859). Köselitz was living at the time in Venice. It is noteworthy that we never encounter a similarly direct rebuke of anti-Semitism in Nietzsche's letters to Schmeitzner.

34. See Nietzsche's postcard from December 2, 1880 (Nr. 70, KSB 6.52), where he informs Overbeck, who assisted Nietzsche with securing and managing his pension, that the deal with Schmeitzner remains as they had arranged it. He instructs Overbeck to stop these loans in August 1881, stating vaguely: "there are reasons to be a little careful; he is rash and does many things without first asking for permission" (August 20/21, 1881, Nr. 139, KSB 6.116–17). Although some commentators claim Nietzsche stopped the payments because of Schmeitzner's anti-Semitic activities, there is nothing in his letter to Overbeck that confirms this sort of rationale.

35. One source of confusion for Nietzsche was the European profile of the journal. It appears that Nietzsche associated anti-Semitism almost exclusively with the racist political scene in Germany, and that he was blind to the international appeal of anti-Semitic thought.

36. Brown, "Friedrich Nietzsche und sein Verleger," 260.

37. Cited in KGB III 7/2.475 (Anhang 10, Paul Heinrich Widemann to Heinrich Köselitz, July 29, 1885).

38. Brown, "Friedrich Nietzsche und sein Verleger," 260.

39. Schmeitzner calls him "the father" of the journal in a letter to Nietzsche in May 1882 (Nr. 121, KGB III 2.253).

40. See David Leopold, "The Hegelian Antisemitism of Bruno Bauer," *History of European Ideas* 25 (1999): 179–206.

41. Douglas Moggach, *The Philosophy and Politics of Bruno Bauer* (Cambridge: Cambridge University Press, 2003), 17.

42. Moggach, *Philosophy and Politics of Bruno Bauer*, 186. See also Douglas Moggach, "Bruno Bauer," *The Stanford Encyclopedia of Philosophy* (Spring 2010 edition), ed. Edward N. Zalta, http://plato.stanford.edu/archives/spr2010/entries/bauer/. See also Ferrari Zumbini, *Die Wurzeln des Bösen*, who notes that Bauer was close to Hermann Wagener, the social conservative editor of the *Kreuzzeitung*, and that Bauer composed all the entries on Jews and Judaism for Wagener's *Staats- und Gesellschaftslexikon*, including "Judaism in Foreign Lands" (*Das Judenthum in der Fremde*), which appeared in 1863 as a separate book (444).

43. Bruno Bauer, *Zur Orientierung über die Bismarck'sche Ära* (Chemnitz: Schmeitzner, 1880), 287.

44. English translation by R. J. Hollingdale from Friedrich Nietzsche, *Ecce Homo: How One Becomes What One Is* (London: Penguin, 1979), 85.

45. Rudolf Lehmann, "Friedrich Nietzsche: Eine Studie," *Schmeitzner's Internationale Monatsschrift* 1, no. 4 (1882): 253–61, and 1, no. 5 (1882): 306–22, here, 313.

46. "Friedrich Nietzsche's neuestes Buch: 'Die fröhliche Wissenschaft,'" *Schmeitzner's Internationale Monatsschrift* 1, no. 11 (1882): 685–95.

47. Paneth departed at the end of March in 1884; Nietzsche's communication with Overbeck in which he laments that anti-Semitism has cost him his financial independence, disciples, Wagner, and his sister was written on April 2.

48. Franz Overbeck, *Erinnerungen an Friedrich Nietzsche* (Berlin: Berenberg, 2011), 77.

49. I am in substantial agreement with Thomas Mittmann, *Judengegner und Antisemitenfeind* (Erfurt: Sutton, 2001), who also deals with the relationship with Schmeitzner (68–82). But Mittmann exaggerates the amount of anti-Semitism in early issues of the *International Monthly* and fails to account for the key role of Bauer in Nietzsche's attraction to the journal and in Nietzsche's recognition of the anti-Semitic nature of the undertaking.

50. See Mittmann, *Judengegner und Antisemitenfeind*, 83–85.

51. Bernhard Förster, *Das Verhältnis des modernen Judenthums zur deutschen Kunst* (Berlin: Schulze, 1881), 36.

52. Janz in *Die Briefe Friedrich Nietzsches* gives an exact account of Elisabeth's stays: approximately forty-two months in the decade of his tenure at Basel (64). When we consider that Nietzsche also visited Naumburg during this period, and that he took leave of his position during the 1870s while he traveled and stayed in Italy, it appears that Elisabeth and Friedrich were together in Basel approximately half of the total time he spent in that city. Elisabeth was also known as an excellent housekeeper. See Angelika Emmrich, "und nun ruht die Obhut über sein Andenken in Frauenhand," in *Friedrich Nietzsche: Rezeption und Kultus*, ed. Sandro Barbera et al. (Pisa: Editioni ETS, 2004), 187–215. Emmrich reproduces part of a letter from Malwida von Meysenbug lauding Elisabeth's talents for the decor in Nietzsche's living quarters (188).

53. See Carol Diethe, *Nietzsche's Sister and the Will to Power: A Biography of Elisabeth Förster-Nietzsche* (Urbana: University of Illinois Press, 2003), 54–60.

54. Ibid., 57. Diethe has the unfortunate habit of making derogatory assertions about Elisabeth and statements emphasizing Nietzsche's derogatory views of her and Förster without sufficient evidence in actual texts.

55. Förster, *Das Verhältnis*, 1–2.

56. In a letter to Malwida von Meysenbug, Nietzsche states that the marriage of his sister will relieve him of a "mortal type of torture"; and to Overbeck he states less dramatically that the marriage may be of advantage to him since Elisabeth will have her hands full and consequently not mix into his affairs (March 26, 1885, Nr. 587, and March 31, 1885, Nr. 589, KSB 7.30, 33). It is difficult to tell whether in these letters Nietzsche is trying to convince himself of the benefits of the impending union, or whether he is reacting to interference he has experienced in the past—and resented. It is quite possibly a combination of both sentiments, but it certainly does not seem to be his dominant feeling about the marriage.

57. Förster explored this region for his colony.

58. Elisabeth obviously considered making her brother their sole heir as a sign of love and respect, although in hindsight, knowing the fate of Förster's financial dealings in the colony, we see that it was a worthless gesture.

59. Erich Podach maintains that the most vehement passages written against Elisabeth in the late 1880s were due to Nietzsche's precarious mental state. These statements have often been used as evidence for Nietzsche's "true" feelings for his sister. But Podach points out that even in the 1880s Nietzsche expressed genuine affection for his sister, and that Nietzsche wrote similarly vehement statements to Malwida von Meysenbug. See Erich F. Podach, "Anhang," in *Friedrich Nietzsches Werke des Zusammenbruchs* (Heidelberg: Wolfgang Rothe Verlag, 1961), 430.

60. There are passages in other letters that are also very harsh, for example, in 1884, when Nietzsche, still angry about Elisabeth's interference in the Lou Salomé affair, writes to Malwida von Meysenbug that he has broken radically from his sister and wants no mediation to restore the relationship: "Between a vengeful anti-Semitic goose and me there can be no reconciliation" (May 1884, Nr. 509, KSB 6.500). As we have seen in the letter to Overbeck, a few months later the siblings were again on intimate terms.

61. The letter he actually sent (June 5, 1887, Nr. 855, KSB 8.83–85) contains his lament that everyone has left him and that even his llama has gone to the anti-Semites. But he adds: "Now I don't say this with the least tone of a reproach; it is far more reasonable to conduct 'Förestry' [a pun Nietzsche uses on the name and forestry] in South American woods on a grand scale than to conduct 'brotherliness' on a small scale." He later writes: "My best wishes to your Dr. Förster on his great undertaking!" In short, he removed the most acerbic comments when he sent the actual letter and added moderate praise of Förster and his venture.

62. Bernhard Förster, *Nachklängen zum Parsifal: Allerhand Gedanken über deutsche Cultur, Wissenschaft, Kunst, Gesellschaft* (Leipzig: Fritsch, 1883).

63. Earlier in the year he had seen that Förster published in the journal and obviously was maintaining his ties with anti-Semitic political movements in Germany.

64. Nietzsche wrote the following emendation for *Ecce Homo*: "The treatment I have received from my mother and my sister, up to the present moment, fills me with inexpressible horror: there is an absolutely hellish machine at work here, operating with infallible certainty at the precise moment when I am most vulnerable.... I confess that the deepest objection to the 'Eternal Recurrence,' my real idea from the abyss, is always my mother and my sister" (Kommentar zu Band 6, Ecce Homo, Warum ich so weise bin, KSA 14.473). Although some English translations have taken this passage into their version of Nietzsche's autobiography, it is unlikely that a sane Nietzsche would have openly criticized his mother and his sister in such a crude fashion. *Ecce Homo* was not a finished work when Nietzsche suffered his breakdown, and these sketches disparaging his closest relatives would almost certainly have had the identical fate to the drafts for letters he thoroughly revised or never sent. The inclusion of the passage in English versions is thus part of the endeavor to discredit Elisabeth in all matters pertaining to her brother.

65. Although Fritsch died in 1933, he was a National Socialist delegate to parliament during the Weimar Republic.

66. The second manuscript, which comprises twenty-three pages, is not included in the KGB.

67. The citation from *Zarathustra* is from the first part in the section "On the Flies of the Market Place" (KSA 4.66).

68. The letter writer misquotes slightly, substituting a present tense for the past perfect that is in the original ("werden" for "geworden sind"). Translation by Walter Kaufmann in his *The Portable Nietzsche* (New York: Viking, 1968), 122.

69. It is unclear whether Fritsch contacted Nietzsche again prior to Nietzsche's second letter. It is difficult to believe he would have continued to correspond with the philosopher after receiving his first dismissive and insulting letter.

70. Förster's article is reprinted in KSB III 7/3,2.888–92 (Anhang 13). Nietzsche had some connection with each of these individuals. He had a personal relationship with Wagner, and in the 1870s he was positively inclined toward Dühring and Lagarde. He had Wahrmund's history of the Greeks in his personal library, although he possessed none of his anti-Semitic writings of the 1880s. Wahrmund was a student of classical and oriental languages who was employed at the Court Library and then at the Oriental Academy in Vienna.

71. Gary C. Fouse, *Erlangen: An American's History of a German Town* (Lanham, MD: University Press of America, 2005), 66–67, 99–100. On Ebrard, see also Karl Eduard Haas, *Reformierte Theologie in Erlangen*, ed., rev., and expanded by Matthias Freudenberg (Nuremberg: Peter Althmann, 2000), http://www.athmann.de/verlag/online/haas/haas104.htm.

72. Nietzsche had in his library one book by Ebrard. It deals with the activities of training medical personnel for the war in 1870–71: August Ebrard, *Bericht des Erlanger Vereins für Felddiakonie über seine Thätigkeit im Krieg 1870–71* (Erlangen: A. Deichert, 1871).

73. Since his mother makes no reference to these outbursts, we can assume that her son, as was his habit, eliminated these sorts of statements when he eventually wrote to her (January 17, 1888, Nr. 514, KGB III 6.147–48).

74. The authenticity of this letter and several others has been called into question because they exist only in copies Elisabeth claimed she made from the originals. Since there is no longer an original manuscript, and since there is evidence that Nietzsche's sister falsified some parts of Nietzsche's correspondence, the editors of the official Nietzsche edition did not include any letters that exist only in Elisabeth's hand. It is unlikely, however, that everything in these letters is a pure forgery. In this particular letter Nietzsche is severely critical of anti-Semitism and his sister's involvement with it. Since her motivation for most of her manipulations was to make her appear closer to her brother than she actually was, she would hardly have considered the inclusion of such a letter in her edition of his correspondence to further that cause. She may have doctored a few sentences in which Nietzsche appears to exonerate her personally for the attitudes of the anti-Semitic party, but much of the substance in the letter resembles closely what Nietzsche drafted to his mother and to Elisabeth during the very same few days.

75. English version is drawn from the translation by Marion Faber in Friedrich Nietzsche, *Beyond Good and Evil* (Oxford: Oxford University Press, 1998).

76. A frequent claim of the anti-Semitic movement was that Germany was in a state of emergency because of Jewish control of the financial world, the press, and cultural affairs.

77. Franz Overbeck and Heinrich Köselitz, *Briefwechsel*, ed. David M. Hoffmann et al. (Berlin: de Gruyter, 1998), 47–48.

78. Overbeck appears to be using the term in scare quotes to indicate its meaning as "anti-Jewish" and to distinguish it from the crude, political anti-Semitism that he and Nietzsche unequivocally oppose.

79. Franz Overbeck, *Erinnerungen an Friedrich Nietzsche* (Berlin: Berenberg, 2011), 77–79.

CHAPTER SIX

1. Heinrich Römer, "Nietzsche und das Rassenproblem," *Rasse: Monatsschrift der nordischen Gedanken* 7 (1940): 59–65.

2. Throughout this chapter English renditions from *On the Genealogy of Morals* are drawn from the translations of Douglas Smith (Oxford: Oxford University Press, 1996). Used by permission of Oxford University Press.

3. There are of course exceptions. Werner Stegmaier, *Nietzsches "Genealogie der Moral"* (Darmstadt: Wissenschaftliche Buchgesellschaft, 1994), provides a differentiated presentation of sections 7 and 8 (109–16).

4. Lawrence J. Hatab, *Nietzsche's* On the Genealogy of Morality: *An Introduction* (Cambridge: Cambridge University Press, 2008), 41.

5. This is true for most of the twenty-four contributions to *Nietzsche, Genealogy, Morality: Essays on Nietzsche's* Genealogy of Morals, ed. Richard Schacht (Berkeley: University of California Press, 1994). Of the fourteen contributions to *Nietzsche's* On the Genealogy of Morality: *A Critical Guide*, ed. Simon May (Cambridge: Cambridge University Press, 2011), only two mention Jews specifically: R. Lanier Anderson writes of "the Jewish priestly nobility" (33), although, as we have seen, there is no mention of Jewish nobility or Jewish priests in the text, just Jews as a priestly people; and Paul Katsafanas places Judaism and Christianity together in remarks on "Judeo-Christian morality" (182–88), although Nietzsche clearly ascribes primacy and priority to Jewry. In David Owen's *Nietzsche's* Genealogy of Morality (Montreal: McGill-Queen's University Press, 2007), and Christopher Janaway's *Beyond Selflessness: Reading Nietzsche's* Genealogy (Oxford: Oxford University Press, 2009) there is similarly no recognition of the anti-Jewish foundation of Nietzsche's reflections on morality. Janaway does refer in section fourteen to the possibility of an "echo of the sweatshops of the Nibelungs in *Das Rheingold*" (103), and therefore a possible proximity to anti-Semitism, but the anti-Jewish underpinnings in sections seven and eight are unnoticed.

6. Exemplary in this regard is Yirmiyahu Yovel's contribution to Schacht's collection: "Nietzsche, the Jews, and *Ressentiment*" (214–36).

7. Nietzsche may very well have been paying tribute to Heinrich Heine in his high praise for the Old Testament. Heine had included similar laudatory passages in the Second Book of *Ludwig Börne: Eine Denkschrift* (1840). See Heinrich Heine, *Sämtliche Werke*, vol. 11 (Hamburg: Hoffmann and Campe, 1978), 40–41, 44.

8. The passage praising the Old Testament in the *Genealogy* (GM, Dritte Abhandlung 22, KSA.392–95) is odd in a number of ways. After praising the "great men," the "heroic landscape," and the "incomparable naïveté" of the Old Testament and condemning the "mere rococo of the soul" in the New Testament, he claims that the latter is "not so much Jewish as Hellenistic." But further on in the same passage, when discussing the "crown of eternal life," he considers these Christian sentiments a sign of "Jewish, not merely Jewish impertinence toward God."

9. Nietzsche is citing Tacitus here, *Annals* 15: 44.

10. Franz Overbeck, *Ueber Entstehung und Recht einer rein historischen Betrachtung der Neutestamentlichen Schriften in der Theologie*," Antritts-Vorlesung gehalten in der Aula zu Basel am 6. Juni 1870 (Basel: Schweighauserische Verlagsbuchhandlung, 1871), 8.

11. Cited from Andreas Urs Sommer, "Zwischen Agitation, Religionsstiftung und 'hoher Politik': Paul de Lagarde und Friedrich Nietzsche," *Nietzscheforschung* 4 (1998): 169–94, here, 177.

12. Sander L. Gilman, ed., *Conversations with Nietzsche* (New York: Oxford University Press, 1987), 76–83. Reuter also considers Nietzsche to have been a disciple of Lagarde, a contention that certainly exaggerates their relationship, even in the mid-1870s.

13. Cosima Wagner, *Diaries*, vol. 1, *1869–1877* (New York: Hartcourt Brace Jovanovich, 1978), 621 (April 8, 1873): "Prof. Nietzsche tells me of a Prof. Paul Lagarde who, on account of a book on church and state, has been completely ostracized." On April 18, 1873, Nietzsche announces his intention to send this work to the Wagners (to Richard Wagner, Nr. 304, KSB 4.145).

14. See Fritz Stern, *The Politics of Cultural Despair: A Study in the Rise of the Germanic Ideology* (Berkeley: University of California Press, 1961), 89–90; and Winfried Schüler, *Der Bayreuther Kreis von seiner Entstehung bis zum Ausgang der wilhelminischen Ära* (Münster: Aschendorff, 1971), 6.

15. See Wolf-Daniel Hartwich, "Die Erfindung des Judentums, Antisemitismus, Rassenlehre und Bibelkritik in Friedrich Nietzsches Theorie der Kultur," *Trumah* 5 (1996): 179–200, here, 184.

16. Paul de Lagarde, *Schriften für das deutsche Volk*, vol. 1, *Deutsche Schriften* (Munich: Lebmann, 1940), 262–65.

17. Ibid., 67–68.

18. See Hubert Cancik, "'Judentum in zweiter Potenz': Ein Beitrag zur Interpretation von Friedrich Nietzsches 'Der Antichrist,'" *"Mit unsrer Macht ist nichts getan ..."*: *Festschrift für Dieter Schellong zum 65. Geburtstag* (Frankfurt: Haag + Herchen, 1993), 55–70, here, 64.

19. Andreas Urs Sommer, "Judentum und Christentum bei Paul de Lagarde und Friedrich Nietzsche," in *Christentum und Judentum: Akten des Internationalen Kongresses der Schleiermacher-Gesellschaft* (Berlin: de Gruyter, 2012), 549–60, writes that Nietzsche used the "latent anti-Semitism" in his transvaluation project: "with Nietzsche anti-Judaism has an anti-Christian function" (560). Both Nietzsche and Lagarde evidence anti-Judaism, but for different purposes.

20. Ernest Renan, *Paulus* (Leipzig: Brockhaus, 1869).

21. See Ernani Chaves, "Das Tragische, das Genie, der Held: Nietzsches Auseinandersetzung mit Ernest Renan in der *Götzendämmerung*," *Nietzscheforschung* 16 (2009): 249–58, here, 249.

22. Gary Shapiro, "Nietzsche contra Renan," *History and Theory* 21, no. 2 (1982): 193–222, here, 193.

23. For an excellent account of Renan's views on Judaism and anti-Semitism, see Paul Lawrence Rose, "Renan versus Gobineau: Semitism and Antisemitism, Ancient Races and Modern Liberal Nations," *History of European Ideas* 39, no. 4 (2013): 528–40; and Richard I. Cohen, "Renan, Ernest (1822–1893), in *Antisemitism: A Historical Encyclopedia of Prejudice and Persecution*, ed. Richard S. Levy (Santa Barbara, CA: ABC-CLIO, 2005), 2: 594–95.

24. Ernest Renan, *Le Judaïsme comme race et comme religion* (Paris: Calmann Lévy, 1883).

25. In a strangely undifferentiated account, however, Weaver Santaniello endeavors to prove Nietzsche's own pro-Jewish sentiments by regarding Renan as an anti-Semite whose ideas Nietzsche contradicts. She thus ignores both Renan's public dissociation from anti-Semitism and the fact that Nietzsche never discusses Renan in the context of anti-Semitism. See Weaver Santaniello, "Nietzsche's Hierarchy of Gods in the *Antichrist*," *Journal of Nietzsche Studies* 19 (2000): 89–102.

26. Ernest Renan, "De l'avenir religieux des sociétés modernes," *Revue des deux mondes* 29 (1860): 765–97. The citation appears on pages 796–97; Nietzsche violates usual practice by leading the reader to believe that the sentences after the ellipsis appear later in Renan's text than the sentences prior to the ellipsis. But the sentences after the ellipsis actually precede the first part of the citation.

27. Translations for *Twilight of the Idols* and *The Antichrist* are based on the renditions of R. J. Hollingdale (London: Penguin, 1968). Translation copyright © R. J. Hollingdale. Reproduced by permission of Penguin Books Ltd.

28. Nietzsche drops the distinction between prophets and priests but retains the general schema. For further insights into the similarities between Christianity and Judaism in Renan's writings, see Schapiro, "Nietzsche contra Renan," especially 204–5.

29. Renan, "L'avenir," 766.

30. See Michael Ahlsdorf, *Nietzsches Juden: Ein Philosoph formt sich ein Bild* (Aachen: Shaker, 1997), 56–57.

31. Julius Wellhausen, *Prolegomena to the History of Ancient Israel* (Edinburgh: Adam and Charles Black, 1885), 361. See also Julius Wellhausen, *Sketch of the History of Israel and Judah* (London: Adam and Charles Black, 1891): "It was not as if Jehovah had originally been regarded as the God of the universe who subsequently became the God of Israel; on the contrary, He was primarily Israel's God, and only afterwards (very long afterwards) did He come to be regarded as the God of the universe. For Moses to have given to the Israelites an 'enlightened conception of God' would have been to have given them a stone instead of bread; it is in the highest degree probable that, with regard to the essential nature of Jehovah, as distinct from His relation to men, he allowed them to continue in the same way of thinking with their fathers" (16).

32. Most evident, as noted above, in aphorism 52 of *Beyond Good and Evil* (KSA 5.72) and in the *Genealogy of Morals* (Dritte Abhandlung 22, KSA 5.393).

33. Wellhausen, *Prolegomena*, 449–51. As Jan Rehmann points out in "Nietzsches Umarbeitung des kulturprotestantischen Antijudaismus—das Beispiel Wellhausen," *Das Argument* 46, no. 2 (2004): 278–91, there are two components of Wellhausen's notion of Judaism: one connected with the priestly introduction of ascetic values; the other associated with the messianic teachings of Jesus (282).

34. For Wellhausen's view of Judaism, see Uwe Becker, "Julius Wellhausens Sicht des Judentums," in *Biblische Theologie und historisches Denken: Wissenschaftsgeschichtliche Studien*, ed. Martin Kessler and Martin Wallraff (Basel: Schwabe, 2000), 279–302. Rehmann obviously believes otherwise, since he characterizes Wellhausen's views as "anti-Judaic."

35. This volume was dedicated to Nietzsche's old nemesis, Ulrich von Wilamowitz–Moellendorf, who had written the scathing review of Nietzsche's *Birth of Tragedy* in 1872.

36. Wellhausen, *Prolegomena*, 341.

37. Ibid., 363–64.

38. Ibid., 359. Nietzsche appears not to distinguish between the prophets and priests, although his preference for the latter after *Beyond Good and Evil* is noticeable. See Ahlsdorf, *Nietzsches Juden*, 88–93.

39. Wellhausen, *Prolegomena*, 409.

40. Ibid., 413.

41. Ibid., 408.

42. See Ahlsdorf, *Nietzsches Juden*, 143–49.

43. Wellhausen, *Prolegomena*, 366.

44. It is revealing that Kaufmann translates the phrase "furchteinflössender Logik" as "awe-inspiring logic," thus ascribing to Nietzsche a much more favorable impression of the Jewish instinct than the German should allow. Friedrich Nietzsche, *The Portable Nietzsche*, trans. Walter Kaufmann (New York: Viking, 1954), 592. See also Cancik, "Judentum in zweiter Potenz," 64.

45. Ahlsdorf points to Max Müller as a possible source for the tenacity of the Jews, and Nietzsche was familiar with Müller's writings on religion, as evidenced in his notebooks from the 1870s. For a general discussion of this motif, see Ahlsdorf, *Nietzsches Juden*, 119–28.

46. See Hal Flemings, *Examining Criticisms of the Bible* (Bloomington, IN: AuthorHouse, 2008), 73–76.

47. See, for example, Robert S. Wistrich, "Between the Cross and the Swastika: A Nietzschean Perspective," in *Nietzsche, Godfather of Fascism?: On the Uses and Abuses of a Philosophy*, ed. Jacob Golomb and Robert S. Wistrich (Princeton, NJ: Princeton University Press, 2002), 144–69, here, 154–59.

48. See Annemarie Etter, "Nietzsche und das Gesetzbuch des Manu," *Nietzsche-Studien* 16 (1987): 341–52.

49. David Smith, "Nietzsche's Hinduism, Nietzsche's India: Another Look," *Journal of Nietzsche Studies* 28 (2004): 37–56, points out how widely known and discussed Manu was in the nineteenth century and cites several places where Nietzsche would have encountered references to Manu prior to 1888 (39–40).

50. (Paris: A. Lacroix, 1876). The notion of legislators is probably where Nietzsche received the impression he was dealing with a "law book."

51. See Thomas Paul Bonfiglio, "Toward a Genealogy of Aryan Morality: Nietzsche and Jacolliot," *New Nietzsche Studies* 6.3/4 and 7.1/2 (2005–6): 170–84, here, 171.

52. Smith puts the matter bluntly: "his Études Indianistes are worthless; however, they sold well" ("Nietzsche's Hinduism, Nietzsche's India: Another Look," 41).

53. See Daniel Caracostea, "Louis-Francois Jacolliot (1837–1890): A Biographical Essay," *Theosophical History* 9, no. 1 (2003): 12–39. Jacolliot is of interest in theosophical circles because Madame Blavatsky read and quotes Jacolliot in her first major work, *Isis Unveiled* (1877).

54. Thomas H. Brobjer, "Nietzsche's Reading about Eastern Philosophy," *Journal of Nietzsche Studies* 28 (2004): 3–35, gives an excellent overview of Nietzsche's preoccupation with texts from the Indian tradition. In his discussion of Manu, Brobjer points out correctly that Nietzsche was critical of the moral code, but he makes too

much of the critical comments in the notebooks (17–18). Nietzsche was critical of all priestly attempts to supervise humanity, but the point is that some sacerdotal codes are preferable.

55. "The order of the castes, the supreme, the dominant law, is merely the sanction of a *natural order*, a natural lawfulness of the first rank, over which no arbitrariness, no 'modern idea' has any power" (AC 57, KSA 6.242). "The order of castes, the *order of rank*, merely formulates the highest law of life" (AC 57, KSA 6.243).

56. Jacolliot, *Les législateurs religieux: Manou, Moïse, Mahomet*, 98–120.

57. This would have been quite impossible since Buddha lived from 563 to 483 BC.

58. One of Nietzsche's notes from 1888 adds a further complication to the terminology of Aryan and Semite: "One speaks today a great deal about the *Semitic* spirit of the *New Testament*: but what one means by this is only priestly—and in the Aryan law book of the purest race, in Manu, this kind of 'Semitism' that is, *priestly spirit* is worse than anywhere else" (Nachlass 1888, 14[204], KSA 13.386). Here we find Nietzsche breaking down the antithesis Aryan/Semitic. The chief characteristic of the Semitic for Nietzsche remains, however, associated with the priests who have brought unnatural morality to the world. As we have seen, the Jews are the prime example of a priestly people, but quite obviously other peoples, even those who consider themselves promoters of Aryanism, can partake in this priestly (and hence Semitic) spirit as well.

CONCLUSION

1. Nietzsche shared this conflicted notion of "anti-Semitism" not only with colleagues like Overbeck but also with many Jewish thinkers of the early twentieth century. We can find anti-Jewish sentiments in writers like Theodor Herzl, Karl Kraus, Kurt Tucholsky, and Sigmund Freud—to name only a few illustrations—accompanied by a simultaneous abhorrence of self-identified anti-Semites and their ideology.

2. See Jonathan M. Hess, *Germans, Jews, and the Claims of Modernity* (New Haven, CT: Yale University Press, 2002), who draws connections between Enlightenment thought and later forms of anti-Semitic discourse.

3. One could argue, of course, that he was obsessed in his last two years with the dominance of "Jewish" values in contemporary Europe.

4. See Martin Heidegger, *Nietzsche*, trans. David Farrell Krell, 4 vols. (San Francisco: Harper and Row, 1979–87).

5. Nietzsche's rehabilitation in postwar Germany was accomplished much more slowly than in the United States, but it accelerated rapidly in the 1960s and 1970s. The *Spiegel* article is reflecting the renewed legitimacy of Nietzsche in Germany while reminding readers of his previous association in the minds of many with the thoughts and deeds of the Third Reich.

6. Jacob Golomb and Robert S. Wistrich, eds., *Nietzsche: Godfather of Facism?: On the Uses and Abuses of a Philosophy* (Princeton, NJ: Princeton University Press, 2002). Although the title is in the form of a question, it is largely a rhetorical one. Almost all contributors to the essay collection would answer in the negative, although

there are some who recognize that Nietzsche's antiliberalism has some affinities with fascist thought.

7. See my "Dialectic of the Biological Enlightenment: Nietzsche, Degeneration, and Eugenics," in *Practicing Progress: The Promise and Limitations of Enlightenment*, Festschrift for John McCarthy, ed. Richard Schade and Dieter Sevin (Amsterdam: Rodopi, 2007), 173–85.

Ahlsdorf, Michael. *Nietzsches Juden: Ein Philosoph formt sich ein Bild*. Aachen: Shaker, 1997.

Andreas-Salomé, Lou. *Lebensrückblick: Grundriß einiger Lebenserinnerungen*. Zurich: Mas Niehans, 1951.

Antisemitische Correspondenz und Sprechsaal für innere Partei-Angelegenheiten. Edited by Theodor Fritsch. Leipzig: Theodor Fritsch, 1885–88.

Aschheim, Steven E. *The Nietzsche Legacy in Germany, 1890–1990*. Berkeley: University of California Press, 1992.

Bach, Hans I. *Jacob Bernays: Ein Beitrag zur Emanzipationsgeschichte der Juden und zur Geschichte des deutschen Geistes im neunzehnten Jahrhundert*. Tübingen: Mohr, 1974.

Baeumler, Alfred. *Studien zur deutschen Geistesgeschichte*. Berlin: Dünnhaupt, 1937.

Barbera, Sandro, et al., eds. *Friedrich Nietzsche: Rezeption und Kultus*. Pisa: Edizioni ETS, 2004.

Bartels, Adolf. "Friedrich Nietzsche und das Deutschtum." *Deutsche Monatsschrift für das gesamte Leben der Gegenwart* 2 (1902): 81–94.

Bauer, Bruno. *Zur Orientierung über die Bismarck'sche Ära*. Chemnitz: Schmeitzner, 1880.

Becker, Uwe. "Julius Wellhausens Sicht des Judentums." In *Biblische Theologie und historisches Denken: Wissenschaftsgeschichtliche Studien*, edited by Martin Kessler and Martin Wallraff, 279–302. Basel: Schwabe, 2008.

Bein, Alex. *Die Judenfrage: Biographie eines Weltproblems*. 2 vols. Stuttgart: Deutsche Verlags-Anstalt, 1980.

Berghahn, Klaus L., and Jost Hermand, eds. *Goethe in German-Jewish Culture*. Rochester, NY: Camden House, 2001.

Bernays, Jacob. *Grundzüge der verlorenen Abhandlung des Aristoteles über Wirkung der Tragödie*. Breslau: E. Trewendt, 1857.

Bernoulli, Carl Albrecht. *Franz Overbeck und Friedrich Nietzsche: Eine Freundschaft*. 2 vols. Jena: Eugen Diederich, 1908.

Boehlich, Walter, ed. *Der Berliner Antisemitismusstreit*. Frankfurt: Insel, 1965.

Bonfiglio, Thomas Paul. "Toward a Genealogy of Aryan Morality: Nietzsche and Jacolliot." *New Nietzsche Studies* 6, no. 3/4, and 7, no. 1/2 (2005–6): 170–84.

Bourel, Dominique, and Jacques le Rider, eds. *De Sils-Maria à Jérusalem: Nietzsche et le judaïsme: Les intellectuels juifs et Nietzsche*. Paris: Les Éditions du Cerf, 1991.

Brann, Henry Walter. *Schopenhauer und das Judentum*. Bonn: Bouvier, 1975.

Brenner, Michael. "Between Revolution and Legal Equality." In *German-Jewish History in Modern Times*, edited by Michael A. Meyer, 2: 291–92. New York: Columbia University Press, 1997.

Brinton, Crane. *Nietzsche*. New York: Harper Torchbook, 1965.

Brobjer, Thomas H. "Nietzsche's Reading about Eastern Philosophy." *Journal of Nietzsche Studies* 28 (2004): 3–35.

Brown, Malcolm B. "Friedrich Nietzsche und sein Verleger Ernst Schmeitzner: Eine Darstellung ihrer Beziehung." *Archiv für Geschichte des Buchwesens* 28 (1987): 213–90.

Brunner, Otto, et al., eds. *Geschichtliche Grundbegriffe: Historisches Lexikon zur politisch-sozialen Sprache in Deutschland*. Stuttgart: Klett, 1972.

Calder, William Musgrave, III. "The Wilamowitz-Nietzsche Struggle: New Documents and a Reappraisal." *Nietzsche-Studien* 121 (1983): 214–54.

Cancik, Hubert. "'Judentum in zweiter Potenz': Ein Beitrag zur Interpretation von Friedrich Nietzsches 'Der Antichrist.'" In "*Mit unsrer Macht ist nichts getan ...*": *Festschrift für Dieter Schellong zum 65. Geburtstag*, 55–70. Frankfurt: Haag + Herchen, 1993.

Caracostea, Daniel. "Louis-Francois Jacolliot (1837–1890): A Biographical Essay." *Theosophical History* 9, no. 1 (2003): 12–39.

Cartwright, David E. *Schopenhauer: A Biography*. Cambridge: Cambridge University Press, 2010.

Chaves, Ernani. "Das Tragische, das Genie, der Held: Nietzsches Auseinandersetzung mit Ernest Renan in der *Götzendämmerung*." *Nietzscheforschung* 16 (2009): 249–58.

Cobet, Christoph. *Der Wortschatz des Anti-Semitismus in der Bismarckzeit*. Munich: Fink, 1973.

Cohn, Paul. *Um Nietzsches Untergang: Beiträge zum Verständnis des Genies*. Mit einem Anhang von Elisabeth Förster-Nietzsche: Die Zeit von Nietzsches Erkrankung bis zu seinem Tode. Hanover: Morris-Verlag, 1931.

Diethe, Carol. *Nietzsche's Sister and the Will to Power: A Biography of Elisabeth Förster-Nietzsche*. Urbana: University of Illinois Press, 2003.

Ebrard, August. *Bericht des Erlanger Vereins für Felddiakonie über seine Thätigkeit im Krieg 1870–71*. Erlangen: A. Deichert, 1871.

Eichstädt, Volkmar. *Bibliographie zur Geschichte der Judenfrage I, 1750–1848*. Hamburg: Hanseatische Verlagsanstalt, 1938.

Emden, Christian J. *Friedrich Nietzsche and the Politics of History*. Cambridge: Cambridge University Press, 2008.

———. *Nietzsche's Naturalism: Philosophy and the Life Sciences in the Nineteenth Century*. Cambridge: Cambridge University Press, 2014.

Etter, Annemarie. "Nietzsche und das Gesetzbuch des Manu." *Nietzsche-Studien* 16 (1987): 341–52.

Feldhoff, Heiner. *Nietzsches Freund: Die Lebensgeschichte des Paul Deussen*. Cologne: Böhlau, 2009.

Ferrari Zumbini, Massimo. "'Ich lasse eben alle Anti-Semiten erschiessen': Anmerkungen zum Thema: Nietzsche und der real existierende Anti-Semitismus." In *Untergänge und Morgenröten: Nietzsche—Spengler—Anti-Semitismus*, 135–50. Würzburg: Königshausen und Neumann, 1999.

———. *Die Wurzeln des Bösen: Gründerjahre des Antisemitismus: Von der Bismarckzeit zu Hitler*. Frankfurt: Klostermann, 2003.

Fischer, Kuno. *Nathan der Weise: Die Idee und die Charaktere der Dichtung*. Stuttgart: Cotta, 1864.

Flemings, Hal. *Examining Criticisms of the Bible*. Bloomington, IN: AuthorHouse, 2008.

Förster, Bernhard. *Nachklängen zum Parsifal: Allerhand Gedanken über deutsche Cultur, Wissenschaft, Kunst, Gesellschaft*. Leipzig: Fritsch, 1883.

———. *Das Verhältnis des modernen Judenthums zur deutschen Kunst*. Berlin: Schulze, 1881.

Förster-Nietzsche, Elisabeth. *Der einsame Nietzsche*. Leipzig: Kröner, 1914.

———. *Das Leben Friedrich Nietzsche's*. 2 vols. Leipzig: Naumann, 1895–1904.

———. *Wagner und Nietzsche zur Zeit ihrer Freundschaft*. Munich: Georg Müller, 1915.

Fouse, Gary C. *Erlangen: An American's History of a German Town*. Lanham, MD: University Press of America, 2005.

"Friedrich Nietzsche's neuestes Buch: 'Die fröhliche Wissenschaft.'" *Schmeitzner's Internationale Monatsschrift* 1, no. 11 (1882): 685–95.

Gilman, Sander L. "Otto Eiser und Nietzsche's Illness: A Hitherto Unpublished Text." *Nietzsche-Studien* 38 (2009): 396–409.

Gilman, Sander L., ed. *Begegnungen mit Nietzsche*. Bonn: Bouvier, 1981.

———. *Conversations with Nietzsche*. New York: Oxford University Press, 1987.

Glagau, Otto. *Der Börsen- und Gründungs-Schwindel in Deutschland*. 2 vols. Leipzig: Frohberg, 1876–77.

Goch, Klaus. "Elisabeth Förster-Nietzsche, 1846–1935: Ein biographisches Portrait." In *Schwestern berühmter Männer*, edited by Luise F. Pusch, 361–413. Frankfurt: Insel, 1985.

Golomb, Jacob, ed. *Nietzsche and Jewish Culture*. London: Routledge, 1997.

Golomb, Jacob, and Robert S. Wistrich, eds. *Nietzsche, Godfather of Fascism?: On the Uses and Abuses of a Philosophy*. Princeton, NJ: Princeton University Press, 2002.

Gossman, Lionel. *Basel in the Age of Burckhardt*. Chicago: University of Chicago Press, 2000.

Groener, Maria. *Schopenhauer und die Juden*. Munich: Deutscher Volksverlag, 1920.

Günther, Hans. "Der Fall Nietzsche." *Unter dem Banner des Marxismus* 9 (1935): 539–82.

———. *Der Herren eigner Geist*. Moscow-Leningrad: Verlagsgenossenschaft ausländischer Arbeiter in der UdSSR, 1935.

Guthke, Karl S. "Zarathustras Tante." *Neue Deutsche Hefte* 29, no. 3 (1982): 470–83.

Haas, Karl Eduard. *Reformierte Theologie in Erlangen*. Edited, revised, and expanded by Matthias Freudenberg. Nuremberg: Peter Althmann, 2000.

Haiser, Franz. *Die Judenfrage vom Standpunkt der Herrenmoral*. Leipzig: Theodor Weicher, 1926.

Härtle, Heinrich. *Nietzsche und der Nationalsozialismus*. Munich: Zentralverlag der NSDAP, 1937.

Hartwich, Wolf-Daniel. "Die Erfindung des Judentums, Antisemitismus, Rassenlehre und Bibelkritik in Friedrich Nietzsches Theorie der Kultur." *Trumah* 5 (1996): 179–200.

Hatab, Lawrence J. *Nietzsche's* On the Genealogy of Morality: *An Introduction*. Cambridge: Cambridge University Press, 2008.

Hayman, Ronald. *Nietzsche: A Critical Life*. New York: Oxford University Press, 1980.

Heidegger, Martin. *Nietzsche*. Translated by David Farrell Krell. 4 vols. San Francisco: Harper and Row, 1979–87.

Heine, Heinrich. *Sämtliche Werke*. Vol. 11. Hamburg: Hoffmann und Campe, 1978.

Herf, Jeffrey. *Divided Memory: The Nazi Past in Two Germanys*. Cambridge, MA: Harvard University Press, 1997.

Herrmann, Dieter B. *Karl Friedrich Zöllner*. Leipzig: Teubner, 1982.

Hess, Jonathan M. *Germans, Jews, and the Claims of Modernity*. New Haven, CT: Yale University Press, 2002.

Hoffmann, David Marc. *Zur Geschichte des Nietzsche-Archivs: Chronik, Studien und Dokumente*. Berlin: de Gruyter, 1991.

Hoffmann, David Marc, et al., eds. *Franz Overbeck Heinrich Köselitz, Briefwechsel*. Berlin: de Gruyter, 1998.

Hollingdale, R. J. "The Hero as Outsider." In *The Cambridge Companion to Nietzsche*, edited by Bernd Magnus and Kathleen M. Higgins, 71–89. Cambridge: Cambridge University Press, 1996.

Holub, Robert C. "The Birth of Psychoanalysis from the Spirit of Enmity: Nietzsche and Psychology in the Nineteenth Century." In *Nietzsche and Depth Psychology*, edited by Jacob Golomb, Weaver Santaniello, and Ronald Lehrer, 149–69. Albany: State University of New York Press, 1999.

———. "Dialectic of the Biological Enlightenment: Nietzsche, Degeneration, and Eugenics." In *Practicing Progress: The Promise and Limitations of Enlightenment*. Festschrift for John McCarthy. Edited by Richard Schade and Dieter Sevin, 173–85. Amsterdam: Rodopi, 2007.

———. "The Elisabeth Legend or Sibling Scapegoating: The Cleansing of Friedrich Nietzsche and the Sullying of His Sister." In *Nietzsche: Godfather of Fascism?: On the Uses and Abuses of Philosophy*, edited by Jacob Golomb and Robert S. Wistrich, 215–34. Princeton, NJ: Princeton University Press, 2002.

———. *Friedrich Nietzsche*. Twayne World Author Series 857. New York: Twayne Publishers, 1995.

———. "Nietzsche: Socialist, Anarchist, Feminist." In *German Culture in Nineteenth-Century America: Reception, Adaptation, Transformation*, edited by Lynne Tatlock and Matt Erlin, 129–49. Rochester, NY: Camden House, 2005.

———. "Nietzsche and the Jewish Question." *New German Critique* 22, no. 3 (1995): 94–121.

———. "Nietzsche and the Women's Question." *German Quarterly* 68, no. 1 (1995): 67–71.

———. "Nietzsche's Colonialist Imagination: Nueva Germania, Good Europeanism, and Great Politics." In *The Imperialist Imagination: German Colonialism and Its Legacy*, edited by Sara Friedrichsmeyer, Sara Lennox, and Susanne Zantop, 33–49. Ann Arbor: University of Michigan Press, 1998.

Janaway, Christopher. *Beyond Selflessness: Reading Nietzsche's* Genealogy. Oxford: Oxford University Press, 2009.

Jacolliot, Louis. *Les législateurs religieux: Manou, Moïse, Mahomet*. Paris: A. Lacroix, 1876.

Janz, Curt Paul. *Die Briefe Friedrich Nietzsches: Textprobleme und ihre Bedeutung für Biographie und Doxographie*. Zurich: Editio Academica, 1972.

———. *Friedrich Nietzsche: Biographie*. 2nd rev. ed. 3 vols. Munich: Hanser, 1993.

———. "Die 'tödliche Beleidigung': Ein Beitrag zur Wagner-Entfremdung Nietzsches." *Nietzsche-Studien* 4 (1975): 263–78.

Jersch-Wenzel, Stefi. "Legal Status and Emancipation." In *German-Jewish History in Modern Times*, edited by Michael A. Meyer, 2: 31. New York: Columbia University Press, 1997.

Jünemann, Ernst. *Dühring und Nietzsche*. Leipzig: Reisland, 1931.

Jung, Jacqueline E. "The Passion, the Jews, and the Crisis of the Individual on the Naumburg West Choir Screen." In *Beyond the Yellow Badge: Anti-Judaism and Antisemitism in Medieval and Early Modern Visual Culture*, edited by Mitchell Merback, 145–77. Leiden: Brill, 2008.

Katz, Jacob. *From Prejudice to Destruction: Anti-Semitism, 1700–1933*. Cambridge, MA: Harvard University Press, 1980.

Kaufmann, Walter. *Nietzsche: Philosopher, Psychologist, Antichrist*. 4th ed. Princeton, NJ: Princeton University Press, 1974.

Klärung: 12 Autoren Politiker über die Judenfrage. Berlin: Wilhelm Kolk, 1932.

Köhler, Joachim. *Nietzsche and Wagner: A Lesson in Subjugation*. New Haven, CT: Yale University Press, 1998.

———. *Zarathustra's Secret: The Interior Life of Friedrich Nietzsche*. New Haven, CT: Yale University Press, 2002.

Krieger, Karsten, ed. *Der "Berliner Antisemitismusstreit," 1879–1881: Eine Kontroverse um die Zugehörigkeit der deutschen Juden zur Nation*. 2 vols. Munich: K. G. Saur, 2003.

Krummel, Richard Frank. "Dokumentation: Josef Paneth über seine Begegnung mit Nietzsche in der Zarathustra-Zeit." *Nietzsche-Studien* 17 (1988): 478–95.

Kuenzli, Rudolf E. "The Nazi Appropriation of Nietzsche." *Nietzsche-Studien* 12 (1983): 428–35.

Lagarde, Paul de. *Schriften für das deutsche Volk*. Vol. 1, *Deutsche Schriften*. Munich: Lehmann, 1940.

Lazare, Bernard. *Anti-Semitism: Its History and Causes*. London: Britons, 1967.

Lehmann, Rudolf. "Friedrich Nietzsche: Eine Studie." *Schmeitzner's Internationale Monatsschrift* 1, no. 4 (1882): 253–61, and 1, no. 5 (1882): 306–22.

Leopold, David. "The Hegelian Antisemitism of Bruno Bauer." *History of European Ideas* 25 (1999): 179–206.

Lessing, Theodor. *Der jüdische Selbsthaß*. Berlin: Jüdischer Verlag, 1930.

Levy, Richard S., ed. *Anti-Semitism: A Historical Encyclopedia of Prejudice and Persecution*. Santa Barbara, CA: ABC-CLIO, 2005.

Liebscher, Martin "'Lauter ausgesuchte Intelligenzen': Admiration for Nietzsche in 1870s Vienna." *Austrian Studies* 16 (2008): 32–50.

Liebeschütz, Hans. "Das Judentum und die Kontinuität der abendländischen Kultur: Jacob Burckhardt." In *Das Judentum im deutschen Geschichtsbild von Hegel bis Max Weber*, 220–44. Tübingen: Mohr, 1967.

Losurdo, Domenico. *Nietzsche, der aristokratische Rebell: Intellektuelle Biographie und kritische Bilanz*. 2 vols. Berlin: Argument, 2012.

Lukács, Georg. "Der deutsche Faschismus und Nietzsche." *Internationale Literatur* 13, no. 12 (1943): 55–64.

———. "Nietzsche als Vorläufer der faschistischen Ästhetik." *Internationale Literatur* 5, no. 8 (1935): 76–92.

———. *Die Zerstörung der Vernunft*. Berlin: Aufbau, 1954.

MacIntyre, Ben. *Forgotten Fatherland: The Search for Elisabeth Nietzsche*. New York: Farrar Straus Giroux, 1992.

Mack, Michael. *German Idealism and the Jew: The Inner Anti-Semitism of Philosophy and German Jewish Responses*. Chicago: University of Chicago Press, 2003.

Magnus, Bernd, and Kathleen M. Higgins, eds. *The Cambridge Companion to Nietzsche*. Cambridge: Cambridge University Press, 1996.

Mandel, Siegfried. *Nietzsche and the Jews: Exaltation and Denigration*. Amherst, NY: Prometheus Books, 1998.

Mann, Heinrich. "Zum Verständnisse Nietzsches." In *Nietzsche und die deutsche Literatur*, edited by Bruno Hillebrand. Vol. 1, *Texte zur Nietzsche-Rezeption, 1873–1963*, 106–8. Tübingen: Niemeyer, 1978.

Marr, W[ilhelm]. *Der Sieg des Judenthums über das Germanenthum*. Bern: Rudolph Costenoble, 1879.

May, Simon, ed. *Nietzsche's* On the Genealogy of Morality*: A Critical Guide*. Cambridge: Cambridge University Press, 2011.

McGrath, William J. *Dionysian Art and Populist Politics in Austria*. New Haven, CT: Yale University Press, 1974.

Mehring, Franz. *Gesammelte Schriften*. Vol. 11. Berlin: Dietz Verlag, 1961.

Misch, Robert. *Kinder: Eine Gymnasiasten Komödie*. Berlin: Harmonie, 1906.

Mittmann, Thomas. *Friedrich Nietzsche: Judengegner und Antisemitenfeind*. Erfurt: Sutton, 2001.

———. *Vom "Günstling" zum "Urfeind" der Juden: Die antisemitische Nietzsche-Rezeption in Deutschland bis zum Ende des Nationalsozialismus*. Würzburg: Königshausen und Neumann, 2006.

Moggach, Douglas. *The Philosophy and Politics of Bruno Bauer*. Cambridge: Cambridge University Press, 2003.

Moore, Gregory. *Nietzsche, Biology, and Metaphor*. Cambridge: Cambridge University Press, 2002.

Müller-Buck, Renate. "'Ach dass doch alle Schranken zwischen uns fielen': Siegfried Lipiner und der Nietzsche-Kult in Wien." In *Friedrich Nietzsche: Rezeption und Kultus*, edited by Sandro Barbera et al., 33–75. Pisa: ETS, 2004.

Nieberle, Sigrid. "'Und Gott im Himmel Lieder singt': Zur prekären Rezeption von Ernst Mortiz Arndts 'Des Deutschen Vaterland.'" In *Ernst Moritz Arndt (1769–1860): Deutscher Nationalismus—Europa—Transatlantische Perspektiven*, edited by Walter Erhart and Arne Koch, 121–36. Tübingen: Niemeyer, 2007.

Niemeyer, Christian. "Nietzsches rhetorischer Antisemitismus." *Nietzsche-Studien* 26 (1997): 139–62.

Nietzsche, Friedrich. *Briefwechsel: Kritische Gesamtausgabe*. Edited by Giorgio Colli and Mazzino Montinari. 24 vols. Berlin: de Gruyter, 1975–85.

———. *Gesammelte Briefe*. 5 vols. Edited by Elisabeth Förster-Nietzsche. Leipzig: Insel, 1902–9.

———. *The Portable Nietzsche*. Translated and edited by Walter Kaufmann. New York: Viking, 1954.

———. *Sämtliche Briefe: Kritische Studienausgabe*. Edited by Giorgio Colli and Mazzino Montinari. 8 vols. Berlin: de Gruyter, 1986.

———. *Sämtliche Werke: Kritische Studienausgabe*. Edited by Giorgio Colli and Mazzino Montinari. 15 vols. Berlin: de Gruyter, 1980.

———. *Werke: Kritische Gesamtausgabe*. Planned ca. 50 volumes, edited by Giorgio Colli, Mazzino Montinari, et al. Berlin: de Gruyter, 1967–.

———. *Werke in drei Bänden*. Edited by Karl Schlechta. Munich: Hanser, 1954–56.

Nirenberg, David. *Anti-Judaism: The Western Tradition*. New York: Norton, 2013.

Nola, Robert. "Nietzsche as Anti-Semitic Jewish Conspiracy Theorist." *Croatian Journal of Philosophy* 3, no. 7 (2003): 35–62.

Nordau, Max. *Degeneration*. Lincoln: University of Nebraska Press, 1993.

Onnasch, Martin. "Naumburg." In *Wegweiser durch das jüdische Sachsen-Anhalt*, 142–49. Potsdam: Verlag für Berlin-Brandenburg, 1998.

Ottmann, Henning. *Philosophie und Politik bei Nietzsche*. 2nd expanded ed. Berlin: de Gruyter, 1999.

Overbeck, Franz. *Erinnerungen an Friedrich Nietzsche*. Berlin: Berenberg, 2011.

———. *Ueber Enstehung und Recht einer rein historischen Betrachtung der Neutestamentlichen Schriften in der Theologie*." Antritts-Vorlesung gehalten in der Aula zu Basel am 6. Juni 1870. Basel: Schweighauserische Verlagsbuchhandlung, 1871.

Owen, David. *Nietzsche's* Genealogy of Morality. Montreal: McGill-Queen's University Press, 2007.

Peters, H. F. *Zarathustra's Sister: The Case of Elisabeth and Friedrich Nietzsche*. New York: Crown, 1977.

Podach, Erich F. *Friedrich Nietzsches Werke des Zusammenbruchs*. Heidelberg: Wolfgang Rothe Verlag, 1961.

———. *Gestalten um Nietzsche*. Weimar: Erich Lichtenstein Verlag, 1932.

"Pogrom in Neustettin (1881)." *Ereignisse, Dekrete, Kontroversen*, 288. Berlin: de Gruyter, 2011.

Poliakov, Léon. *The Aryan Myth: A History of Racist and Nationalistic Ideas in Europe*. New York: Barnes and Noble, 1996.

Pulzer, Peter, *The Rise of Political Anti-Semitism in Germany and Austria*. Rev. ed. Cambridge, MA: Harvard University Press, 1988.

Rabe, Johanness E., ed. "Kasperl und Abraham." In *Kasper Putschenelle: Historisches über die Handpuppen und althamburgische Kasperszenen*, 178–86. Hamburg: C. Boysen, 1912.

Ratner-Rosenhagen, Jennifer. *American Nietzsche: A History of an Icon and His Ideas*. Chicago: University of Chicago Press, 2012.

Rée, Paul. *Basic Writings*. Translated and edited by Robin Small. Urbana: University of Illinois Press, 2003.

Rehmann, Jan. "Nietzsches Umarbeitung des kulturprotestantischen Antijudaismus—das Beispiel Wellhausen." *Das Argument* 46, no. 2 (2004): 278–91.

Renan, Ernest. "De l'avenir religieux des sociétés modernes." *Revue des deux mondes* 29 (1860): 765–97.

———. *Le Judaïsme comme race et comme religion*. Paris: Calmann Lévy, 1883.

———. *Paulus*. Leipzig: Brockhaus, 1869.

Römer, Heinrich. "Nietzsche und das Rassenproblem." *Rasse: Monatsschrift der nordischen Gedanken* 7 (1940): 59–65.

Romero, Simon. "German Outpost Born of Racism in 1887 Blends into Paraguay." *New York Times*, May 6, 2013, A4.

Roos, Richard. "Les derniers écrits de Nietzsche el leur publication." *Revue philosophique* 146 (1956): 262–87.

————. "Elisabeth Förster-Nietzsche ou la sœur abusive." *Études Germanique* 11, no. 4 (1956): 321–41.

Rose, Paul Lawrence. "Renan versus Gobineau: Semitism and Antisemitism, Ancient Races and Modern Liberal Nations." *History of European Ideas* 39, no. 4 (2013): 528–40.

Roux, Georges. *Ancient Iraq*. London: Penguin, 1992.

Rybak, Jens. "Ernst Moritz Arndts Judenbilder: Ein unbekanntes Kapitel." *Hefte der Ernst-Moritz-Arndt-Gesellschaft* 6 (1997): 102–37.

Santaniello, Weaver. *Nietzsche, God, and the Jews: His Critique of Judeo-Christianity in Relation to the Nazi Myth*. Albany: State University of New York Press, 1994.

————. "Nietzsche's Hierarchy of Gods in the *Antichrist*." *Journal of Nietzsche Studies* 19 (2000): 89–102.

————. "A Post-Holocaust Re-Examination of Nietzsche and the Jews: Vis-à-vis Christendom and Nazism." In *Nietzsche and Jewish Culture*, edited by Jacob Golomb, 21–54. London: Routledge, 1997.

Schaberg, William H. *The Nietzsche Canon: A Publication History and Bibliography*. Chicago: University of Chicago Press, 1995.

Schacht, Richard, ed. *Nietzsche, Genealogy, Morality: Essays on Nietzsche's* Genealogy of Morals. Berkeley: University of California Press, 1994.

Scheuffler, Gottlieb. *Friedrich Nietzsche im Dritten Reich: Bestätigung und Aufgabe*. [Erfurt-Melchendorf: E. Scheuffler], 1933.

Schickedanz, Arno. *Sozialparasitismus im Völkerleben*. Leipzig: Lotus-Verlag, 1927.

Schirmacher, Wolfgang, ed. *Schopenhauer, Nietzsche und die Kunst*. Vienna: Passagen Verlag, 1991.

Schlechta, Karl. *Der Fall Nietzsche*. Munich: Hanser, 1958.

Schmeitzner's Internationale Monatsschrift: Zeitschrift für allgemeine und nationale Kultur und deren Litteratur. In 1883 subtitled *Zeitschrift für die Allgemeine Vereinigung zur Bekämpfung des Judenthums*. Chemnitz: Verlag von Ernst Schmeitzner, 1882–83.

Schmidt, Hermann Josef. *Nietzsche absconditus, oder, Spurenlesen bei Nietzsche*. 2 vols. Berlin: IBDK Verlag, 1990–93.

Schmidt, Jochen. *Kommentar zu Nietzsches* Die Geburt der Tragödie. Berlin: de Gruyter, 2012.

Schopenhauer, Arthur. *Zürcher Ausgabe, Werke in zehn Bänden*, edited by Arthur Hübscher. 10 vols. Zurich: Diogenes, 1977.

Schüler, Winfried. *Der Bayreuther Kreis von seiner Entstehung bis zum Ausgang der wilhelminischen Ära*. Münster: Aschendorff, 1971.

Seligmann, Caesar. "Nietzsche und das Judentum." In *Judentum und moderne Weltanschauung: Fünf Vorträge*, 69–89. Frankfurt: Kauffmann, 1905.

Shapiro, Gary. "Nietzsche contra Renan." *History and Theory* 21, no. 2 (1982): 193–222.

Sherratt, Yvonne. *Hitler's Philosophers*. New Haven, CT: Yale University Press, 2013.

Singer, Isidore, et al., eds. *The Jewish Encyclopedia*. New York: Funk and Wagnalls, 1901–6.

Small, Robin. *Nietzsche and Rée: A Star Friendship*. Oxford: Clarendon Press, 2005.

———. *Nietzsche in Context*. Burlington: Ashgate, 2001.

———. "Nietzsche, Zöllner, and the Fourth Dimension." *Archiv für Geschichte der Philosophie* 76 (1994): 278–301.

Smith, David. "Nietzsche's Hinduism, Nietzsche's India: Another Look." *Journal of Nietzsche Studies* 28 (2004): 37–56.

Sommer, Andreas Urs. "Judentum und Christentum bei Paul de Lagarde und Friedrich Nietzsche." In *Christentum und Judentum: Akten des Internationalen Kongresses der Schleiermacher-Gesellschaft*, 549–60. Berlin: de Gruyter, 2012.

———. "Zwischen Agitation, Religionsstiftung und 'hoher Politik': Paul de Lagarde und Friedrich Nietzsche." *Nietzscheforschung* 4 (1998): 169–94.

Spengler, Oswald. *The Decline of the West*. Vol. 1, *Form and Actuality*. New York: Knopf, 1926.

Stegmaier, Werner. *Nietzsches "Genealogie der Moral."* Darmstadt: Wissenschaftliche Buchgesellschaft, 1994.

Stegmaier, Werner, and Daniel Krochmalnik, eds. *Jüdischer Nietzscheanismus*. Berlin: de Gruyter, 1997.

Stern, Fritz. *The Politics of Cultural Despair: A Study in the Rise of the Germanic Ideology*. Berkeley: University of California Press, 1961.

Strathern Paul. *Nietzsche in 90 Minutes*. Chicago: Ivan R. Dee, 1996.

Strauß, David Friedrich. *Nathan der Weise*. Bonn: Emil Strauß, 1877.

Tönnies, Ferdinand. *Der Nietzsche-Kultus: Eine Kritik*. Berlin: Akademie-Verlag, 1990.

Tucholsky, Kurt. "Fräulein Nietzsche." *Gesammelte Werke*. Vol. 10, 9–15. Hamburg: Rowohlt, 1960.

Venturelli, Aldo. "Asketismus und Wille zur Macht: Nietzsches Auseinandersetzung mit Eugen Dühring." *Nietzsche-Studien* 15 (1986): 107–39.

———. "Nietzsche in der Berggasse 19: Über die erste Nietzsche-Rezeption in Wien." *Nietzsche-Studien* 13 (1984): 448–80.

Volkov, Shulamith. *Antisemitismus als kultureller Code*. Munich: Beck, 1990.

Von Müller, Hans, "Nietzsches Vorfahren." *Nietzsche-Studien* 31 (2002): 253–75.

Wagner, Cosima. *Diaries*. 2 vols. New York: Harcourt Brace Jovanovich, 1978 and 1980.

Wagner, Richard. *Gesammelte Schriften und Dichtungen*. Leipzig: Fritzsch, 1887–88.

———. *Das Judenthum in der Musik*. Leipzig: J. J. Weber, 1869.

Weimer, Wolfgang. "Der Philosoph und der Diktator: Arthur Schopenhauer und Adolf Hitler." *Schopenhauer-Jahrbuch* 84 (2003): 157–67.

Wellhausen, Julius. *Prolegomena to the History of Ancient Israel*. Edinburgh: Adam and Charles Black, 1885.

———. *Sketch of the History of Israel and Judah*. London: Adam and Charles Black, 1891.

Whyte, Max. "The Uses and Abuses of Nietzsche in the Third Reich: Alfred Baeumler's 'Heroic Realism.'" *Journal of Contemporary History* 43, no. 2 (2008): 171–94.

Willingham, Robert Allen, II. "Jews in Leipzig: Nationality and Community in the 20th Century." PhD. diss., University of Texas, 2005.

Winteler, Reto. "Nietzsches Bruch mit Wagner: Zur Plausibilität seiner späteren Stilisierung." *Nietzsche-Studien* 40 (2011): 256–72.

Wistrich, Robert S., "The Cross and the Swastika: A Nietzschean Perspective." In *Nietzsche, Godfather of Fascism? On the Uses and Abuses of a Philosophy*, edited by Jacob Golomb and Robert S. Wistrich, 144–69. Princeton, NJ: Princeton University Press, 2002.

Wollkopf, Roswitha. "Die Gremien des Nietzsche-Archivs und ihre Beziehung zum Faschismus bis 1933." In *Im Vorfeld der Literatur: Vom Wert archivalischer Überlieferung für das Verständnis von Literatur und ihrer Geschichte*, edited by Karl-Heinz Hahn, 227–41. Weimar: Verlag Hermann Böhlaus Nachfolger, 1991.

Young, Julian. *Friedrich Nietzsche: A Philosophical Biography*. Cambridge: Cambridge University Press, 2010.

Yovel, Yirmiyahu. "Nietzsche contra Wagner on the Jews." In *Nietzsche, Godfather of Fascism? On the Uses and Abuses of a Philosophy*, edited by Jacob Golomb and Robert S. Wistrich, 126–43. Princeton, NJ: Princeton University Press, 2002.

Zimmermann, Moshe. *Wilhelm Marr: The Patriarch of Anti-Semitism*. New York: Oxford University Press, 1986.

the right wing to integrate Nietzsche as one of theirs, 7–11; in Bayreuth, 91–92; birthplace of (Röcken), 32; boasting of, 112, 235n51; break of with Lipiner, 107–8; break of with Rée, 101–2, 233n30–31; central issues of concerning Judaism, xviii–xix; on Christian priests, 229n47; claims of concerning his noble Polish ancestry, 31, 111, 234–35n49; commentaries on contemporary life in Germany, 67; and the concept of chandala, 198, 199–203; correspondence of with Busse, 152–55; and the "cultural code" of anti-Semitism, xvii, 57, 71, 75, 83–88, 205; demands of as an author as to the appearance of his published works, 132; distaste of for Karl Mendelssohn-Bartholdy, 59–60; on the distinction between anti-Semitism and anti-Jewish attitudes, 161–162, 231n12; drafts of letters written by differing from the final letters themselves, 20; and eugenics, 113–14; as an existentialist, 26; and fascism, 212–14; formation by as a teenager of the "Germania" club, 50; friendship of with Burckhardt, 63; friendship of with Lipiner, 103–9, 124, 205; friendship of with Overbeck, 62, 159; friendship of with Paneth, 109–15, 124, 133–34, 205; friendship of with Rée, 96–103, 124, 205; general views of on anti-Semitism, 125–26, 128, 131, 159, 160–161, 239n35; on Germany and Jewish immigration, 121–23; on the goal of humankind, 86–87; and the goals of German militarism, 10, 217–18n24; influence of on culture and politics, 9; insanity/madness of, 116, 241n64; intellectual program of (early 1870s) to promote the Wagnerian renaissance, 66–74; interest of in Schopenhauer's philosophy, 45–47; on journalism, 84; lack of direct mention of Jews or Judaism in his work, 70–71; lawsuit of against Schmeitzner, 139–40; "legend" concerning, 223n81; limited exposure of to Jews and Judaism in his youth, 34–35; as a "modish" philosopher, 5; move of to Naumburg, 33–34; on the old Teutons and modern Germans, 16, 219n42; opinion of Auerbach, 56; opinion of Bauer, 138; opinion of Meyerbeer, 56–58;

opinion of Renan, 181–82; oppositional animus in his work, 7; opposition of to National Socialism, 213; on pain, 113, 235n58; patriotism of, 14; as a "philo-Semitic," 126; physical illnesses of, 91–92, 93–94, 107, 234n37; preoccupation of with Indian texts, 246–47n54; Protestant upbringing and family of, 31–32; as a "proto-Nazi," 27; and racism, 15; reception of in his early career, 2–3; rejection of by Communists, 23; rejection of the Grecophilic view of Greece, 229n43; rejection of ultranationalist political movements in Germany, 123; reputation of as a right-wing advocate of racism, xv; and scientific knowledge, 112–13; self-publishing of, 132; "silent community" of, 111–12; on slavery, 85; on the sole virtue of modern times, 88; support of for the notion of *Bildung*, 106–7; stylistic ambiguity of, 9; texts of as akin to the Bible, 9; transfer of to the University of Leipzig, xvi; and "untimeliness," 86; use of the term "Misojuden" by, 128, 237n18; and Viennese Jewry, 112, 139; views of on Jews/Judaism and his philosophy, 209–10; *völkisch* values of, 10; on the will to power, 21, 115, 116, 177, 186, 189, 192, 213, 220–21n57. *See also* Andreas-Salomé, Lou: relationship of with Nietzsche; Jewish Question, the: in Nietzsche's writings and life; Nietzsche, Friedrich, as an anti-Jewish; Nietzsche, Friedrich, break of with Wagner; Nietzsche, Friedrich, on the history of religion and morals; Nietzsche, Friedrich, as an opponent of anti-Semitism; Nietzsche, Friedrich, postwar rehabilitation of; Nietzsche, Friedrich, relationship of with the Försters; Nietzsche, Friedrich, relationship of with Wagner; Nietzsche, Friedrich, at the University of Basel; Nietzsche, Friedrich, at the University of Bonn; Nietzsche, Friedrich, at the University of Leipzig

Nietzsche, Friedrich, as an anti-Jewish, xi–xii, xiv, xviii, 13, 15, 48, 102–3, 126, 206–7, 211–12; anti-Jewish song refrain found in Nietzsche's notebooks, 35–36; attack of on Goldschmidt's translation of Dostoevsky, 116, 160; descriptions of Nietzsche's negative bias toward Jews, xiv; disparaging

Volkmann, Richard von, 64, 71
Voltaire, 89
Voltmar, Marie, 235–36n66

Wagener, Hermann, 239n42
Wagner, Cosima, xvi, 52, 80, 82, 89–90, 94, 99, 205; anti-Jewish convictions of, 49; diaries of, 71–72, 95–96, 230–31n63, 244n13; on the loss of major newspapers to the Jews, 84; marriages of, 226n1; opinion of Auerbach, 55–56; reaction of to Nietzsche's "Socrates and Tragedy," 69–70
Wagner, Ottilie, 80
Wagner, Richard, xiii, xv, 28, 45, 116, 152, 156, 157, 205; anti-Semitism of, 52–55; on assimilation of the Jews, 61; association of with Jews, 227n17; attack of on Auerbach, 55–56; attack of on Mendelssohn and Meyerbeer, 55, 58; attacks on journals and newspapers that belong to "Israel," 83–84; belief that Germans should be emancipated from Jews, 54; celebrity of, 90; criticism of Jewish musical culture, 77–78; critique of modernity by, 2; cultural mission of, 79; disparagement of the appearance of Jews, 54; disruption of Wagnerian operas by Jews, 71–73; on the educated Jew, 55; on the emancipation of the Jews, 53–54; embrace of Christianity by, 93; ideological convictions held by, 130; interference of with Nietzsche's medical diagnosis, 94; on Jewish control of the press and the economy, 60; Jewish friends of, 103; on Jewish occupation of the German artistic realm, 61; on Leipzig as a "world city of Jewish music" (Juden-musikweltstadt), 60; mistakes made mixing politics with art, 74; music of, 50–51; reaction of to Nietzsche's "Socrates and Tragedy," 68–69; on Semitic speech and music, 54–55; and socialism, 207–8; weakness of in underestimating his enemies, 73–74. See also Nietzsche, Friedrich, break of with Wagner; Nietzsche, Friedrich, relationship of with Wagner

Wagnerians, 18, 129, 130, 140, 179; association of with Jews in Berlin, 230n54; Nietzsche as a "Wagnerian," 51–52; traits associated with Jews according to academic Wagnerians, 81
Wahrmund, Adolf, 156, 157, 242n70
Walküre (Wagner [1870]), 50
Wars of Liberation, 33
Weimer Republic, xv, 8; Nietzsche and the right wing in, 11–14
Wellhausen, Julius, xix, 187, 189, 202, 245n31, 245n33; on the character of Jehovah, 184–85; on the denaturalization of religion and religious practices, 184–85; the "documentary hypothesis" of, 183; influence of on Nietzsche, 182–85, 186; respect of for Judaism, 184; on self-denial, 183; as a source for Nietzsche's thought in The Antichrist, 192–94; Wellhausen's view of Judaism, 183–85, 245n33
Wideman, Paul Heinrich, 132, 135, 136, 137, 138
Wilamowitz-Moellendorf, Ulrich von, 80, 81, 98, 245n35
will to power, 21, 115, 116, 177, 186, 189, 192, 213, 220–21n57; Spengler's "national" will to power, 10
Will to Power, The (Nietzsche [Elisabeth Förster-Nietzsche's edition of]), 17, 25, 27, 28–29, 223–24n84
Winckelmann, Johann, 76
Windisch, Ernst, 51
Winteler, Reto, 231n8
Wolff, Julius, 152–53
Wolzogen, Hans von, 99
World as Will and Representation, The (Schopenhauer), 45
World War I, 10
World Zionist Organization, 4

Young Hegelians, 40

Zimmern, Helen, 233n36
Zionist Congress (1897), 62
Zöllner, Johann, 130